Principles and Practices of Teaching Civics and Citizenship Education

Principles and Practices of Teaching Civics and Citizenship Education

J. C. Aggarwal

SHIPRA

ISBN: 978-81-7541-497-6

First Published in India in 2010

Principles and Practices of Teaching Civics and Citizanship Education

Published by:
SHIPRA PUBLICATIONS
H.O.: LG 18-19, Pankaj Central Market, Patparganj,
I.P. Ext., Delhi-110092, Tel: 91-11-2223 5152, 2223 6152
Br.Off.: 115, Munish Plaza, 20, Ansari Road, Darya Ganj,
New Delhi-110002, Tel: 6594 6453, 9810522367
E-mail: info@shiprapublications.com
www.shiprapublications.com

Preface

With the introduction of Women Reservation Bill, the subject itself stands to gain more importance.

The present book is designed to serve a dual purpose.

First, it should be useful to the prospective teachers by virtue of its extensive coverage.

Second, it should serve as a useful reference book to the practising teachers.

With a view to facilitating easy comprehension, each topic is divided into suitable heads and subheads. Material has been organized in the context of examination requirement. Various methods of citizenship education and training are discussed in detail. The entire approach is in the context of contemporary societies.

The author is grateful to all the publishers and authors where works he has consulted in the preparation of this book.

J. C. Aggarwal

Contents

1

Meaning, Importance and Place of Civics in the School Curriculum

1.1 MEANING OF CIVICS

In simple language, Civics is the study of human relations in terms of 3Rs—Rights, Responsibilities and Relationships. Man is a social being. He is born in society, lives in society and dies in society. It is, therefore, very important that he is acquainted with society's institutions. Of course, Civics deals with elementary matters.

With a view to have a wider and meaningful knowledge of various dimensions of Civics, its important definitions are given here:

1. '*Columbia Encyclopaedia*' defines Civics as a frame of learning that treats the relationship between citizens, their society and state. Originally it was called civil government. It became a subject in secondary schools of the U.S.A. in the second half of the 19th century.

2. According to '*American Heritage Dictionary of English Language*', Civics means a branch of political science that deals with civic affairs and the rights and duties of citizens.

3. *Wikipedia* regards Civics as the science of comparative government. It further its as a part of politics.

4. *Paul Monore* in '*A Cyclopaedia of Education*' refers to Civics as the teaching of civil government in over elementary and secondary schools and colleges. The term civil government which was formerly very commonly used for describing this study has ban abandoned, because in its interpretation it was usually narrowed down to a study of the mere framework of government. The word 'Civics' is said to have been introduced by Henry Randall Waite and has the advantage over the "civil government in that it is now generally understood to include: (1) ethics or the doctrine of duties in society; (2) civil polity, or governmental methods and machinery; (3) history of civic development and movement".

5. *F.G. Gould* regards Civics is the study of institutions, habits, activities and spirit by means of which a man or a woman may fulfil the duties and receive the benefits of the membership of a political community.

6. *Oxford Dictionary* explains Civics as the science which studies the conditions of best possible social life.

7. *Beni Prasad* states that in the context of social relationships there are many duties to be performed and correspondingly many rights to be respected, it is with them that Civics is mainly concerned.

8. *Puntambekar* considers Civics as the science and philosophy of citizenship.

9. *A.T. Shah* defines Civics as that branch of human knowledge which deals with rights and duties of man, living as a member of a group of people politically organised.

10. According to *E.M. Whyte*, Civics is more or less a useful branch of human knowledge which deals with everything (e.g. social, intellectual, economic, political and even religious aspects) relating to a citizen; past, present and future, local, national and human.

11. *The Dictionary of Education* by *C.V.* gives the following meaning of Civics, "(1) the elements of political science or the branch of political science dealing with the rights and duties of citizens; (2) since about 1915, the accepted title for studies in government, used especially in secondary schools, replacing the former designation 'civil government' but with a current tendency for the content to be included in courses with changed titles such as "problems in democracy"; (3) a course of study, usually in the junior high school, fusing political, social, and economic phases of group life".

1.2 IMPORTANCE OF CIVICS

It is through its schools, that a society prepares its future citizens. Hence a school cannot be concerned merely with the teaching of school subjects; it has also to shape the minds of young people so that the life and culture of the society of which it is a part, may flourish. In a developing society like ours this responsibility of the school is greater, because the school should not only transmit, from one generation to the next, our tradition and culture, but help in the process of modernisation. The young person of today should not just be the old one of tomorrow. Considering the rapid changes in the world of today, he should know the world he lives in and particularly the directions in which we as a nation have to advance so that we can fulfil our "tryst with destiny", as Nehru announced on the midnight of August 15, 1947. For discharging this responsibility, the school depends, among other things, heavily on the teaching of Civics, the central concern of which is to understand the relationship between man and his society.

The study of Civics has special significance for a developing democracy like India. India became a sovereign democratic republic in 1950 and adopted a democratic way of life. India, immediately after independence had to face many social, economic and political problems. It needed really a well-disciplined, educated and enlightened citizenship which could understand its responsibilities towards the nation and also as an electorate for electing representatives for central, state and local bodies. Majority of Indians were illiterate, orthodox, caste ridden, blind followers and believed in untouchability, child marriage, etc. They needed the development of basic qualities of a good citizen. Civics enables us to develop those habits, attitudes which are necessary to develop a broad, rational, national and secular outlook".

Any worthwhile programme of the teaching of Civics is designed to enable the student to gain certain basic understandings, to acquire necessary skills and develop attitudes that are needed for effective citizenship in a democratic society.

A. Developing the Students' Understanding of:

1. Major aspects of social development.
2. Major aspects of physical development.
3. Interdependence of peoples and nations.
4. Ways in which man has coped with his environment.
5. Ways in which man has governed and is governed.
6. Social control functions performed by groups.
7. Reciprocal relationships between the individuals and society.
8. How man provides for his basic needs.
9. Major developments in the growth of civilisation.
10. Attitudes that go to make one's personality.

B. Objectives of Acquiring Skills by Students in:

1. Critical thinking.
2. Analysing and resolving problems.
3. Locating and gathering information.
4. Organising and evaluating information.
5. Reading, listening, speaking and writing intelligently.
6. Interpreting maps, globes, charts and graphic materials.
7. Using time concepts.
8. Participating in group activities.

C. Objectives of Developing Attitudes in Students by:

1. Respecting the dignity of the individual.
2. Believing in the equality of opportunity for all people.
3. Upholding the law.
4. Working cooperatively for the good of all.
5. Willingly assuming civic responsibilities.
6. Having faith in the democratic processes.
7. Believing that man is capable of self-government.
8. Believing that social problems are susceptible to rational analysis and solution.

Summing up: The following points sum up the importance of Civics:

1. The primary responsibility of the school is to prepare the pupils for life. The school must, therefore, see to it that they acquire the knowledge and attitude necessary for adjustment to the environment. In the present times the world is changing fast. The school must, therefore, lay the foundations of the preparation for the understanding of, adjustment to and participation in the process of change.

The environment in which the child is born is the product of social and physical conditions. The environment influences our life. Through Civics we acquaint children with the environment and at the same time develop in them the skills which help them to become responsible citizens.

2. The independence we enjoy bestows on us a number of rights and a number of responsibilities. To discharge these responsibilities effectively it is necessary to be equipped with the related knowledge and a suitable frame of

mind. Civics supplies this knowledge and also attempts to lay the foundation of desirable habits and attitudes through a suitable programme of activities.

3. To make the nation strong and prosperous we are taking several steps through developmental plans and programmes. Pupils should possess a working knowledge of the plans and projects so that, as adults, they can make maximum contribution to the progress and prosperity of the country. Civics serves this purpose.

4. For peaceful coexistence people of the world must have mutual trust and cooperation. Civics can help in promoting an attitude of national and international understanding.

1.3 BRIEF HISTORY OF CIVICS

Encyclopaedia of Educational Research, edited by Chester W. Harris has, traced the History of Civics and Political Science as, "By 1900, a course in civil government was widely taught in the secondary schools, with 20 per cent of all students taking it. The course was formal and descriptive, with most of the content devoted to structure of the national government but with some attention to state government. Gradually, courses in government and Civics changed to present government as functional process, with an emphasis on local community. By 1914, the term 'Civics' had come into wide use in describing courses in government. By 1920, the titles 'Vocational Civics' and 'Community Civics' had become popular almost one fifth of all high school students studied some variety of Civics. Content varied greatly. Community Civics tended to be placed in grade IX. An advanced civic course, frequently given in the twelfth grade, emphasised national government. However much duplication existed. As the twelfth-grade problems of democracy course grew in popularity, it tended to draw much of its material from the area of Civics. The boundary line of Civics courses are still not clear, and there has been a great increase in the number of new topics introduced in recent years."

1.4 PLACE OF CIVICS IN SCHOOL CURRICULUM

Civics occupies an important place on the school as it attempts to train students in the qualities of good citizens.

A good citizen:

1. Believes in equality of opportunity for all people.
2. Values, respects, and defends basic human rights and privileges guaranteed by the Indian Constitution.
3. Respects and upholds the law and its agencies.
4. Understands and accepts the following democratic principles as guides in evaluating his own behaviour and the policies and practices of other persons and groups, and judges his own behaviour and the behaviour of others by them:
    (a) that each individual possesses dignity and worth as a person and is entitled to consideration as a person,
    (b) that governments exist by the consent of the governed,
    (c) that each citizen has certain civil liberties guaranteed by the Constitution,

(d) that government is by law, not by men,
(e) that in a large nation with diverse social and economic groups compromise is frequently necessary,
(f) that, since the people are intelligent enough to govern themselves, they do not need protection by censorship—hence free speech, a free press, and academic freedom are necessary.

5. Understands that, in the long run, people will govern themselves better than any self-appointed group would govern them.
6. Puts the general welfare above his own whenever a choice between them is necessary.
7. Feels that he has inherited an unfinished experiment in self-government, which is his duty and privilege to carry on.
8. Exercises his right to vote.
9. Accepts civic responsibilities and discharges them to the best of his ability.
10. Knows techniques of social action and can cooperate with other in achieving such action.
11. Accepts the basic idea that in a democracy the majority has the right to make decisions under the Constitution.
12. Assumes a personal responsibility to contribute toward a well-informed climate of opinion on current social, economic, and political problems or issues.
13. Realises the necessary connection of education with democracy.
14. Respects property rights, meets his obligations in contracts and obeys regulations governing the use of property.
15. Supports fair business practices and fair relations between employers and employees.
16. Assumes a personal responsibility for the wise use of natural resources.
17. Accepts responsibility for the maintenance and improvement of a competitive economic system assisted and regulated when necessary by governmental action.
18. Knows in general how other economic systems operate, including their political and social consequences.
19. Knows about, critically evaluates, and supports promising efforts to prevent war, but stands ready to defend his country against tyranny and aggression.
20. Is deeply aware of the interdependence of people and realises that a good life can be attained only by the organised cooperation of millions of people all over the world.
21. Understands cultures and ways of life other than his own.
22. Cultivates qualities of character and personality that have a high value in his culture.
23. Is a responsible family member and assumes his full responsibility for maintaining the civic standards of his neighbourhood and community.
24. Recognises taxes as payment for community services and pays them promptly.

1.5 VALUES OF TEACHING CIVICS

Basis of Democratic Behaviour

The major responsibility for the pattern of development of democratic behaviour in pupils falls upon the programmes related to Civics. Civics is a very valuable subject because in a large measure it contributes to the development of an enlightened citizenship. Civics when taught effectively in the schools, it will result in the following outcomes:

1. *Development of Desirable Attitudes*: The development of attitudes is important because they are significant factors of behaviour. Desirable attitudes are based upon an appreciation of what things are worthwhile in life. Social mindedness is one of the most important attitudes that will result from the teaching of Civics. Such an attitudes will bring about in the pupil the desire to play an important part in creating a better society.

2. *Positive Understanding*: Civics is not the mere transmission of unrelated isolated facts. Understanding relevant to the organised set of facts is very important. With the provision of relevant experiences and activities inside and outside the classroom, there will be development of proper understanding of the subject matter which will result in proper utilisation of the development of society on the basis of their applicability.

3. *Development of Competence in Problem Solving*: Civics is helpful in providing training to the child to solve the problems. It would help in development the skill of self-reliance. It can lead to a sense of responsibility. The young generation will begin to feel that it is capable of doing things. This will enable it to solve the problems in the near future also.

4. *Knowledge Structure*: The subject of Civics includes content based on facts and information related to human beings and the environment in the context of time and space. Thus the structure of the subject content in the relevant sequence assists to develop the knowledge structure in the minds of the pupils.

5. *Training in Cooperation*: Civics provides opportunities to pupils to learn that whenever there is a challenging situation faced by the society, how it is solved by the cooperative efforts of the people. Teaching of Civics by virtue of its content matter and methods adopted by the teacher offers several opportunities to get optimum cooperation from students.

6. *Character Development*: Teaching of Civics will help in inculcating high ideals and civic standards in preparing pupils to take their place in a democratic society.

7. *Development of Social Understanding*: Civics provides social education. The social education and social awareness will save the child from anti-social influences and help in building up his social understanding which is necessary for the success of democratic nation.

8. *Training in Responsible Group Participation*: Participating competently in group problem solving requires the students to apply various types of knowledge and thinking skills such as the abilities to lead, organise, bargain, reconcile and manage a group discussion cooperatively and effectively.

9. *Development of Thinking and Reasoning Power*: Civics develops the power of reasoning and independent thinking in the children. It stimulates the mental processes of the students. They reflect as how the society has grown out of the past and how it has undergone changes needed in the present age for the development of future.

10. *Development of International Understanding*: Civics provides opportunities to students to understand the need of cooperation for promoting world peace. They come to know that there is interdependence and interrelation between man to man and nation and nation. It teaches children to show reverence to people of different religions and regions. It builds child's ability to understand global relationship.

11. *Development of Values of Adjustability and Flexibility*: The social environment is changing at a rapid rate on account of the impact of scientific inventions and technical advances. These changes help the child in developing a flexible outlook which will enable him to adjust himself to the changes that will take place in his adult life. It will train him how to participate intelligently in that process and how to adjust himself properly to the changing environment.

12. *Development of Values of Tolerance and Open-mindedness*: In Civics there are various problems raised by the teacher before the students to give their views. Students also feel free to put questions and explore various types of evidences. Group decision making activities require the values of tolerance and openness to a variety of opinions and judgments.

13. *Development of Healthy Teacher Pupil Relationship*: Civics brings the teacher and pupils more close to each other. A healthy relationship is established between the two as the two engaged themselves whole heartedly in a wide range of activities. By providing stimulation and motivation the teacher will help in maintaining close relationship with the pupils.

14. *Development of Skill in Enquiry and Decision Making*: The skills related to enquiry and decision-making can be acquired through guided discovery learning.

15. *Development of Various Learning Skills*: Civics help in developing skills which pertain to organising, sifting, interpreting and evaluating information, interpreting maps, tables, graphs, charts, time line, distinguishing facts from fiction, summarising data, etc.

16. *Basis for Specialisation*: Civics develops different subjects like history, geography, political science, economics, etc. It helps in selecting the subject for specialisation at higher level.

We may conclude that Civics is a very useful subject and it plays an important role in the development of desirable pattern of conduct of the pupil. It is intended to promote the values of humanism, secularism, socialism and democracy. The teacher must provide a supportive learning environment that may enable the students to develop these values in them.

In short, each letter of the term denotes values as listed below.

C — stands for citizenship

— stands for courtesy
— stands for cooperation
— stands for courage of conviction
I — stands for inquiring mind
V — stands for vision
I — stands for intelligent thinking
— stands for interrelations
C — stands for critical thinking
— stands for constructive attitude
— stands for civic sense
S — stands for self-discipline
— stands for social attitude
— stands for social efficiency
— stands for social relationships
— stands for sensitivity to social issues
— stands for social commitment

1.6 SCOPE OF CIVICS

Scope of Civics is very vast. It touches almost all aspects of social, political and economic life in form or the other. It draws its material from all other social sciences. It deals with the social environment which is influenced by a multitude of factors.

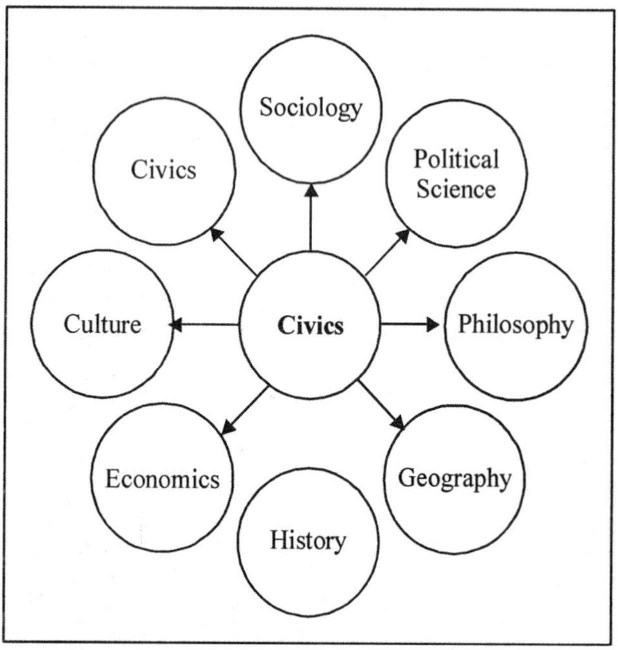

Fig. 1.1: The Scope of Civics

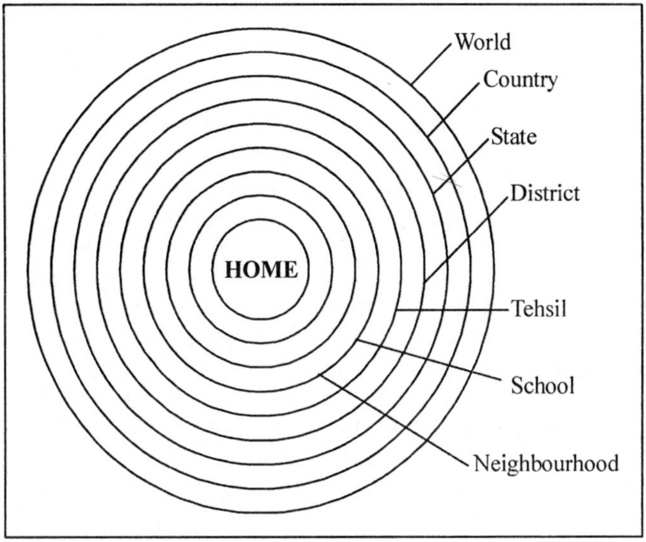

Fig. 1.2: The Expanding Environment

1.7 A BRIEF HISTORY OF THE PLACE OF CIVICS IN THE SCHOOL CURRICULUM IN INDIA:

Basic System of Education (1938)

The basic system of education included social studies as a compulsory subject in the curriculum. Excepting for a brief period of two years' rule of Congress Ministries (1937-39), it did not make any headway in independent India.

Secondary Education Commission (1952-53)

At the middle stage of education, it recommended social studies (including History, Geography and Civics). At the secondary stage (classes IX to XI), it suggested seven streams (groups of subjects). In the humanities stream it included History, Geography and Elements of Economics and Civics.

The recommendations of the Commission could not be implemented and Civics remained a separate subject in classes IX and X.

Education Commission (1964-66)

At the lower primary stage (classes I-V), Study of the Environment (covering Science and Social Studies) in classes III to IV/V was recommended. At the higher primary stage (classes VI-VIII), Social Studies (History, Geography and Civics) was recommended as a compulsory subject.

At the lower secondary stage (classes IX-X), History, Geography and Civics were recommended.

Ishwarbhai Patel Committee (1977)

The Committee included History, Civics, Geography, Economics and

Commerce as separate constituents of Social Studies at the secondary stage (classes IX and X). It clearly mentioned the inclusion of History, Civics and Geography in middle classes (VI to VIII).

1.8 DIMINISHING PLACE OF CIVICS AS A SEPARATE SUBJECT IN CURRICULUM BUT MORE IMPORTANCE TO ITS CONTENTS

According to modern thinking among educators, Civics, History and Geography as separate disciplines have no place in the curriculum. They consider these subjects as pieces of incoherent information and knowledge. Their view is that knowledge should be given to the students in an integrated manner and this could be incorporated in the subject titled 'Social Studies'/ 'Social Sciences'. However, the situation is that although the contents generally included in Civics, History and Geography are also included in Social Studies but are called units. Thus the situation is very paradoxical. It is not very clear as to why discard the names of the subjects and to include their contents under units. For all practical purposes, teachers in the classroom in general follow the traditional nomenclature of subjects, i.e., History, Geography and Civics.

1.9 National Curriculum Framework for School Education (2000)

It included the compulsory study of Social Sciences in classes VI to X. The social studies drew its contents mainly from Geography, History, Civics and Economics. It also included some elements of Sociology. The concerns and issues of the contemporary world were also kept in view the Curriculum discarded the nomenclature of Civics and names units 1, 2 and 3. It emphasised the importance of Civics and its contents in these words, "In a democratic set-up with decentralisation of power, local governments such as 'Panchayati Raj' has gained importance. It aims at raising the levels of participation and involvement of people. In order to make optimum utilisation of resources for development, the local governance has to be more responsive and efficient. The learners, therefore, are to be equipped well to understand the process of development, its need and implications as well as the system of governance at all levels – local, state and national and their own place in it. This would necessitate considerable increase in the coverage of courses in Civics".

1.10 National Curriculum Framework 2005

National Curriculum Framework, 2005 prepared by NCERT observed, "Instead of Civics, the term 'Political Science' be used. Civics appeared in the Indian school curriculum in the colonial period against the background of increasing 'disloyalty' among Indians towards the Raj. Emphasis on obedience and loyalty were the key features of Civics. Political science treats civil society as the sphere that produces sensitive, interrogative, deliberate, and transformative citizens". Thus the national curriculum framework was a sort of 'death-warrant to Civics'.

Accordingly the syllabus formulated by the NCERT in 2005 discarded the term Civics and instead used the terms History: our pasts (Class VI: Our Pasts-I; Class VII: Our Pasts-II; and Class VIII: Our Pasts-III). It discontinued the three traditional categories, i.e., Ancient India, Medieval India and Modern India. For Geography it has used these terms – Class VI: The Earth – Our Habitat; Class VII: Our Environment; Class VIII: Resources and Development.

For Civics, it has used the term 'Social and Political Life'. Further for class VI, the title is 'Diversity and Interdependence' for class VII it is 'Democracy and Equality' and for class VIII, it is 'Rule of Law and Social Justice'.

2

Objectives of Teaching Civics

2.1 BROAD CATEGORIES OF OBJECTIVES OF TEACHING CIVICS

Objectives of teaching Civics may broadly be divided into two categories:

1. General Objectives of Teaching Civics
2. Specific Objectives of Teaching Civics

2.2 GENERAL OBJECTIVES OF TEACHING CIVICS

1. *Strengthening Democracy*: We adopted a democratic system of government in 1950. By all standards, ours is young democracy. We have to do everything to strengthen it. A study of Civics can help to develop proper attitudes in the young pupils, which can ultimately strengthen this democracy.

2. *Strengthening Secularism*: India is a secular democracy. The secular character of this democracy is well-enshrined in our Constitution. However, there are forces in the country which are communal in nature. They often fan the feelings of religious and communal fanaticism and threaten the idea of secularism. Civics will teach the young pupils to rise above narrow communal considerations.

3. *Strengthening Socialism*: Thirdly, India is wedded to Gandhian Socialism and Sarvodaya. It is a way of life also. Civics is a subject which can teach this way of life deeply rooted in Indian culture.

4. *Strengthening National and Emotional Integration*: India is a vast country. There are numerous forces which still indulge in fissiparous tendencies and adopt practices and actions which often threaten the unity of the country. This is a serious problem. A proper teaching of Civics can create a sound base for the continued oneness and unity of the country.

5. *Promoting Rational Outlook*: There are numerous other evils also which eat into the vitals of the society. Untouchability, regionalism and casteism are a few of them. Attempts are, being made to fight them through many sources. A sound base against them, however, can be laid in the minds of the people in their young age. Civics is a subject which can play a leading role in this direction.

6. *Strengthening International Understanding*: In fostering internationalism—that is, educating people with a broad outlook and an international view of the world free from nationalistic views on sentiments—the contribution of all school subjects is important. But the most important school subject of all is Civics. The content of Civics course has a direct influence on the formation of pupil's scientific world outlook, on their view

of the world and their attitudes to people in their own country and elsewhere. Teaching of Civics must be aimed at educating pupils in a spirit of respect and friendship for other people. Students must understand that all forms of aggression and racial hatred or racial discrimination are inimical to humanity and constitute a crime against it. Enormous harm is done to the spirit of peace and mutual understanding whenever Civics directly or indirectly, is used to kindle narrow nationalism.

7. *Strengthening Common Ideas of Various Faiths*: These are as under:

Buddhism: Hurt not others with that which pains yourself.

Christianity: All things whatsoever ye would wish that men should do to you, do ye even so to them; for this is the law of the prophets.

Confucianism: Is there anyone maxim which ought to be acted upon throughout one's whole life? Surely the maxim of loving-kindness is such. Do not unto others what you would not they should do unto you.

Judaism: What is hurtful to yourself, do not to your fellow man. That is the whole of the Torah and the remainder is but commentary. Go learn it.

Hinduism: That is the sum of duty: do naught to others which is done to the would cause the pain.

Islam: No one of you is a believer until he loves for his brother what he loves for himself.

Taoism: Regard your neighbour's loss as your loss.

8. *Citizenship Education*: Every country employs a wide range of social institutions to induct new members into its society, to transmit the cultural heritage to the young and to develop in its people a feeling of national pride. The major means for accomplishing, these goals is through its educational institutions, both formal and informal. Within the schools, the major responsibility falls upon the Civics programme.

Education for citizenship is not the exclusive property of Civics. Other subjects also contribute, but Civics has a special role. From their Civics course students learn how the government is organised and the roles they are expected to play as citizens, and they learn the ideology which binds citizens together and gives meaning and purpose to their national identity.

2.3 SPECIFIC OBJECTIVES OF TEACHING CIVICS

To teach any subject effectively it is essential to know why it is taught and what difference it is likely to make in the pupil's knowledge, understandings, skills, habits and values. Given below are some important objectives of teaching Civics. This account will assist the teacher in teaching and evaluating his work in the classroom.

2.4 DEVELOPMENT OF UNDERSTANDING

Teaching of Civics should enable the pupils to understand that:

1. The basic needs—food, clothes and shelter of man all over the world are the same and man always seeks the help of others in meeting these needs.

2. Man's life on earth is intimately connected with his physical environment. His activities are to a large extent conditioned by it, though he has always been striving, with varying success to turn it to his advantage also.

3. Man's life is made possible by the use of physical resources, like soil, water, forests, minerals. Man needs these resources, badly and it is his duty, therefore, to conserve them and to put them to the best possible use.

4. Man lives in society. He has to depend on others for his needs. Thus members of a family, states of the country and different countries of the world are dependent on one another. Life is impossible without cooperation.

5. Mutual cooperation, goodwill, trust and a sense of responsibility are an essential prerequisite, for smooth and peaceful life in the society.

6. In the democratic, socialist, secular republic of India all citizens have equal rights and duties. Students should understand these fully and discharge them conscientiously.

7. There is a great diversity among the people in the different parts of our country with respect to languages, food habits, dresses and religious beliefs. In spite of all these differences we all are Indians and make one nation.

8. India has a culture of her own, and we as Indians cherish certain values. In order to preserve and modify our culture and values it is essential to know these.

9. Several great men have contributed to the development of Indian culture. We should also know about these great men.

10. There is a great diversity in different countries but all countries are a part of one world. Each country has some important contribution to make to the world. We should show the same respect to the people of each country and should honour the differences in their religious beliefs and faiths.

2.5 DEVELOPMENT OF SKILLS AND ABILITIES

1. While taking part in meetings and working in groups children should be able:

- to explore themselves clearly and logically through speech or writing.
- to listen to others with due respect and attention.
- to use respectful language during conversation and to speak on one's turn.
- to discharge assigned responsibilities, to cooperate with others and to be able to lead others.
- to take active part in meetings, debates dramas and other activities and to work systematically.
- to arrange exhibitions.
- to collect information from different sources, to present it, to use it and to write brief reports.

2. While visiting important places of neighbourhood, children should be able:

- to plan tours and excursions.
- to be courteous and respectful towards others.
- to cooperate and to share things with others.
- to understand the traffic signs and follow the traffic rules.

3. While using maps, charts, graphs and globes, children should be able:

- to identify, read and compare different types of maps.
- to measure the distance between two places on the map.

- to locate different places on the map.
- to read directions on the map.
- to know and understand the meaning of colours and symbols used in maps.
- to understand the difference between a globe and a map.
- to read easy and simple arts and graphs.
- to prepare simple charts and models.
- to arrange in the album pictures, flowers, leaves and newspaper clippings.

2.6 DEVELOPMENT OF ATTITUDES

The teaching of Civics should develop in the pupil the following attitudes:

1. Respect for people of different religions, communities, language and occupations.
2. Respect for and pride in the national goals and values.
3. Faith in country's unity.
4. Respect for national symbols.
5. Accepting small responsibilities for the sake of the country.
6. Keen desire to preserve country's independence.
7. Willingness to share responsibility to preserve personal or government property and the natural resources of the country.
8. Respect for law and government.
9. Respect for teachers and elders.
10. Sympathy for the poor and the helpless.
11. Faith in international understanding and cooperation.
12. Appreciation of natural beauty.
13. Awareness towards change.
14. Self-reliance.

(Adopted from *Social Studies Teaching Manual*, NCERT, New Delhi, 1972).

2.7 OBJECTIVES OF TEACHING CIVICS FOR CLASSES III TO V

NCERT syllabi for Classes III to V in accordance with the nationally developed curriculum for the ten-year school states:

For Classes III, IV and V, a course in Environmental Studies I (social studies) would be introduced. This course at this stage consists of a broad and composite instructional area which draws its information from different social sciences such as History, Geography, Civics and Economics in order to develop social values and attitudes which are in conformity with the cultural heritage of our society and its accepted goals. The general objectives for teaching this course at the primary school stage are as follows:

1. to help the child to explore and understand his social and cultural environment;

2. to develop in the child a sense of belongingness to the society through a gradual widening of his mental horizons — from his home and school to the wider world;

3. to acquaint the child with the world of work and to develop in him respect for human labour;

4. to encourage the child to understand that we are striving to build a better life for all;

5. to impress on the child's mind, as he grows, that ours is a rich and composite culture in the formation of which people of different faiths, regions, and linguistic groups have made valuable contributions;

6. to develop among children respect for all religions and their places and ways of worship;

7. to encourage the child to understand that we are all equal irrespective of sex, creed, language, etc. and that there are no superior or inferior people and that we all cooperate and organise ourselves to solve our problems; and

8. to impress on the child that India, in keeping with its cultural heritage, is one of the important countries of the world that is active in promoting peace, understanding and cooperation among the nations of the world.

2.8 OBJECTIVES OF TEACHING CIVICS IN CLASSES VI TO VIII

Civics as a constituent of Social Sciences: NCERT Syllabi (1976) for Classes VI to VIII in accordance with the nationally developed curriculum for the ten-year school gives the following objectives:

The course in Civics has the major responsibility of promoting well-informed and intelligent citizens who have the ability to participate in the affairs of their community effectively. From this point of view, the course at this stage aims mainly at imparting training in civic life rather than mere scholarship. It contains such socially imperative knowledge which would also provide training in the development of civic competencies. Some practical aspects of citizenship education have also been incorporated from the point of view of adopting a functional approach. Thus the syllabus in Civics at the middle stage has the following objectives:

1. to provide the student with intelligent understanding of the 'various social responsibilities and civic processes;
2. to help the student understand our constitution and the values enshrined in it;
3. to acquaint the student with the machinery of the government at different levels;
4. to make the student conscious of the actual problems that are facing our country today and instil in him a sense of responsibility towards the community;
5. to make the student identify with the people and their institutions; and
6. to inculcate in the student the values of democracy, secularism, socialism and national integration.

Project Work: The student who is a citizen in training, needs help in getting experience and insight into the process of citizenship. Under this scheme an opportunity should be provided to the student to develop abilities which are essential for any active citizen in India.

It is suggested that 20 per cent of the total marks allotted to Civics should be assigned to the project work. Every student should take up at least two practical activities every year and prepare a short write-up or report on his project. The reports of the students should be evaluated on the basis of three components:

1. collection of data;
2. analysis and interpretation of data; and
3. conclusions drawn on the basis of this interpretation.

List of Projects:

(i) Sanitation problem of any town of the area.

(ii) Management and maintenance of civic amenities in the area and the related problems.

(iii) Functioning of police in the area.

(iv) Distribution and location of educational institutions in the area—nursery, primary, middle, secondary, technical; aided and unaided, for boys and girls, etc.

(v) Organising school, government and national festivals.

(vi) Election process from nomination to declaration of results of elections of students' union, village panchayats, municipal committees.

(vii) Study of some major developments in the national life, e.g., electrification, nationalisation of banks, nuclear experiment, food, population, green revolution, white revolution, impact of 20-point programme in the locality, study of local historical events connected with the Indian Independence Movement.

(viii) Participation of local people in war effort during Indo-Pak and Sino-Indian Wars.

(ix) Achievements and problems of any one of the following:

- (a) Village Panchayat/Municipal Committee or Corporation.
- (b) Block Samiti.
- (c) Zila Parishad.

Note: Not an exhaustive list, other projects of such type could also be taken up.

2.9 OBJECTIVES OF TEACHING CIVICS IN CLASSES IX AND X

The Curriculum for the ten-year school—A framework of NCERT (1975) states the objectives of Civics as under:

The major objective of the study of the social sciences is to acquaint the child with his past and present geographical and social environment. An effective programme of teaching of the social sciences in schools should help the pupils to take a keen interest in the ways people live and function through various socio-economic and political institutions. It should also help children to develop an insight into human relationship, social values and attitudes. These are essential to enable the growing citizen of tomorrow to participate effectively in the affairs of the community, the state, the country, and the world at large.

The teaching of the social sciences should enable children to appreciate India's rich cultural heritage as also to recognise and get rid of what is undesirable and antiquated, especially in the context of the social change.

The schools should see that narrow parochial, chauvinistic and obscurantist tendencies are not allowed to grow in our pupils. The schools should endeavour to develop a will and ability in every pupil to participate in the most important task of the reconstruction of our society and economy with a sense of social commitment. Children should also develop a faith in the destiny of our nation in terms of promoting a spirit of tolerance and assimilation, and peace and harmony among the peoples of the world. Thus instruction in the social sciences should promote the values and ideals of humanism, secularism, socialism and democracy. It should inculcate attitudes and impart the knowledge, necessary for the achievement of the principal values of just world order, maximisation of economic and social welfare, minimisation of violence and maximisation of ecological stability.

The study of the social sciences in Classes I-X should include the study of history, geography, Civics and economics. In view of the limited time that will be available for each of these branches, it would be desirable to integrate their teaching in a way that the pupils develop a proper understanding of the facts and problems in the right perspective without causing any damage to the totality of the individual disciplines. This would require identifying the essential units in each of the subjects and then into an integrated syllabus for the social sciences.

Since Classes V, VIII and X are the terminal classes for a large number of students, it is necessary to develop self-contained courses of study for each stage, and at the same time the courses should be such as to lay the foundation for the subsequent stage. While following this principle, it is also necessary to avoid repetition and waste of time and energy as far as possible.

2.10 NEW DEVELOPMENTS AND THEIR IMPLICATIONS FOR TEACHING OF CIVICS IN INDIA

As we think about the present and future, we need to examine what 'new' developments are likely to make impact on the teaching of Civics in India.

	Apparent Trend	*Implications for the Teaching of Civics*
1.	Increasing interdependence of India with other parts of the world.	More thorough study of all the major areas of the world.
2.	Increasing importance of science and technology.	Examination of social implications of science and technology.
3.	Increasing demand for a higher standard of living.	Exploitation of resources and their wise use.
4.	Increasing number of persons in India living close to each other.	More attention to the skills and attitudes involved in human relations.
5.	Increasing urbanisation and sub-urbanisation with large centres for work.	More knowledge of the local community. Desire to work at the local level for civic improvement.
6.	Increasing mobility of the population.	The need to develop roots in the families and to know about new co-mmunities.

(Contd.)

	Apparent Trend	*Implications for the Teaching of Civics*
7.	Increasing pace of life.	More emphasis on mental health and human relations.
8.	Increasing changes in family.	As thorough a study of family life as possible.
9.	Increasing leisure and length of life.	Importance of life-education and further education. Knowledge of ways of spending leisure time wisely.
10.	Increasing role of the arts.	Encouragement to cultural pursuits.
11.	Increasing powers of the mass media of communication and of pressure groups.	Development of critical thinking about the mass media and pressure groups.
12.	Increasing facility of communication.	Making use of modern means of communication—radio and T.V., etc.
13.	Increasing recognition of rights of minorities.	Inculcating a desire to help them to develop their rightful place in a society of equals.
14.	Increasing centralisation of society, government with more and more planning.	An examination of the problem as well as the benefits of such planning.
15.	Increasing facilities for education through life.	Development of an attitude of wanting to continue some form of education.
16.	Increasing conflicts in value system.	A careful search for values and philosophy of life with stress on freedom.

2.11 INSTRUCTIONAL OBJECTIVES OF CIVICS

1. To acquire the knowledge (information) of facts, terms, concepts, conventions, trends, principles, generalisations, assumptions, hypotheses, processes, etc. in Civics.
2. To develop an understanding of facts, terms concepts, conventions, trends, principles and generalisations, assumptions, hypotheses, processes, etc. in Civics.
3. To apply the acquired knowledge of Civics and its understanding in unfamiliar situations.
4. To acquire practical skills essential for the study of Civics.
5. To develop interest in the subject and problems related to civic and political life of the people of one's country and of those of the world.
6. To develop desirable positive attitudes necessary for developing a broader outlook.

Objectives and Their Specifications

1.0 Objective: To acquire the knowledge (information) of facts, terms, concepts, conventions, principles, generalisations, assumptions, hypotheses, problems, processes, etc. in Civics.

Specifications of the Objective: To demonstrate the achievement of the above objective, the pupil:

1.1 recalls facts, terms, concepts, principles, trends, etc.
1.2 recognises facts, terms, concepts, principles, trends, etc.
1.3 reads information from various forms of representation of data, i.e., maps, charts, diagrams, graphs, etc.

2.0 Objective: To develop an understanding of facts, terms, concepts, conventions, trends, principles generalisations, assumptions, hypothesis, processes, etc. in Civics.

Specifications of the Objective: To demonstrate the achievement of the above objective, the pupil:

2.1 discriminates.
2.2 classifies.
2.3 compares and contrasts.
2.4 identifies relationships.
2.5 detects the points of emphasis and the trends of arguments.
2.6 cites illustrations.
2.7 detects errors and fallacies and corrects them.
2.8 explains (analyses or gives meaning or clarifies or elucidates).
2.9 gives reasons or advances arguments.
2.10 interprets data presented in different forms.

3.0 Objective: To apply the acquired knowledge and its understanding to unfamiliar situations.

Specifications of the Objective: To demonstrate the achievement of the above objective, the pupil:

3.1 analyses the unfamiliar situations or problems and:
   (a) finds out what is given and what is required.
   (b) recalls knowledge relevant to the situation.
   (c) judges the sufficiency or insufficiency, inadequacy of data or any other evidence for solving the problem.
3.2 establishes relationships.
3.3 suggests alternative methods for solving a particular problem.
3.4 selects the most appropriate method of attack.
3.5 draws inferences and makes generalisations.
3.6 makes predictions regarding the probable outcome of a given situation.

4.0 Objective: To acquire practical skills essential for the study of Civics.

Specification of the Objective: To demonstrate the achievement of the above objective, the pupil:

4.1 draws maps, charts, tables, diagrams, graphs, etc. from the given data.
4.2 translates data from one form of presentation to another.
4.3 prepares models.

5.0 Objective: To develop interest in the subject and problems related to the civic and political life of the people of one's country and of those of the world.

Specifications of the Objective: To demonstrate the achievement of the above objective, the pupil:

5.1 voluntarily studies literature related to Civics and tries to know about the inherent issues and problems.
5.2 spends leisure in trying to know about civic problems and issues and exerts in finding solutions to them.
5.3 closely observes civic and political processes and changes at local, national and international levels.
5.4 discusses and is able to communicate various aspects of every day civic problems and their implications.
5.5 enthusiastically participates in excursions, visits and field-trips to places of civic and political activities (e.g., Panchayats, Municipalities, Assemblies, etc.).
5.6 enjoys attending and participating in debates, symposium, discussions on civic and political problems.
5.7 enjoys writing articles and preparing pamphlets, brochures, etc. on topics related to Civics.
5.8 enjoys preparing display-materials related to civic and political life and events.
5.9 enjoys collecting information about other political systems and facts about other location regions and countries.

6.0 Objective: To develop desirable positive attitudes necessary for developing a broader outlook.

Specifications of the Objective: To demonstrate the achievement of the above objective, the pupil:

6.1 respects the views, opinions and problems of others and displays sympathy and fellow-feeling towards them:
  (a) shows tolerance.
  (b) controls emotions and displays restraint.
  (c) develops social awareness.
6.2 is able to present situations in the light of a historical perspective.
6.3 develops a sense of law-abidingness.
6.4 assumes responsibility in cooperative and civic activities.
6.5 judges issues objectively and on their merits.
6.6 displays abhorrence towards 'socio-economic malpractices like hoarding, profiteering, black-marketing, smuggling, bribery for votes, etc.
6.7 shows sympathetic understanding of the problems of people belonging to different social, religious, linguistic and cultural groups.
6.8 realises the importance of the contributions made by the leaders of the nation in different spheres.
6.9 develops a sense of respect for the National Flag, the National Anthem, the National Emblem and the Constitution of one's own country and those of other countries of the world.
6.10 develops faith in democratic values.

(*Source*: 'Instructional Objectives in School Subjects', NCERT)

3

Correlation of Civics with other Social Sciences

3.1 KNOWLEDGE IS ONE WHOLE

Any piece of knowledge or experience or activity is not to be treated in isolation or in a fragmented manner. Mind is not composed of different faculties of branches which are unrelated. Each branch of knowledge is influenced and influences the other in one or the other form. Cohesion is the power of mind which integrates influences and impressions. Similar elements, experiences, ideas, activities and knowledge are stored in an integrated way. Correlation is the technique with the help of which we can get unified and integrated knowledge.

Life has varied facets. We undertake different kinds of activities related to our cultural, economic, political or social needs. Outwardly they appear to be isolated ones but in reality they are related to each other.

3.2 MEANING OF CORRELATION

Education is considered as life centric. Education is for life and life is very complex and full of several problems which are interlinked. The study of a particular problem requires the study of a number of subjects or disciplines. Clothing, for example, is related to industry—cottage, small scale or large scale. Production of cotton depends on the state of agriculture which in its turn depends on government policies and political set-up. So it is quite clear that the study of one area is closely linked with the other areas. It, therefore, becomes necessary to correlate the study of one subject whenever possible with other subjects.

Correlation brings about clarity, comprehension and consolidation of knowledge. It provides unity and purpose.

According to K.G. Saiyidain, the primary objective of correlation is a better integration of knowledge and experience and an economy of time and experience (Fig. 3.1).

3.3 DIFFERENT TYPES OF CORRELATION

(1) Correlation of the subject with life

(2) Correlation of the subject with other subjects

(3) Correlation of the contents of a subject among themselves

(4) Correlation of the subjects/subject with craft

(5) Correlation of the subject with the environment

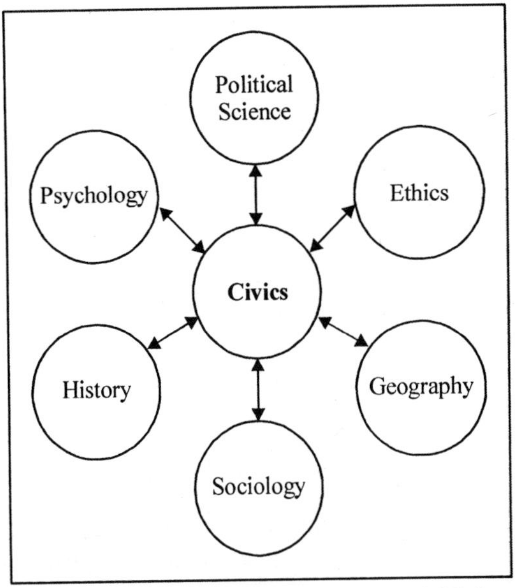

Fig. 3.1: Co-relation of Civics with Other Social Sciences

3.4 POLITICAL SCIENCE AND CIVICS

Political science is concerned with human relations in their political aspects, i.e., political structure and political processes which are carried out through various forms of political organisations at the local, state, regional, national and international level. All of these have their origin in the study of Civics. Whereas the political scientist studies these in detail the theoretical differences, the student of Civics makes an elementary but practical study of the various aspects. Both however study forms of local government, state legislature and federal type of national government.

3.5 CIVICS AND HISTORY

Civics and History are interdependent. It is accepted that a study of contemporary society is incomplete without an account of its development in the previous times. But by itself, the picture is not complete. The study of history would be incomplete without the study of the perspective of the present society. History without Civics has no fruit, Civics without History has no roots. Separating Civics and History, one becomes cripple, if not a corpse and the other a will of the wisp. History is the laboratory and library of Civics. A study of History is absolutely necessary to understand civic institutions. History places at the disposal of a 'Civic Scientist' a very useful fund of information about man's civic activities in the past. History provides invaluable raw material to the civic scholar.

History is also indebted to Civics. History fades into mere literature when it loses to sight its relation to civic institutions. Without description and analysis of civic events, history tends to become a mere fiction. Civic ideas, thoughts and motives contribute to shaping the human history.

Without understanding the concepts like democracy, liberty, equality, etc. it is not possible to understand the historical process. Civic institutions have contributed in making the history of societies. American history begins with the American Revolution which primarily was the outcome of several matters of civic importance. French history begins with the revolution of 1889 and modern Russian history with the 1917 resolution and 1990. All these events were closely related to matters connected with Civic administration.

Following points regarding the relationship of History and Civics may be mentioned:

1. History provides material for Civics.
2. History is the laboratory of Civics.
3. Civics makes History interesting.
4. Civics enables History to bear fruit.

3.6 CIVICS AND ECONOMICS

Economic situations have a great bearing on the civic life of a country. Economic conditions in Russia brought about a new form of political government. Similarly civic institutions of a country have greatly affected the economic conditions of the people. Every political party is supposed to have its political agenda.

Aristotle, in his book '*Politics*' described in detail economic problems of the State. Chanakya's book entitled '*Arthasastra*' discusses various civic aspects like justice and peace side-by-side agriculture, currency and commerce, etc.

Movements of civic reforms are profoundly influenced by economic causes and economic life is conditioned by civic institutions and ideas.

There is no doubt that many of the problems of the State are economic ones and the State works for their solution.

3.7 CIVICS AND SOCIOLOGY

Sociology studies the factors which are responsible for bringing about civic changes. Sociologists like Auguste Comte and Max Weber greatly influenced the thinking on Civic matters by their sociological approach. They discussed in detail the impact of the changing society on the character of the State and its various civic institutions. Civics help sociology by furnishing the details about State and government, which are essential in understanding sociological problems.

Following points may be mentioned regarding the relationship of Civics and Sociology.

1. Civics recognises the facts established by Sociology.
2. Civic institutions are various social institutions.
3. Civic life is a part of social life.
4. Social conditions influence the nature of civic institutions and organisations.

3.8 CIVICS AND ETHICS

Plato established an intimate connection between Civics and Ethics when he observed that citizens can be formed only in a good State. He regarded

State to be a moral and ethical institution and stated his ideals from the moral point of view. Gandhiji observed that what is morally wrong cannot be politically correct. Several civic laws of the State intend to improve the ethical plane of society. Without high ethical standards, civic institutions cannot function effectively. Transparency in them leads further civic values.

Civic institutions are idle institutions without an ethical code.

3.9 CIVICS AND PSYCHOLOGY

It has been observed by Prof. Garner that government to be able and really popular must express the mental ideas and moral sentiments of those who are subject to its authority. In short it must be in harmony with 'mental set-up' of the race. A great significance is given by civic institutions to solve the civic problems of the society by psychological methods. It is believed that several problems originate through human nature. Civic institutions cannot be analysed without an analysis of man. It is of great importance to note that three sessions of the American National Conference on the Science of Politics which were held in 1923, 1924 and 1925 were attended by leading psychologists like L.L. Thurstone of Chicago University and Floyed Allport of Syracuse.

3.10 SOCIAL STUDIES AS AN INTEGRATED SUBJECT AND NOT HISTORY, GEOGRAPHY AND CIVICS

The teaching of History, Geography and Civics only imparts miscellaneous and unrelated information and throws very little light and does not provide insight into social conditions and problems. The study of these subjects does not create the desire to improve the existing state of things.

Whole group of studies has, therefore, to be viewed as a compact whole whose object is to adjust the students to their environment which includes the family, community, State and Nation—so that they may be able to understand how society has come to its present form and interpret intelligently the matrix of social forces and movements in the midst of which they are living.

There are six important reasons which necessitate that History, Geography and Civics should not be introduced as separate subjects:

1. We cannot expect from these subjects the same social concepts and skills as we expect from a unified course of Social Studies.
2. Up to the secondary stage of school education, the aim is to give only general and liberal education and this is possible only through an integrated course of Social Studies which not only includes the knowledge of civic, cultural, economic, physical and social experience of man but also the development of attitudes and skills.
3. In the past, the family and the community provided various experiences to the child but now it is not possible. This task is to be performed by the present day school and only an integrated course in the school can fulfil this responsibility.
4. Social problems and skills cannot be treated in isolation. The complexity of modern industrial, economic and social life demands that the entire outlook must be changed. This is possible only through a unified course of Social Studies.
5. Isolated subjects fail to develop enlightened citizenry. An integrated

course of Social Studies help to build up in pupils a widespread interest in current affairs.

6. Social Studies can serve as a safe foundation on which the specialisation in History, Geography and Civics can be built at a later stage.

The Secondary Education Commission (1952-53) has observed, "It is not often realised that the complaint of over-crowding is largely due to the multiplicity of subjects, presented in separate entries, without bringing out their organic inter-relationship. So, in framing the curriculum an attempt should be mate to see whether certain subjects can be grouped in large, organically related units dealing with certain broad areas of human knowledge and interest. Thus, it is psychologically preferable to present subjects round the study of the social environment and human relations under the comprehensive heading of "Social Studies" than to teach a number of separate subjects like History, Geography, Civics and Economics in watertight compartments".

Social Studies helps the student to discover and explain how this adjustment has taken place in the past and how it is taking place today. Through it the students should be able to acquire not only the knowledge but also the attitudes and values which are essential for successful group living and civic efficiency. It should endeavour to give the students not only a sense of national patriotism and an appreciation of national heritage, but also a keen and lively sense of world unity and world citizenship.

Correct Concept of Social Studies

An analysis of the foregoing paragraphs brings out the following characteristics of Social Studies:

1. Social Studies deals with the inter-relations that develop between and among people and those that develop between people and their environment.
2. Social Studies is a broad and composite instructional area which draws its contents from different social sciences.
3. Social Studies is a compound rather than a mixture where the ingredients lose their identity and something tangible and worthwhile emerges out of the combination. It differs from the teaching of History, Geography, Civics, Economics, etc. in the same sense in which the taste of ice-cream differs from that of its ingredients like sugar, cream, milk, etc. tasted in isolation.
4. Social Studies aims at enabling the students to adjust to their social environment which includes the family, community, state and nation and in fact the entire humanity.
5. Social Studies deals with the art of living.
6. Social Studies deals with those areas of curriculum that enable the students to interpret intelligently the matrix of social force and movements in the midst of which they are living.
7. Social Studies establishes relationships between present, past and future.
8. Social Studies integrates the knowledge of all social sciences and is, therefore, called 'Coordinate' and 'Coordinating'.
9. Social Studies is the applied branch of Social Sciences, introduced in the school curriculum with a view to developing proper attitudes, sensibilities and skills in future citizens.

10. The materials of Social Studies are useful for general education at school level, before collegiate education starts so that pupils can learn them with sufficient ease and interest.

11. The contents of Social Studies are continuously growing and changing with the changing social process. Hence, its contents will have to be revised periodically.

12. Social Studies cover the study of communities at all levels local, regional, national and international with focus on man and his social environment.

13. Social Studies stresses contemporary human life and its problems rather than the past history of man.

Social Studies includes material from various disciplines as indicated below:

1. *Geography*: To exist, man must utilise natural resources.
2. *History*: The life of man has been and is influenced by change.
3. *Economics*: Productive resources are scare and human wants are unlimited.
4. *Civics*: Man seeks to establish and maintain a public authority through which to govern and be governed.
5. *Psychology*: Man's behaviour is purposive and goal-oriented.
6. *Sociology*: Man is a social being.
7. *Anthropology*: Man is a man, yet everywhere he is unique.
8. *Social Psychology*: Man as a social being is both an individual amid a member of group.

4

Curriculum and Principles of Curriculum Construction

4.1 MEANING OF CURRICULUM

Curriculum as the 'Social Environment in Motion'. Curriculum may be defined as the 'social environment in motion'. It is the sum total of all planned and directed purposeful learning activities and experiences provided by the school to the learners for achieving the desired objectives. It is made up of everything that surrounds the learners in the classroom, the library, the laboratory, the workshop, the hobbies club, the school farm, the school playground, etc. It comprises all the opportunities for learning which the school provides to learners to meet their varying needs. These opportunities relate to much more than the courses of study. The courses of studies are merely a suggestion for curriculum activities and procedures, a guide for the teacher to follow. Curriculum includes any materials or activities that affect the learning, development, attitudes, skills and behaviour of the children in the school.

Curriculum is the pivot and the hub around which all activities in the school revolve. It is the 'warp and woof' of the process of education.

Curriculum in Political Science and Civics is that part of the school curriculum which includes the subject-matter and experiences that is intended to acquire an understanding of human relations, give knowledge of the basic principles and values of the society, inculcate right attitudes, develop appropriate skills, teach tolerance cultivate a forward outlook, impart mental training, help resolving contemporary individual and social problems, foster national feelings and develop international understanding.

Etymologically the term curriculum is derived from the Latin word 'currere' which means a run-way course. Thus curriculum "is a run-way course which one runs to reach a goal—a course of study".

4.2 DEFINITIONS OF CURRICULUM

Following are the important definitions of curriculum:

1. *A. Alberty* and *E. Alberty* in their publication '*Reorganising the High School Curriculum*' (1959) observes, "Curriculum is the sum total of student activities which the school sponsors for the purpose of achieving its objectives".

2. '*Blond's Encyclopaedia of Education*' (1969) defines curriculum "as all the experiences which a pupil has under the guidance of a school".

3. *Bossing, L. Nelson* state in '*Principles of Secondary Education*' (1965) "Popularly the curriculum has been thought of as those compendiums of information and skills which the school has made available for study....... It consists of experiences the learner has under the direction of the school."

4. '*A Dictionary of Education*' by *Derek, Rowntree* (1981) reads as, "Curriculum can refer to the total structure of ideas and activities developed by an educational institution to meet the learning needs of students and to achieve desired educational aims."

5. '*Good's Dictionary of Education*' (1980) gives these meaning, "Curriculum is a body of prescribed educative experiences under school supervision, designed to provide an individual with the best possible training and experience to fit him for the society of which he is a part or to qualify him for a trade or profession."

6. *The Education Commission* (*1964-66*) or the *Kothari Commission* views curriculum as, "We conceive of the school curriculum as the totality of learning experiences that the school provides for the pupils through all the manifold activities in the school or outside, that are carried on under its supervision. From this point of view, the distinction between curricular and extra-curricular work ceases to exist, and a school camp and games and sports are curricular or rather co-curricular activities."

7. *Hills, P.J.* in '*Dictionary of Education*' (1982) writes, "A simple way of considering the curriculum is to see in terms of four facets: content, methods, purposes, evaluation."

8. *Johnson, M. Jr.* in *Definitions and Models in Curriculum Theory* (1967) states, "Curriculum is a structured series of intended learning outcomes. Curriculum prescribes (or at least anticipates) the result of instruction."

9. *Saiyidain, K.G.* provides the following concept of curriculum in his *Education, Culture, and the Social Order* (1952), "The curriculum is primarily an aid in the process of adjusting the child to the environment in which he functions from day-to-day and in the environment in which he will have to organise his activities later."

10. According to the *Secondary Education Commission 1952-53*, "It includes the totality of experience that a pupil receives through the manifold activities that go on in the school—in the classroom, library, laboratory, workshop, playground and in the numerous informal contacts between teachers and pupils. In this case the whole life of the school becomes the curriculum which can touch the life of the students at all points and help in the evolution of balanced personality".

Summing Up—Thus broadly speaking, curriculum is the blue print or plan of the school that includes experiences for the learners. It is a means to achieve the ends of education. Guidance of the school staff plays an important part in providing suitable experiences to the learners.

From above, the concept of curriculum may be explained as:

1. A curriculum includes all the subjects activities and experiences for the developments of the child.
2. All these subjects, activities and experiences are under the guidance and supervision of teacher.

3. All these subjects, activities and experiences are offered in the school inside the classroom, in the farm, the laboratory in the workshop, in the playground, etc.
4. Some portion of the curriculum is for all pupils while other portions may be in accordance with individual needs.
5. A diversified curriculum is provided in Class XI in the 10+2 pattern of education.

4.3 SIGNIFICANCE AND NEED FOR THE CURRICULUM

The child of today is the builder of tomorrow. It is only through a well-designed and effectively implemented curriculum that the child can be equipped to realise his inner potential and to contribute meaningfully to nation-building. Curriculum is basic to the aesthetic, emotional, ethical, intellectual, physical, social, spiritual and vocational development of the child.

As observed by *William J. Bennet* (*1984*), "If the teacher is the guide, the curriculum is the path. A good curriculum marks the points of significance so that the student does not wander aimlessly over the terrain, dependent solely on chance to discover the landmarks of human achievement".

According to Cunnigham it is a tool in the hands of the artist (the teacher) to mould his material (the pupil) in accordance with his ideal in his studio (the school).

4.4 NATIONAL DEVELOPMENT AND CURRICULUM

Curriculum and modernisation of society. The modernisation of a society is tied up with the contents of the curriculum. Broadly speaking this implies in terms of curriculum objectives:

1. The development of a scientific outlook from early childhood.
2. Loosening of bonds of dogmatism and dispelling of superstition, fatalism, dogmatism and passive resignation.
3. Promoting the capacity to think rationally to enquire and judge for himself and to contribute to the stock of human knowledge.
4. The development of productive capacity.
5. The development a synthesising attitude towards science and culture.
6. Development of values of a secular, socialist and a democratic state.
7. Development of values of emotional integration and national unity.

4.5 ISSUES AND QUESTIONS INVOLVED IN CURRICULUM CONSTRUCTION AND IMPLEMENTATION

Following are the basic questions that should be taken into consideration while constructing the curriculum:

1. *Why to Formulate the Curriculum*? Curriculum is framed to realise the aims of education. This, therefore, includes taking into consideration the aims of education. The educator and the learner must be clear about the aims of education so that right efforts are made in this direction.

2. *For Whom to Formulate the Curriculum*? The curriculum is to be formulated for the learner. It is, therefore, very important that curriculum should be formulated according to the various stages and age groups. Curriculum should cater to the individual differences of the learners.

3. *What to include in the Curriculum*? This leads to the content of the

curriculum which has been described as 'the environment in motion'. In a broader sense it includes all the courses, readings, clubs and activities in the school.

4. *Where to Use the Curriculum*? The curriculum is used in and outside school—in the classroom, library, laboratory, workshop, playgrounds and in the numerous informal contacts between teachers and pupils etc.

5. *When to Use the Curriculum*? This is concerned with the different stages of the child so that 'motivational aspects' may be handled satisfactorily.

6. *How to Use the Curriculum*? This involves the knowledge and techniques of various methods of teaching-learning for making the teaching-learning process dynamic, effective and inspirational.

7. *Who is to Use the Curriculum*? The teacher and the students are the main consumers. The teachers must understand themselves also.

8. *Who is to Formulate the Curriculum*? Formulation of curriculum is a joint enterprise in which teachers should play a dominant role. The views of the learners should also be given their due importance.

9. *What type of Resources to be Used in the Curriculum*? With the rapid advances in sciences and technology new learning resources are coming into use. A judicious use of the traditional and modern audio-visual aids should be made.

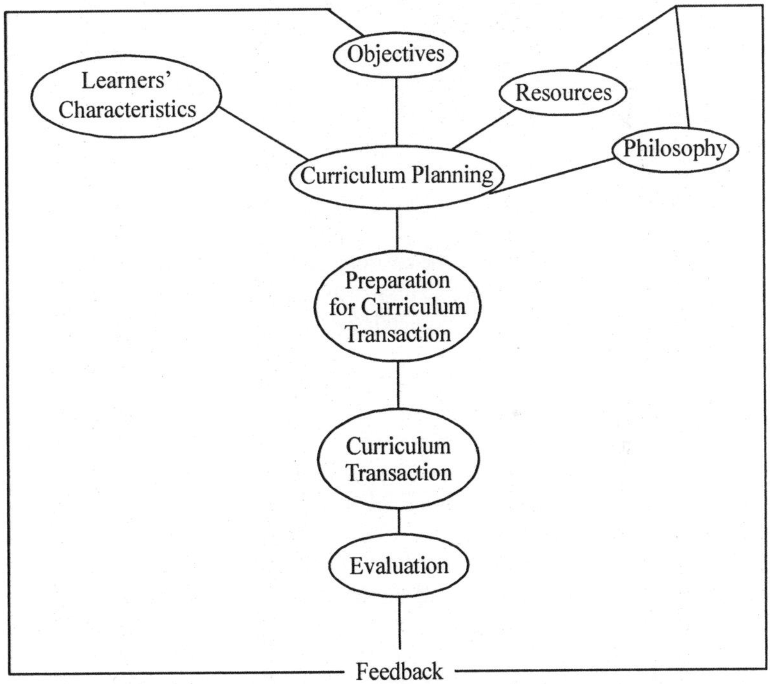

Fig. 4.1: A Typical Flow Chart of Activities Relating to Curriculum

10. *How to Evaluate the Outcomes of the Curriculum Implementation*? This is concerned with the success of the learners as well as of the teachers. Outcomes are evaluated by a number of tests.

11. *How to Bring About the Required Changes in the Curriculum*?

Curriculum must be evaluated from time to time so as to make it in conformity with the changing needs.

4.6 BASIC PRINCIPLES OF CURRICULUM CONSTRUCTION

The curriculum is meant to reflect the pattern of life in a society—a carefully selected pattern. It is not a mere scheme of studies or a list of subjects but an entire range of activities and experiences which considerably help to inculcate those standards of moral action which are essential for successful living in society and for getting true satisfaction out of life. It is, therefore, very essential that it should be constructed on sound principles.

The need of the society and the needs of the students (macro level needs and micro level needs) are the two primary considerations in the selection of the content:

Following are the basic principles of curriculum construction.

1. *The Conservative Principles*: It has been stated that 'nations live in the present, on the past and for the future'. This means that the present, the past and the future needs of the community should be taken into consideration. The past is a great guide for the present as it helps us to decide what has been useful to those who have gone before and what will be useful to those who are going through now.

This principle will be of help only when we carefully select as to what things of the past are likely to help us in the present. All the things of the past may not suit us. It is, therefore, essential that we should select only those subjects and activities, which are required by the present generation.

2. *The Forward-looking Principle*: Children of today are the future citizens of tomorrow. Therefore, their education should be such as it enables them to be progressive-minded persons.

3. *The Creative Principles*: In the curriculum that content should be included which enables the child to exercise his creative and constructive powers. The objective of education is to discover and to develop his special interests, tastes and aptitudes.

4. *Child-Centred Content or Interest-Centred Content Principles*: It is true that the child is to be prepared for life. But this does not mean that his immediate interests should be sacrificed for the sake of the future which is indefinite. As Ryburn puts, "The best preparation for life that we can give a child is to help him to live fully and richly his life at that stage at which he is."

5. *Principle of Individual Differences or Principle of Flexibility*: Individuals differ in taste, temperament, skill, experience, aptitude, innate ability and in sex. Therefore, the content should be adapted to individual differences. It should not be rigid.

6. *Principle of Preparation for Life*: We have to prepare the child in such a way as he is capable of facing the various challenges of the complex problems of the future.

7. *Principle of Maturity*: Content should be adapted to the age of the pupils and to their stage of mental and physical development.

8. *The Activity Principle*: The content must ensure the activity of body and mind. It should be the centre of the curriculum. All modern methods of

teaching, i.e., Kindergarten, Montessori, Project, Basic etc., are based on this principle of activity.

9. *Principle of Linking with Life or Principle of Utility*: The community needs and characteristics should be kept in view while selecting the content.

10. *Principle of Comprehensiveness and Balance*: The content should be selected in such a way as every aspect of life, i.e., economic relationships, social activities, occupations and spiritual life, is given due emphasis.

11. *Principle of Loyalties*: The content should be selected in such a manner that it teaches a true sense of loyalty to the family, the school, the community, the town, the province, the country and the world at large. It should enable the child to understand that there is unity in diversity.

12. *Vertical and Horizontal Articulation*: On the one hand each year's course should be built on what has been done in previous years and at the same time should serve as basis for subsequent work. It is absolutely essential that the entire content should be co-ordinated.

13. *Principle of Significance*: Content should take into consideration the special needs and circumstances of the pupils and the community. Curriculum of the girl may not always be identical with that of boys. The special needs of both the sexes should be given their due consideration.

In general the content of the village and the urban school will be the same but there might be variation according to the specific needs of the locality.

14. *Principle of Core or Common Subjects*: There are certain broad areas of knowledge, skill and appreciation with which all the children must be made conversant and these should find a place in the curriculum. This is more important at higher secondary stage where there are diversified courses. These subjects are to be common to all groups. They are known as core subjects. Mother tongue or regional language, social studies (general course), general science including mathematics and one craft are expected to be the core subjects.

15. *Principle of Workability*: It should be possible to translate into action the content in the light of existing resources.

16. *Principle of Authenticity*: The content should be as objective and true as possible.

17. *Principles of Self-sufficiency or All-around Development*: After going through the course or content, the learner should develop self-reliance and self-confidence.

18. *Principle of Globalisation*: Curriculum should reflect world ethos.

19. *Principle of Reconciliation*: At the core of the things, curriculum should harmonise 3 contradictions.

(i) A synthesis of western values of efficiency—a concern for ends and eastern values and ethos—an equal concern for means.

(ii) Co-existence of collaborative and competitive modes—striving for individual excellence and yet reinforcing the 'group culture' through daily activities.

(iii) Commitment to material advancement along with sensitivity to distributive justice.

5

Organisation of Curriculum in Civics

5.1 APPROACHES OF ORGANISATION OF CURRICULUM

Organisation of the subject matter for different stages and classes in Civics is an important problem. It has to be organised in such a way as it is taught effectively and in a coherent way. It is, therefore, very essential that organisation of the subject-matter must be comprehensive and continuous. Generally, three approaches are adopted for organising the subject-matter in Civics. They are:

1. Unit Approach.
2. Concentric Approach.
3. Topical Approach.

5.2 UNIT APPROACH

The unit approach is based on the growing acceptance of the Gestalt-Organismic-Field Theories of learning which emphasise the 'wholeness' nature of learning. This approach is contrary to the older atomistic conception of learning according to which learning was a matter of adding one small item of knowledge to another bit by bit. The new approach is based upon the assumption that effective learning takes place in an environment in which the goals are clearly perceived and every phase of the operational procedure is viewed as a relational part of the total learning situation. The underlying assumption is that the learner reacts to the situation as a whole and not to parts in isolation.

Definition of a Unit

Few terms in modern educational usage have been more extensively used with as much disagreement as to meaning as has the term 'unit'.

According to *Bossing*, "A unit of comprehensive series of related and meaningful activities so developed as to achieve pupil purposes, provide significant educational experiences, and result in appropriate behavioural changes."

The Dictionary of Education defines a unit as "an organisation of varied activities, experiences and types, learning around a central problem or purpose, developed cooperatively by a group of pupils under teacher leadership, involves planning, execution of plans and evaluation of results".

James High defines unit approach in *Teaching Secondary School, Social Studies* as, "It is more than a mere technique and is often called the unit approach rather than method. The primary requisite is a point of view that will allow the imaginative instructor to arrange and organise all available and pertinent information around a nuclear idea and then select and provide references, aids and activities that will enable his students to master the basic material."

H.C. Morrison (1871-1945), a Professor of the University of Chicago has explained the 'unit method' in detail in his book "*The Practice of Teaching in Secondary School*" published in 1926. The unit method is very popular and frequently used in U.S.A.

According to *Morrison*, "Unit is a comprehensive and significant aspect of the environment of an organised science and art."

According to *Wesley*, "Unit is an organised body of information and experience designed to effect significant outcomes of the learner."

Jarolimek John defines unit, "as a means of organising materials for instructional purposes which utilises significant subject matter content, involves pupils in learning activities through active participation intellectually and physically and modifies the pupil's behaviour to the extent that he is able to cope with new problems and situations more competently."

Richard Survey has pointed out in *Social Studies Instruction in Elementary School* as, "A teaching unit in social studies is a comprehensive instructional plan specifying the 'what', the 'how' and the 'when' of teaching a big idea".

According to *East S. Johnson*, "Unit is a segment of experience which is cut for study, within it, i.e. method employed. It is my understanding that every unit is a 'project'. It is a project in the sense that one projects enquiry into it. Furthermore, every unit has a topic, theme or careful tendency or whatever name you choose to call it, otherwise it could have no unity. Every unit is a 'contract' in the sense that the student enters upon a contract or obligation to study how the things which it contains are related, how they work, how cause and effect are identified and related and how a conclusion is reached. Every unit is also a 'problem', a problem of significance and meaning in some unknown or less than thoroughly known phase of human experience."

Hanna, Hagemann and Potter state, "A unit can be defined as a purposeful learning experience focused upon behaviour of the learner and enabling him to adjust a life situation more effectively."

Elements of a Teaching Unit

A good teaching unit has nine elements but the sequence of those elements is not fixed. Following sequence is generally followed:

1. *Overview*: This implies the consideration of the needs of the students while formulating the objectives of teaching unit.

2. *Inventory or Background*: This element is concerned with exploring the entering behaviour of the students. The teacher is required to establish the behaviour repertoire by linking the new knowledge with the previous knowledge of the students.

3. *Presentation*: This element is concerned with providing new experiences to the learners. It includes an analysis and presentation of the elements of teaching units in a logical sequence so that they are helpful to the students. With a view to encourage students' participation in teaching, question-answer strategy is employed.

4. *Motivation*: This element of the teaching unit is concerned with the creation of motivational situations to facilitate learning.

5. *Summarisation*: This element of the unit is concerned with providing a summary of the unit.

6. *Drill*: This element provides an opportunity to the students for drill or practice which enables them to retain longer what is learnt.

7. *Review*: This implies giving the salient features of the unit orally.

8. *Organisation*: This element involves giving assignments to the students to organise their learning experiences on their own.

9. *Evaluation*: This element of the teaching unit consists of ascertaining how far the teacher has been successful in achieving the objectives of the lesson, i.e., to what extent students have grasped, the content and developed meaningful behaviour.

Characteristics of a Good Teaching Unit

A good teaching unit possesses the following characteristics:

1. A teaching unit consists of meaningful elements.
2. A teaching unit arranges all elements in such a manner as the students can understand the whole.
3. A teaching unit provides the starting point of teaching activities.
4. A teaching unit provides the ending point of activities.
5. A teaching unit has a broad and comprehensive structure.
6. A teaching unit has a practical form rather than theoretical.
7. A teaching unit provides for various activities so as to create appropriate learning structures by the teacher.
8. A teaching unit provides for the interaction of the teacher-taught.
9. A teaching unit includes appropriate techniques of reinforcement.
10. A teaching unit presents the basis for evaluating the performance of the students.
11. A teaching unit reveals the forms of teaching activities and selects appropriate teaching strategies, tactics and teaching aids.
12. A teaching unit is economical from the point of view of time and energy.
13. A teaching unit is flexible and provides opportunities in adapting teaching to individual differences of children.

Classification of Units

Units may be classified into four types:

1. Subject-matter Units
2. Experience Units
3. The Adaptive Units or Units of Adaptation
4. The Resources Units

1. *Subject-matter Units*: In these units emphasis is more on the subject-matter than the learner. The wholeness or integration is achieved through large bodies of information or subject-matter to be acquired or achieved. It has three types as follows:

The Topical Unit: It is like the traditional topical organisation of the subject-matter. It differs from that only in degree. It is not recommended by modern educators, as teachers in this approach are apt to include too much or too little and thereby confuse the students.

The Generalisation Unit: This is based on the understanding of some principle. For example, a principle of utility could be selected in economies as the central factors.

The Environment Unit: This was developed by Morrison of University of Chicago and is, therefore, also known as the Morrison Unit. Morrison defined it as "A comprehensive and significant aspect of the environment of, an organised science, of an art or of conduct, which when learned results in adaptation in personality". An environmental unit is organised around an important aspect of the environment or culture.

2. *Experience Units*: These art based upon the experiences of the learner on certain life situations or problem situations. The learner fully reacts to situation he is confronted with. The learner's needs, purposes and interests determine these experiences. Need, purpose or interest is the binding and motivating force. This results in greater effort, knowledge and understanding on the part of the learner. Experience unit is of three types as: (a) Student-interest unit, (b) Student-purpose unit, (c) Student-need unit.

An important limitation of the student interest is that all areas of curriculum cannot be planned on this basis. The learner may not be interested in all the areas at the curriculum. Student-purpose and student-need units cannot be planned in advance. They have to be continuously planned as they develop.

3. *The Adaptive Units*: In the words of *Jones* of the University of Pennsylvania who is the originator of the unit, "a unit consists of a group or chain of planned coordinated activities undertaken by the learner in order to obtain control over a type of life situation". The central point in the adaptive unit is that it is the 'general ability' that should be developed to meet specific life situations, resulting in greater adjustment or adaptation or integration of the individual. The development of acquisition of skills, habits, knowledge, each as a separate aspect of learning does not result in unification or integration of the individual.

4. *The Resources Units*: A resource unit like the 'subject-matter type' or of the 'experience type' is not planned for a specific group of pupils in a particular school and for a definite time. It is concerned with a broader field and, in fact, it serves as a guide for teachers working at different places. This unit is generally built by a group of teachers who operate in a workshop guided by specialists and helped by the extensive library facilities. Once built up, they are mimeographed and made available to other teacher of the concerned subject. A resource unit serves as a teacher's guide in planning his programme. It includes: (i) Statement of objectives concerning the theme; (ii) Problem; (iii) The approach or initiation; (iv) Content of subject matter basic to the area of study; (v) Direct and related experiences; (vi) Organising and summarising experiences; (vii) Evaluation of learnings; and (viii) A collection of instructional resources.

Implication and Working of Unit Approach

The centre of interest usually offers an opportunity to cover a considerably wide area. For instance, a child in the first class is interested in knowing more and more about his own school. Obviously 'school' is his centre of interest. Therefore, for him, 'school' may be a suitable unit of work. The topic provides both intellectual and manual work. Also, it offers opportunities for him to work individually and in cooperation with his classmates. This unit of work is broken up into a few sub-units, each covering an important aspect of the main problem or a topic, in which a child is profoundly interested. Thus the unit can be conveniently broken up into sub-units such as (a) The school is our home; (b) How do we come to school? (c) Annual day of the school; and (d) To be a good boy or a girl at home and at school.

In other words, a unified course in civics consists of a series of problems or units of study, drawn from the major areas of the daily living. Information from all subjects contributes to the solution of the problem. It thus cuts across the subject boundaries and presents a content in a composite and united form, centred around children's typical interests.

The choice of the units of study or of unit work is based on the following criteria:

(a) The unit is related to the current needs and problems of the society.
(b) It is appropriate to the physical and mental development of the children, their needs and interests at the particular age level.
(c) It is conducive to achieve lifelike, practical and creative learning.

The organisation of the subject of civics into a series of a units of work offers the best transition from a more verbal learning of a practical approach. The unit of work offers many opportunities for learning through activity and provides for constant correlation with the physical, social and cultural environment, and even with crafts, wherever possible. A unit of work, moreover, is realistic and functional in nature.

The Sequence of the Civics Programme

The sequence of the programme in Civics in the present NCERT syllabus is based on the studies of child growth and development. These suggest that children should first deal with direct experience and with the simpler aspects of their own environment. Then, they are prepared to progress gradually, to its more remote and complex aspects.

Another pedagogical consideration in determining the grade-placement of various units of work, is to group the units of work for each grade, so as to develop a central theme, or a big idea, throughout the year. Thus an attempt is made to develop, also, the grade-themes for each grade or class.

The sequence of the grade-themes, again is based on the principle of widening children's mental horizon, gradually from the immediate to the remote and from the the simple to the complex aspects of our living. In fact, an attempt is made to fit every unit in a sequence both horizontal and vertical.

For instance, transport is one of the major areas of our daily living. The problem listed under this are: (a) How do we come to school? (b) How do people travel in town and village? (c) Avoiding road accidents. (d) Undertaking a rail journey. (e) How do goods come from abroad? and (f) The age of aeroplanes or a shrinking world.

The units, in the order they are stated, represent a vertical sequence from grade to grade. They are in conformity with the pedagogical principles as such 'from immediate to remote' and 'from simple to complex'.

Merits of Unit Approach

1. It is based on Gestalt Psychology which emphasises the 'Wholeness' nature of learning.
2. Since the subject matter is divided into small units, it leads to easy comprehension.
3. In the unit approach, learning does not remain just 'memorisation'. It develops understanding.
4. On account of the delimitation of the learning contents and specification of the unit objectives, teaching and learning becomes more objective.
5. Division of the learning material into small units and sub-units makes the task of teaching-learning easy, interesting and simple.
6. All the steps in the unit approach are directed to achieve the desired mastery.
7. This approach encourages the habit of independent and self-study among the students.
8. By providing adequate opportunities to the students to remain active, this approach leads to healthy interaction between the students and teachers.
9. Learning process becomes organised, systematic and sequenced.

Limitations of Unit Approach

1. Unit approach is time consuming.
2. This approach is more suitable in the case of intelligent students.
3. This approach puts heavy demands upon the teachers.
4. The present syllabus is very heavy and with this approach it is very difficult to complete in time.

5.3 CONCENTRIC APPROACH

This is based on the psychological principle that children come to know things in the first instance as 'wholes' and gradually learn to analyse them. The subject-matter in Civics at each succeeding stage gradually increases in difficulty but the developing and growing child seems to be ready for comprehending each new aspect. The approach provides for adequate repetition for fixing events. This approach resolves, to some extent, the problem of adaptation of the teaching material to the age and understanding of the student. In the first year, the review of the entire subject-matter is very sketchy, every subsequent year means the provision of greater detail. In the initial stages, thinking is at a simpler level. As the pupil advances in age and understanding, he develops his capacity of thinking in abstract terms and greater detail. The learning sequence progresses from the simple to be more detailed sequence.

Merits

1. It proceeds from 'simple to complex' and 'whole to parts'.
2. It arouses interest and revision becomes easy.
3. It follows a simpler path.
4. It covers the course during the course of a few years.
5. It takes into consideration the mental growth of the child.

Demerits

1. Repetition is sometimes cumbersome. Some facts are repeated again and again.
2. The presentation lacks novelty and freshness. A sense of boredom and dullness is inherent as the children go through the whole course more than once.
3. This approach makes it difficult so develop time and space sense in the pupils.
4. A passing reference to the topic is not helpful in understanding the complex problem.
5. Very capable teachers are needed for following this approach.

5.4 TOPICAL APPROACH

Topical approach implies the revolving of the contents of Civics around a series of topics connected together. Topics of study suitable for the age, ability and interests of students make up the entire syllabus. These topics are also called 'linked' lessons. Each topic stands by itself. According to the topical approach, particular topics are taken as the central theme of work in social sciences.

This approach takes different forms. The teacher may announce a topic. The students tell what they know about the topic, ask questions, raise doubts and take part in lively discussions. The teacher notes down the questions which the students are not able to answer.

The teacher notes the questions, selects the questions according to the mental growth of the students and answers are provided by the students and the teachers in a cooperative way. Learning takes place spontaneously as the students are motivated.

A teacher may introduce the topic with the assistance of a material aid. Topics can be picked up from daily routine, life situations and environment.

Merits

Topical approach has the following merits:

1. Integrated knowledge is imparted to the pupils.
2. Learning is related to life and environment.
3. Pupil's interest and motivation remain aroused.
4. Correlation of different subjects takes place.
5. The approach helps the pupils to understand the facts in their development setting.
6. The approach can be adapted according to the age, ability and aptitude of the children.

Demerits

Limitation of this approach are as follows:

1. Approach is rather difficult to be adapted.
2. This approach pre-supposes good library facilities.
3. This approach requires very competent resourceful teachers.
4. Appropriate instructional materials are not readily available.

Organising the Syllabus in Different Ways

The Education Commission, 1964-66 observed, "The social studies syllabus may be organised in different ways, and both the integrated approach which seeks to combine the knowledge and skills provided by the separate subjects of history, geography, economics and civics, and the traditional method according to which these subjects are treated as separate disciplines, have their own place in a balanced school curriculum.

"At the lower primary stage, the integrated approach is desirable. Instead of giving the pupils miscellaneous and unrelated bits of information in History, Geography and Civics, it is far better to provide a coordinated programme of social studies centering round the study of man and his environment. In the upper classes of the primary school, the content of social studies may still be organised as an integral whole in connection with the treatment of certain topics, but the pupils should be gradually introduced to an appreciation of History, Geography and Civics as separate subjects. In the secondary school, these subjects will be studied as separate disciplines and form the basis of specialised studies in social sciences at the higher secondary stage."

6

Curriculum of Civics at Different Levels

6.1 NCERT CURRICULUM (1976)

The NCERT prepared the curriculum in the light of the 10+2+3 system of education.

6.2 CURRICULUM APPROACH AT THE PRIMARY STAGES

The Curriculum for Ten Years (1976) has observed that the primary concern of the school at this stage should be to develop the necessary social skills, values and attitudes that would enable the child to contribute his mite, as he grows, towards the development of the society to which he belongs.

During the five years of primary school the child's mental horizon would be gradually widened from the home to the school and the local community to the world. In the process, the child would begin to appreciate the geographical elements of his environment. Various human activities, which help him to understand how the gifts of nature are processed to produce goods for serving the various needs of man, would also be studied. He would also get an idea of the social and cultural life in different parts of the country as well as of some different ways of living, in certain parts of the world. Stories and narratives about personages and events that have contributed to our national heritage and human heritage will also be studied. In addition to these, the child would get ample opportunities to develop socially desirable habits, attitudes and values besides becoming broadly acquainted with the functioning of political and social institutions.

6.3 CURRICULUM APPROACH AT THE MIDDLE AND HIGH SCHOOL STAGE

For the organisation of content in social sciences, comprising History, Geography, Civics and Economics, in the next two stages of school education, three different approaches can be visualised.

History, Geography and Civics may be introduced as separate discipline in the middle classes and carried over as such to high school classes, while Economics may be introduced at the high school stage as a separate discipline.

History and Civics may form one group and Geography and Economics another group, and these two groups may be introduced right in Class VI and carried up to Class X.

The contents of History, Geography, Civics and Economics may be identified in an integrated manner for all the five years taken together.

While the first two approaches are common today and do not need any elaboration, except that they contribute to the isolation of the disciplines amongst themselves and of disciplines from problems or situations, in the third approach, it would be necessary to identify essential units in each subject in two cycles of three years and two years. The units thus identified for the first cycle of three years may be integrated and arranged sequentially between and within subjects in the form of a common syllabus for social science. For the next two years of education, a similar exercise may be done treating the earlier cycle as the base. Some old units may be taken at a greater depth while new ones may be introduced in each subject so as to lead to a slightly more advanced integrated syllabus in these subjects. While selecting units from individual subjects, care may be taken to preserve the general structure of the discipline and include those facts and principles which are useful to a growing adolescent and serve as a base for a systematic study.

6.4 ENVIRONMENTAL STUDIES AND SOCIAL SCIENCES

The NCERT syllabi (1976) has used the term Environment Studies for Classes I to V and Social Sciences for Classes VI to VIII.

The curriculum in environment studies for the primary stage aims at introducing the pupil to his environment, both physical and social. After the first two years of an integrated curriculum in environmental education, the pupils will be introduced to a composite course in Environmental Studies I (Social Studies) in Classes III, IV and V where he would get an understanding of the geographical setting in which he lives and that of his social and cultural environment. In this course, the pupil would be gradually introduced to the life in his home and family, school neighbourhood, the state, the country and the world at large.

At the middle school stage (Classes VI-VIII) it has proposed to introduce a course in Social Sciences drawing elements primarily from History, Economics and Sociology. Elements drawn from these different subjects will be taught separately (under three subjects—History, Geography and Civics). Elements from Economics and Sociology would be integrated in these three subjects. although these three subjects would be taught separately, they would help to relate various elements from these subjects to understand the life and problems surrounding the pupil. The focus of this course would be interaction between man and his physical and social environment, and the relationship between man and his social and cultural heritage, and the community of which he is a part. Such a course will help the pupil to understand various aspects of the contemporary problems in their totality.

The teaching of Social Sciences at the middle school stage should aim at the realisation of following objectives:

1. to help the pupil understand the inter-relationship between man and environment;
2. to promote an understanding of the major stages in the evolution of Indian society through the ages;

3. to promote an understanding of the civic processes and to provide training in the development of civic competencies; and
4. to develop an understanding of the economic forces that influences the everyday life of citizens.

Keeping in view the above objectives, elements of History, Geography and Civics may comprise the curriculum in Social Sciences at this stage. Wherever possible, these may be taught in an integrated manner.

In each subject, ten periods have been suggested for doing various kinds of practical and project work each year. These may consist of a variety of practical activities, inside and outside the school, library work, visits, surveys, preparation of reports, etc. Wherever possible, activities in various subjects may be taken up in an integrated manner. The main purpose of these activities should be to make the student an active participant in the teaching-learning process.

6.5 OBJECTIVES OF TEACHING CIVICS IN MIDDLE CLASSES

The course in Civics has the major responsibility of promoting well-informed and intelligent citizens who have the ability to participate in the affairs of their community effectively. From his point of view, the course at this stage aims mainly at imparting training in civic life rather than more scholarship. It contains such socially imperative knowledge which would not only impart understanding of the civic processes but would also provide training in the development of civic competencies. Some practical aspects of citizenship education have also been incorporated from the point of view of adopting a functional approach. Thus the syllabus in civics at the middle stage has the following objectives:

1. to provide the student with intelligent understanding of the various social responsibilities and civic processes;
2. to help the student understand our Constitution and the values enshrined in it;
3. to acquaint the student with the machinery of the government at different levels;
4. to make the student conscious of the actual problems that are facing our country today and instil in him a sense of responsibility towards the community;
5. to make the student identify with the people and their institutions;
6. to inculcate in the student the values of democracy, secularism, socialism and national integration.

6.6 CURRICULUM APPROACH TO CIVICS IN MIDDLE CLASSES

The course envisages the study of local government and the Indian Constitution in Classes VI and VII, respectively; and in the last year, i.e., in Class VIII, the students would study the actual problems that are facing India today. In the course, some practical aspects of citizenship education and the elements of economics should also be incorporated to adopt a functional and integrated approach.

Though many of the activities and topics of study included under this scheme may be organised by the teacher in the class or school, it is suggested that the training would be more fruitful if the students are taken out of the classroom and involved in real life situations.

Class VI—Civic Life in the Community

Unit 1. Preservation of property of the community (10 periods)
Unit 2. Development of the community (10 periods)
Unit 3. Local government: rural (10 periods)
Unit 4. Local government: urban (10 periods)
Unit 5. Project work (10 periods)

Class VII—Our Constitution

Unit 1. Chief features of our Constitution (10 periods)
Unit 2. Law making process (10 periods)
Unit 3. Executing laws (10 periods)
Unit 4. Interpreting laws (10 periods)
Unit 5. Project work (10 periods)

Class VIII—Independent India

Unit 1. Our national goals (10 periods)
Unit 2. Strengthening our democracy (10 periods)
Unit 3. Social and economic reconstruction (10 periods)
Unit 4. Defence of the country (10 periods)
Unit 5. India and the world (10 periods)
Unit 6. Project work (10 periods)

Project work. The student who is a citizen in training, need help in getting experience and insight into the process of citizenship. Under this scheme an opportunity should be provided to the student to develop abilities which are essential for any active citizen in India.

It is suggested that 20 pr cent of the total marks allotted to Civics should be assigned to the project work. Every student should take up at least two practical activities every year and prepare a short write-up or report on his project. The reports of the students should be evaluated on the basis of three components as: (1) collection of data; (2) analysis and interpretation of data; and (3) conclusions drawn on the basis of this interpretation.

List of Projects

(i) Sanitation problem of any town of the area.
(ii) Management and maintenance of civic amenities in the area and the related problems.
(iii) Functioning of police in the area.
(iv) Distribution and location of educational institutions in the area—nursery, primary, middle, secondary, technical, aided and unaided, for boys and girls, etc.
(v) Organising school government and national festivals.
(vi) Election process from nomination to declaration of results of elections of Students' Union, Village Panchayats, Municipal Committees.

(vii) Study of some major developments in the national life, e.g., electrification, nationalisation of banks, nuclear experiment, food, population, green revolution, white revolution, impact of 20-point programme in the locality, study of local historical events connected with the Indian Independence Movement.

(viii) Achievements and problems of any one of (i) Village Panchayat/ Municipal Committee or Corporation, (ii) Block Samiti, (iii) Zila Parishad.

Note: This is not an exhaustive list. Other projects of such type could also be taken up.

In Classes IX and X, the two major objectives of teaching Civics should be: (i) to promote an active and intelligent citizenship, and (ii) to develop an intelligent understanding of the structure and working of the social and political institutions. In addition to this, an understanding that the UNO is playing a significant role in strengthening world peace and cooperation should also be promoted.

From this point of view, the course in Class IX should include the meaning and scope of civics, community life, form of government, rights and duties and democracy in action. In Class X, the students would study the structure and functions of political and social institutions in India and the role of UNO in maintaining world peace. Some basic elements of sociology should also be introduced.

6.7 CBSC SYLLABI AND COURSES IN CIVICS FOR CLASSES IX AND X

The Central Board of Secondary Education (CBSE) prescribed the following syllabi and course for All-India Secondary School Examination 1983 and 1984.

Unit I. Man as a Social Being:

(i) Man is a social being.
(ii) Family, his relationship with his family, how decisions are taken in the family.
(iii) His relationship with the community such as neighbourhood, school community and village community.

Unit II. Man as a Citizen:

Man as a citizen.
(a) Who is a citizen?
(b) The citizen and government. The necessity and meaning of government, the citizen and the government; from non-participation to participation. What the government does for its citizen?
(c) What the citizen owes to his government?

Unit III. Government at the Local Level:

The citizen and his local government:
Study of his immediate local government, e.g., the Village Panchayat or

the Municipal Committee, Corporation, etc. with special reference to its composition, powers and functions, administrative machinery, etc.

Unit IV. Government at the State and National Levels (with reference to India)

(i) The citizen and his State Government:
   (a) The State Government—Legislature, Executive and Judiciary. Administration of Union Territories.

7

Civics Curriculum Suggested by Review Committee (1977)

7.1 BACKGROUND OF THE APPOINTMENT OF THE REVIEW COMMITTEE

With the formation of the Janata Government, in March 1977 the Education Minister appointed this Committee. The Education Minister had received many letters and comments from different sources regarding the introduction and the implementation of the new pattern of education. The Education Minister desired to have a review of the new pattern.

In the 1968 National Policy Resolution, it was outlined that "the Government of India will make a review of the scheme every five years". It was also envisaged that other recommendations of the Kothari Commission as well as various guidelines issued for implementation of the recommendations would also be reviewed. Since no such review had been done so far, it was considered very appropriate to have this review.

The Review Committee was appointed in 1977 under the Chairmanship of Dr. Ishwarbhai Patel, Vice-Chancellor, Gujarat University to review the syllabuses and text-books prepared by the NCERT for 10+2 system of school education. The terms of reference of the Review Committee were:

1. To review the stage-wise and subject-wise objectives identified in the NCERT document the curriculum for the 10-year school.

2. To scrutinise the NCERT syllabuses and text-books in the light of the review as per (1) above.

3. To scrutinise the scheme of studies, as given in the said documents and examine whether any suitable modifications in either the scheme of studies or the time-table or both should be made and to propose suitable staffing pattern.

4. To review the present scheme of studies and the time allocated for various subjects with a view to ensure that:

(i) the institution/teacher has adequate time for experimentation, creative work, remedial instruction, etc.

(ii) to accommodate the needs of the bright child for advanced level courses; the specific interest and aptitude, or the lack of it, in children, in only certain subject areas, keeping in view the national goals of development and objectives of education.

7.2 RECOMMENDATIONS OF THE COMMITTEE REGARDING CURRICULUM, TEXT-BOOKS AND METHODS OF TEACHING

History, Civics, and Geography

We are of the view that the one area in which the present scheme is overloaded is in 'social studies' or 'social sciences'. In some of the courses prescribed by examining bodies under one or the other of these headings, the subjects included are History, Civics, Geography, Economics, Commerce and Psychology.

We agree with the conclusions of the Kothari Commission that History, Civics and Geography only should be taught in this area of the curriculum and that such correlation as is natural and possible should be introduced.

We have, therefore, recommended definitely that a course in History, Civics and Geography should be included in the scheme as, we believe, that such a course will, with the other areas of study, be sufficient to provide a broad-based general education.

Syllabus Frames

We have given syllabus frames in most subjects and not detailed syllabuses. The frames give the main topics in each subject and it will be for the states, local authorities, education/examination boards and schools to plan and fill in the details.

We believe that uniform courses of study designed to serve the needs of average schools cease to be meaningful as there is a large variety of schools in each state and there are many variable factors, such as, the quality of teachers, facilities available and the needs of children to be taken into consideration.

A single rigid scheme of studies for all schools may prove to be beyond the competence of some schools and may not provide a sufficient challenge to other schools.

The content of the courses finally framed must be capable of being taught or studied within the time allotted per week as given in the scheme. We believe that in each subject, only the main ideas should be introduced; these should be few and important and that in teaching they should be thrown into every possible combination so that the children will make these ideas their own and understand their application. In the words of a distinguished educationist:

"We enunciate two educational commandments: 'Do not teach too many subjects' and again 'what you teach, teach thoroughly'."

We believe that the main concepts in each subject should be studied and that unnecessary details, which overload the syllabus, instead of developing knowledge, inevitably lead to the memorising of scraps of information, never interconnected, never utilised.

Another value of providing syllabus frames only lies in the fact that the limits of knowledge to be expected at the end of the ten-year period will be clear to those responsible for framing courses at the higher secondary stage.

Freedom to Develop Text-Books

We are also of the view that by not giving details of the courses, but only the main topics, it will be possible for education authorities to prepare text-book material to suit the needs of schools under their control.

We recommend that NCERT should concentrate on the production of instructional material and that state governments, education/examination boards. Schools and other educational agencies should be free to adapt and develop this material to suit their particular needs.

Experimentation and creative work.

It is our view that in the conditions prevailing in the majority of schools experimentation and creative work depend on factors other than time.

A young teacher full of enthusiasm and brimful with ideas arrives to find that the school is a shed or a dingy, depressing building. The classroom is ill-ventilated and badly lighted. In the average classroom situation he finds himself surrounded all day by 40 to 50 lively and active children. When the load of daily corrections is added to this, the urge to experiment and undertake creative work is progressively reduced.

We, therefore, feel that while teachers should be made aware of the areas of experimentation which require their creative effort, help through guidebooks, frequent seminars and conferences is essential to foster new ideas and to sustain interest in heir work.

We are of the view that schools should be encouraged to frame their own curriculum and courses of study and that teachers should be encouraged and helped to attend seminars and in-service courses and to visit other schools.

We feel that if teaching conditions are made reasonably congenial, creative and experimental work will develop and thrive.

History, Civics and Geography as one Course (3 hours per week)

7.3 CLASS VI—OUR CIVIC LIFE

1. *Development of the Community*
   Scheme—Cooperatives—Community Development.
2. *Local Government: Rural*
   Need—Structure and Functions.
3. *Local Government: Urban*
   Structure and Functions.
4. *District Administration*
   Law and Order—Civic Amenities.
5. *Preservation of Property of the Community*
   Public property, its preservation—historical monuments.
6. *Project Work*
   Opportunities to develop abilities which are essential for any active citizen in India. Problems.

7.4 CLASS VII—OUR CONSTITUTION

1. Chief Features of Our Constitution

Basic Principles—National Government—State Governments, Rights-Duties, Directive Principles, National Symbols.

2. Law-Making Process

Parliament—State legislature, How Laws are made.

3. Executing Laws

President, Prime Minister and the Council of Ministers, Governor, Chief Minister and the Council of Ministers, Public Services.

4. Interpreting Laws

Supreme Court, High Courts and Subordi-Courts.

5. Project Work

7.5 CLASS VIII—INDEPENDENT: INDIA: ACHIEVEMENTS AND CHALLENGES

1. Our National Goals

Democracy, Socialism, and Secularism, International Cooperation.

2. Strengthening Our Democracy

Citizenship in a democracy—Literacy in India.

3. Social and Economic Reconstruction

Poverty—Population—Unemployment Casteism.

4. Five Year Plans: Achievements and Failures

Agriculture—Industry—Rural Life.

5. Defence of the Country

Armed Forces—Territorial Army, Border Security Force, N.C.C., A.C.C., Citizens and defence.

6. India and the World

Need for cooperation, coexistence, the United Nations.

7. Project Work

7.6 CLASSES IX AND X

1. Man as a social being.
2. Man as a citizen.
3. Local self-government.

4. State and national government.
5. Rights and duties of a citizen.
6. Democracy in India.
7. India as a nation: unity in diversity.
8. Social and economic challenge before our country.
9. India and the world.
10. India and the United Nations.
11. Project work.

7.7 CRITICAL ANALYSIS OF THE CURRICULUM AS SUGGESTED BY THE ISHWARBHAI PATEL COMMITTEE (1977)

(1) Pragmatic Approach: The Patel Committee took note of the prevailing criticism levelled against the overloaded curriculum as prescribed under the new scheme of education popularly known as new pattern or 10+2+3 pattern of education. It rightly suggested the deletion of some material which was hardly needed in social studies. The Committee emphatically observed, "We are of the view that one area in which the present scheme is overloaded is 'social studies' or 'social sciences'." The Committee, therefore, recommended the inclusion of courses in History, Civics and Geography and excluded subjects like Economics, Commerce and Psychology in the pattern of general education for Classes IX and X.

(2) Curriculum According to the Maturity Level: Curriculum of social studies and social sciences is psychologically sound as it has taken into consideration the level of maturity of the students. Social studies are to be taught as the part of the study of environment in classes one and two, social studies as an integrated subject in Classes 3 to 5 and separate discipline at middle and high school stage.

(3) Syllabus Frames: The Committee has suggested frames and topics and not detailed contents of the syllabus. It has been left to the education departments, examination boards and schools to decide the details of the schools content, in relation to their particular needs and in keeping with the facilities available.

(4) Curriculum Related to the Community: The curriculum takes care of the specific needs of the community. Significant social and economic problems form an important part of school curriculum.

(5) Well-knit Curriculum: The curriculum for each class is fairly connected.

(6) Flexibility of the Curriculum: Care has been taken to ensure that the contents of the curriculum are so arranged and kept flexible as to suit the needs of individual learners. The curriculum is capable of catering to the requirements of a wide range of learners and learning circumstances. It is suggestive and illustrative rather than prescriptive or restrictive.

(7) Self-contained Courses: The courses are self-contained as well as the foundation of the subsequent stage. The curriculum provides for a minimum but sufficient broad knowledge for those who may not continue their education after the secondary stage.

(8) Development of Basic Understandings, Skills and Attitudes: The contents of the programme have been planned in such a manner as to provide adequate opportunities for the development of basic understandings, skills and attitudes needed for the realisation of the ideals of democracy, secularism and socialism.

(9) Promotion of National and International Understanding: There is sufficient scope for the development of right attitudes of national and international understanding.

(10) Emphasis on Various Sources of Learning: The curriculum does not consider classroom as the only place or source from which students learn. It rightly states that the environment and society are also sources from which children acquire understanding, skills and attitudes. It provides scope for the arranging of educational programmes in such a way that all these factors are fully utilised. The curriculum focuses attention on the practical aspects.

Conclusion: The curriculum integrated, as it is, with its many and varied objectives and comprehensive programmes, concerning the whole area of experiences—the family, the community, the nation and the world—is aptly suited to bridge the wide gulf between the schools and the outside world. It provides for sufficient scope for the students to be able to understand how society has come to its present form. They will also be able to interpret intelligently and rationally the matrix of social forces and movements in the midst of which they are living. Adequate emphasis has been laid on making the knowledge as relevant to life as possible by weaving the content around day-to-day problems. Attempts have been made to make knowledge functional and relevant. To broaden the outlook, developments in other parts of the world have been in a proper perspective.

8

Curriculum of Civics at Different Levels

8.1 CURRICULUM OF CIVICS AT THE MIDDLE SCHOOL LEVEL

Following points regarding curriculum in Civics are stated in brief:

1. Main objectives of Civics curriculum.
2. Rationale of introducing Civics in Class VI.
3. Curriculum contents.

8.2 MAIN OBJECTIVES OF CURRICULUM OF CIVICS AT THE MIDDLE SCHOOL LEVEL

- To enable students to make connections between their everyday lives and the issues discussed in the text-book;
- To have students imbibe the ideals of the Indian Constitution;
- To have children gain a real sense of the workings of Indian democracy: its institutions and processes;
- To enable students to grasp the interconnectedness between political, social and economic issues;
- To have them recognise the gendered nature of all of the issues raised;
- To have them develop skills to critically analyse and interpret political, social and economic developments from the point of view of the marginalised;
- To have them recognise the ways in which politics affects their daily lives.

8.3 CURRICULUM OF CIVICS FOR CLASS VI

Diversity and Interdependence

Rationale

In the first year of the new subject area, 'Social and Political Life' the themes of diversity, interdependence and conflict are to be focused on. This is done through first elucidating aspects of social diversity through a discussion of linguistic diversity as well as the diversity of art forms. In discussing these topics the idea is to celebrate diversity and interdependence while also highlighting that this can be zone for conflict. The idea of government is introduced at this grade and then elaborated upon through a discussion of the types of government at the local level, as well as different aspects of their functioning. Through focusing chapters on concrete, though narrativised, examples of land administration in the rural context and sanitation services in the urban one, the attempt is to have the child gain an experiential understanding of the ways in which local government functions. The last chapter through its focus on how people make a living in the rural and urban context discusses issues of the diversity of livelihoods.

Curriculum includes the following units:

Unit 1: Diversity
Unit 2: Government
Unit 3: Local Government
Unit 4: Make a Living

Themes	*Objectives*
Unit 1: Diversity In this unit we focus on various aspects of diversity. The first section begins by having the child recognise diversity as a fact of being human and understanding diversity as different ways of doing the same thing. The second section builds on this by having the child interrogate societal prejudices against diversity, recognising that the self can be made up of multiple identities and that the Constitution compels us to respect diversity. ***Section 1*** ■ Diversity as a fact of being human. ■ What diversity adds to our lives. ■ Diversity in India. ***Section 2*** ■ Prejudice and discrimination. ■ Inequality and discrimination. ■ Recognition of multiple identities in oneself. ■ The Constitution and respect for diversity.	To enable students to: ■ understand and appreciate various forms of diversity in their everyday environments, ■ develop a sensitivity towards pluralism and interdependence, ■ understand how prejudice can lead to discrimination, ■ understand the difference between diversity and inequality, ■ recognise that there are multiple identities within ourselves that we use in different contexts and that these can come into conflict with each other, ■ understand that the Constitution compels us to respect diversity.
Unit 2: Government This unit introduces the student to the idea of government. The first section focuses on the need for it, the history of adult franchise, the various types of governments that exist at present. The second section discusses the key elements that influence the functioning of democratic government.	To enable students to: ■ gain a sense of why government is required, ■ recognise the need for universal adult franchise, ■ appreciate need to make decisions with collective sanction, ■ understand key elements that influence the functioning of democracy.

(*Contd.*)

Themes	Objectives
Section 1 ■ The need for government. ■ Decision-making and participation. ■ The quest for universal adult franchise through examples of the sufferagate movement and the anti-apartheid struggle. ■ Various forms of government and absence of collective sanction. ***Section 2*** ■ Key elements that influence the functioning of democratic government: ■ Participation and accountability. ■ Resolution of conflict. ■ Concerns for equality and justice.	
Unit 3: Local Government This unit familiarises the student with both rural and urban local government. It covers the Panchayati Raj, rural administration and urban government and administration. The effort is to have the child draw contrasts and comparisons between the ways in which urban and rural government function. ***Section 1: Panchayati Raj*** ■ Description of panchayat including electoral process, decision-making, implementation of decisions, ■ Role of a gram sabha ■ Women and the panchayat. ***Section 2: Urban Local Government*** ■ Municipal corporation elections, decision-making structures ■ The provision of water and the work of the municipal corporation ■ Citizens protests to get their grievances addressed ***Section 3: Rural Administration*** ■ Focus on a land dispute and show the role of local police and patwari. ■ On land records and role of patwari. ■ On the new inheritance law.	To enable students to: ■ understand local level of government functioning, ■ understand the workings of the Panchayati Raj and appreciate its importance, ■ gain a sense of who performs what role within the local administration, ■ understand how the various levels of administration at the local level are inter-connected, ■ understand the intricacies involved in the local administration's provision of water.

(Contd.)

Themes	*Objectives*
Unit 4: Making a Living This unit focuses on individuals earn a livelihood both in the rural and the urban context. The rural context focuses on various types of farmers and the urban one on various types of occupations people engage into earn an income. The student should be able to compare and contrast the urban and the rural context. ***Section 1: Rural Livelihoods*** ■ Various types of livelihoods prevalent in a village. ■ Different types of farmers: middle farmer, landless labourers and large farmers. ***Section 2: Urban Livelihoods*** ■ Difference between primary, secondary and tertiary occupations. ■ Descriptions of various types of livelihoods including vegetable vendor, domestic servant, garment worker and bank employee. ■ Differences between self-employed, regular employment and wage employment. ■ The inter-linkage between rural and urban lives through a discussion of migration.	To enable students to: ■ understand conditions that underline and impact life strategies of various groups of people, ■ understand that these conditions and opportunities for making a living are not equally available to all.

8.4 CURRICULUM OF CIVICS FOR CLASS VII

Democracy and Equality

Rationale

Democracy and Equality are the key ideas to be engaged with this year. The effort is to introduce the learner to certain core concepts, such as, equality, dignity, rule of law etc. that influence Democracy as a political system. The role of the Constitution as a document that provides the guiding framework to function in a democratic manner is emphasised. This section deals with making the link between democracy and how it manifests itself in institutional systems in a concrete and live manner through case studies and real experiences. The objective is not to represent democracy as a fixed idea or system, but one that is changing and evolving. The learner is introduced to a wide range of institutions—the government, the bureaucracy and civil society organisations like the Media so that she can develop a broad understanding of the relationship between the State and Citizens.

Equality as a value is explored in some detail, where its relationship with democracy is highlighted and the challenges or questions it raises on inequities and hierarchies that exist at present in society is also discussed. An analysis of everyday experiences in the domain of gender enable the learner to understand how these are related to the creation of differences that are discriminatory in nature.

Following are the Units in Class VII:

Unit 1: Democracy

Unit 2: State Government

Unit 3: Markets Around Us

Objectives

The specific objectives of the course, where it is not clear from the rationale of the approach, are indicated beside the themes to be taught in the course.

Themes	*Objectives*
Unit 1: Democracy This unit will focus on the historical as well as the key elements that structure a democracy. The structures in place to make people's representation a reality will be discussed with reference to its actual functioning. ***Section 1*** Why Democracy Two main thrusts ■ Historical What were some of the key junctures and transformation in the emergence of democracy in modern societies. ■ **Key Features** — The different systems of power that exist in the world today. — Significant elements that continue to make democracy popular in the contemporary world. ■ Formal equality. ■ Decision making mechanisms. ■ Accommodation of differences. ■ Enhancing human dignity. ***Section 2*** ***Institutional Representation of Democracy*** ■ Universal adult franchise. ■ Elections. ■ Political parties. ■ Coalition governments.	To enable students to: ■ develop an understanding of the rule of law and our involvement with the law, ■ understand the Constitution as the primary source of all laws, ■ develop the ability to distinguish between different systems of power, ■ understand the importance of the idea of equality and dignity in democracy, ■ develop links between the values/ideas of democracy and the institutional forms and processes associated with it, ■ understand democracy as representative government, ■ understand the vision and the values of the Constitution.

Unit 2: State Government

This unit will focus on the legislative, executive and administrative aspects of state government. It will discuss processes involved in choosing MLAs, passing a bill and discuss how state governments function through taking up one issue. This unit might also contain a section on the nation-state.

Section 1: Its working

- Main functionaries-broad outline of the role of the Chief Minister and the Council of Ministers.

Section 2: Its Functioning

Through one example:
Land reform/irrigation/education/ water/ health discuss

- The nature of the role played by the government – regarding resources and services.
- Factors involved in distribution of resources/services.
- Access of localities and communities to resources/services.

To enable students to:

- gain a sense of the nature of decision-making within state government,
- understand the domain of power and authority exercised by the state government over people's lives,
- gain a critical sense of the politics underlying the provision of services or the distribution of resources.

Unit 3: Understanding Media

In this unit the various aspects of the role of a media in a democracy will be highlighted. This unit will also include a discussion on advertising as well as on the right to information bill.

Section 1: Media and Democracy

Media's role in providing the following:

- providing information,
- providing forum for discussion/ debate creating public opinion.
- Media ethics and accountability
- Relationship between Government and Information
- A case study of the popular struggle that brought about the enactment of this legislation.

Section 2: On Advertising

- Commercial advertising and consumerism,
- Social advertising.

To enable students to:

- understand the role of the media in facilitating interaction between the government and citizens,
- gain a sense that government is accountable to its citizens,
- understand the link between information and power,
- gain a critical sense of the impact of media on people's lives and choices,
- appreciate the significance of people's movements in gaining this right.

Unit 4: Unpacking Gender

This unit is to understand the role gender plays in ordering our social and economic lives.

Section 1: Social Aspects

Norms, values that determine roles expected from boys and girls in the:

- family,
- community,
- schools,
- public spaces,
- understanding inequality: the role of gender in creating unequal and hierarchical relations in society.

Section 2: Economic Aspects

- gender division of labour within family,
- value placed on women's work within and outside the home,
- the invisibilisation of women's labour

To enable students to:

- understand that gender is a social construct and not determined by biological difference,
- learn to interrogate gender construction in different social and economic contexts,
- to link everyday practices with the creation of inequality and question it.

Unit 5: Markets Around Us

This unit is focussed on discussing various types of markets, how people access these and to examine the workings of an actual market.

Section 1

- On retail markets and our everyday needs.
- On role and impact of wholesale markets how are these linked to the above.
- People's access to markets depends upon many factors, such as, availability, convenience, credit, quality, price, income cycle, etc.

Section 2

Examine the role of an observable wholesale market, such as, grain, fruit, or vegetable to understand the chain of activities, the role of intermediaries and its impact on farmer-producers.

To enable students to:

- understand markets and their relation to everyday life,
- understand markets and their function to link scattered producers and consumers,
- gain a sense of inequity in market operations.

8.4 CURRICULUM OF CIVICS FOR CLASS VIII

Rule of Law and Social Justice

Rationale

The theme of law and social justice for Class VIII attempts to connect constitutional values and vision to the reality of contemporary India and to look at the constitution as an inspiring and evolving document. Some provisions of the constitution relating to fundamental rights, parliamentary form of government, role of the judiciary and economic role of government are the topics discussed in this light. The attempt is to move from listing rules and functions to discussing some of the key ideas underlying the working of these institutions. The role of people as desiring and striving for a just society and hence responding and evolving laws and structures that govern us is brought forth.

Objectives

The specific objectives of the course, where it is not clear from the rationale of the approach, are indicated beside the themes to be taught in the course.

Curriculum of Civics in Class VIII is divided into the following units:

Unit 1: The Constitution

Unit 2: Parliamentary Government

Unit 3: The Judiciary

Themes	*Objectives*
Unit 1: The Constitution This unit focuses on the Constitution through first highlighting why there is a need for laws and then showing how the Constitution is the framework that determines the making of laws in this country. Aspects of secularism as well as economic justice are highlighted with respect to the Constitution. ***Section 1*** The Role of the Constitution and the Need for Laws ■ On need for laws discussed through an example like dowry, ■ Role of Constitution in determining the authority/legitimacy of the law, ■ Laws and Dissent: Salt Satyagraha and a post-1947 example such as anti-liquor agitation. ***Section 2*** ■ Vision set forth in the Indian Constitution with a focus on secularism. ■ On how an ideal of the Constitution translates into a law. ■ On how ideals of secularism got translated into fundamental rights.	To enable students to: ■ develop an understanding of the rule of law and our involvement with the law, ■ understand the Constitution as the primary source of all our laws, ■ understand laws as evolving and subject to change, ■ understand the vision and the values of the Constitution, ■ develop an appreciation of human rights guaranteed in the Constitution ■ appreciate our continuous involvement with the Constitution as a living document.

(*Contd.*)

Themes	*Objectives*
■ On Fundamental rights as human rights. ■ On Fundamental Duties. ■ On whether the fact that a law exists to secure certain right mean that in effect these sight have been realized for all. This will be discussed with examples from current efforts of various marginalized communities to realise their rights.	
Unit 2: Parliamentary Government In this unit the functioning of parliamentary government and the roles and responsibilities of the various individuals involved in explained in context. In addition the workings of the central government are explained through the steps involved in passing a new law that arose out of people's struggles. ***Section 1*** ■ Reasons why parliamentary form chosen in India. ■ Main features of composition of Parliament and its role in debating a bill. ■ Accountability of the government to the Parliament. ■ Role of President, PM and the Council of Ministers. ***Case Study***: Debate between Nehru and Rajendra Prasad on the real powers of the president. ***Section 2*** ■ Understand central government through issue of minimum wages or other struggles keeping following in mind. ■ Translation of felt need into law and the critical features of the legislation. ■ Implication of law.	To enable students to: ■ understand why India chose a parliamentary form of government, ■ gain a sense/rationale of the essential elements of the parliamentary form of government, ■ analyse the role of people's agency in placing demands for legislation, ■ understand the ways in which the government and other groups respond to such issues.
Unit 3: The Judiciary This unit focuses on understanding the judiciary through tracing a case from the lower to the higher courts. It also examines the difference between civil and criminal cases and the difference between the police and the courts as well as provides information on an FIR. ***Section 1*** ■ The structure and process followed by the judiciary: Trace a case from lower to higher courts. ■ Distinguish between civil and criminal cases. ■ Indicate the rationale of the process.	To enable students to: ■ understand the main elements of our judicial structure, ■ appreciate the need for the processes followed, ■ understand what an FIR is and how to file one.

(*Contd.*)

Themes	*Objectives*
Section 2 Difference between the roles of the police and that of the courts ■ Role of the Public Prosecutor. ■ On an FIR: filing one, on the legality of the police not accepting an FIR and the Supreme Court's directive on this.	
Unit 4: Social Justice and the Marginalised This unit focuses on issues of social justice and the marginalised. It first provides an understanding of what is meant by 'marginalised' groups. It then discusses-in-depth the issue of untouchability and reservations. ***Section 1*** A brief explanation of what is meant by marginalised. Include how various communities (SC, ST, OBC, minorities) fit in. ■ Forms of social inequality – Constitutional provisions relating to social justice. ■ Effect of social inequalities on economic inequalities. ■ On reservations. ***Section 2*** Different forms of untouchability that continue to exist. ■ The law on manual scavenging with reference to existing realities in rural and urban areas.	To enable students to: ■ understand what is meant by marginalised, ■ gain a critical understanding of social and economic injustices, ■ develop skills to analyse an argument from the marginalised point of view.
Unit 5: Economic Presence of the Government Introduction of various ways by which government is engaged in developmental activities, especially in infrastructure and social sectors. Explain with an example from this area why we need the government, how is the provision done, how does it impact upon people. Transport, communication and trade.	To enable students to: ■ think about the role of government in the economic sphere, ■ see some links between people's aspirations/ needs and role of government. To explain the importance of transport and communication in the ever shrinking world; To understand the role of trade in the economic development of a country and analyse the changing. *Periods 5*

Contd.

Themes	*Objectives*
Project/Activity ■ Learners may collect photographs of typical rural houses, and clothing of people from different regions of India and examine whether they reflect any relationship with the climatic conditions and relief of the area. ■ Learners may write a brief report on various irrigation practices in the village and the change in cropping pattern in the last decade.	
Posters ■ Pollution of water in the locality. ■ Depletion of forests and the greenhouse effect. *Note*: Other similar activities may be taken up.	

Source: Courses and Syllabi, NCERT (2005)

9

Curriculum in Political Science—Classes IX and X as Suggested by NCERT and CBSE

9.1 NCERT CURRICULUM

In class IX and X, the NCERT has avoided the term 'Civics' but the subject-matter related to Civics constitutes in a large measure the subject of Political Science.

The NCERT in its *National Curriculum Framework* (2005) has recommended the curriculum as given below.

9.2 RATIONALE OF INTRODUCING SOCIAL STUDIES

Secondary stage provides the last opportunity to all the students to engage with Social Sciences. Following an elementary introduction to the Social and Political life and functioning of Indian democracy in Classes VI to VIII, the process of understanding, critical reflection and analysis of the political life will be taken to a higher level at the secondary stage. Political Science at this stage will introduce the young citizens to the political phenomenon by taking up the central theme of democratic politics. This course shall draw upon from the various sub-disciplines of political science — political theory, contemporary world, Indian constitution and Indian government and politics — but from the vantage point of democracy. The course seeks to introduce the students to the Constitution of India, without getting into technicalities of the constitutional provisions. The course has been structured to give students a basic orientation and opportunities to reflect and debate on their own experiences and values in relation to the Indian Constitution and democratic politics. It would further develop their capacities and skills to weave interconnections between the personal and the political.

9.3 OBJECTIVES OF SOCIAL STUDIES

The specific objectives of the course, where it is not clear from the rationale of the approach, are indicated beside the themes to be taught in the course.

9.4 CLASS IX DEMOCRATIC POLITICS I

Class IX includes the following themes:

1. Democracy in contemporary world
2. What is democracy? Why democracy?

3. Designing of democracy in India.
4. Electorate politics in democracy.
5. Institutions of Parliamentary democracy.
6. Citizen's rights in democracy.

Themes	*Learning Objectives*
1. Democracy in contemporary world	
How has democracy expanded in the world in recent times? In which ways has this expansion changed the world? Is this expansion changing democracy itself? Are we moving towards global democracy?	■ Develop a comparative historical sense of the spread of democracy. ■ Analyse the functioning of global institutions such as U.N. ■ Skills of comparison and evaluation.
2. What is democracy? Why democracy?	
What are the different ways of defining democracy? Why has democracy become the most prevalent form of government in our times? What are the alternatives to democracy? Is democracy superior to its available alternatives? Must every democracy have the same institutions and values?	■ Develop conceptual skills of defining democracy. ■ Understand how different historical processes and forces have promoted democracy. ■ Developing a sophisticated defence of democracy against common prejudices.
3. Designing of democracy in India	
How and why did India become a democracy? How was the Indian Constitution framed? What are the salient features of the Constitution? How is democracy being constantly designed and redesigned in India?	■ Develop a historical sense of the choice and nature of democracy in India. ■ Introduction to the process of Constitution making. ■ Develop respect for the Constitution and appreciation for Constitutional values. ■ Recognise that Constitution is a living document that undergoes changes.
4. Electoral politics in democracy	
Why and how do we elect representatives? Why do we have a system of competition among political parties? How has the citizens' participation in electoral politics changed? What are the ways to ensure free and fair elections?	■ Introduce the idea of representative democracy via competitive party politics. ■ Familiarise with our electoral system and reasons for choosing this. ■ Develop an appreciation of citizen's increased participation in electoral politics. ■ Recognise the significance of the Election Commission.

(*Contd.*)

Themes	*Learning Objectives*
5. Institutions of parliamentary democracy	
How is the country governed? What does Parliament do in our democracy? What is the role of the President of India, the Prime Minister and the Council of Ministers? How do these relate to one another?	■ Provide an overview of central governmental structures. ■ Sensitive to the key role of the Parliament and its procedures. ■ Distinguish between nominal and real executive authorities and functions. ■ Understand the parliamentary system of executive's accountability to the legislature.
6. Citizens' rights in democracy	
Why do we need rights in a Constitution? What are the fundamental rights enjoyed by the citizen under the Indian Constitution? How does the judiciary protect the fundamental rights of the citizen? How is the independence of the judiciary ensured?	■ Develop a citizens' awareness of their rights. ■ Introduction to and appreciation of the fundamental rights. ■ Recognition of the ways in which these rights are exercised and denied in real life situations. ■ Introduction to judicial system and key institutions like the Supreme Court, High Courts and National Human Rights Commission.

9.5 CLASS X: DEMOCRATIC POLITICS II

Themes and Learning Objectives

Following are the themes in Class X:

1. Working of democracy
2. Power sharing mechanisms in democracy
3. Competition and contestations in democracy
4. Outcomes of democracy
5. Challenges to democracy

Themes	*Learning Objectives*
1. Working of democracy	
Are divisions inherent to the working of democracy? What has been the effect of caste on politics and of politics on caste? How has the gender division shaped politics? How do communal divisions affect democracy?	■ Analyse the relationship between social cleavages and political competition with reference to Indian situation ■ Understand and analyse the challenges posed by communalism to Indian democracy. ■ Understand the enabling and disabling effects of caste and ethnicity in politics. ■ Develop a gender perspective on politics.

(Contd.)

Themes	*Learning Objectives*
2. Power sharing mechanisms in democracy	
Why and how is power shared in democracies? How has federal division of power in India helped national unity? To what extent has decentralisation achieved this objective? How does democracy accommodate different social groups?	■ Introduce students to the centrality of power sharing in democracies. ■ Understand the working of spatial and social power sharing mechanisms. ■ Analyse federal provisions and institutions ■ Understand the new Panchayati Raj institutions in rural and urban areas.
3. Competition and contestations in democracy	
How do struggles shape democracy in favour of ordinary people? What role do political parties play in competition and contestation? Which are the major national and regional parties in India? Why have social movements come to occupy larger role in politics?	■ Understand the vital role of struggles in the expansion of democracy. ■ Analyse party systems in democracies. ■ Introduction to major political parties in the country. ■ Analyse the role of social movements and non-party political formations.
4. Outcomes of democracy	
Can or should democracy be judged by its outcomes? What outcomes can one reasonably expect of democracies? Does democracy in India meet these expectations? Has democracy led to development, security and dignity for the people? What sustains democracy in India?	■ Introduction to the difficult question of evaluating the functioning of democracies. ■ Develop the skills of evaluating Indian democracy on some key dimensions: development, security and dignity for the people. ■ Understand the causes for continuation of democracy in India.
5. Challenges to democracy	
Is the idea of democracy shrinking? What are the major challenges to democracy in India? How can democracy be reformed and deepened? What role can an ordinary citizen play in deepening democracy?	■ Distinguish between sources of strength and weaknesses of Indian democracy. ■ Reflect on the different kinds of measures possible to deepen democracy. ■ Promote an active and participatory citizenship.

9.6 CONTENTS RELATING TO CIVICS IN THE SOCIAL SCIENCES AS OUTLINE BY CBSE (CLASS IX AND X)

Nomenclature: Absence of Civics as a Separate Discipline

There is no subject of Civics in secondary classes. Of course, its subject matter is covered under the title 'Unit 3 Democratic Politics I and Democratic

Politics II. As already stated the present trend is not to use the nomenclature Civics. Even the term 'Political Science' is also not used.

Rationale of Introducing Social Sciences as a Compulsory Subject at the Secondary Level of Education Classes IX and X.

Social Sciences is a compulsory subject up to secondary stage of school education. It is an integral component of general education because it helps the learners in understanding the environment in its totality and developing a broader perspective and an empirical, reasonable and humane outlook. This is of crucial importance because it helps them grow into well-informed and responsible citizens with necessary attributes and skills for being able to participate and contribute effectively in the process of development and nation-building.

The social sciences curriculum draws its content mainly from Geography, History, Civics and Economics. Some elements of Sociology and Commerce are also included. Together they provide a comprehensive view of society over space and time, and in relation to each other. Each subject's distinct methods of enquiry help the learners study society from different angles and form a holistic view.

Objectives

The main objectives of this syllabus are:

- to develop an understanding of the processes of change and development—both in terms of time and space, through which human societies have evolved.
- to make learners realise that the process of change is continuous and any event or phenomenon or issue cannot be viewed in isolation but in a wider context of time and space.
- to develop an understanding of contemporary India with its historical perspective, of the basic framework of the goals and policies of national development in independent India, and of the process of change with appropriate connections to world development.
- to deepen knowledge about and understanding of India's freedom struggle and of the values and ideals that it represented, and to develop an appreciation of the contributions made by people of all sections and regions of the country.
- to help learners understand and cherish the values enshrined in the Indian Constitution and to prepare them for their roles and responsibilities as effective citizens of a democratic society.
- to deepen the knowledge and understanding of India's environment in its totality, their interactive processes and effects on the future quality of people's lives.
- to facilitate the learners to understand and appreciate the diversity in the land and people of the country with its underlying unity.
- to develop an appreciation of the richness and variety of India's heritage–both natural and cultural and the need for its preservation.
- to promote an understanding of the issues and challenges of contemporary India—environmental, economic and social, as part of the development process.

- to help pupils acquire knowledge, skills and understanding to face the challenges of contemporary society as individuals and groups and learn the art of living a confident and stress-free life as well as participating effectively in the community.
- to develop scientific temper by promoting the spirit of enquiry and following a rational and objective approach in analysing and evaluating data and information as well as views and interpretations.
- to develop academic and social skills such as critical thinking, communicating effectively both in visual and verbal forms—cooperating with others, taking initiatives and providing leadership in solving others', problems.
- to develop qualities clustered around the personal, social, moral, national and spiritual values that make a person humane and socially effective.

Class IX: Democratic Politics I

Following themes are included:

1. What is democracy? Why democracy?
2. Designing of democracy in India.
3. Electoral politics in democracy.
4. Institutions of parliamentary democracy.
5. Citizens' rights in democracy.

Themes	*Learning Objectives*
1. What is democracy? Why democracy?	
What are the different ways of defining democracy? Why has democracy become the most prevalent form of government in our times? What are the alternatives to democracy? Is democracy superior to its available alternatives? Must every democracy have the same institutions and values?	■ Develop conceptual skills of defining democracy. ■ Understand how different historical processes and forces have promoted democracy ■ Developing a sophisticated defence of democracy against common prejudices.
2. Designing of democracy in India.	
How and why did India become a democracy? How was the Indian Constitution framed? What are the salient features of the Constitution? How is democracy being constantly designed and redesigned in India?	■ Develop a historical sense of the choice and nature of democracy in India. ■ Introduction to the process of Constitution making. ■ Develop respect for the Constitution and appreciation for Constitutional values. ■ Recognise that Constitution is a living document that undergoes changes. ■ Introduce the idea of representative democracy via competitive party politics.

(Contd.)

Themes	*Learning Objectives*
3. Electoral politics in democracy	
Why and how do we elect representatives? Why do we have a system of competition among political parties? How has the citizens' participation in electoral politics changed? What are the ways to ensure free and fair elections?	■ Familiarise with our electoral system and reasons for choosing this. ■ Develop an appreciation of citizen's increased participation in electoral politics. ■ Recognise the significance of the Election Commission. ■ Provide an overview of central governmental structures.
4. Institutions of parliamentary democracy	
How is the country governed? What does Parliament do in our democracy? What is the role of the President of India, the Prime Minister and the Council of Ministers? How do these relate to one another?	■ Sensitive to the key role of the Parliament and its procedures. ■ Distinguish between nominal and real executive authorities and functions. ■ Understand the parliamentary system of executive's accountability to the legislature. ■ Develop a citizens' awareness of their rights. ■ Introduction to and appreciation of the fundamental rights.
5. Citizens' rights in democracy	
Why do we need rights in a Constitution? What are the fundamental rights enjoyed by the citizen under the Indian Constitution? How does the judiciary protect the fundamental rights of the citizen? How is the independence of the judiciary ensured?	■ Recognition of the ways in which these rights are exercised and denied in real life situations. ■ Introduction to judicial system and key institutions like the Supreme Court, High Courts and National Human Rights Commission.

Class X—Unit 3: Democratic Politics II

Class X includes the following themes:

1. Power sharing mechanisms in democracy
2. Working of democracy
3. Competition and contestations in democracy
4. Outcomes of democracy
5. Challenges to democracy

Themes	*Learning Objectives*
1. Power sharing mechanisms in democracy	
Why and how is power shared in democracies? How has federal division of power in India helped national unity? To what extent has decentralisation achieved this objective? How does democracy accommodate different social groups?	■ Analyse the relationship between social cleavages and political competition with reference to Indian situation ■ Understand and analyse the challenges posed by communalism to Indian democracy. ■ Understand the enabling and disabling effects of caste and ethnicity in politics. ■ Develop a gender perspective on politics.
2. Working of democracy	
Are divisions inherent to the working of democracy? What has been the effect of caste on politics and of politics on caste? How has the gender division shaped politics? How do communal divisions affect democracy?	■ Introduce students to the centrality of power sharing in a democracy. ■ Understand the working of spatial and social power sharing mechanisms. ■ Analyse federal provisions and institutions ■ Understand the new Panchayati Raj institutions in rural and urban areas.
3. Competition and contestations in democracy	
How do struggles shape democracy in favour of ordinary people? What role do political parties play in competition and contestation? Which are the major national and regional parties in India? Why have social movements come to occupy larger role in politics?	■ Understand the vital role of struggle in the expansion of democracy. ■ Analyse party systems in democracies. ■ Introduction to major political parties in the country. ■ Analyse the role of social movements and non-party political formations.
4. Outcomes of democracy	
Can or should democracy be judged by its outcomes? What outcomes can one reasonably expect of democracies? Does democracy in India meet these expectations? Has democracy led to development, security and dignity for the people? What sustains democracy in India?	■ Introduction to the difficult question of evaluating the functioning of democracies. ■ Develop the skills of evaluating Indian democracy on some key dimensions: development, security and dignity for the people. ■ Understand the causes for continuation of democracy in India.

(Contd.)

Themes	*Learning Objectives*
5. Challenges to democracy	
Is the idea of democracy shrinking? What are the major challenges to democracy in India? How can democracy be reformed and deepened? What role can an ordinary citizen play in deepening democracy?	■ Distinguish between sources of strength and weaknesses of Indian democracy. ■ Reflect on the different kinds of measures possible to deepen democracy. ■ Promote an active and participatory citizenship.

9.7 EVALUATION OF CURRICULUM

Merits

1. *Curriculum According to Maturity Level*: Curriculum is psychologically sound as it takes into consideration the level of maturity of the students. It is also suitably graded.

2. *Curriculum Related to Community*: The curriculum takes note of the specific needs of the community. It includes activities and programmes which have great potential to link the school with the community.

3. *Emphasis on Various Sources of Learning*: The curriculum does not consider classroom as the only source of learning. It very rightly states that the environment and the society are important sources from which students acquire appropriate understanding, skills and attitudes.

4. *Focus on Practical Aspects*: The curriculum provides for undertaking several types of projects which are very meaningful and purposeful.

5. *Well-knit Curriculum*: There is continuity of the curriculum. The curriculum for each class and each stage is fairly connected.

6. *Self-contained Themes*: The themes in the curriculum are given in such a manner that they provide for a minimum but basic knowledge for even those students who may not continue their education after the secondary stage.

7. *Development of Basic Understandings, Skills and Attitudes*: The contents of the programme are planned in such a manner as to provide adequate opportunities to the students for the development of basic understandings, skills and attitudes needed for the ideals and values of democracy, secularism and socialism.

8. *Promotion of International Understanding*: There is sufficient emphasis on the development of values of international understanding and peace. The curriculum highlights the contribution of great thinkers and statesmen etc. who have worked for the betterment of the human race.

9. *Flexibility of the Curriculum*: The curriculum caters to the requirement of a wide range of learners and learning situations. It is suggestive and illustrative rather than prescriptive or restrictive.

10. *Cultural Heritage*: The curriculum notes that the nations live in the present or the past and for the future. It is backward-looking, modern-looking and forward-looking. It keeps in forefront the issues and concerns of the contemporary society. At the same time it accepts that past developments and to be studied for developing a historical perspective.

11. *Emphasis in the Process of Learning*: The curriculum emphasises the importance of process of learning and thinking rather than mere learning of facts.

12. *Emotional and National Integration*: It includes all the core components such as history of India's freedom movement, constitutional obligation, content essential to nurture natural identity, equality of sexes, removal of social barriers, fundamental duties and rights etc.

13. *Integrated Approach*: In the organisation of content, inter-relatedness of ideas and comprehensibility have been given due importance.

14. *Balance Struck*: The curriculum strikes a balance on the glory of ancient India and the new demands of modern times. It duly takes note of new forces of information and communication technology, economic liberalisation and globalisation.

Limitations and Shortcomings of the Social Sciences Curriculum

1. '*Old Wine in New Bottles*': The contents of Units in Classes VI to VIII clearly denote, that they relate to Geography, History and Civics. No useful purpose could be served by eliminating or discarding the names of the subjects and substituting them by Units I, II and III. By and large, a similar approach is followed in Classes IX and X.

2. *Omission of Significant Elements*: Some significant elements are missing in the content of the curriculum at the upper primary stage and secondary stage. For instance no mention is made of the Aryans and Asoka. Likewise, the contribution of freedom fighters does not find any place in the curriculum at the secondary stage. India's contacts in ancient India with the Eastern World have not been given their due importance.

There is no reference to population planning.

While discussing the industries of India in Unit II of the Upper Primary Stage, role of cottage and small scale industries has not been highlighted.

3. *Unbalanced Units*: Some units are too sketchy to serve any useful purpose.

4. *Ambiguous Terminology*: Curriculum at some places is laced with language and phrases which normally are beyond the easy comprehension of the students.

Summing up—Notwithstanding certain gaps, the curriculum on the whole is balanced and integrated. Adequate stress has been laid on making the knowledge relevant to life by weaving the content around day-to-day experiences.

While discussing various dimensions of curriculum, it must be remembered that even a poorly constructed curriculum can yield the desired results when implemented by a seasoned teacher and on the other hand a balanced curriculum may lose its utility at the hands of an indifferent teacher. As observed by the Secondary Education Commission, "Even the best curriculum and the most perfect syllabus remains dead unless quickened by the right methods of teaching". This however, does not mean that adequate care need not be exercised in constructing.

10

Methods of Teaching Civics

10.1 SIGNIFICANCE OF DYNAMIC AND PROGRESSIVE METHODS OF TEACHING

There is no single road to successful teaching. There are many road—highways and by-ways, royal roads and narrow lanes, delightful paths and rugged and rough ones, functional and decorative, passive and dynamic, conservative and progressive. The choice of a suitable method depends upon many factors such as the learner, the nature of the subject and the topic, the facilities available and above all the attitude of the teacher. A method is not a mere mechanical device for passing on facts and figures. It is a means of creating the right reaction and response and improving the values of learning and fostering right attitudes. To quote the Secondary Education Commission, "Any method, good or bad links up the teacher and his pupils into an organic relationship with constant mutual interaction; it reacts not only on the mind of the students but on their entire personality; their standard of work and judgement, their intellectual and emotional development, their attitudes and values. Good methods which are psychologically and socially sound may raise the whole quality of life; bad methods debase it. So, in the choice and assessment of methods, teachers must always take into consideration their end products, namely the attitudes and values inculcated in them consciously or unconsciously."

The Secondary Education Commission has further emphasised the need for right methods of teaching in these words, "Every teacher and educationist of experience knows that even the best curriculum and the most perfect syllabus remains dead unless quickened into life by the right methods of teaching and the right kind of teachers. Sometimes even an unsatisfactory and unimaginative syllabus can be made interesting and significant by the gifted teacher who does not focus his mind on the subject matter to be taught or the information to be imparted but on his students—their interests and aptitudes, their reaction and response. He judges the success of his lesson not by the amount of matter covered but by the understanding, the appreciation and the efficiency achieved by the students."

In the words of *Herbert Ward and Frank Roscoe*, "While it is true that good method is not merely a collection of artifices or mechanical devices and that every teacher must device his own method, it is important to remember that good method can result only from the constant observation of certain broad principles. These include orderly procedure in teaching, an arrangement of the subject mater which will avoid waste of time and energy and a distribution of emphasis which will secure the greatest cooperation from the pupils and maintain their active interest."

10.2 HISTORICAL DEVELOPMENT OF METHODOLOGY

The origin of modern methodology may be traced to *Great Didactic of Johann Amos Comenius* who lived in the seventeenth century. Comenius believed that all instruction should be carefully graded and arranged in a natural order. He advocated that the teacher, in his methods, should appeal through sense perception to the understanding of the child. He set forth his principles in his Great Didactic. The work of Comenius, however, like that of other educators of his time was buried beneath the sea of religious controversy and bigotry of his age.

Emile of Rousseau in the second half of the eighteenth century laid the foundations of the methodology and became the inspiration of forward looking and progressive educators. Comenius provided some ideas, Rousseau improved and enlarged and others worked them and put them into practice. In his chief educational work *Emile*, Rosseau begins with his principle, "Everything is good as it comes from the hands of the Author of Nature; but everything degenerates in the hands of man." He points out that there are three great teachers, "nature, man and things."

Johann Heinrich Pestalozzi attempted to "psychologies instruction". He declared that education was a drawing out process and not a pouring in process, that the basis of all education lay in the nature of the child and that methods of instruction must be sought and constructed to that end.

Wilhem August Froebel and Johann Friedrich Herbart, disciples and followers of Pestalozzi developed elaborate systems of education. The work of Froebel dealt largely with the Kindergarten stage. Herbert gave his famous 'Herbartian Steps' which cast a flood of light on existing methods. Herbartian steps became the stimulators of various other movements in the field of education. Herbert condemned the rote method and stressed comprehension and association. The concept that the outcome of education was not the strengthening of the mental faculties but rather the building up of an "appreceptive mass" of ideas was very revolutionary. Herbartian theory and practice became popular in Germany between 1865 and 1885. Teachers and students from many lands studied at Jena, a centre of Herbartian teaching. By 1890 these ideas were brought to America where they received an almost universal acceptance.

The period of Herbartian influence, on the whole, was a transitional one. It prepared the way for newer and better concepts of education. By 1910, Herbartian as a system of education was quite generally criticised. Herbartianism stressed the teacher and the formal procedure of teachings; the new theories of educational philosophy and psychology emphasised the pupils. Emphasis during recent years has been on individual instruction in the classroom but the socialisation of the individual is not to be neglected. Almost all modern methods and procedures can be used to promote both. It is believed that socialisation can be used in connection with individual development. In the social studies and social sciences, socialisation is very necessary. Through his own activities intermingled with the activities of the group, the pupil can learn and develop. Education must begin with the child and must be adapted to the needs and requirement of the child as he grows. Only in this manner, according to this philosophy, can the individual be made socially efficient.

10.3 CHIEF FEATURES OF GOOD METHODS OF TEACHING

1. They should aim at inculcating 'love of work'.

2. They should aim at developing the desire to do work with the highest measure of efficiency of which one is capable. The motto of every school and its pupils should be "everything that is worth doing at all is worth doing well". Whether it be making a speech, writing a composition, drawing a map, cleaning the classroom, making a book rack or forming a queue.

3. They should provide numerous opportunities of participation in freely accepted projects and activities in which discipline and cooperation are constantly in demand.

4. They should aim at developing the capacity for 'clear thinking' which distinguishes every truly educated person, "whether a student is asked to make a speech in a debating society or to write an essay or to answer a question in History, Geography, or Science or to experiment, the accent should always be on clear thinking and on lucid expression which is a mirror of clear thought."

5. The methods of teaching should expand the range of students interest. "We would urge all schools to provide in the time-table, at least one free period every day in which student may pursue their favourite hobbies and creative activities individually or in groups, preferably under the guidance of some interested teacher", recommended the Secondary Education Commission.

6. They should aim at providing opportunities to pupils to apply practically the knowledge that has been acquired by them. They should aim at transforming present bookish schools into "work schools" or "activity schools".

7. They should aim at the quickening of interest and training in efficient techniques of learning and study.

8. They should train the students in the art of study. They should train the students in the use of reference material such as the list of contents and index in books, the dictionary, the atlas, and reference books like the encyclopaedia.

9. They should be adapted to suit different levels of intelligence.

10. They should be such as they balance the claim of individual work with cooperative or group effort. The training of emotions, attitudes and social capacities take place best in the context of projects and units of work undertaken cooperatively. The Secondary Education Commission has recommended that the teachers should be so trained that they are able to visualise and organise at least a part of the curriculum in the form of projects and activity-units which groups of students may take up and carry to completion.

10.4 FLEXIBILITY AND RESEARCH IN THE USE OF METHODS

To quote the Education Commission Report, "It has to be remembered that advances in classroom practices occur on a broad front, with all the teachers and the schools moving forward in unison... But the work of the best teachers can be crippled, if they are not permitted, encouraged and helped to go beyond the departmental prescriptions. The success of an educational reform will depend upon the flexible approach where the good school or the good teacher is able to go ahead and the necessary supports are provided to the weaker institutions to introduce the reform gradually." The Commission has again observed, "In a modern society where the rate of change and growth of knowledge is very rapid, the educational system must be elastic and dynamic. It must give freedom to its basic units, the individual pupil in a school, the individual teacher among his colleagues and the individual school (cluster of schools) within the system to move in a direction or at a pace which is different from that of similar other units within the system without being unduly hampered by the structure of the system as a whole. In this process the freedom of the teacher is the most vital, it is almost synonymous with the freedom of the school for the pupils can rarely be freer than the men and women who teach them. It will, therefore, be quite in order to equate the elasticity of dynamism of educational systems basically with the freedom of the teachers."

10.5 CLASSIFICATION OF METHODS OF TEACHING CIVICS

The methods of teaching of Civics and other subjects are classified in a number of ways:

Classification No. I

1. Traditional Methods of Teaching, and
2. Modern Methods of Teaching.

Classification of Methods—No. I

1. *Methods based upon equipment*
   - Text-book method
   - Library method
   - Laboratory method
   - Construction projects
2. *Methods based upon approach*
   - Verbal-Bookish
   - Graphic representations
   - Specimens
   - Excursions
   - Participation for purpose of training
   - Participation for social helpfulness
3. *Methods based upon organisation of material*
   - Genetic
   - Chronological
   - Psychological
   - Logical
   - Topical
   - Subjects
   - Correlation
   - Integration

- Fusion
- Units
- Problems
- Contracts

4. *Methods based upon teacher purpose*
   - Explanatory
   - Appreciation
   - Reasoning
   - Diagnostic
   - Developmental
5. *Methods based upon pupil purpose*
   - Problem
   - Project
   - Socialised
6. *Methods based upon teacher-pupil relationship*
   - Assigned lesson
   - Supervised study
   - Freely chosen project
7. *Methods based upon pupil-pupil relationship*
   - Individual activity
   - Committee activity
   - Class activity
   - Cooperative activity
8. *Methods based upon the pupil participation*
   - Dogmatic
   - Occasional participation by pupils
   - Systematic participation
   - Socialised recitation
   - Pupil-planned activity (problems, projects, etc.)
9. *Methods based upon the degree of independence of thought*
   - Authoritarian
   - Tentative conclusions
   - Heuristic
   - Freedom of procedure but predetermined conclusions
   - Experimental
10. *Methods based upon manner of checking*
    - Oral recitation
    - Written reports
    - Written tests
11. *Methods based upon physical senses*
    - Visual
    - Auditory
    - Motor
12. *Methods based upon theories of learning*
    - Drill
    - Problem solving
    - Activity

13. *Methods based upon goals of education*
    - Democratic
    - Authoritarian
    - Laissez-faire
    - Cooperative group work
    - Creative self-realisation

Classification of Methods—No. II

Methods of Teaching of Civics may be classified into the following:

- Methods based upon equipment.
- Methods based upon approach.
- Methods based upon organisation of material.
- Methods based upon teacher purpose.
- Methods based upon pupil purpose.
- Methods based upon teacher-pupil relationship.
- Methods based upon pupil-pupil relationships.
- Methods based upon the degree of pupil participation.

Classification of Methods—No. III

It may be useful to understand the various pedagogical methods using some common dimensions, so that we may have a broad understanding of the classification of these modalities and methods on some basis. Three dimensions to be kept in view while classifying the training modalities and methods are as under:

(a) The amount of participant activity allowed in the modality or method;
(b) The amount of emphasis on cognitive learning; and
(c) The amount of emphasis on providing experience to and scope for experimentation by the learners.

The learner-activity is not necessarily in conflict with teacher activity. The teacher's role remains central; he directs and controls all the learning activity. Even then the learning activity can be either high or low. The concern with cognitive activity is that the various kinds of learning should lead to the formation of new ideas and concepts, their reformation in a better understanding of certain phenomena. Emphasis on experience and experiment on the part of the learner indicates the position that learning cannot be effective unless the learner is able to experience and also take initiative in experimenting either with outside phenomena (usually material) or with own behaviour.

Combining these three dimensions a cube may be constructed. Each dimension may be conceived as a continuum from high to low. In order to simplify the understanding of the combination of the three dimensions, it is proposed that each dimension can be divided into two, high or low. A combination of these may give us three different typologies of training modalities and methods. These are shown in Figure 9.1. The figure shows eight different typologies of such methods. These are briefly discussed below:

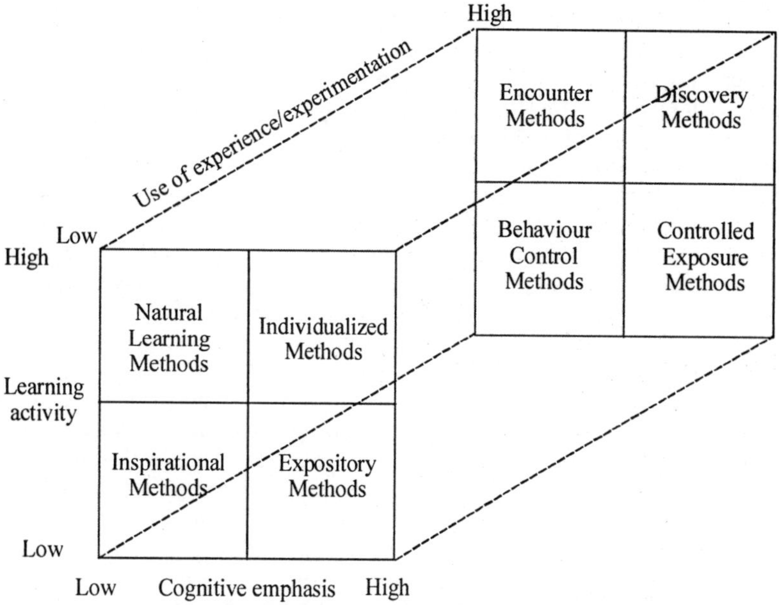

Fig. 10.1: Typology of Pedagogical Methods

1. *Inspirational Methods*: These methods are primarily based on high activity on the part of the teacher. Giving a sermon or talk to a group of learners in the hope that this will change their attitudes and behaviour, is a good example of this methodology. In this methodology all the three dimensions are low.

2. *Expository Methods*: In these methods cognitive emphasis is very high, while teacher activity and emphasis on experiences is low. A good example of expository is the lecture method in which the teacher takes the main active part, and the main emphasis is on imparting cognitive information to the learners. The learners remain comparatively passive, and they have no opportunity to experiment or experience things.

3. *Natural Learning Methods*: The main rationale of these methods is that learning takes place in a natural way and in a natural setting, and that planning for learning is not necessary. Learners are left on their own, with free and unplanned activity. The emphasis on learner activity is high, whereas it is low on planned experience or on cognitive inputs. The following modalities are worth mentioning in this regard:

(a) *Trial and Error Learning*: Under this learning no planned activity is done, and the learner is left to try on his own learning from the mistakes and then try out new ways until he has learned the phenomenon.

(b) *On the Job Training*: In this modality the learner is put on the job which he is required to do, and he learns from whatever experience he gains from the job. There is no emphasis on planned experiences or planned experimentation. All experience is in the natural form. The main emphasis is on learning from the natural setting of the job.

(c) *Discussion Methods*: Seminars, symposia and other forms of discussions can also be classified under this category. Natural groups are organised to discuss various topics and people express their views, share several things with each other, and they learn whatever they can from such discussion. It is hoped that providing such an opportunity will help people to learn.

4. *Individualised Methods*: These methods are quite well known mainly through the popularity of the programmed instruction. The main characteristic of these methods is the guided search encouraged by the instructor or the programme. These methods are low on providing experience or experimentation by the learner, and are high on both participant activity and cognitive emphasis.

The following individualised modalities are worth mentioning:

(a) *Programmed Instruction*: The essential characteristic of programmed instruction is that it takes the participant at his own pace. The programmed instruction material are prepared with great care, after analysing the content of a programme. The programme instruction methods, whether in the form of programmed books, or teaching machines, are characterised by the following:

(i) an ordered sequence of items of learning, taking the learner step by step, questions to be answered by the learner, immediate feedback whether the answer is right or wrong and why, minimising chances of learners making mistakes, and providing enough practice of correct responses.

(ii) Programmed instruction requires thorough preparation of material. Specialised techniques have been developed to prepare such material.

(b) *Training through Mass Media*: The use of mass media like radio and television is also included in this method. It has its own limitations. Some teaching can be conducted through radio, television and other mass media like journals, news-letters being issued by the department of education, circulars and regular ways of communicating with the large number of people through some written media or oral form like the radio programmes. Such programmes are being repeatedly used to supplement teaching.

5. *Behaviour Control Methods*: These methods are based on the rationale that behaviour can be changed only by understanding how behaviour develops and why some behaviour gets stabilised in people so that it becomes a part of their habits. The use of psychology of learning is made in these efforts. These methods are very low on cognitive dimension and on the active participation of the learner. The main emphasis is on helping the learner experience, and experiment with, some behaviour. Two methods are worth mentioning here. In a recent survey of various methods used for training social skills, it has been observed that the two most effective methods of training of social skills are modelling and the reinforcement of behaviour. These are mentioned below:

(a) *Behaviour Reinforcement*: This method is based on the theories of learning like those of Pavlov (conditioned reflex), or its further development and refinement by Skinner (called operational conditioning). According to these concepts such behaviour, if appropriately reinforced (rewarded in some form), a learner can acquire that behaviour very fast. The method used to change behaviour, therefore, is to prepare a schedule of reinforcement (reward) for the behaviour which is meant to be learnt. According to the schedule, each act of desired behaviour is reinforced (rewarded) and each act which is not in the desired direction is not reinforced or rewarded. A continuous schedule of this type helps in developing proper behaviour. The application of this technique may be in the form of preparing several systems of reward and reinforcement for appropriate learner behaviour in the organisation, and lack of reinforcement for behaviour which is not appropriate. This may help the learners acquire desired behaviour. As is obvious, this teaching does not produce any cognitive understanding in the learner, nor is the learner actively involved in generating situations. However, the learner is certainly experiencing various phenomena, and indirectly is encouraged to experiment.

(b) *Modelling*: The second method which has been found to be most effective in training of skills is that of modelling. The influence of the teacher has been recognised for a long time. However, in the past it was not realised that the participants are not influenced only by the individual teacher, but by the entire training atmosphere. In the training situation people learn from what is not directly taught much more than from what is directly taught in the classroom. They unconsciously learn many things from the experience they have of the teacher, the total group of faculty in an institution, the behaviour of the head of the institution, the general climate prevailing in the institution, and norms of behaviour which are practised rather than taught or talked about. The conscious efforts of presenting desirable behaviour either of the individual or of the group is called modelling. One implication of this method is that the educational institutes have to pay attention to how they operate and what is done in the institutes. It also means that they have to consciously examine and analyse the possible or probable effects of various aspects of individual teacher's behaviour or of the total institute on the learners.

6. *Controlled Exposure Methods*: The low level of participation by the learners, and a high emphasis on experience and cognitive learning characterises these methods. Several methods expose the learners to new experiences, but do not have scope for the participants to directly manage their own experience. These methods have been called controlled exposure methods. We mention two such methods below:

(a) *Demonstration*: This method has been very widely used in teaching agriculture, education, science and engineering. Demonstration can range from a very simple one in the classroom, when a teacher shows some action and the learner who observe to complex demonstrations of certain things in a controlled area where experiments have been going on and where people can go and see for themselves the results of such experiments.

For example, in the teaching of agronomy or agricultural extension, experimental fields are prepared where a particular crop is grown or other practices are applied. People are taken to these fields to see for themselves the results of the new seed or other practices. This method is very effective in agricultural extension. The farmers who see the actual results of a particular variety of seed in a field are convinced about its usefulness; it may help them in adopting that variety. The main characteristic of this method is controlled experimentation or research of a particular practice, developing the experiment carefully, exposing the participants to such experiment and experience, and helping them to understand why the experiment succeeded.

(b) *Films*: The use of films, or such other material like the closed circuit television, is another example of controlled exposure. When people cannot be taken out for demonstration because such well-controlled experience may not be available, or it may be too expensive to take people to a place where such experience is available, the same experience can be brought to the classroom through a film. When properly chosen, films help the learner to become aware of certain experiences and experiments, and they are able to see for themselves certain things which make an impression on them. Increasingly more and more films are being used in the classroom for demonstration.

The use of films has a great potential in teaching. For example, it is useful to prepare films on various important topics like elections. Once energy, time and resources are invested in making the films these are available to a large number of teachers for their teaching. Such an investment may be worthwhile. One danger in the use of films is that unless such films are developed for a particular country, or adapted from the existing films, or at least tested vigorously for their application, people are likely to use films developed in the western context by commercial organisations, and they may have limited value for developing countries. Selection of the films therefore is a very important dimension.

7. *Encounter Methods*: These methods emphasise both experiencing by the learner as well as learner-activity. These methods are based on the assumption that learning can be achieved more effectively if the learner are able to experiment and prepare their own training material. Such methods are not high on cognitive learning. In fact, the main aim of these methods is to help the learner earn new behaviour and practise it. Several methods have been developed based on this concept. We mention below only a few important ones.

(a) *Laboratory Training*: The purpose of laboratory training is to provide to a group of learners an intensive experience about how they work together, compete with each other, and learn from each other. This is called T (standing for teaching) or L (standing for learning) groups. Such groups have to be small, between 8 to 15. The main focus of T-groups or L-groups is to help the learners experience the process of dealing with authority, develop leadership behaviour, experience various methods of leadership development in the group, and experiment with their own behaviour as well as with the development of maturity in the group. This method seems to be very effective for producing basic attitudinal changes amongst learners, and in helping them in further learning.

A good laboratory training can produce same basic changes in the attitude and behaviour of the learners. It can help them to learn further. The emphasis of laboratory training is on learning how to learn. One limitation of laboratory training is the need of a well-trained and effective faculty. Unless those who run the laboratory training are thoroughly trained in the techniques of conducting such programmes, laboratory training may do more damage than good. Availability of such people may be a problem. The second limitation is the high cost of this training in terms of the number of days required for the training and the condition of the group being small for this purpose.

(b) *Assertion Training*: Some outer methods have been used to help people learn how to assert themselves without being aggressive, in modest, and at the same time not yielding to the ideas and pressures of others. A variety of methods have been used in this regard. A similar type of training is called value clarification training, mainly designed to help people understand and develop their values effectively. In assertion training, the main approach is to help the learner understand his current mode and behaviour and learn how this can be changed to a more aware and assertive one. Exercises for developing an assertive belief system, and procedures for cognitive restructuring, behavioural rehearsal, modelling and assessment are used.

(c) *Motivation Development*: Some programmes have been developed to increase motivation of people. The main rationale of these programmes is that people behave in a particular way, because their thinking is dominated by some needs. These needs are reflected in the imagery they may create during day-dreams, dreams, or creative expressions like writing of stories, poems, dreams, paintings, etc. The main approach of this method is to help the learners analyse their motivation by taking samples of their imagery, and later to help them increase a particular content of motivation (need) in their imagery. The limitation of this method is the availability of well-trained people to conduct such programmes.

(d) *Creativity Training*: In creativity training the emphasis is more on helping people recognise their level of creativity, and develop an insight into the blocks which prevent them from being creative. Once they are able to have this insight, they experiment with the help of various techniques to become more creative in general, and in particular on their jobs. Creativity in work situation takes the form of non-confirmative behaviour. Creativity training may be useful if the teachers have an opportunity not only to experiment with new practices, but also when they have opportunities to develop and use such practices. The limitation of this method is also non-availability of well-trained faculty to conduct such programmes.

8. *Discovery Methods*: When the emphasis is high on all the three dimensions, i.e., cognitive learning, activity by the learner, and experience and experimenting by the learner, we have methods in which people discover knowledge for themselves. These methods are very effective in producing change in behaviour. The rationale of these methods is that change in behaviour does not occur only by new experience and reinforcement, but also by the development of proper cognitive framework so that people learn why certain things happen, and they may be able to understand and advance their insight further. Several such methods are available as mentioned below:

(a) *Experiments*: Some methods may encourage learners to experiment and learn from such experiments. The best examples are the experiments done in the science laboratory.

However in Political Science and Civics experiments can be conducted in self-government practices in schools.

(b) *Field Training*: Field training is increasingly being used in the teaching of Civics. Students go to a particular field, and observe for themselves, learn from such experiences, and bring their observations to review what they have learnt in detail. This method has great value. Without such practical experience and training, students may not be able to learn many things.

(c) *Case Teaching*: When people cannot be taken to a field for studying some complex phenomena, the field can be brought in the classroom. This is done through the use of cases in training. A case describes an actual situation and its dynamics, and the various aspects of the situations are properly selected to help people learn a few things. Then the learners discuss the various dimensions of the case and learn for themselves various aspects involved in the case.

(d) *Role Playing*: Role playing has been more extensively used in educational training. A particular situation created in the classroom on a limited basis, and the roles involved in the situation are developed by giving proper instructions (role brings) to the participants. Then the participants take up these roles and actually sit and work as if the situation was real, and play these roles to solve a particular problem, or deal with a particular situation. Role play has great advantage. It requires a very careful planning. Again, we shall have opportunity to discuss this in more details in the next section.

(e) *Behaviour Simulation*: When an entire experience is recreated in the classroom it is called simulation. Stimulation means preparing a particular experience and reproducing it in an artificial way. This is done through a game, or an exercise, or through the use of computers. People then experience in a controlled way some aspects of the situation. Simulation has several advantages.

10.6 THE BALANCE SHEET OF THE METHODS

Table 9.1 gives a comparative view of eight training methods on the ten criteria as given on p. 86. It may be seen from this that the least effective method is "lecturing", and yet it is the most widely used method. It is necessary to move more and more towards participative methods—the methods in which individual participants are involved in some activity, and which can provide them opportunity to experience and experiment.

To quote the Education Commission Report, "It has to be remembered that advances in classroom practices never occur on a broad front, with all the teachers and the schools moving forward in unison... But the work of the best teachers can be crippled, if they are not permitted, encouraged and helped to go beyond the departmental prescriptions. The success of an educational reform will depend upon the flexible approach where the good school or the good teacher is able to go ahead and the necessary supports are provided to the weaker institutions to introduce the reform gradually." The Commission has again observed, "In a modern society where the rate of change and growth of knowledge is very rapid, the educational system must be elastic and dynamic. It must give freedom to its basic units, the individual pupil in a school, the individual teacher among the colleagues and the individual school (cluster of schools) within the system to move in a direction or at a pace which is different from that of similar other units within the system without being unduly hampered by the structure of the system as a whole. In this process the freedom of the teacher is the most vital, it is almost synonymous with the freedom of

Table 10.1: Comparison of Some Training Modalities and Methods on Criteria of Learning

	Criteria	*Seminars, etc.*	*Programme Instruction*	*Lecture*	*Encounter Groups*	*Demonstrative Films*	*Behaviour Simulation*	*Case Teaching*	*Field Training*
1.	Know	4	5	5	1	2	4	4	2
2.	Experience	2	1	1	5	1	5	4	5
3.	Experiment	2	1	1	5	1	4	3	3
4.	Reflect	2	2	1	5	2	5	4	3
5.	Practice	1	5	1	5	1	3	3	3
6.	Relate	2	2	2	3	4	4	4	5
7.	Pace	1	5	1	4	2	2	2	3
8.	Ger reinforced	1	5	1	5	1	4	4	3
9.	Share	5	1	1	5	3	5	5	4
10.	Belong	4	3	3	5	3	3	3	3
	Total	**24**	**30**	**17**	**43**	**20**	**39**	**36**	**34**

(Adopted from handbook for Training in Educational Management, UNESCO Regional Office for Education in Asia and the Pacific, Bangkok, Thailand, 1981)

the school for the pupils can rarely be freer than the men and women who teach them. It will therefore be quite in order to equate the elasticity of dynamism of educational systems basically with the freedom of the teachers".

10.7 LEARNING BY DOING (ACTIVITY METHOD)

Children have been endowed by nature with tremendous vitality. They have within them the springs of youth, joy and vigour. They possess curiosity and wish to know things for themselves. In the words of T.S. Avinashilingam, "The great Ganga of life flows majestically on. But if anyone tries to retain and dam it, the dam will break unless attempts are simultaneously made to divert it into other channels. These waters can only be diverted, but cannot be dammed indefinitely. If anyone tried to do the impossible, it would be at his peril, for the dam will break, sooner or later. So is the nature of children. The great vitality of our children cannot be permanently restrained without providing a positive purpose. In ordinary bookish classroom education, the teacher teaches, learners are but passive listeners. Their energy is not to be restrained by fear, inducement or punishment. This is against their nature and that is why we see much outbursts of so-called indiscipline. But, on the other hand, if we provide such activities in which the children themselves can take part, we will find that discipline becomes natural. Thus, providing for various types of activities which will interest the children and give them opportunities for observation and the use of their hands is to offer them the fulfilment and satisfaction, which nothing else confers".

The principle of 'Learning by Doing' has been accepted by all the progressive educators and in all the progressive countries. All educationists recognise that activity is an important instrument of education.

Comenius's View: According to him, "impression must be ensured by expression and what has to be done must be learnt by doing".

Rousseau's Views: Rousseau protested against the traditional methods of teaching very vehemently and he declared, "Children are first restless and then curious. Instead of making the child stick to his books, I keep him busy in workshop, his hands will work to the profit of his mind."

Pestalozzi's Views: He called the traditional system as 'the wordy system of teaching'. According to him, "Our unpsychological schools are essentially only artificial stifling machines for destroying all the results of the power and experience, the nature herself brings to life in them... After they enjoyed sensuous life for five years, we make all nature round them vanish before their eyes: tyrannically to the delightful course of their unrestricted freedom; peg them up like sheep; pitilessly chain them for hours, days, weeks, months, years to the contemplation of unnatural and unattractive letters."

10.8 LEARNING BY PLAY

Froebel's views. "Play is the chief activity of childhood", which Froebel considers as, "the highest phase of child development... for it is self-active representation of the stage... It gives, therefore, joy, freedom, contentment, inner and outer rest, peace with the world. It holds the source of all that is good." But, "without rational conscious guidance", says Froebel, "childish activity degenerates into aimless play instead of preparing for those tasks of life for which it is designed."

10.10 LEARNING BY EXPERIENCE

Dewey's views. Dewey endeavoured to substitute bookish learning by experience. He strongly recommended investigation and experimentation. According to him the school is a 'special environment' where a certain quality of life and certain types of activities and occupations are provided with the object of securing children's development along desirable lines. "The teacher", according to him," is a guide and director, he steers the boat but the energy that propels it must come from those who are learning."

10.11 LEARNING BY SELF-EDUCATION

Madam Montessori's Views: She shifted the emphasis from 'teaching to learning'. She believed that self-education is the best method by which the child learns in his own way and at his own rate. She used the word 'Directress'.

James Welton's Views: The teacher is like a guide and the pupil like a traveller in an unknown country. The traveller knows where he wants to go, but knows neither the way nor the exact character of the place he wishes to go... But unless the traveller that is the pupil takes the journey himself, nothing is accomplished. Many a lesson is too much like a guide describing the journey to the would-be traveller who sits and listens but does not leave his chair to undertake it. In other lessons, the guide himself laboriously takes the journeys again and again, but the traveller that should be, remains inert. In short, no matter how admirably a lesson is planned, there is no really methodical teaching unless the pupils by their own efforts pass along the road traced for them; for as has been said, "true teaching is nothing but arousing and directing learning activity of another."

Gandhiji's Views: "Let us now cry a halt and concentrate on education of the child properly through manual work, not as a side activity but as a prime means of intellectual training."

Thus we find that a long line of distinguished experts in education have advocated that knowledge can best be given through constructive activities suitable to the child. These new ideas on education have brought a new and hopeful message to our children.

10.12 MERITS OF LEARNING BY DOING ACTIVITY METHODS

1. *Instinctive Tendencies*: Children are active by nature. Constructions is a powerful drive roused in childhood. The hands of the child are ever ready to make new things. If he does not find material to construct, he begins to destroy. In fact, construction and destruction are the aspects of the same activity. The teacher should utilise this instinct by encouraging children to construct and create things.

Children Possess Curiosity: They want to understand the environment and put hundreds of questions to teachers, parents and friends. This urge must be exploited. Children are fond of collecting things. They should be encouraged to collect useful things for their museum.

2. *Self-motivation*: Motivation facilitates the process of learning by doing. It arouses the interest of the child and once interest is aroused, the child becomes active, attentive and learns by doing.

3. *Purposeful-activities*: Abstract things cannot be followed and understood by children. Mental activities should be followed by concrete activities, and this gives them the idea about what they are doing and with what purpose and aim.

4. *Utilisation of All Senses*: The children are required to utilise all of their senses in learning by doing. They have to be attentive in learning, seeing, feeling, smelling and sometimes tasting even. This makes learning fruitful.

5. *Close Relation of Mind and Body*: Mental activities alone fail to develop harmoniously the mind and body which are closely related. By doing the hand and the head work in close cooperation the learning becomes successful.

6. *The Principle of Linking with Life*: Learning is linked with the life and the environment of the child and thus it becomes part and parcel of his nature. In a lesson on gardening, if we take the students to a garden and explain to them the relevant topic, it creates more impression and the students learn it easily.

7. *Lessening of Fatigue*: Undoubtedly mental work is more fatigue-giving than the manual one and if children are kept busy in purely mental activities, they feel mental fatigue. But when we coordinate both mental and manual work, fatigue is lessened to a great extent.

8. *Social Development*: Social development is as important as individual development, children want to work in groups. In learning by doing they learn from each other and thus develop qualities like cooperation. Sometimes learning by doing takes the form of productive activities as is the case in basic education work experience and socially useful productive work. The students then produce things for society. Thus they develop feelings of being a part of the community and try to be useful for it.

9. *Inferiority Complex Resolved*: Learning by doing affords opportunities to backward children in studies to show their talents in various kinds of productive and constructive activities. This helps them in gaming confidence which further assists them in resolving their inferiority complex and they succeed in mental activities also.

10. *Use of All the Theories of Learning*: Various theories of learning have been put forward. 'Learning by trial and error', 'learning by imitating' others and 'learning insight'—all are employed in learning by doing. Thus learning becomes quicker, easier and more effective.

Learning by Doing and the Different Stages in the Education Ladder

This method can be employed at all stages of education. In the primary classes some manual work or craft work is at the centre. This may take the form of making envelopes. It may take the form of action songs, games clay modelling, paper-cutting, etc. The use of apparatus as devised in Kindergarten and Montessori systems also implies learning by doing. The project method is also an activity method which provides life situations and presents purposeful activities.

Middle and Higher Secondary Classes: The principle of learning by doing takes various forms in the higher secondary classes. Dalton Plan is an activity method which provides many opportunities to do work independently, to find out answers to a large number of questions by studying various types of instructional material. It also provides for conferences and discussion work. The Heuristic method places the children in the position of discoverers, inventors and experimenters.

Principle of Learning by Doing and Out-of-class Activities: The scope of this principle is not related only to the learning of various subjects in the class but also to the out-of-class activities. Students should be engaged in debating, editing, scouting, dramatising, etc. Games and sports are other fields. Students should be provided opportunities to render social service to the community. Social education centres, social service clubs, etc, should be started. NCC, BSS, all provide useful channels to harness the energies of the youth and thereby sublimate the instincts of the students.

Learning by Doing in Social Studies: The principle can be employed in all the school subjects.

History: Children should be taken to places of historical interest, i.e., ancient monuments, caves, forts, ruins, edicts, museums, etc. Charts and models of the various battles should be prepared. Maps of various dynasties and the extent of empire should be prepared.

Historical plays may be dramatised. The students may be encouraged to read historical novels.

Geography: Excursions to the places of geographical interest should be arranged. The students should be asked to prepare geographical maps, models and charts to show geographical facts in colours and lines on paper as well as on earth.

Civics: Visits to the meetings and sessions of Village Panchayat, District Boards, State Assemblies, etc. may be arranged.

11

Project Method and Source Method

11.1 MEANING, ORIGIN AND SIGNIFICANCE OF PROJECT METHOD

Project Method is a natural, whole-hearted problem solving and purposeful activity carried to completion by students in a social environment under the guidance of their teacher.

Project method is the outcome of the pragmatic educational philosophy of Dewey, the well-known American philosopher-cum-educationist. It was developed and perfected by Dr. William Head Kilpatric of the University of Columbia. It is a revolt against the traditional environment of the school which is usually marked by listlessness and passivity and which lacks keenness and real life. Much of the subject matter taught and many habits formed in school do not conform to desirable social life in the outside world. The project method is the expression of the wide spread dissatisfaction against the bookish, encyclopaedic passive method, whereby children as obedient masses are carefully drilled and spoon fed with fact and information. The modern educators speak in no uncertain terms about these disconnected facts, disconnected subjects, water-tight compartments and pigeon hole time-tables. "Ignore these" they say, "Give the class a real life project to bite at and watch the result".

11.2 DEFINITION OF THE PROJECT METHOD

Project Method has been defined by various educationists as:

1. *Ballard.* A project is a bit of real life that has been imported into the school.
2. *Burton.* The problem is a project which results in doing. The motor element is not what makes the activity a project, but the problem-solving of a practical nature accompanying the activity.
3. *J.A. Stevenson.* A project is a problematic act carried to completion in its natural setting.
4. *Snedden.* Project is a unit of educative work in which the most prominent feature is some form of positive and concrete achievement.
5. *W.W. Charters.* In the topical organisation principles are learned first while in the projects the problems are proposed which demand in the solution the development of principles by the learner as needed.

The following points have been stressed in the above-mentioned definitions of the project:

1. A project is a problematic act.

2. A project is a purposeful activity.
3. A project is a whole-hearted activity.
4. A project is an activity in a natural setting.
5. A project is an activity in a social environment.
6. A project is a bit of real life introduced in school.
7. A project is a problem-solving of a practical nature.
8. A project is a positive and concrete work.
9. A project is an activity through which solution of various problems are found out.

11.3 MAIN PRINCIPLES OF THE PROJECT METHOD

1. *The Principle of Purpose*: Knowledge of purpose is a great stimulus which motivates the child to realise his goal. The child must have an ideal. "Why is he doing certain things?" Purpose-motivates learning. Interest cannot be aroused by aimless and meaningless activities.

2. *The Principle of Activity*: Children are active by nature. They love activity. The instincts of curiosity, construction, pugnacity and herd make them active by nature. Therefore, such opportunities should be provided to them that make them active and learn things by doing. Physical as well as mental activities are to be provided to them. They are to be allowed to 'do' and to 'live through doing'.

3. *The Principle of Experience*: Experience is the best teacher. What is real must experienced. The children learn new facts and information through experience.

4. *The Principle of Social Experience*: The child is a social being and we have to prepare him for social life. Training for a corporate life must be given to him in his childhood. In the project method, the child works in groups.

5. *The Principle of Reality*: Life is real and education to be meaningful must be real. The child who is to live in a life of reality must be trained as such through his education. The project method is a method of educating the child and, therefore, it must also be real. Real life situations should be presented in the life of the school.

6. *The Principle of Freedom*: The desire for an activity must be spontaneous and not forced by the teacher. The child should be free from imposition, restrictions or obstructions so that he may express himself fully and freely. He must be given the freedom to choose an activity, to do an activity according to his interests, needs and capacities.

7. *The Principle of Utility*: Knowledge will be worthwhile only when it is useful and practical. The traditional system of instruction simply stressed formal and vital information, for its own sake, is of little utility. The project method develops various attitudes and values which are of great significance from the practical point of view.

11.4 DIFFERENT TYPES OF PROJECTS

W.H. Kilpatrick mentions four types of projects:

1. 'The Producer Type', in which the emphasis is directed towards the actual construction of a material object or article.

2. 'The Consumer Type', where the objective is to obtain either direct or vicarious experience, such as, reading and learning to stories, listening to a musical delectation, etc.

3. 'The Problem Type', in which the chief purpose is to solve a problem involving the intellectual processes, such as, determining the density of a certain liquid.

4. 'The Drill Type', where the objective is to attain a certain degree of skill in a reaction—as learning a vocabulary.

11.5 VARIOUS STEPS IN A PROJECT

These steps are given below:

1. *Providing a Situation*: It is not right to force a project on the unwilling students. The students themselves should define, state and choose their problems. Of course, the teacher's function would be to provide real and worthwhile situations. He would discover the tastes, temperaments and needs of the students and would provide situations wherein the students feel a spontaneous urge to carry out projects according to their felt needs. Stevenson taught the uses of the electric bell to his high school students by the project method. The necessity of completely overhauling the bell system in the school building arose and this occasion was utilised in providing a situation.

2. *Choosing and Purposing*: Purposing is very important. It is the centre round which a project moves. The project selected must be such as to satisfy a definite need or purpose. This purpose, as far as possible, must be acceptable to all the students of a class. Dr. Kilpatrick remarks, "The part of the pupil and the part of the teacher in most of the school work depend largely on who does the purposing. It is practically the whole thing." The students themselves should choose the project. The teacher should not be in a hurry to choose the project. Better results and better satisfaction can be had only through self-choice. Many situations should be provided to children. These situations should be discussed and the teacher should give useful suggestions. Decision should always be democratic. The teacher should merely guide and not thrust his opinion. The children must feel that the project is of their own choice.

3. *Planning*: When the decision of a project has been arrived at, the next problem is of planning. The teacher should draw the attention of the students to the need of planning before undertaking any activity. The task of planning is quite difficult. Good planning leads to better results. Each child should be encouraged to give his suggestions. The teacher should point out to the students to take into consideration their resources. Different proposals should be discussed and alternatives considered. The best plan is agreed upon after a good deal of discussion, suggestions and counter suggestions, rejections, and then students should be asked to write down the plan in their project book.

It must be stressed that the teacher must be ready with some proposals regarding the plan beforehand so that it may be possible for him to help the students in the best possible manner.

4. *Executing the Plan*: This step is the longest of all and requires a lot of work. The whole project is to be executed through the cooperative efforts

of all students. The various activities of the project should be divided according to the individual interests and abilities of the different children in the class.

The teacher should give sufficient guidance to the students. He should not dictate them.

This is the stage at which the students perform many activities and learn various useful experiences. The children keep themselves busy in collecting information, reading and writing in various languages, keeping accounts, calculating prices, looking up maps, collecting specimens of different things, measuring length and area, visiting markets, museums and zoos, visiting fields and crops, seeking help from others and the like.

5. *Judging*: The work is to be reviewed when it is completed. Lessons must be learnt from the mistakes that have been made in the various steps of a project. The students must learn to criticise constructively their own work. Self-criticism is a valuable form of training. The students should find out what things they have learnt from the project.

6. *Recording*: A complete record of all activities connected with the project must be maintained. The project book should be well maintained. All the details in the various steps should be noted down. The project book should give a comprehensive picture of the project as a whole. It should give the procedure of providing a situation and of choosing the project, duties assigned, difficulties felt and experience gained, etc.

11.6 ESSENTIALS OF GOOD PROJECT

These factors are given below:

1. *Timely*: Project should be related directly to the lesson and vocational interest. Project should suit the particular mental and chronological ages of the students.

Environmental and seasonal factors should also be taken into consideration. It is a well-known fact that there are definite relationships between the seasons of the year and current community interests and those of pupils. Projects should be timely.

2. *Usefulness*: Practical aim of the project should not be lost sight of. It must fulfil a long-standing need. The learning experiences in a project must be capable of being applied in life.

3. *Interesting*: Projects should be interesting to students. They must make an appeal to the emotional hungers or drives of the students.

4. *Challenging*: Projects should neither be too simple and easy nor too long and difficult. They should be challenging. It is an admitted fact that the youth wants to do tasks which are challenging in nature.

5. *Economical*: The projects should be economical. They should not unnecessarily tax the energy and pocket of the students. There should be the least wastage of time also.

6. *Rich in Experiences*: Many experiences of the sociable nature should be provided in a project. The project selected should be capable of correlating different subjects and practical activities of life.

7. *Cooperativeness*: The students should be allowed to think and plan

independently and cooperatively. The project should be executed in such a way as the students are kept active both physically as well as mentally.

11.7 MERITS OF PROJECT METHOD

Following are the merits of the Project Method:

1. Based on the Laws of Learning: It is in accordance with the psychological laws of learning. It is based upon:

(a) *The Law of Readiness*: According to this law, we learn most when our minds are ready to receive. The project method prepares the mind of the students by providing them with suitable situation.

(b) *The Law of Exercise*: Learning to be effective must be practised. The project method affords many opportunities to the students to learn by doing.

(c) *The Law of Effect*: This law states that if learning is to be effective and fruitful, it must be accompanied by satisfaction and happiness. The students derive immense pleasure when they manipulate their own activities.

2. Related with Life: Learning becomes practical and intimately related with life when meaningful and purposeful activities are provided to the students. The children get opportunities to acquaint themselves with the real problems of life. The students learn the practical usefulness of different subjects of the curriculum.

3. Correlation of All the Subjects: The project method gives unity to the curriculum. The water-tight treatment of the various subjects which is commonly found in our schools gives way to an integrated programme. Subjects do not remain isolated. Learning comes as a by-product of purposeful activity.

4. Training for a Democratic Way of Life: The method provides sufficient opportunities to the students to work cooperatively for a common purpose. Decisions are arrived at democratically. The students have a say in the activities they choose, plan and execute.

5. Training in Citizenship: This method imparts training to the students to inculcate in them primary virtues like tolerance, independence, open-mindedness, resourcefulness, etc.

6. Dignity of Labour: Dignity of labour is engendered through the project method. The students have to perform their activities with their own hands and thus they develop a taste for all kinds of work. They learn that there is nobleness in working and doing things with their own hands.

7. Stress on Problem-solving: It discourages cramming and memory work. It stresses problem-solving. It develops the thinking and reasoning powers of the students.

8. A Source of Happiness for the Backward: The project method provides a great relief to the backward children by providing them opportunities of participation in practical situations. Such children as are incapable of thinking abstract things keep themselves busy in concrete and practical situations.

9. Freedom: The students work with great enthusiasm for the completion of their self-chosen project. They do not feel tired as there is a good deal of variety in their work and atmosphere is full of freedom.

10. Constructive Discipline: As the children remain busy with their self-chosen work they do not get opportunities to think of anti-social ways.

11.8 DEMERITS, LIMITATIONS AND DIFFICULTIES

These are given below:

1. *Neglect of Intellectual Work*: There is a wide-spread misconception that the project method glorifies hand work at the cost of intellectual work. The critics argue that the children are kept busy in model-making and the like.

2. *Haphazard and Unconnected Teaching*: Projects many a time do not keep the examination and curriculum in view.

It is not possible to deal with all the subjects in a single project.

There are many topics which cannot be taught through this method.

This difficulty can be met with by setting aside some periods in which the gaps may be covered up.

3. *Upsetting of Time-table*: In a project method it is not possible to follow a rigid time-table. It upsets the routine work of the school.

4. *Neglect of Drill Work*: This method neglects practice and the development of skill in various subjects. The students do not get adequate drill in arithmetic, reading, spelling, drawing, etc.

5. *Difficulty in Getting Suitable Text-books*: Preparation of books suitable for the project method is by no means an easy task. Moreover material required for the implementation of a project is very costly. The method is not suitable for ordinary schools.

6. *Artificial Correlation*: Sometimes teachers show over-enthusiasm in stretching the projects upon which the class is working beyond its natural limits and try to connect those topics which have remote connections with the project in hand.

7. *Unsuitable for the Shirkers and Shy*: Some students who are not inclined to take responsibility may remain in the background and do very little work.

8. *Too Much Reliance on Young Children*: It is not wise to depend too much on the choice of the children.

9. *Lack of Competent Teachers*: For the successful working of this method, learned, efficient and resourceful teachers are needed. The method imposes heavy burden and responsibility upon the teachers.

10. *Unsuitable for Transfers*: A chief reading in an ordinary school finds it very difficult to adapt himself to a school that follows project method and vice versa.

Concluding Observations: A review of the above brings us to the conclusion that most of the limitations are unreal and without much significance. Whenever a new method is suggested, criticisms are unnecessarily levelled. Traditional methods have been tried and found unsuitable to the changing needs of the time. New methods must be tried and if found suitable should be accepted even if they are a bit expensive.

11.9 PROJECT METHOD AND NORMAL CLASSROOM TEACHING: ROLE OF THE TEACHER

The project to be successful must be based on a definite procedure. The first and the main responsibility of a teacher is to provide those situations to the students wherein they should feel a spontaneous urge to solve some of their practical problems. The teacher must be on the lookout of discovering their interests, tastes, aptitudes and needs. There are different methods of providing situations. As far as possible, problems or situations which are provided to the students should be social ones. These provide better social training and give more satisfaction.

The teacher may converse with the class on different topics of interest to them. Pictures of different scenes may be shown to them. Surveys of the surrounding conditions may be undertaken. The projects for study and work may arise out of the festivals like Diwali or Dussehra. The teacher must tap all resources to provide worthwhile situations.

Most of the educators are of the view that projects should be selected by the students themselves. They think that this will stimulate pupil purposing and that they will be more interested in their work if they have a share in determining what they are to undertake.

Others who think that the teachers should select the projects argue that this method will ensure that the students undertake only those projects which are within their reach. Students are immature and they require adequate guidance to select their projects.

However, the safer course would be to arrive at a compromise. According to this, the 'planning' and 'doing' should be under the guidance of the teachers. There should be no hard and fast rules in selection of the project.

The relation of the teacher with his students is very closer in the project method than in the ordinary class teaching. The teacher is like a friend an elder brother who works together with the students and helps them to gain rich experiences. He must stimulate the shy students to put in their best. He must help the students to help themselves. He must see that the project is carried on in a democratic way. He must read intensively as well as extensively. He should have adequate patience, skill, knowledge, tact and sincerity.

11.10 PROJECT VILLAGE SURVEY

History: History of the village, if any, relics and monuments, dwellings of primitive man—caves, huts, etc. houses through different ages and at different places.

Geography: Source of water supply, climate, crops, fruits, vegetables and other products.

Economics: Occupation of the people, agricultural yield per acre, village handicrafts, rural indebtedness, cooperative societies.

Civics: Working of the Village Panchayat, cooperative store, educational facilities.

General Science: Health and sanitation of the village, water facilities, causes of diseases, village dispensary, ventilation, etc.

Arithmetic: Estimate of the cost of the village drainage system, calculation of the per capita income of the villager, measurement of land holding, calculation of different items in the family budgets, total area of the village land, area sown and cultivated, calculating agricultural produce per acre.

Language: Description of the various details of the survey.

Art Work: Preparation of charts depicting conditions of an ideal village.

11.11 SOURCE METHOD

11.12 MEANING OF SOURCE METHOD OF TEACHING SOCIAL STUDIES

Source method implies the use of original material and original sources in the teaching of political science and civics. A source method provides first hand experiences and leads to better understanding of the subject. Sources may be divided into two categories:

(a) Primary sources.

(b) Secondary sources.

(a) *Primary Sources*. These include as given below:

(i) Physical remains or relics or unconscious testimony in far off historical sites, roads, pyramids, human remains, clothing, food, fortification, utensils, pottery, building, implements, machinery, furniture, weapons, fine arts and museum pieces of many kinds inscriptions, chiselled stories, monuments, tombs, coins, stamps, tapestrips, scenery and portraits, sculptures, historical paintings, etc.

(ii) Consciously transmitted information in the form of oral or written testimony. Written sources include constitutions, charters, court decisions, official minutes or records, autobiographies, letters, diaries, geneologies, contracts, deeds, wills, permits, licences, affidavits, depositions, declarations, proclamations, certificates, bills, receipts, magazines and newspapers, accounts, advertisements, maps, diagrams, books, pamphlets, films, catalogues, paintings, inscriptions, recordings, transcriptions and research reports. Oral tradition includes ballads, anecdotes, tales and saga.

(b) *Secondary Sources*: These are those sources which are written by those who are not on the scene of the event. They simply describe the reports of those persons who either participated in an event or were eye-witnesses of the events. Gradually they are several times removed from the original first hand account of events and as such they are usually of limited worth.

An act passed by the Parliament is a primary data whereas is extracts published in newspapers are covered by the secondary data. The report of the University Education Commission is primary data but contents published in text-books form the secondary data. Many text-books and encyclopaedias are examples of secondary sources.

11.13 USES OF SOURCE METHOD

It can be used at the following stages of the lesson:

(1) *Pre-lesson Use of Resources*: Visits to actual sites of monuments, forts or museums may be arranged. The teacher can ask the students to read selected passages connected with the lesson beforehand.

(2) *Mid-lesson Use of Resources*: Extracts from original or secondary sources can be read during the course of the lesson. They create real situations, impart reality and vividness to the lesson and reinforce the impact of teaching.

(3) *Post-lesson Use of Resources*: Pre-lesson use of resources can also become the post-lesson use of resources and vice versa. Students may be given assignments which need the use of resources and vice-versa. They may

be encouraged to pursue their interest in a particular topic, do some critical thinking and analysis and prepare their own account.

Advantages of the Source Method

The following advantages may be derived occasionally by following the source method:

(1) It would make facts appear real, as they are gathered from sources which can be seen or studied directly. The learner acquires, greater conviction in regard to the truth of happenings.

(2) The source method provides an opportunity to the pupils to learn civics and political science by 'doing'. It is an activity method. The activities may take very interesting shape in the form of visits to museums actual handling of things in the school museum, etc.

(3) The source method offers scope for group work—there may be a workshop for building up history in regard to a particular topic with the help of sources.

(4) This method gives the pupil an insight into the process of gathering facts and it develops the historical sense in them. The sense of objectivity which is so very important to a student of civics and political science can be particularly developed through this method.

(5) This method also gives the pupils some idea about the method of historical research, however, rudimentary the idea might be. As such this method may make some contribution in developing the interest of pupils in research though they may undertake it at a much later date.

(6) Though the source method may be more suitable to the pupils of higher classes, it can also be utilised with advantage by pupils of primary classes, who may be studying political science and civics through the source method. The source method would make their study more concrete and more meaningful.

(7) It supplements classroom lesson.

(8) It develops elementary skills of collecting data sifting the relevant and organising the same.

(9) Learning becomes functional because it is gained in the real situation.

(10) It provides opportunities for useful mental exercises right thinking and imagining, comparing and analysing, drawing inferences, etc.

11.14 STEPS TO BE FOLLOWED IN SOURCE METHOD

The steps, which may be followed in studying a topic through the source method are indicated below:

(i) The unit for study, with problems and source materials through which answers are to be sought, should first be presented to the pupils. References in regard to the source materials may also be given to the pupils.

(ii) If it is proposed to follow the workshop technique, the class should be divided into groups with assignment of specific responsibilities, i.e., each group should be given a few specific questions whose answers it may try to find out with the help of source materials.

(iii) At the next stage the pupils should be introduced to the sources (excursions to sites, visits to museums and the student or group should seek the solution of the problems assigned to them (the group may make its own sub-division of responsibilities among its members).

(iv) One or two class periods may then be provided to the groups for editing the notes (taken while in direct contact with the sources) and for preparing written answers to the questions assigned to them.

(v) The answers may be mutually corrected by the group according to the procedure suggested before; the teacher may also go through the answers, select the best ones and keep them in a convenient place for use by the pupils.

(vi) One class period (if it can be spared) may be devoted to the discussion of some of the controversial findings arrived at by the groups, with a view to stimulate greater interest in the work.

(vii) The groups may also be encouraged to write articles for the civics wall newspaper on the basis of their findings.

11.15 LIMITATIONS OF THE SOURCE METHOD

1. It is very difficult for the school teachers to have an easy access to original sources.
2. Utilisation of original sources is a very difficult task for the school students as they lack the requisite training.
3. The method is very complex and technical.
4. There is the difficulty of languages. Almost all the original sources are in Sanskrit, Pali, Arabic or Persian and a few in English.
5. Contemporary authors and writers have given their own prejudices, preferences and limitations with the result that it becomes very difficult to sift fact from fiction. The students are, thus, lost in the maze of conflicting views about the same event or movement.
6. Source method of teaching is very expensive.
7. Source method of teaching is time consuming.

11.16 HOW TO MAKE SOURCE METHOD EFFECTIVE?

The students should be encouraged to study the resource books in the library. Educational tours to places of importance may be arranged. The students may be asked to write their own impressions and inferences about the places they visit. Copies of important extracts from the relevant records may be pasted on the blackboard for the use of students.

Dr. Keatings thinks that original sources can be used for creating suitable environment in the lower form. Well planned, purposive and well directed efforts have to be made by the teacher in the use of this method. By suggesting the use of resource method we do not aim at making our students research scholars. Use of the method in selected topics is likely to make the study of political science and civics more meaningful and real.

12

Problem Solving—Deductive and Inductive Methods

12.1 MEANING AND SIGNIFICANCE OF PROBLEM SOLVING

Life is full of problems and a successful person in life is one who is adequately equipped with knowledge and reasoning power to tackle problems rationally. The function of education is to prepare children for life. Problem solving, therefore, must be encouraged in school. Problem solving may be defined as a planned attack upon a difficulty or perplexity in which a person uses his ability and capacity to find a suitable and satisfying solution. The teacher motivates the pupils to make conscious, planned and purposeful efforts to arrive at an explanation or solution to some educationally significant difficulty. Yoakam and Simpson define it as "a problem that occurs in a situation in which a felt difficulty is clearly present and recognised by the thinker. It may be a purely mental difficulty or it may be physical and may involve the manipulation of data. The distinguishing thing about a problem, however, is that an individual who meets it as needing a solution, recognise it as a 'challenge'. It is a method in which some difficulty to act in an educational setting is felt and an attempt is made in a conscious, planned and purposeful way to find its solution".

Dewey observes, "Whenever—no matter how slight and common place is character—a difficulty perplexes and challenges the mind so that it makes belief at all uncertain—there is a genuine problem". He further ties problem solving with reflective thinking in these words, "The problem fixes the end of thought and the end controls the process of thinking".

Gates has defined the problem thus, "A problem exists for an individual when he has a definite goal and he cannot reach by the behaviours pattern which he already has available."

Problem solving is not merely a method of teaching. It is in fact a method of organisation of a subject-matter. It is an approach to deal with the subject-matter. The researches of Quitten and Hanne reveal that as compared to the chronological and tropical treatment, problem approach in social sciences is much more useful.

Children are curious by nature. They want to find out answers of many questions which sometimes are puzzling even to the adults. Nevertheless, they must be helped to satisfy their curiosity, whenever possible, by solving various problems. We must teach the pupils how to think so that they are able to transfer these techniques to a vast number of varied problem situations.

12.2 STEPS IN PROBLEM-SOLVING

1. *The Formation and Appreciation of the Problem*: The nature of the problem should be made very clear to the students. They must also feel the necessity of finding out a solution for the problem.

2. *The Collection of Relevant Data and Information*: The students should be simulated to collect data in a systematic manner. Full cooperation of the students should be secured. They may be invited to make suggestions as to how they could collect the relevant data. The teacher may suggest many points to them. He may ask them to read extra books. He may also ask them to organise a few educational trips to gather the relevant information.

3. *Organisation of Data*: The students should be asked to sift the relevant material from the superficial one and put in a scientific way.

4. *Drawing of Conclusions*: Discussion should be arranged collectively or individually with each pupil. Panton suggests, "the teachers aim should be to secure that, as far as possible, the essential thinking is done by the pupils themselves and that their educative process produces the particular solution, formulation or generalisations at stake." Care should be taken that judgement is made only when sufficient data is collected.

5. *Testing Conclusions*: No conclusion should be accepted without being properly verified. The correctness of the conclusion must be proved. The students must be taught to be critical, to examine the truths which they discover to see whether they fit all the known data. We should have our minds free from every bias in the process of problem-solving.

12.3 TEACHER'S ROLE IN PROBLEM-SOLVING

Valentine Davis quotes Professor Pasher who suggests the following points in problem-solving:

1. Give them (the students) a chance to define the problem clearly.
2. Aid them to keep the problem in mind.
3. Get them to make many suggestions by encouraging them:
   (a) to analyse the situation in parts,
   (b) to recall previously known similar cases and general rules that apply,
   (c) to guess courageously and formulate guesses clearly.
4. Get them time to evaluate each suggestion carefully by encouraging them:
   (a) to maintain a state of doubt or suspended conclusion,
   (b) to criticise the suggestion by appeal to know facts, minister experiments, and scientific treatises.
5. Get them to organise the material by proceeding:
   (a) to build an outline on the board,
   (b) to use diagrams and graphs,
   (c) to formulate concise statement of the net outcome of the discussion.

It may be stated that for the success of the problem-solving teaching technique, we need "a teacher who has the ability to see problems clearly, the power to analyse with a keen discernment and the facility to synthesise and draw conclusions with an uncanny accuracy."

12.4 DEDUCTIVE AND INDUCTIVE METHODS

Broadly speaking there are two general approaches or procedures in problem solving—the Inductive and the Deductive. In fact, the entire process of teaching and learning is based on induction and deduction.

The Inductive Method

The inductive method is a method of development. In the inductive method, the child is led to discover truth for himself. The various processes in the inductive method are: (i) observation of the given material; (ii) discrimination and analysis of differences and similarities; (iii) classification; (iv) abstraction and generalisation; (v) application or verification.

In the inductive method, the pupils are led from particular instances to general conclusion. Concrete examples are given and with their help students are helped to arrive at certain conclusions or principles. In the teaching of science including geography, mathematics and languages, this method is very helpful. The students, by examining a number of examples in science, conclude that heat expands and cold contracts.

In a geometry lesson the students by measuring the angle of a triangle come to the conclusion that their sum is equal to two right angles.

In a geography lesson the students by examining the heights of the places located at high places conclude that temperature decreases as height increases. The students may examine the heights and temperature of places like Simla, Nainital, Dalhousie, Darjeeling, etc.

In an economics lesson the students by examining a number of cases, may conclude that agriculturists in India are in debt. The process runs like this. Ram is in debt. Sham is in debt. Krishan is in debt and so on. Ram is an agriculturist. Sham is an agriculturist. Krishan is an agriculturist and so on. From this, it will be concluded that all these persons are agriculturists and are in debt.

In a language lesson, the teacher while teaching proposition may give examples like 'Ram is in the room'. 'The cat is under the table'. 'The book is on the table' and may lead the students to find out the definition of 'proposition'.

We find that a crow is black; we find another crow also black; still another crow black and so on and say that all crows are black.

This method is more useful in lessons where rules, definitions, generalisations, laws and casual connections between facts are to be established.

Merits of the Inductive Method

Following are the merits of the inductive method:

1. Knowledge is self-acquired and is soon transformed into 'wisdom'. 'General truths in order to be learned must be earned' is a famous saying and the inductive method is true to it.

2. It promotes mental activity on the part of the pupils and makes them active participants in the teaching-learning process.

3. It makes the lesson interesting by providing challenging situation to the students.

4. The method affords opportunities to the students to be self-dependent. It helps them develop self-confidence.

5. The student's curiosity is well-kept up till the end when generalisations are arrived at.

6. The child learns how to tackle problems. He not only acquires mere facts but also learns the way of acquiring facts and which proves him useful for practical life.

7. The method is based on sound psychological principles. Learning by doing is the basis of this method.

Demerits of Inductive Method

Following are the demerits of inductive method:

1. There is every possibility that the students may draw conclusions very hastily and these may be based on insufficient data and therefore may be wrong.
2. The method is very slow and lengthy.
3. It is not very helpful in the case of small children.
4. It is not suitable in the teaching of subjects in which there is more stress on the teaching of facts.
5. The inductive method is not a complete method in itself. It has been said, "Induction does not prove but only provides the material to prove, it only discovers". When we have discovered a principle, we have to apply it again on some concrete instances for its verification. Therefore, we need deductive method to ensure the value of inductive process.

The Deductive Method

This method is the other way round. In the deductive method, rules, generalisations and principles are provided to the students and then they are asked to verify them with the help of particular examples. The students are told that places situated at high attitudes are cold and then particular examples are taken to prove it. Such examples can be multiplied.

Merits of the Deductive Method

The merits of the Deductive Method are as below:

1. The teacher's work is much simplified. He gives general principles and the students verify them.
2. This method is very economical. It saves time and energy both of the students and the teachers. Many principles for the discovery of which mankind has taken a lot of pains can be told to the students very easily.
3. It is very suitable for small children who cannot discover truths for themselves. They get ready-made material.
4. There is no danger of arriving at wrong and incomplete conclusions.

Demerits and Limitations of the Deductive Method

These are as follows:

1. Knowledge is not self-acquired and, therefore, not assimilated properly.
2. The child is deprived of the pleasure of self-activity and self-effort as ready-made formulas, principles and rules are given to him.

3. It encourages memorisation of facts which are soon forgotten and, therefore, knowledge is rendered useless.

4. This method is unnatural and unpsychological for the students who do not possess ability to appreciate abstract ideas in the absence of concrete examples.

5. It fails to develop motivation and interest in the learning as the truths are not of much value to them.

6. It fails to develop self-confidence and initiative in the students.

Combination of Deductive and Inductive Method

According to I.E. Miller, induction is the making of the tools of thought and deduction is the using of tools. Both supplement each other and are not opposite things. Both are wanted for the discovery of truth as both legs are wanted for walking.

Induction should be followed by deduction and deduction by induction. Our approach should be inductive-cum deductive.

12.5 DEDUCTIVE AND INDUCTIVE METHOD COMPARED

	Deductive		*Inductive*
1.	General laws are first stated and particular cases are taken as examples to prove them.	1.	First particular cases are dealt with and then laws are derived from them.
2.	It does not lead to new knowledge.	2.	It leads to new knowledge.
3.	It is a method of verification and explanation and, therefore, it is a method of instruction.	3.	It is a method of discovery and, therefore, it is a method of education.
4.	This method is very quick. The child gets ready-made knowledge and he makes use of knowledge acquired by others.	4.	This method is very slow. The child acquires first-hand information by actual observation of a lot of material.
5.	This method encourages dependence upon others as it is based on borrowing from others.	5.	This method gives training to the child to depend upon himself and develops self-confidence and initiative.
6.	It is a downward movement of thought and leads to a more perfect comprehension of the principle of generalisation.	6.	It is an upward movement of thought and leads to rules, definitions or, principles.

12.6 A FEW ILLUSTRATIONS OF PROBLEMS

1. What does a citizenship mean?
2. What does the government do to protect our life and property?
3. How can we attain a well-rounded life?
4. What does the community do in helping character formation?
5. What is meant by public opinion?

6. How are our governments financed?
7. In what ways has man conquered time and space?
8. How are human needs satisfied?
9. How is man today extremely dependent upon his fellowmen for his existence?
10. How do we pay for goods and services?
11. How are products and goods distributed?
12. What are the various means of making a living?
13. What was the impact of Industrial Revolution in England?
14. How did America gain independence?
15. What were the effects of French Revolution?
16. What were the outcomes of the Russian Revolution?
17. What is the contribution of UNO to world peace?

13

Socialised Recitation and Supervised Study

13.1 MEANING AND SIGNIFICANCE OF SOCIALISED RECITATION

In the words of Yoakam and Simpson, socialised recitation is an educational programme of the school in which, "children are discussing, questioning, reporting, planning, working in natural ways. The teacher is a guide, counsellor, advisor, contributor and director in the best sense of the word, trying to get children to discover things for themselves rather than to have them merely listening to him." The programme aims at the socialisation of children by developing in them the traits of initiative and responsibility and harmony with group interests. Training children for democracy by giving them training in democracy is the all absorbing purpose of socialised class procedures. 'Cooperative enterprise' is the 'keynote' of the method. According to Schorling, "The main purposes of the socialised recitation are to develop techniques useful in group work, to stimulate reflective thinking, to supplement previous knowledge, to encourage creative expression, to develop desirable social attitudes by providing practice in a large variety of socialised situations and above all, practice in the technique of cooperative thinking."

13.2 WHY SOCIALISED RECITATION?

The traditional type of procedure of teaching does not provide for the active participation of the child in the learning-teaching process. It considers the child as a passive being. It does not provide sufficient opportunities for the child to express himself. Students usually learn by heart the subject-matter without understanding its meanings and significance. Ready-made knowledge is given to them. There is a lack of incentive for exercising initiative, originality and independent thinking. There is always the possibility that the child recites correctly and yet fails to comprehend the real meaning of what he has committed temporarily to memory.

Education for democracy is of recent origin. In the past the social aspect was not stressed. But now it is recognised that there must be a proper social setting and through education the child is to be prepared for social participation. Teaching as well as learning are seen in a social setting under the impact of sociological approach. Gandhiji said, "I value individual freedom but you must not forget that man is essentially a social being. He has risen to his present status by learning to adjust his individualism to the requirements of social progress." Child being a social animal should be prepared for 'social participation'. He is to be equipped with skills and abilities that would make him a better and useful member of the society. In the past such a conception of education was not taken into consideration in the educative process. Socialised recitation is one of the techniques of developing social understanding in children.

13.3 OBJECTIVES OF SOCIALISED TECHNIQUES

1. To make teaching real, interesting and natural by increasing activity on the part of the pupils and by adopting the techniques of learning by doing.
2. To develop social consciousness among the students by providing opportunities to them to work together in a friendly and cooperative manner.
3. To give the students a training for social responsibility.
4. To reduce the social distance between the teacher and the taught by minimising the formalities.
5. To provide opportunities to the shy pupils to become more self-confident.
6. To give opportunities to students to understand each other in a better way.
7. To assist the students to express themselves freely and to develop the capacity to think clearly and in a concise way.
8. To assist the students to decide by collective discussions and to be benefited by each other's contribution and also share each other's experiences.
9. To help students utilise and develop their natural interests.

13.4 VARIOUS FORMS OF SOCIALISED TECHNIQUES

(a) *The Informal Group Plan*: The teacher and the taught talk about the experiences and problems in an informal manner. There is no ad hoc agenda. Any member of the group may initiate a discussion. Every member of the group is at liberty to ask questions, to ask for explanation and classification.

(b) *Formal Group Techniques*: Such techniques are organised on the pattern or a club, council, a senate or a committee. It becomes desirable to elect or nominate office-bearers of the group. Proper records of the minutes of the discussions are maintained. Such techniques impose heavy responsibilities and they must see that every pupil is provided opportunity to get chance to assume leadership. It can be further divided under the following heads:

(i) The panel discussion.
(ii) The symposium.
(iii) The seminar plan.
(iv) The workshop techniques.

(i) *The Panel Discussion*: The panel usually consists of four to eight persons, a chairman and the audience. In a panel discussion, the representatives of the large group participate. The aim is to provide the features of a small group for the benefit of a large group.

A stage may be erected or a raised platform used for the panel personnel to sit. Seats may be arranged in a semicircular form to enable the audience to see and hear clearly the panel personnel. The discussion is opened by the chairman who explains the whole problem and coordinates the discussion and brings to a close the panel discussion by summarising the proceedings. The listeners should be given an opportunity to ask questions and make contributions.

Long speeches and debates are not allowed in a panel discussion. The members of the panel should be fully prepared for the discussion.

(ii) *The Symposium*: In a symposium two or more persons prepare their papers or speeches and present them to the audience. All the speakers talk about the various phases of the same problem and thus provide enough material to think about. Audience may be allowed to take part when the speeches or papers have been read. A chairman is also selected.

(iii) *The Seminar Plan*: Generally advanced students who possess advanced knowledge and intellectual maturity can be benefited through the seminar. A number of students investigate a problem and report their findings. The students may investigate problems individually or jointly. Reports are presented which are critically evaluated in the conference. The participants are free to ask for clarification of certain points. The teacher is the leader of the seminar. He must see that everyone gets some chance to contribute towards the seminar discussion.

(iv) *The Workshop Techniques*: It is a recent innovation. Many techniques are adopted in a workshop. Papers may be read, speeches may be made and discussions may be held. Practical work may be provided for the participants.

13.5 MERITS OF SOCIALISED TECHNIQUES

Yoakam and Simpson give the following advantages of socialised techniques:

1. Pupils learn to plan activities.
2. Common interests and purposes are discovered.
3. Practice in leadership is gained.
4. Initiative is encouraged.
5. Independence of thought is achieved.
6. Training in courtesy is given.
7. Ability to report is developed.
8. Pupils learn how to take part in discussion.
9. Practice is bad in passing judgement.
10. Extensive experiences are made possible.
11. Self-confidence is gained.
12. Respect for others is developed.
13. Cooperation is learnt.
14. Teachers know pupils better.
15. Pupils have greater admiration and respect for teachers.
16. Learning is more highly motivated.

13.6 HOW TO MAKE SOCIALISED RECITATION EFFECTIVE?

(1) Topics to be discussed should be interesting and at the same time educative.

(2) Proper seating arrangements should be made.

(3) Adequate preparation on the part of the teacher is absolutely essential. He must find out ways and means to ensure total participation by pupils.

(4) The atmosphere of friendship should prevail. Every participant should realise that ideas may be attacked and not people. Each child should be made to feel that his views are given their due recognition.

(5) The teacher is expected to play the role of a guide-cum-counsellor-cum-director-cum-contributor. It is his responsibility to see that the discussion is not off the track.

(6) The discussion must end with some conclusions. It should give the solution of a problem or a plan of action, the formulation of a policy, the evaluation of an issue or the acquisition of more knowledge about a topic.

(7) Reliance should be made on the interests, experiences and ability of the participants and should be supplemented by factual information supplied by teachers or leaders.

(8) Conversational tone is preferable to set speeches.

(9) All should be patient and tolerant of other's view-point.

(10) It should be used as a supplementary device.

13.7 WHAT SOCIALISED CLASSROOM TECHNIQUE SHOULD NOT BE?

(1) It should never be used to propagate certain ideas.

(2) Certain pupils should not be allowed to misuse their privilege by making it difficult for others to get to a fair dealing.

(3) The group should not be forced to arrive at any definite decision at the time of discussion.

(4) 'Heated' arguments for the purpose of overcoming one's opponent should not be allowed.

Teacher's Task in the Socialised Method

(1) He should enable the pupils to prepare themselves for classroom discussions by offering suggestions for reading or by questioning them.

(2) He must assume full control of the discussion and should also possess the ability to accept the position as one among the students' without surrendering his 'control'. He must acquire the art of making himself useful at the proper time.

(3) The teacher should ensure that the students go with right conclusion when the discussion is over.

(4) The teacher should assess the outcomes of the socialised techniques through devices like asking the students to summarise, to draw charts, maps, etc. of the principles of knowledge acquired through such techniques.

In the words of Yoakam and Simpson, "The teacher is a guide, counsellor, adviser, contributor and director in the best sense of the word, trying to get children discover things for themselves rather than to have them merely listening to him".

13.8 DEMERITS OF SOCIALISED RECITATION

There are some drawbacks also which are given below:

1. It is wasteful of time. It requires long periods of study.
2. It does not develop adequate mastery of the subject-matter.
3. There is a tendency of the class to wander from the subject.
4. It runs the risk of futile discussion.
5. In a socialised recitation there is always the danger that a few pupils will dominate the lesson.

Concluding Remarks: The teacher leads the students into thinking about and discussing various issues and often a tangible result in the form of a set of behavioural standards is produced. For example, the class may establish the following standards of leadership behaviour:

When I am a leader
I give everyone a chance to speak,
I listen to others,
I help others decide what to do,
I help others in a nice way to do things, and
I help our work going.

When I am in a group
I wait my turn to speak,
I speak quietly,
I give ideas,
I listen to others, and
I work with the leader and others to get the job done.

13.9 SUPERVISED STUDY

13.10 MEANING AND SIGNIFICANCE OF SUPERVISED STUDY

Arthur C. Bining and David H. Bining describe the meaning of supervised study as, "By supervised study, we mean the supervision by the teacher of a group or class of pupils as they work at their desk or around their tables. In this procedure, we find pupils busy at work that has been assigned to them by the teacher. When they meet a difficulty that they cannot overcome, they ask the teacher for direction and assistance. The teacher, when not called upon, walks quietly up and down the classroom or remains at his desk watching the pupils do their work continually alert for any wrong procedures that the pupils may follow. He is always ready to direct and aid them".

Individual Attention: Supervised study is an aid in helping to solve the problem of individual differences. Supervised study aids in preventing failures. The pupil works along his own mental level and at his own capacity. Assignments can be given to meet all levels of ability.

Better Pupil-teacher Relations: Another good feature of supervised study is seen in the better pupil-teacher relations that it promotes. In the usual class teaching procedure, the teacher is frequently considered a hard task master and the procedure often produces a 'class versus teacher' attitude. Under the supervised study programme, he appears in the role of a helper and guide. There is greater opportunity for the display of sympathy and understanding. The teacher is able to understand the pupil and his difficulties better and in a position to spur him on to a greater effort.

Development of Skills: There are certain skills which can best be developed under this procedure. A thorough use of the supervised method would reveal weaknesses in the learner. Following skills can be developed easily:

(a) Skills as to how to read instructional material.
(b) Skills as to how to use encyclopaedias.
(c) Skills as to how to use dictionaries.

(d) Skills as to how to use maps, atlases, indexes and almanacs.
(e) Skills as to how to read graphs.

13.11 LIMITATIONS OF SUPERVISED STUDY

1. Some investigations have concluded that the bright pupil is not helped, under this method and in some cases in even hindered by the method.
2. Supervised study requires the lengthened school day and which is not possible due to various pressures of co-curricular activities.
3. Supervised study is a costly method. It would necessitate an increase in the teaching force that would mean an increased cost of education.
4. Supervised study depends too much on the initiative and enthusiasm of the students which they seldom display.
5. Supervised study destroys the supremacy of the teacher as he plays a secondary role in the teaching-learning process.

13.12 SUPERVISED STUDY AND SOCIALISED RECITATION

Bining and Bining have explained the difference. "The socialised recitation has been used successfully with a supervised study procedure. In a class period of sixty minutes, however, it would be better to use a simplified form of socialised recitation. The first part of the period can be devoted to the socialised study. For example, the procedure could be as follows. During the socialised recitation, the direction of the class is under a pupil Chairman and a discussion leader. The Chairman first calls upon a pupil, previously chosen by the Chairman, teacher or class, for review of the work of the preceding day. Corrections and additions are then voluntarily made. The Chairman next calls for the topic or problem of the day, in order to be sure that subject is clearly in the minds of the members of the group. The discussion leader now takes charge. Each phase of the topic or problem is then discussed by the group, under the direction of the leader. After the discussion the teacher examines or comments on any points that have not been clearly brought out. This ends the socialised procedure, and the teacher makes the assignment for the investigation or supervised study period. Under such a procedure as this, it is better to keep the same Chairman for a week and to have a new discussion leader each day".

13.13 PARTICIPATION OF STUDENTS

Meaning of Student Participation: Student participation involves discovering, analysing and learning the 'what', 'why' and 'how' of political science and civics. The spirit of enquiry prevails throughout what happened. Why did it happen? Why did it happen at a particular time? What is the signification of the event? How can we have first hand experiences of a particular event.

Idea Behind Student Participation: The idea behind student participation is to provide children with first hand stimulating learning experiences. Here learning teaching is not teacher-dominated and the students are not passive listeners. The teacher does not lecture. He causes students to learn. He exposes students to a variety of multiple educational media. Learning and assimilation accrue through a process of interaction between the teacher and the taught. Learning is vicariously acquired and shared.

Why Students' Participation?: Text-book learning, teacher-telling lecturing and factual achievement tests—all indicate the overwhelming emphasis on the mastery of information in the present system of education and especially teaching of political science and civics. These methods of teaching do not facilitate the achievement of desirable teaching skills, attitudes and behaviours.

Political science has now assumed a scientific character. It is no longer expected to provide amass of unrelated information about the past or to fit facts into a preconceived pattern. Its purpose now is taken to deepen man's understanding of societies and the process of change. It involves rational explanation and interpretation. If taught properly it can provide us with the right perspective for a better appreciation of the ideas and principles of all facets of our political and civic life. This needs developing motivation among the students by providing them appropriate channels to participate in various programmes.

The Teacher's Role in Student Participation: The quality of student participation depends on the depth or knowledge, and the quality and quantum of interaction which the teacher brings forth during the learning process. The pupils have to be trained for purposeful self-study and group participation in realising objectives. The teacher's role lies in directing discussions, organising the responses of pupils and giving suggestions on the use of resource-materials, care should be taken that there is no digression and irrelevance. Activity should not degenerate into a mere mechanical process. The teacher must decide with the collaboration of the students what activities will be undertaken by the pupils either individually or in group, what materials will be necessary and how they can be procured.

The teacher must keep in view that 'discovery' and 'enquiry' are inseparable, this is the realisation of new relationships. In the selection and presentation of facts, he should be neither doctrinaire nor dogmatic. His skills include the ability to stimulate interest when it flags, to recognise hurdles as they present themselves, to raise provocative and productive questions, and to guide discussion.

13.14 COMPARISON BETWEEN FORMAL TEACHING AND SOCIALISED CLASSROOM RECITATION

	Formal Teaching	*Socialised Classroom Recitation*
	The Process of Education	
1.	Considers future needs.	Takes into account present needs.
2.	Develops individuality.	Develops social attitude.
3.	Provides formal learning.	Provides real experience.
4.	Uses text-books.	Uses many instructional aids.
5.	Makes acquisition of subject matter as an end.	Includes commitment learning.
6.	Adopts logical order.	Adopts psychological order.
7.	Imparts information.	Imparts information, develops attitudes.

(Contd.)

	Formal Teaching	Socialised Classroom Recitation
	Role of the Pupil	
1.	Passive listener	Active participant.
2.	Under heavy strain.	Makes efforts.
3.	Memorising individual.	Thinking individual.
4.	Reciting individual.	Expressing individual.
5.	Dependent.	Less dependent.
6.	Passive attitude.	Constructive attitude.
7.	Non-social conduct.	Social conduct.
8.	Imposed control.	Self-control
	Role of the Teacher	
1.	Makes artificial setting.	Creates material setting.
2.	Dictates artificial tasks.	Guides natural activities.
3.	Takes interest in the subject-matter only.	Takes interest in children.
4.	Concentration on the subject matter.	Concentrates on desirable ends.
5.	Takes pride in his wisdom.	Gives due consideration to students.

14

Lecture Method, Text-book Method and Heuristic Method

14.1 LECTURE METHOD

14.2 SIGNIFICANCE OF LECTURE METHOD

It is the oldest teaching method given by idealism. As used in education, the lecture method refers to the teaching procedure involved in the clarification or explanation to the students of some major idea or theory or principle. This method lays emphasis on the presentation of the content by the teacher through talking. Teacher is more active and students are passive but he uses the question-answer procedure to keep them attentive in the class. It is used to clarify matters, to expand content and motivate the students. By changing his voice, by impersonating characters, by shifting his position and by using simple devices, a teacher can deliver his lesson effectively. While delivering his lecture, a teacher can indicate by his facial expression, gestures and tones the exact shade of meaning that he wishes to convey.

14.3 MERITS OF THE LECTURE METHOD

1. It is economical as it needs no apparatus and no laboratory. A large number of students can be taught at a time.
2. It saves time and covers syllabus in a limited time.
3. It is very effective in giving factual information and in relating some of the thrilling anecdotes. The life stories of great adventurers, experimenters, investigators and thinkers can become very interesting and valuable talks by a teacher.
4. Lecturing makes the work of the teacher very simple. He need not make elaborate arrangements.
5. A good lecture not only stimulates the students but also lingers long in their imagination. It motivates students to become good orators.
6. It provides better scope for clarification and for laying stress on significant ideas.
7. It brings a personal contact and touch to impress or influence the pupils.
8. It provides flexibility. As the teacher is in close and intimate contact with his pupils, he can adjust his technique in accordance with their abilities, aptitudes and interests.
9. It gives the students training in listening.

10. It gives the students training in taking notes rapidly.
11. It develops good audience habits.
12. It provides opportunities of correlating events and subjects.
13. It enables the linkage of previous knowledge with the new one.

14.4 LIMITATIONS OF THE LECTURE METHOD

1. There is very little scope for pupil activity.
2. It does not take into consideration individual differences.
3. Lecturing is against the principle of 'Learning by Doing'.
4. It spoon-feeds the students without developing their power of reasoning.
5. Speed of the lecture may be too fast for the learners to grasp the line of thought.
6. An average student may not be able to fix up his attention to a lecture of forty to forty-five minutes.
7. A lecture is likely to cover more content without realising that little learning takes place.
8. A lecture may become monotonous to the students after a while. Very few teachers can keep the interests of the students upon the end.

14.5 MAKING LECTURE METHOD EFFECTIVE AND INSPIRATIONAL

The following points should be kept in view in using the lecture method:

1. Matter should be arranged in such a way as to leave a single clear impression on the minds of the students.
2. The teacher should have pause in between the lesson so that the students may learn the new knowledge bit by bit.
3. The rate of exposition should be slow when the class is weak. The teacher should utilise different ways of presenting the same information.
4. There should be abundant repetition but it should be in a new way so that the class may not feel dullness.
5. Children's way of looking at things should be considered.
6. Language used should be familiar and suitable.
7. The lesson should be divided into sections which have a logical sequence. This will enable the students to understand easily and also train them in systematic thinking besides assisting them to put their own thoughts logically.
8. The rate of exposition and the size of the subject matter are determined by the individual capacity of children and teacher's natural rate of speech.
9. Proper use of the blackboard should be made.
10. Actual objects, models, diagrams, sketches, etc. should be used.
11. Students should be encouraged to ask questions. This will enable them to get their doubts removed.
12. Verbal illustrations such as examples, comparisons, etc. should be used to enable the students to grasp the exposition.
13. Pictorial illustrations, such as pictured, maps and charts should be freely used as these help in motivating the students.
14. The aim of the lesson should be kept in view and the students fully made conversant with the aim.

14.6 TEXT-BOOK METHOD

Meaning of Text-book Method

Text-book method consists of asking a few students to read about the prescribed text and thereafter explaining the main points by the teacher.

Traditional Method. Text-book method is the traditional method. It is still and in a number of schools.

Merits of the Text-book

(Discussed separately)

Limitations of the Text-books

1. Students, by and large, remain passive listeners.
2. There is very little intellectual activity in the class.
3. The teacher may also remain busy with some other work.
4. The classroom environment is generally dull and lifeless.

How to Make Text-book Method Effective?

1. The teacher himself should explain the main points/terms and concepts etc.

2. Before taking up the lesson, the teacher may ask the students to go through the text-book at their homes. This will motivate the students to ask questions when the lesson is actually taken up in the class.

3. After the lesson is over, students may be given home assignments from the text-book.

14.7 HEURISTIC METHOD

14.8 MEANING OF HEURISTIC METHOD

Meaning of Heuristic Method

Spencer wrote, "Children should be told as little as possible and induced to discover as much as possible". The extreme application of this dictum is to be found in the heuristic method developed by Professor Armstrong. The method was first used in the teaching of science but later on was adopted in the teaching of all subjects in the curriculum. The word 'heuristic' comes from the Greek work 'heurisco' or 'heuriskein' which means 'to find out'. Hence the heuristic method is the method in which children find out things for themselves are placed in the position of discoverers or inventors. The heuristic method is a method of learning from nature advocated by Rousseau in his *Emile.*

14.9 OBJECTIVES OF THE HEURISTIC METHOD

In the words of Ryburn, "The object of teaching by the heuristic method is not so much to teach facts ... as to teach how knowledge of facts may be obtained, of how they can be systematised and of how they may be used.

Pupils who are taught in this way learn to be observant, exact and to think for themselves." The method aims at developing a scientific and critical attitude and spirit in the students. An eminent educationist has pointed out that the object of the heuristic method is, "to make pupil more exact, more truthful, observant, thoughtful and dexterous, to lay the solid foundation for future self-education and to encourage the growth of a spirit of enquiry and research."

14.10 PRINCIPLES OR PSYCHOLOGICAL BASIS OF HEURISTIC METHOD

1. Principle of activity or learning by doing.
2. Principle of experience.
3. Principle of freedom.
4. Principle of play-way.
5. Principle of purpose.

The students acquire knowledge through their personal experience and remain busy in some form of activity. It awakens a spirit of enquiry through observation and fact finding. It utilises the instinct of curiosity of the children and prompts them to find facts through their own efforts. The children work in an atmosphere of freedom and in a play-way spirit.

The children are not mugging up certain facts. They have to exert themselves and therefore learning becomes meaningful to them.

14.11 PROCEDURE IN THE HEURISTIC METHOD

Inductive process is the form of process in this method. It involves very little telling by the teacher. The pupils are required to be active and enabled to acquire knowledge through their own efforts from a book or using some apparatus or carrying out experiments. The child is in the position of research student.

The same problem may be given to the entire class to work on and each child made responsible for finding out something for himself. The students are allowed to discuss freely and there is no restriction on their movements whether in classroom or laboratory.

14.12 PLACE OF THE TEACHER IN THE HEURISTIC METHOD

The students need the active help and guidance of the teacher as they cannot discover facts all alone by themselves. The teacher is not to give the finished product of his own thinking but is only to act as a guide.

The teacher should possess ample knowledge and information. He should be a great reader who learns himself all the time, replenishes and keeps his store of knowledge up-to-date.

The teacher must be imbued with curiosity and observation. He must possess a spirit of scientific investigation so that he may instil these qualities in his students.

The teacher must be adept in the art of questioning for an efficient and skilful use of this device leads to the success of this method. He should encourage the students to ask questions.

The teacher must be sympathetic to the students and maintain an atmosphere of freedom in the classroom.

The teacher should possess sufficient patience. He should help the children in discovering the flaws and drawbacks in their self-discovered conclusions. Opportunities should be provided to them to correct their mistakes.

The teacher should plan and devise problems which are in accordance with the age, aptitude, interest and ability of the students.

In short, the teacher should be more active, alert, learned, and watchful in this heuristic method.

14.13 USE OF HEURISTIC METHOD IN DIFFERENT SUBJECTS

The above discussion makes it abundantly clear that the heuristic method is in reality not a method but an attitude which must be maintained during the teaching-learning process. This attitude is an essence of all the methods and must pervade all teaching and learning in the classroom.

14.14 MERITS OF THE HEURISTIC METHOD

1. It develops a scientific and critical attitude of mind in the students.
2. It arouses the spirit of enquiry in the students.
3. It develops habit of hard work among the students by keeping them busy to find out the required solutions.
4. It fosters self-activity in the students.
5. It helps to develop the power of initiative and self-confidence and self-reliance among the students by encouraging them to draw their own conclusions through their own efforts.
6. The students learn the art of planning their programmes.
7. It makes learning more effective and permanent. The students learn facts through their own labour and, therefore, retain them much longer.
8. It helps to develop good relationship between teacher and pupils and among pupils themselves.
9. The method provides enough training to the students to prepare themselves for life. The students learn how to handle different situations and how to arrive at certain conclusions. This experience helps them in later life.
10. The fear of the home task disappears. The students are not to memorise facts at home but to find facts in the classroom or the laboratory.
11. The students feel the pleasure and joy of achievement and sense of originality.
12. The problem of discipline is solved as the students remain busy in their work.

14.15 DEMERITS, DIFFICULTIES AND LIMITATIONS OF HEURISTIC METHOD

T. Raymont writes that we should avoid all wild statements to the effect that the pupil must be told nothing. He quotes, "The best of teachers will tell a class some fact in natural history, when he might have taken them into the fields to observe it for themselves. The fact is wanted then and there; to observe it directly would cost half a day; to omit all mention of it would be to omit a necessary qualification of an important principle which is being worked out. If we are to make our natural science absolutely for ourselves, we must be prepared to spend some centuries upon it."

The fact that the 'apperception masses' of children are scanty and ill-organised puts heavy responsibility upon the teachers and their business is not to have them fumble their way as best as they can but to give them just as much help as will enable them to make real and encouraging progress in the paths of simple research.

Following are some of the main demerits of the heuristic method:

1. The pupils are immature and we cannot put them in the position of discoverers or inventors.

2. It is a very slow method and it is not possible to finish the curriculum in time.

3. This method requires teachers who are very enthusiastic in their work and who are very resourceful and hardworking. But there is a scarcity of such teachers.

4. This method cannot be used in large classes as it involves a close supervision on the part of the teacher.

5. This method is not suitable for primary classes.

6. This method cannot be used at all occasions and all the time. There will be numerous occasions when it becomes absolutely essential for the teacher to give direct information.

7. We cannot expect all the children to become discoverers and inventors because there are many children who are mentally deficient.

8. Wrong generalisations may be arrived at and thus a lot of time and energy may be wasted.

9. There is a great shortage of text-books written on the lines as required in the heuristic method.

10. The child possesses a social heritage and he has every right to make full use of it. It is more foolishness to make him repeat all the mistakes and hardship of the race.

In the end we may state that the heuristic attitude should pervade all teaching in the classroom. If the teacher is successful in maintaining this attitude, better and quicker results will be achieved.

15

Assignments, Home Work and Dictating Notes Methods

15.1 ASSIGNMENTS

15.2 SIGNIFICANCE OF AN ASSIGNMENT

Following quotes bring out clearly the significance of an assignment:

1. *N.L. Bossing* has observed, "The central position of the assignment in the techniques of teaching has remained unquestioned."

2. *G.H. Betts* asserts, "Upon the proper assignment of the lesson depends much of the success of the recitation, and also much of the pupil's progress in learning how to study."

3. *W.N. Drum* suggests, "Teachers generally do not appreciate the importance of the assignment and the work of the pupils probably suffers as much from hasty or careless assignment as from any other single cause."

4. *H.R. Douglass and others* are of the view, "The assignment represents one of the most important phases of teaching."

15.3 TYPE OF ASSIGNMENT

N.L. Bossing has listed the following types:

1. *Page or Paragraph Assignment*: This is often thought of as the text-book assignment. Unfortunately, this is still widely used as recent studies have revealed.

2. *Chapter Assignment*: This is another form of the text-book assignment though vastly different from the page or paragraph form. Chapters usually are of a unitary nature and involve some elements of completeness within themselves.

3. *Topical Assignment*: This type may or may not centre about a single chapter in a text-book. It has a wealth of possibilities in the social sciences particularly.

4. *Problem Assignment*: Where an arbitrary distinction is set-up between a problem and a project, the type becomes a very valuable form of assignment.

5. *Project Assignment*: Adapted especially to the workshop, natural sciences, and in some measure to the social sciences its special appeal is through the natural motor activity required.

6. *Exercise*: Most frequently used in mathematics it represents the old traditional approach to teaching although if used in combination with other types, this form can be used very effectively.

7. *Individual or Group Report Assignment*: Used as a device to supplement other types and to provide for individual differences in interests and capacities within the class becomes very effective.

8. *Unit Assignment*: It may apply to any extensive segment of classroom activity that presents factors of cohesion and a relatively complete ideational element around which the unit may resolve itself as a core. A rather pretentious problem may serve as this unitary core.

9. *Experimental Assignment*: This is a form of the problem and project type characteristic of the science laboratory. Too often in practice it does not represent either an experiment or a problem in the true sense. It can be made a vital instrument of educational training if properly used.

10. *Practice Assignment*: This type represents an assignment of repetitions of activities designed to produce mental or motor skills. Mastery of the simple combinations in arithmetic, memorisation of a poem, or practice in speed on the typewriter are examples of this type of assignment.

15.4 ESSENTIALS OF AN ASSIGNMENT

The assignment should be clear and definite; the assignment should be concise but sufficiently detailed to enable each student to understand the task assigned; the assignment should anticipate special difficulties and suggest ways to remove them; the assignment should relate the new unit to past experience; students should understand the importance of the assignment; the assignment should arouse interest in advance work; the assignment should provide for differences in the ability and interest of students; the assignment should be motivated chiefly by the hope of worthwhile achievements, rather than scholastic reward or the fear of punishment; the assignment should stimulate thought; the assignment should provide necessary and specific directions for the study of the lesson; the assignment should be adjusted to the time and opportunity of the class; materials of the assignment should be varied and adaptable to the needs and interest of the students.

15.5 DIFFICULTY IN THE PREPARATION OF A GOOD ASSIGNMENT

Fleming and Woodring have listed the following difficulties:

1. Insufficient thought and preparation on planning the assignment.
2. Inability to obtain an acceptable by the pupil of a worthy purpose for performance of the task.
3. Stimulation of preparation of the assignments by appealing to the interests of adolescents and by providing for real needs growing out of pupil experience.
4. Prevention of loss of interest due to too long phase of time between the assignment and preparation.
5. Avoidance of assignment for so long that successful accomplishment is impossible in the time available for preparation, with consequent loss of interest.
6. Guarding against too many and too varied activities, resulting in dividing interests with consequent bad habits of work, and unsatisfactory accomplishments.
7. Difficulty in presenting work to be done so that it is clearly understood

by the pupils; also, the difficulty of ascertaining whether every pupil understands.

8. Gauging the difficulty of work so that success is possible for each pupil.

9. Determining essential requirements, and differentiation of assignments to suit the various levels and types of ability existing in the class.

10. Inclusion of challenges to mental exploration by the pupil, thereby stimulating real thinking.

11. Provision for continuity of work by presenting new problems as a continuation of previous experience and anticipation of future problems.

12. Correlating with other subjects and outside activities.

13. Focusing attention on important elements in the new problem or task, and directing the attack in such a way as to increase interest rather than lessen it, to stimulate effort, and to overcome seeming obstacles to accomplishment.

14. Providing the necessary tools for preparation by training in study procedures and techniques, and in selection, organisation and use of material, thereby developing effective habits of independent work.

15. Giving to pupils devices for checking the mastery and performance of work undertaken.

16. Evaluating the effectiveness of an assignment by the quality of response during the presentation of the assignment and by the adequacy of pupil preparation.

17. Providing sufficient time for adequate consideration of the assignment and determining the psychological moment for its presentation.

15.6 SUGGESTED ASSIGNMENT PROCEDURE

The procedure suggested for the preparation of a good assignment is as follows:

1. Analyse the nature of the learning process required in the advance unit. This is without exception the first step in a good assignment procedure. Much of what follows in any good assignment depends upon this analysis.

2. Study the various types of assignments available and select the one, or modified form of it, that appears to fit best the learning situation. Some assignment types are admirably adapted to one form of learning or teaching but not to others.

3. Provide the essential background for the advance work where uncertainty exists that such background obtains. At this point too many teachers are likely to assume the adequacy of this background when in fact it may not exist. Scarcely can one emphasise too strongly the apperceptive preparation for the new.

4. Whether this is the next step in the assignment procedure or not, it is obvious that very early in the assignment phase the teacher must throw out a challenge to the student that will enlist his interest and maximum efforts in the new unit.

5. Outline in sufficient detail the advance unit to be studied.

6. Suggest some plan of attack upon the new unit. It is well to remember one caution that do not do for the student that which he be led to do for himself. This suggests the desirability of leading the class in a cooperative discovery of desirable leads for the general attack upon the new.

7. Where reference to source material other than the text-books is necessary, this should be made specific. The most satisfactory plan in the large unit assignment is to provide the select list of available sources in mimeographed or hectographed form with chapter or inclusive page references given. Some points of interest concerning the author, the authoritative or popular nature of the reference may give the student valuable hints on the proper evaluation of the sources used.

8. It is desirable in the long unit assignment especially to indicate the approximate length of time that may properly be devoted to various phases of the assignment.

9. The final step in any assignment procedure is the check upon the students' grasp of the work ahead. Many devices are available for this. Pivotal questions about the assignment may detect any lack of a fundamental grasp of the advance work. Or a pupil apparently uncertain of the significance of the assignment may be asked to summarise the main points of the assignment for the class. Many teachers safeguard against misunderstanding or forgetfulness by requiring a supplemental notebook in which the student notes explanations and amplifications or any mimeographed outlines or written directions passed out to the class.

10. A suggested technique for the assignment procedure that deserves much more extensive use than it now receives is the use of the blackboard. Reinforcement of the ear through the eye is sound psychology. Its application to an assignment procedure is equally sound pedagogy.

15.7 HOME ASSIGNMENT OR HOME WORK

Whether or not home work should be given to the students is a controversial point. Extreme views have been expressed regarding the usefulness of home work. The assignment of home task has been emphatically denounced by Bray. He writes, "Under normal conditions a reasonable day's work for a child has been done at the close of the afternoon and home work as it is generally organised does more harm than good as a rule in this country except perhaps from the point of view of examination success." On the other hand, P.C. Wren commends the assigning of home work. An average guardian also feels that some work should be given to the student which he should do at home.

15.8 PURPOSES OF HOME TASK

1. To provide opportunities to students to work independently and thereby to develop in them self-reliance and initiative.
2. To develop habits of reading regularly among the students.
3. To provide opportunities to the students to utilise their leisure time profitably. It is generally seen that our school children waste their precious time in loitering about or making mischiefs when no such work is given to them.
4. To give them opportunity to revise what is done in the school.
5. To finish the prescribed courses in time. The syllabi is too heavy to finished in the classroom work.
6. To serve as a link in the parent-teacher cooperation. It enables the parents to know that regular work is being done in the school.

7. To develop permanent interests and to train the students in the profitable use of leisure.
8. To enable the child to revise his previous lesson and prepare the next one.
9. To provide remedial measure for backward children.
10. To give a chance to every child to progress at his own speed.

15.9 TYPES OF HOME WORK

These are:

1. Writing of essay-type answer to questions arising out of the subject-matter already done in the class.
2. Verbal memorising work pertaining to curricular and co-curricular activities. It may take the form of cramming facts, principles, poems, spelling, etc. of memorising work in respect of dramatics and debates, etc.
3. Practical work, e.g., preparation of charts, maps, knitting, sewing and drawing, etc.
4. Transcription, calligraphy, etc.
5. Advance preparation for the coming lesson.

15.10 DISADVANTAGES AND OBJECTIONS

1. It deprives the children from participating in recreational activities when it imposes heavy demands upon them.

2. It is a great hindrance in the way of the students in enjoying family and social life.

3. It deprives children of the opportunity to help their parents in supplementing their income.

4. It imposes a great physical strain on small children and thus endangers their health.

5. It becomes a constant source of fear and worry to the students and therefore it endangers their emotional stability.

6. Children are tempted to copy whenever they find that the home task is difficult to do.

7. Sometimes children are tempted to tell a lie that due to certain reasons they have failed to do home task.

8. Unhealthy home conditions make study more harmful than profitable. There is a lack of adequate light and quietness in a large number of Indian homes and the atmosphere is not congenial for study.

9. Too much of home work develops on attitude of indifference on the part of the pupils and they become careless.

10. Lack of proper correction by the teacher sometimes gives rise to carelessness on the part of the pupils. It also develops wrong habits of work if the work is not properly checked.

11. Too much work is set by some over-enthusiastic specialist teachers in their subjects completely disregarding what other teachers of the same class might have set for the same day.

12. Home task is generally too academic in nature and ignores those activities which are needed most for an all-round development of the personality of the child.

13. It is not properly adjusted to pupils needs and capacities.

15.11 PRINCIPLES OF ASSIGNING HOME WORK

1. The nature of the home work should be such as it does not require any kind of assistance from a private tutor or guardian.
2. It should not be purely mechanical, i.e., requiring no general knowledge on the part of the child.
3. Home work should also aim at developing the taste of the individual child. This purpose can be very conveniently realised if home work is in the nature of hobbies.
4. Home work should be very definite.
5. It should be supplementary rather than preparatory as far as possible.
6. A single assignment for the whole class may not be considered as appropriate. It should vary according to the mental and physical make-up of the students.
7. Home work in different subjects should be coordinated. Home work time-table should be framed so as to avoid confusion.
8. While assigning home work 'principle of sliding scales' should be adopted. The primary classes might be given home task to keep them busy for about half an hour or so; in the middle one hour and in secondary and senior secondary classes time involved in doing home task should not extend two hours.
9. Home task should not be set as a punishment.
10. Home task should be properly checked.
11. Library books should be given for reading at home as a home task.
12. Copies of the home work time-tables may be sent to the parents to seek their cooperation which is very important.
13. While assigning home work the teacher should take into consideration the home conditions of the child.
14. 10 percent marks should be reserved for the evaluation of the student's work based on the assignments done throughout the year.

15.12 METHODS OF CORRECTION

The following methods of correction may be adopted: correction by the teacher; correction with the help of the bright students in the class; corrections with the help of the blackboard; correction by interchanging the exercise books among the students; glance checking and signing by teachers.

At the primary stage teachers should correct all the assignments without any help from the children. At this stage it is not possible for the children to do any self-correction.

15.13 DICTATING NOTES

Dictating notes, by and large, has become a coaching and not a teaching device. However, used properly it has a great significance in the teaching of Political Science. It is used due to the following:

1. Lack of suitable text-books.
2. Pressure of work with the teacher and less time for preparing the lesson.
3. Shortcut to finish the over-crowded subject-matter.

4. Short cut to pass the examination.
5. Lack of adequate power of expression of the teacher.

Methods of Dictating Notes

1. Detailed notes on important topics after discussing the topics in the class.
2. Notes in the question-answer form primarily from examination.
3. Explanatory notes and summaries on the blackboards.

Defects in the Method of Note Dictation

1. It does not provide training to the students in the use of their abilities.
2. Note dictation makes teaching synonymous with memorisation of facts communicated by the teacher.
3. Note dictation fails to develop proper insight into the subject.
4. Note dictation proves to be a great hindrance in developing the habit of consulting reference books and text-books also.

Instead of dictating notes to the students, they should be encouraged to prepare their own notes.

16

Dalton Plan and Discussion Method

16.1 DALTON OR LABORATORY METHOD

16.2 ORIGIN AND SIGNIFICANCE OF DALTON PLAN

The plan is named not after its originator Miss Helen Parkhurst but after the name of the town in which it was first adopted in a high school. It is also called a Laboratory Plan as Miss Parkhurst attaches importance to the use of the word 'laboratory'. She writes, "I cling to it in the hope that it may gradually shift the educational point of view away from the atmosphere of prejudice which the word 'school' calls up in our minds. Let us think of school rather as a sociological laboratory where the pupils themselves are the experimenters, not the victims of an intricate and crystallised system in the evolution of which they have neither part nor lot. Let us think of it as a place where community conditions prevail as they prevail in life itself." Her aim was to 'create a new type of educational society' by putting boys and girls under entirely different conditions of living from those provided in the ordinary classroom and to reorganise the community life of the school.

16.3 PRINCIPLES UNDERLYING THE DALTON PLAN

1. *The principle of individual work.* Johan Adams says, "It is the most dramatic and systematic break away from the class-teaching unit." It is now generally accepted that the students differ in various respects and it is not fair to tag them together for keeping pace in studies. The plan aims at providing equal opportunities to all pupils to work at their own rate and speed. The time taken is not necessarily equal but a minimum uniform achievement is required. In the words of Miss Parkhurst, "It is a piece or machinery for putting into operation the principle of individual work".

2. *The principle of freedom.* Children work well when they are allowed freedom to do so. There are no arbitrary fixed periods. There are no classroom restrictions or rigidity of discipline. In the Dalton Plan children are free to move about, to consult one another and to work in any particular subject. In the words of an educationist, "It aims at giving to the older child that freedom for self-development which has proved so valuable in the school life of the infant while at the same time ensuring that he shall master thoroughly the academic work required by the curriculum of the school."

3. *The principle of self-effort.* Learning to be effective must be the product of one's own self-efforts. In the Dalton Plan, the child learns through his own efforts.

4. *The principle of cooperation.* In a subject laboratory pupils of different age groups not only assist each other when occasions demand but are very much helped in turn, without being distracted; the task of a companion being similar if not identical. According to Miss Parkhurst, "the school can only reflect the social experience of the community when all its parts or groups develop the same intimate relations with one another as is found in society as a whole. The schools should be organised in such a way as the pupils and teachers come in close interaction with one another as is found in society, as a whole. The schools should be organised in such a way as the pupils and teachers come in close interaction with one another." Miss Parkhurst has used the term "interaction of group life". The students live and work together with the same teaches, in the same shared common workshops or laboratories.

5. *The principle of setting goals.* The child is enabled to survey the whole field, to see the goal at which he is aiming and thus a stimulus is provided to him and he takes up the work bit by bit thereby increasing and ensuring better learning.

16.4 HOW THE PLAN WORKS?

1. *Assignment or Contracts*: The teachers outline the work of the year to be done in their respective subjects to enable the students to know about the scope and the nature of the work they are required to complete in each subject. The work is further sub-divided into suitable monthly units by the subject teachers. While preparing the assignment the teachers bear in mind factors like holidays, time available, revision at various stages, co-curricular activities and the demands of other subjects.

Each unit of work is accepted by the pupil as a contract and he promises to complete the work and to satisfy the teacher before going to the next unit.

Each subject has its separate assignment. The child is given the new assignment only when he has completed his assignments in all the subjects. A pupil is not allowed to do more than the month's work in a single subject unless he finishes the month's contract in every other subject. The child is free to undertake an assignment of a month in any manner he likes, i.e., he may devote one week completely to complete his assignment in one subject and may ignore assignments in other subjects during that particular week and take up assignments in other subjects in the second, third or the fourth week. He may spend his whole day in one assignment of a subject and so on. The only limitation is that he must finish the whole contract, i.e., monthly assignments in each subject for a particular month, before the second contract is entered upon.

2. *Subject Teachers*: The Dalton Plan does away with class teachers and accepts specialist teachers. Each specialist teacher supervises each child in his subject and guides his work. He renders all possible help to the child to complete his assignment in time.

3. *Subject Rooms*: The plan scraps classrooms and gives their place to

subject rooms which are called subject-laboratories. Each specialist is the in-charge of his room. Each subject room is adequately equipped with the material required in that subject. It contains books and magazines, charts, maps, models, apparatus and appliances, etc. concerning that subject.

There is no fixed time-table and no fixed period. Each student is free to devote more time to the subject in which he is weak and less in which he is up to the mark.

4. *Records*: Graphs are kept to show the work done by each child and each subject so that the pupil himself and the teacher may know how he is progressing. Two records are maintained by the pupil himself; one showing his progress in each subject and the other in all subjects. The third record is kept by the subject teacher himself and is hung in the subject room.

The records serve as a mirror to indicate the work of the pupils and are kept up-to-date. These serves as a link also between the teacher and the pupil and bring them in close cooperation for effective learning. The graph, in fact, is a constant reminder of the 'contract' or 'promise' and helps to make one conscious of the extent to which the progress is made and is to be made.

5. *Conferences*: Usually the morning time before recess is devoted to individual work by each child or may be devoted for voluntary group work. The afternoon time may be used by the teacher for oral lessons in his subject. Group discussions under the guidance of the teacher may be held. These oral lessons or group discussions are called 'conferences'. These conferences may be devoted to remove common difficulties or to explain certain items of common interest and importance.

16.5 DUTIES OF A TEACHER

The duties of a teacher in the Dalton Plan may be summed up as under:

(i) Preparation of assignments and giving them to the pupil as and when required.

(ii) Keeping an atmosphere of study in the room.

(iii) Giving explanations of any details of the assignment and removing the difficulties of the pupils.

(iv) Giving information with regard to the use of relevant equipment and material.

(v) Ensuring that each assignment is finished properly before the new assignment is given to the pupil.

(vi) Keeping full records of the progress made by pupils in different classes.

(vii) Keeping the subject-library and other equipment up-to-date and in proper order.

The teacher, in the Dalton Plan, is "a helper, not a driver; the pursued, not the pursuer."

16.6 MERITS OF THE PLAN

The plan has the following advantages:

(1) *Individualised Teaching*: Each pupil is permitted to work as his own rate. The plan approaches teaching and instruction from the point of view of the pupil. The weak are not hurried along at the speed of other pupils and the

bright are not kept back by their slow class-fellows. The teacher pays individual attention to each child.

(2) *Continuity of Work*: There is no waste of time as is usually the case in the conduct of various examinations for promotion or other purposes. There are no failures and the promotions from grade to another may take place at any time.

Absence from school of a child due to ill-health or otherwise does not stand in his way of working smoothly. He can start the work just from where he had stopped and can make up his deficiency in his own way and at his own speed. There is no danger that some courses have been covered in his absence and he has missed them.

(3) *Development of Qualities Like Self-efforts and Self-confidence*: There is absolutely no spoon-feeding in the Dalton Plan. Ready-made knowledge is not given to the child. He has to depend upon himself in the solution of his problems. He has to consult suitable books and other reference material. He himself has to experience difficulties and to solve his problems. All this makes him self-confident.

(4) *Purposeful Learning*: Student's contract or assignment is like a project in front of him and for its completion, he tries his best and devotes his heart and soul into the work. Thus learning becomes motivated and purposeful.

(5) *Development of Desirable Study Habits*: The students have to make use of a variety of material to complete their assignment. They have to study reference books, source books, etc. and all this help to develop desirable study habits in them.

(6) *Development of a Sense of Responsibility*: The contract is a constant reminder to the children to complete their work in time. They feel that they must fulfil their responsibility that they have accepted in entering upon the assignment.

(7) *Solving the Problem of Home Task*: There is no need to burden a child with home task. The child in order to complete his assignment may of his own accord devote extra time in the subject-laboratory. Thus compulsory home work loses its terror in the school.

(8) *Solving the Problem of Discipline*: No restrictions are put on children. They work in an atmosphere of freedom. They accept their own responsibility and work for its fulfilment. There is no rigid time-table and the students are not forced to attend to studies according to a set time-table. Problems of truancy, mischief and delinquency are rare.

(9) *Simplification of the Problem of Evaluation*: The graph system is a valuable check on the progress of each child. The records show the progress of each pupil and enable him to know where he stands. In a way records can help to give incentives to him. There is no necessity of frequent tests and awarding of marks.

(10) *Better Pupil-teacher Relationships*: The plan enables the teacher to know the child individually. Every child is free to seek the teacher guidance at any point when a difficulty occurs. The teacher is essentially a guide and a helper.

16.7 LIMITATIONS AND DIFFICULTIES

The limitations of Dalton Plan are:

1. *Not Suitable for the Average Child and a Shirker*: The clever and the bright, students can derive a lot of benefit from this scheme. It is not possible for the average child to learn new principles without a formal lesson. The shirkers also find opportunities to develop the attitude of postponement.

2. *Development of Individualistic Tendencies*: As a child has his own assignment to do, he may not like to help his other friends if he is required to do so on the plea that he is absorbed in his own work. Pinkevitch observes, "We cannot but express the fear that it will be instrumental in developing individualistic tendencies in children."

3. *Purely Intellectual Plan*: The plan fails to provide for liberal group activities. There is little scope for social service activities. Dr. Cox states, "the Dalton Plan is highly inadequate for social education."

4. *Unsuitable for Lessons that Require Inspirational Treatment*: There are certain subjects which require collective lessons for appreciation purposes. Physical training, music and drill in languages need group teaching. Therefore the plan is unsuitable for these subjects.

5. *Lack of Suitable Teachers*: For the successful working of the plan, competent, liberal and progressive teachers are required. The plan puts heavy demands upon the teachers who are expected to prepare good assignments and to be able to guide and help the pupils if and when much guidance or help is needed. Teachers must be in a position to inspire students to work hard independently. It is very difficult to get such teachers.

6. *Lack of Well-equipped Libraries*: Most of the libraries of our schools are not adequately equipped and are without any trained librarians. But under the Dalton Plan, we require a wide variety of suitable text-books, source books and other relevant material so that the children may prepare their assignments.

7. *Unsuitable for Junior Classes*: The plan is more suitable for children above nine years of age.

8. *Very Costly*: The plan is very expensive. It requires many more teachers and well-equipped libraries and other equipment.

9. *No Provision for Individual Differences*: It is very difficult to change the attitude of the teachers who are accustomed to old methods of class teaching. They do not like sweeping changes. Moreover, they do not like to give freedom to the pupil.

A review of the limitations and difficulties of the Dalton Plan shows that it is not possible to introduce this plan in its entirety in our schools. However, there is much that can he introduced in ordinary teaching. We should try to evolve some system in which class teaching may be done in the morning and individual teaching in the afternoon. More individual attention should be given to the students. They should be encouraged to read extra books and a record of that should be kept. Some short of day-to-day assessment should be made of the work done by each child and the results communicated to them so that they may be motivated to work harder.

16.8 DISCUSSION METHOD

16.9 MEANING AND SIGNIFICANCE OF DISCUSSION METHOD

Discussion has been described as a thoughtful consideration of the relationships involved in a topic or problem under study. It is concerned with the analysis, comparison, evaluation and conclusions of these relationships. It aims at uniting and integrating the work of the class. It is carried out by organising, outlining and relating the facts studied. It encourages the students to direct their thinking process towards the solution of a problem and to use their experiences for a further clarification and consolidation of learning material.

Discussion is to be distinguished from debate in which the participants seek to prove a point rather than to discover a truth. Debate may also be marked by uncontrolled exchange of verbalism.

Discussion is very important in stimulating mental activity, developing fluency and ease in expression, clarity of ideas in thinking and training in the presentation of one's ideas and facts. An exchange of ideas and opinions offers valuable training to students in reflective thinking.

16.10 ESSENTIAL ELEMENTS OR CONSTITUENTS OF DISCUSSION

These are as under:

1. The leader—the teacher
2. The group—the students
3. The problem or the topic
4. The content—body of knowledge
5. Evaluation—change in ideas, attitudes, etc.

The teacher leads the students into thinking about and discussing these issues. Often a tangible result in the form of a set of behavioural standards is produced. For example, the class may establish the following standards of leadership behaviour:

When I am leader
I give everyone a chance to speak,
I listen to others,
I help others decide what to do,
I ask others in a nice way to do things, and
I keep work going.

The class may define followership behaviour in this way:

When I am in a group
I wait my turn to speak,
I speak quietly,
I give ideas,
I listen to others,
I work with the leaders, and
Others to get the job done.

16.11 MERITS OF DISCUSSION

1. It helps in clarifying issues.
2. It helps children in crystallising their thinking.

3. It helps students in discovering what they do not know and what they have overlooked.

4. It engenders more reflection. It is farther from rote learning.

5. It represents a type of pooled knowledge, ideas and feelings of several persons.

6. It develops team spirit.

7. It engenders toleration of views which are at variance.

8. It affords opportunities to the students to learn together, make suggestions, share responsibility, comprehend the topic, evaluate the findings and to summarise results.

9. It provides opportunities to the students to speak distinctly, stand and sit correctly respect the ideas of others, share interests, ask pertinent questions and comprehend the problem before the group.

10. It helps the teacher in discovering talented students who have potential for becoming good leaders.

16.12 LIMITATIONS OF DISCUSSION

1. It is not suitable in all topics.
2. It is likely to be dominated by a few students.
3. It is likely to go off the track.
4. It may lead to unpleasant feelings.
5. It may create emotional tensions.
6. It may involve unnecessary arguments.

16.13 ORGANISATION OF DISCUSSION

Following are the main techniques of organising a discussion:

1. Introducing a topic or a problem by the teacher by giving points or explanations to serve as the basis of discussion.

2. Calling upon a pupil by the teacher to give facts, describe a scene or situation, explain an incident, event or happening for getting the discussion started.

3. Preparing an outline of points cooperatively by the teacher and a few students which may become the starting point for discussion.

4. Asking the students to describe their own experiences connected with the subject, topic or problem and making them points for discussion.

5. Presenting detailed papers by the teacher and discussions thereon.

6. Presenting detailed papers by the students and discussing them in the class.

7. Showing special works and projects to the class and discussing them.

8. Showing some pictures, charts, diagrams or any audio-visual material and discussion about them.

Directing Group Discussions

The teacher has to show immense patience and skill to ensure that discussion takes place on right lines and in the appropriate environment. Following points may be considered in this respect:

1. Students should be well-acquainted with the significance of the topic; its nature and scope and causes why the class should discuss it.
2. Discussion should be confined to important aspects.
3. Students should be encouraged to participate in the discussion.
4. Ideas may be invited without pressure or embarrassment.
5. Explanations, where needed, should be provided.
6. Personality cult should be avoided.
7. Cooperation rather than competition should be encouraged.
8. Efforts should be made to develop team spirit.
9. Doubts, mistakes and wrong interpretation should be made clear by the teacher.
10. Facts and points should be evaluated.
11. Facts and points should be summarised.
12. Students should be guided to honour difference of opinion and views.
13. Goals of discussions should be kept in view.
14. Only a few students should not be allowed to dominate classroom discussion.
15. Shy students may be given training in discussion in small groups so that their hesitation is removed while participating in bigger groups.

16.14 PANEL DISCUSSION

Advantages of Panel Discussions

1. They stimulate the group.
2. They give depth to learning.
3. They provide leaders a chance to lead a group.
4. They provide the quieter students a chance to talk in smaller group.
5. They provide opportunities to the students to practise skills that will be useful in adult life.
6. They provide variety and change in the teaching-learning situation.

Who should be the Members of the Panels

1. Every student over a period of weeks or months.
2. Students who are usually quiet in the large class discussion but who have something to say.
3. Students who have done special work.
4. Students who need experience in leadership roles.
5. Students who have worked on committees.

Who should be the chairman of a panel

1. The teacher, if the class does not have adequate experience.
2. More mature students.
3. Students who are to be trained for this kind of experience.

How to Conduct Proceedings Effectively

1. There should be adequate preparation.
2. Physical conditions should be conducive to group discussion.

3. Students should be provided with a chair and table.
4. Students should be seated in a semi-circle so that they can talk to each other and can be heard by the entire group.
5. A list of questions for the panel may be useful.
6. Students may use notes but should be discouraged from reading prepared speeches.
7. There should be no digression from the topic.
8. First speaker should be selected carefully so as to set the ball rolling.
9. A time limit should be put on the speakers.

17

Play-Way in Education

17.1 ORIGIN, DEFINITION, MEANING AND PRINCIPLES OF PLAY-WAY

Origin of Play-way

Play-way approach to teaching is based on the philosophical thought of Caldwell Cook. According to him, good work is more often the result of spontaneous effort and free interest than of compulsion and forced application." This means that teaching should characterise the elements of 'spontaneous effort' and 'free interest'. Since these two characteristics are inherent in play, this approach or method of teaching is called play-way. Having discovered the unwillingness and distaste of his pupils for lessons in English literature, he employed a method by means of which the boys showed a keen interest in the subject. The Shakespearean plays, meanings of which were generally memorised without any interest and understanding came to be treated like real plays when 'dramatised' by the pupils. An open-air theatre was organised in the school. Literature now acquired a new meaning for them and lessons acquired the spirit of play. Similarly, activities were planned for grammar and composition lessons. The pupils participated eagerly in the lesson and were allowed to express their ideas freely. Thus, the English period was welcomed with joy. Gradually the scope of play-way became enlarged and it began to be applied to the teaching of other subjects. The play-way approach aims at introducing the elements of freedom, interest, realism and spontaneity into the entire school work.

Definition and Meaning of Play

With a view to have a comprehensive understanding of the play-way, it is felt appropriate to consider the definitions of play and the keywords understanding this concept.

Crow and Crow observe, "Play can be defined as the activity in which a person engages when he is free to do what he wants."

Dewey defines play as, "Activities not necessarily performed for the sake of any result beyond themselves."

Froebel notes, "Play is the purest, most spiritual activity of man at this stage (childhood). It gives, therefore, joy, freedom, contentment, inner rest and peace with the world."

Good defines play as, "Any pleasurable activity carried on for its own sake, without reference to the ulterior purpose or future satisfaction."

Gullicks writes, "Play is what we do when we are free to do what we will." Hurlock states, "Play relates to any activity engaged in the environment it gives, without consideration of the end results." Montessori visualised play as "When a child plays it resembles the never ending activity of the flowering stem of the growing tree."

Nunn holds that "play is a profound manifestation of creative activities."

Ross regards play as "joyful, spontaneous, creative activity, in which man finds his fullest expression".

Ryburn writes, "Play is a way, a means which is used by the self when the different instinctive urges are trying to express themselves."

Stern regards play as " a kind of voluntary self-constrained activity."

Thomson looks upon play as "the impulse to carry out certain instinctive action."

Principles of Play-Way

(i) The play-way is based on the principle that learning takes place through doing.
(ii) It is based on the principle that learning takes place in an environment of freedom.
(iii) It is based on the principle that learning should be adapted to life situations and not to books.
(iv) It is based on the principle that the method should be suited to the needs and interests of the students.
(v) It is based on the principle that the child should be freed from authoritarianism.
(vi) It is based on the principle that the child should themselves take upon the responsibility of learning and progress in studies.
(vii) It is based on the principle that ample opportunity should be provided to children for self-expression.

Educative Value of Play-Way

Play-way is important on account of the following:

(a) Play-way is a great motivating force. Play-way activities are based on the natural urges of the children. They put their heart and soul into work.

(b) Play-way kills drudgery and boredom. The students willingly undertake to do a piece of work.

(c) Doing and practice occupy the first place and telling the second and an unimportant place.

(d) The method is based on the laws of learning and it provides a great incentive to original creative work.

(e) Play-way provides opportunities for the sublimation of various instincts of children.

(f) Play-way assures maximum freedom for the child with the result that he develops originality, power of reasoning, imagination and insights.

(g) Play-way helps in sublimating the emotions of children. It provides suitable outlets which help in overcoming shyness, moodiness, timidity and sensitiveness.

(h) Play-way provides opportunities to the students to learn to cooperate, to take the lead and also to follow.

Play-Way Materials

These include—(1) Gifts of Froebel, (2) Sand play, (3) Water-play, (4) Wooden toys, (5) Rubber toys, (6) Glass toys, (7) Plastic toys, (8) Pictures, (9) Picture book puzzles, (10) Cut-outs, (11) Card board games, (12) Doll and doll house, (13) play-ground games, (14) Story telling, (15) Dramatics, (16) Art work, (17) Excursions, (18) Dancing, (19) T.V., (20) Community work etc.

17.2 APPLICATION OF PLAY-WAY ATTITUDES

The application of the principles of play-way is found in all the progressive methods of education and other school activities in one way or the other.

1. *Project Method*: 'Purpose element' is used to secure the interests of the students. The play-spirit pervades throughout the various activities connected with the completion of the project. The students work in an atmosphere of reality, freedom and responsibility.

2. *Kindergarten Method*: Froebel's Kindergarten provides a lot of action for children. Doing, singing, acting and playing are its chief characteristics. Gifts are given to the students with the help of which they learn the ideas of shape, colour, number and weight etc.

3. *The Montessori Method*: Didactic apparatus imparts training in various fields. With the aid of this apparatus children learn reading, writing and arithmetic. The Children's Home provides an atmosphere of complete and unrestricted freedom. Children are kept active and playing while learning.

4. *The Dalton Plan*: The children are free from the tyranny of the time-table. They work according to their own rate and speed of learning. They are at liberty to move from room to room and laboratory to laboratory. A sense of self-help and responsibility is generated in the students. The students take a real pleasure in studies.

5. *Gary System, Winnetke Plan, etc.*: All these methods are based on the play-way principles. School becomes the hub of activities in which children take keen interest.

6. *The Heuristic Method*: This method places the child in the position of a discoverer. Thus he acquires and learns some of the most fundamental skills through his own effort. The child is always mentally active as he wants to satisfy his curiosity.

7. *Basic System of Education*: This is a revolt against the verbal and bookish system of education. Here too the child learns by doing and thus derives immense pleasure side-by-side.

7. *School Life*: The play principle should be at work in all aspects of school life. The work of the educator is to make more and more use of this technique. The following play-way activities may be mentioned:

(a) *Self-Government in Schools*:This is very helpful in sublimating the various instincts of children—self-assertion, gregariousness, self-submission and pugnacity. Students develop valuable social and civic virtues. They themselves frame their rules.

(b) *The Boy-Scout and Girl Guide Movement*: This movement makes the life of children full of activity, competition and cooperation. Students learn valuable social, intellectual and civic lessons through camping and tracking etc.

(c) *Dramatics*: Students prepare the stage, learn their parts and prepare costumes. They are working, but it is play.

(d) *NCC, Excursions, School Celebrations etc.*: All these are examples of play-way spirit.

17.3 PLAY-WAY SPIRIT AND TEACHING OF VARIOUS SUBJECTS AND EXPERIENCES

Play-way spirit can be utilised in many practical ways in the teaching of different subjects.

Languages and Mother Tongue

Dramatics, magazines and games are the different ways of introducing the spirit of play-way in teaching of the mother tongue and other languages. Mock interviews, mock parliament, debates and panel discussions provide play-way means of training in oral expression in languages.

Mathematics

Running a school shop is the best way of teaching mathematics in a play-way spirit. Homely and practical examples should be selected. Surveys provide many opportunities.

History

The teaching of history provides a great scope for introducing the spirit of play-way. The school library should contain a good collection of books on history. Biographies, letters, historical atlases, historical albums and memories, etc. must find a place in the library or history room. Historical plays should be staged. Visits to picture galleries and museums create an environment of reality. A pageant on the life of Lord Buddha may be prepared. Scenes from the lives of great freedom fighters of India may be depicted. Historical poems may be narrated. Debates on historical events can be made a popular form of activity in schools.

Geography

The use of films and slides is very helpful in providing a clear and vivid picture of the lives of remote and distant areas. Visits to canals, dams and rivers give vivid glimpses.

Nature Study

Specimens of leaves, flowers, plants, feathers may be collected by children. Opportunities for observing natural phenomena may be provided to the students.

Science

Illustrative scientific journals and books should be made available in the school library. Books on the lives of great scientists and discoverers should find a prominent place. Scientific hobbies should be encouraged. Science clubs may be organised effectively. Experiment work should be taken up in abundance.

Moral and Social Training

Various co-curricular activities like self-government, student parliament, scouting, cooperative store, cleanliness campaigns in the school and the community etc., provide useful training in moral and social values.

Various Play-Way Activities

1. *Dramatic Play*: Dramatic play is basically an exercise of the imagination, at the same time, it can also be a valuable learning experience. To a young child, a doll is not just a doll. It is like a real person. A toy telephone can be used to call and talk with someone.

2. *Games*: Games may be simple games, guessing games or more lively games, such as, musical chair. Several types of inexpensive educational games are available in the market.

3. *Watching the Television*: Television programmes can be educational-cum-recreational. Conducting of quiz programmes on a variety of topics is very helpful in enriching the experiences of students.

4. *Projects*: Projects provide immense scope for doing and learning.

5. *Celebration of Days*: Literacy Day, Girl Child Day, Aged Day, Prohibition Day, Cleanliness Day, Republic Day etc. are full of providing rich educational experiences.

6. *Educational Tours and Excursions*: All these if properly planned and executed are full of educational potentials.

17.4 PLAY-WAY AND SOFT PEDAGOGY

It is wrong to regard play-way as soft pedagogy. It is in the words of Smith and Harrison, "an all absorbing activity in which initiative, forethought, control and skill can be exercised in full measure." Emphasis on play does not mean absence of serious work. On the other hand, introduction of the play-way spirit in work reduces drudgery. Play-way is an approach to do a difficult and boring tasks in an interesting way.

Play-way puts heavy demands on the teacher. It requires a lot of imagination and a real zeal on the part of the teachers as well as students. A teacher has to plan and execute activities, teaching points and projects very carefully and skilfully. Thus play-way is by no means a soft pedagogy. As observed by Griffith, "Play is the child's characteristic mode of behaviour and any system of education which hampers this natural direction for the expanding of energy endangers the health-mental and physical of the child." Indeed play-way has a unique place in dynamic and progressive teaching.

18

General Principles, Maxims and Techniques of Teaching

18.1 GENERAL PRINCIPLES OF TEACHING

Successful teaching necessitates that the teacher comes down to the level of the pupils and at the same time assists them in rising above it. To a great extent, the principles of teaching to be followed depend upon the age of the pupils, the subjects and topic of the lesson. However, there are certain general principles which should underline the teaching of all subjects. As already stated, there is no clear-cut dividing line between psychological and general principles of teaching.

1. Principle of Definite Goals or Objectives: Destination or goals of teaching-learning must be clear to the teachers and students. Goals and objectives keep the teachers and students on the track. Definiteness of goals helps in planning, executing and evaluating every step, phase or act of the teaching-learning process.

2. Principle of Child-centredness: The entire teaching endeavour is for the child. Therefore, it is essential that teaching strategies should cater to the aptitude, interest and abilities of the students. In the drama of education, child should be assigned the role of a 'hero'.

3. Principle of Linking with Life: Teaching can never be performed in a vacuum. It is always in a social context. In the teaching of all the school subjects, examples from everyday life should be given their due place.

4. Principle of Correlation: Knowledge is one 'whole'. Various ideas and events are interrelated. There exist links among various subjects and events. Correlation of the present events can be made with the past. Similarly future can be visualised on the basis of the present happenings or state of affairs. Gandhiji propounded his system of basic education with correlation as its cornerstone-correlation with the craft, correlation with the physical environment and correlation with social environment.

5. Principle of Active Involvement and Participation of Students: Teaching-learning is a two-way traffic. Traditional teaching was almost teacher-centred. There was very little scope for the involvement of the students. The teacher taught and the students listened to him passively. The new teaching emphasises that the students must actively participate in all the stages and steps of teaching-learning.

6. Principle of Cooperation: Classroom environment becomes lively when the teacher and the taught work in unison, helping each other in carrying out the task of teaching and learning. All the participants have the same common interest. Naturally, they must cooperate with teacher.

7. Principle of Remedial Teaching: All students do not learn with the same speed and achievement. Some lag behind and need extra coaching. The teaching has to find out where the fault lies and think for positive measures. He may have to arrange for remedial or compensatory or extra teaching for any particular group of students for removing their specific difficulties.

8. Principle of Creating Conducive Environment: Physical as well as social environment of the classroom plays a vital role in motivating the learners. Arrangement of light and furniture etc. should be properly attended to. There should be proper discipline and order. The teacher should be sympathetic but firm.

9. Principle of Planning: Planning determines the quality or success of any task. Planning in teaching involves the preparation of the lesson notes, provision of teaching aids and working out strategies to be adopted in the delivery of the lesson.

10. Principle of Effective Strategies: Teaching process to be effective must adopt proper means, strategies and tacts. A teaching strategy is a generalised plan for a lesson which includes structure, desired learning behaviour in terms of goals of instruction and an outline of planned tactics necessary to implement the strategy.

11. Principle of Flexibility: Strategies should serve as guides for effective teaching. Strategies may have to be changed if the classroom situations so warrant. Teaching is a complex task and a live phenomenon. The possibilities of alternation in planned strategies cannot be ruled out at the execution side. A teacher must be quite imaginative and resourceful for adapting himself and his teaching to the requirements of the teaching-learning environment.

12. Principle of Variety: A variety of teaching aids and strategies should be adopted to motivate and sustain the interests of the students. Variety serves as great tonic for creating fresh environment and checking boredom and lethargy.

18.2 MAXIMS OF TEACHING

Significance of Maxims of Teaching

The maxims of teaching are very helpful in obtaining the active involvement and participation of the learners in the teaching-learning process. They quicken the interest of the learners and motivate them to learn. They make learning effective, inspirational, interesting and meaningful. They keep the students attentive to the teaching-learning process. A good teacher should be quite familiar with them. Now we proceed to discuss them.

1. *Proceed from the Known to the Unknown*: The most natural and simple way of teaching a lesson is to proceed from something that the students already know to those facts which they do not know. What is already known to the students is of great use to the students. This means that the teacher should

arouse interest in a lesson by putting questions on the subject-matter already known to the pupils. The teacher is to proceed step by step to connect the new matter to the old one. New knowledge cannot be grasped in a vacuum. A civic lesson on the powers of the President of India may start from the powers of the President of Municipal Board or of the President of Village Panchayat. A lesson on profit and loss in arithmetic can easily be taught to the pupils by referring to the shopkeepers who make profit. A history lesson on Lord Ram may be taken up with the celebration of Ram Lila.

2. *Proceed from Simple to Complex*: The simple task or topic must be taught first and the complex one can follow later on. The word simple and complex are to be seen from the point of view of the child and not that of an adult. We would be curbing the interest and initiative of the children by presenting them complex problems before the simpler ones are presented. In a lesson on nature study, for instance, a child will understand the concept of a flower first and thereafter its various parts. Similarly in a geography lesson the teacher will take up the general study of a region or country first and later on a detailed and specific study.

3. *Proceed from Easy to Difficult*: We must graduate our lessons in order of ease of understanding them. Students' standard must be kept in view. This will help in sustaining the interest of the students. In determining what is easy and what is difficult we have to take into account the psychological make-up of the child. Logically viewed one skill or idea may be easy but psychologically it may be difficult. There are many things which look easy to us but are in fact difficult for children. The interest of the child has also to be taken into account. Lines are very easy to draw but a child may not like to draw lines. He may try to draw an animal. There is no doubt that it is difficult, but it is more interesting to him and so is easy for him. We should encourage him to do so and our approach will be psychological instead of logical.

4. *Proceed from the Concrete to the Abstract*: A child's imagination is greatly aided by a concrete material. "Things first and words after" is the common saying. Rousseau said, "Things. Things. Things." Children in the beginning cannot think in abstractions. Small children learn first from things which they can see and handle. Very young pupils learn counting with the help of pebbles etc. A child understands an aeroplane with the help of a model. Actual visits to canals and rivers provide a clear idea of them.

A lesson in geography can be made interesting with the help of models, pictures and illustrations of bridges, rivers and mountains etc. Care must be exercised to ensure that the students do not remain at the 'concrete stage' all the time. This is only the initial step for children with a view to reach the higher stage of 'abstraction' they advance in age.

5. *Proceed from Particular to General*: Before giving principles and rules, particular examples should be presented. As a matter of fact a study of particular facts should lead the children themselves to frame general rules. The rules of arithmetic, of grammar, of physical geography and almost of all sciences are based on the principle of proceeding from particular instances to general rules.

6. *Proceed from Indefinite to Definite*: Ideas of children in the initial stages are indefinite, incoherent and very vague. These ideas are to be made definite, clear, precise and systematic. Effective teaching requires that every word and idea presented should stand out clearly in the child's mind. For classifying ideas, adequate use must be made of actual objects, diagrams and pictures. Every possible effort should be made to make the children interested in the lesson.

7. *Proceed from Empirical to Rational*: Observation and experience are the basis of empirical knowledge. Rational Knowledge implies a bit of abstraction and argumentative approach. The general feeling is that the child first of all experiences knowledge in his day-to-day life and after that he feels the rational basis. For instance, plane geometry makes better sense when taught in the context of everyday life instead of it in the format of a highly abstract theory. It is always better to begin with what the children see, feel and experience than arguing and generalising.

8. *Proceed from Psychological to Logical*: Logical approach is concerned with the arrangement of the subject-matter. Psychological approach looks at the child's interests, needs, mental make up and reactions. When we treat a subject logically, we are usually thinking of it from our own point of view and not from the point of view of the child. In psychological approach, we proceed from the concrete to the abstract, from the simple to the complex and from known to unknown. We start reading by teaching the child to read a whole sentence, as for him the unit is the sentence, not the word or the letter as it is for the adult. This is psychological approach. In a drawing lesson a child has little sense in lines and curves. Logically we start with simple lines and curves but psychologically we start with drawing a whole animal.

9. *Proceed from Whole to Parts*: Whole is more meaningful to the child than the parts of the whole. J.P. Guildford, E.B. Newman and May Seagoe conclude after their research that the whole approach is generally better than 'part' learning because the material to be learnt 'makes sense' and its parts can be seen by the learner as interrelated. The learner sees a relationships between the central idea of the material to be learned. The 'whole' unit or passage for slow learners should be smaller than the 'whole' for the fast learners.

10. *From Near to Far*: A child learns well in the surroundings in which he resides. So he should be first acquainted with his immediate environment. Gradually he may be taught about things which are away from his immediate environment. In a geography lesson we start from the local geography and then take up tehsil, district, state, the country and the world gradually.

11. *From Analysis to Synthesis*: Analysis means breaking a problem into convenient parts and synthesis means grouping of these separated parts into one complete whole. A complex problem can be made simple and easy by dividing it into units.

12. *From Actual to Representative*: When actual objectives are shown to children, they learn easily and retain them in their minds for a long time. This is, especially suitable for younger children. Representative objects in the form of pictures, models etc. should be used for the grown-ups.

13. *Proceed Inductively*: This maxim includes almost all the maxims stated above. In the inductive approach, we start from particular examples and establish general rules through the active participation of the learners. In the deductive approach, we assume a definition, a general rule or formula and apply it to particular examples. An example will make this distinction very clear. 'The farmers in India are very poor' is a general statement in the deductive type of reasoning. The inductive will follow thus: Ram is a farmer. He is very poor. Shyam is a farmer. He is very poor. Krishan is a farmer. He is very poor. In this way from several such examples it will be evident that farmers are poor. Thus we derive generalisations. Both of the approaches i.e., the deductive and inductive have their own importance. However in general, inductive approach is considered a better one.

Conclusion: In the ultimate analysis it must be observed that the maxims are meant to be our servants and not masters. Moreover, by and large all are interrelated. It is also to be kept in view that children differ in their aptitudes, capacities, interests, mental and physical make up. Different maxims suit different situations and different children. It is, therefore, essential that a judicious use should be made of each maxim.

18.3 TECHNIQUES OF TEACHING

Following techniques of teaching are discussed:

1. Description
2. Dramatisation
3. Narration
4. Excursion and Field Work
5. Story Telling

18.4 DESCRIPTION

Description and narration are quite similar terms and there is not much difference between these two terms. Description demands a more effective use of the language than needed in narration. We usually describe a 'thing' or an 'object' and do not use the word 'narrate' to portray a thing. We describe an event. We also narrate events. According to the dictionary meaning "to describe" is "to set forth, define, depict or portray in words" and "description" is defined as "the act of representing a thing by words; account of the properties or appearance of something."

Description is needed in most of the lessons of almost all the subjects and especially in the case of Science, Geography and History.

The following points should be kept in view while using this device in teaching:

1. As far as possible, the teacher should try to see the object before describing it. A history teacher will not be able to present a vivid picture of the Red Fort until he sees it.

2. It may be borne in mind that without forming a clear visual image of the object or event in mind, it is not possible to describe an object or event or

place in an effective manner.

3. Language employed should be very clear and simple.

4. It is preferable to give first a broad general view of the whole object and then field in the details.

5. Too many details at a time should be avoided for those may baffle the students imagination.

6. Key points should be stressed and repeated.

7. A definite order may follow in giving description.

8. Verbal description should be supplemented with diagrams, modes and pictures, etc.

9. The use of homely illustrations, such as, metaphors and similar helps to provide a vivid account of an object.

10. The aim of the description should be made very clear to the students in the very beginning of the lesson.

18.5 DRAMATISATION

Meaning

Dramatisation has been described as "a synthetic art", involving the purposive coordination and control of the delicate organs of speech and muscles of the body combined with a sense of rhythm, with a view to free and intelligent expression of emotions and ideas.

Dramatic art affords innumerable opportunities for the correlation of a large number of subjects. In the preparation of their roles, the students indirectly and unconsciously improve their speech habits and language. A systematic study of historical events has to be made when pageants of the life of great persons are prepared, i.e., pageant on the life of Buddha, Chandragupta, Vikramaditya, Gandhiji etc. Children prepare costumes suiting different ages and thus come to know about the dresses of the people during different periods of history. Dramatics also add to the geographical knowledge of the students. Carpentry and other mechanical arts facilitate the work of construction of the stage. Dance and music add to the beauty of a drama.

Drama has its great social value. It is a cooperative enterprise and develops qualities of cooperation and social understanding. It helps in fostering '*espirit de crops*' among the students. In various school functions, dramas form the chief items of the programme. For the honour of the school, every student works to the best of his capacity.

Dramatics afford the students many opportunities for training in teamwork. They are very helpful in providing the students with opportunities for the release of the inhibitions to which they are subjected by the conventions of society.

There are many activities in a drama and as such students of diverse aptitudes get chances to choose items for which they are best suited and satisfy their urges, e.g., self-expression through the various activities of a drama.

Conditions for Success

A number of rehearsals bring grace and success to the play when it is staged. Pupils should prepare as much stage material as they can.

Children should be encouraged to write their own plays. The usual participants in this activity should be given opportunities to play different roles. The same pupils as far as possible should, however, not be allowed to play the role of a villain.

Selection of Play

1. Plays chosen should depict the evils of the social customs.
2. A play should have a literary value also.
3. The students should be able to understand and appreciate the play.
4. It should have entertainment value.
5. It should be free from objectionable subject-matter.
6. There should be no vulgarity in the play.

18.6 EXPLANATION

The main objective of explanation is to enable the children to take an intelligent interest in the lesson, to grasp the purpose of what is being done and to develop their insight and understanding of how to do it.

According to Panton, "Explanation forms a kind of bridge between telling and revealing knowledge of the lesson, and it involves a number of other techniques as well as narration and description.

Following suggestions are offered:

1. The librarian should behave very sympathetically with the students.
2. The school library should be kept open during the vacation and long holidays.
3. The beautiful picture-cuttings from newspapers and illustrations from current events and topics should be displayed on the library bulletin boards.
4. Books suiting different tastes and interests should be provided in large numbers.
5. The furniture should suit the needs of the students.
6. A catalogue of library books should be available in the library for ready reference.
7. Library day may be organised once a year to popularise the school library.
8. Completed projects of the students can be exhibited in the library.

We may sum up the discussion with a quotation from Tagore, "In order to bring a library into the fullest use, it is necessary that its contents should be clearly and specifically brought to notice, otherwise it is difficult for the ordinary man to find his way about them, and the library is left as a city of vast accommodation that lacks sufficient means of communication. Those who frequent visit libraries on some special quest of their own may manage to make a track for themselves by dint of the urgency of their particular pursuit. But the library itself should recognise its share of responsibility in the matter. Because it has the books, it is incumbent on the library to get them read, for then alone it is justified. It is not enough that it passively permits visitors; its invitation should be active. For, as the Sanskrit proverb tells us *tannashtamyannadiyate*, that which is not given is wasted". These views are applicable to school libraries also.

18.7 NARRATION

Narration is an indispensable device of communicating knowledge. According to *Panton, I.H.*, "Narration is an art in itself which aims at presenting to the pupils, through the medium of speech, clear, vivid, interesting, ordered sequence of events, in such a way that their minds reconstruct these happenings and they live in imagination through the experiences recounted either as spectators or possibly as participators." The skill of narration enables the teacher to come very close to the hearts of the students and thereby to attract the undivided attention. The art of narration involves the use of pictorial word images, a certain dramatic element in delivery and the ability to conjure up one picture after another. To be a good narrator, a teacher should know the skilful use of language.

Some teachers are born narrators and they are very fortunate in this respect. However, the art of narration can be cultivated through the following measures:

1. By observing skilful narrators.
2. By listening to speeches of good orators.
3. By critically observing one's own performance with the help of tape recording and making use of this feedback.
4. By studying the work of effective writers of children's literature.
5. By using appropriate beginning and concluding statements.
6. By explaining links in the form of suitable words and phrases.
7. By using proper gestures.
8. By using common metaphors and similes.
9. By Story telling.

Some Dont's in Narration

1. Do not use irrelevant or vague statements.
2. Do not allow any missing link or break in the logical sequence of interrelated statements.
3. Do not use fumbling ideas.
4. Do not utter incomplete or half sentences.

18.8 EXCURSION AND FIELD WORK

It is rightly believed that observation under the careful guidance of a civics teacher proves very effective in the process of learning, and facts, skills and behaviour learnt are retained for a long period. Observation or direct experience or visits to actual places, say, Village Panchayat, State Assembly, Parliament, a monument, a fort, a field, a river, a temple, an institution, etc. provide ample opportunities to students for 'seeing', 'hearing', 'examining', 'gathering data' and 'asking' questions. Visits to hospitals, telephone exchanges, telegraph offices, study trips to airports, etc. show how people and goods are transported from one place to another. Pupils understand better the working of markets, cooperative stores and factories when they see their working and thus acquaint themselves with the processes of production, distribution, exchange and consumption. Such experiences are most conducive to learning. Concrete data on cultural, industrial, political and geographical facts and relationship being more 'tangible', 'visible' and 'describable' serve as a great motivating force for further enquiry in social sciences. Observation lends vitality to the subject matter of social studies.

Techniques of Observation Method

Following techniques are adopted in the observation method:

1. Field Trips or Educational Excursions.
2. Community Surveys.
3. Community Service Projects.

Educational Trips in the Teaching of Civics

Advantages

1. They provide opportunities for first-hand observation.
2. They provide new information.
3. They broaden the background and outlook of students and provide new vistas.
4. They provide common experiences for a group.
5. They provide experiences in planning.
6. They enable the teacher to observe behaviour of the students, in new situations.
7. They build group morale.
8. They provide social experiences for learning social skills.

Criteria for Selecting Excursion and Field Work

1. A trip should be related to the topic under discussion or as a motivation for a new topic.
2. It should provide something that can be learned better by direct experience then by text-books, films and other methods.
3. It should give those experiences to students that they cannot easily have alone or with parents or in very small groups.
4. The distance between the school and the place to be visited should not be too long for the time available.
5. The expenses should be low.
6. It must have the approval of the parents and school administration.

Preparation Needed for Excursion and Field Work

1. Obtaining clearance from parents and administrators. Clearance from parents usually involves permission slips.
2. Undertaking visit by the teacher in advance if possible.
3. Framing simple rules of conduct.
4. Prescribing simple rules for dress.
5. Carrying a safety or first-aid box.
6. Issuing directions about what to do when get lost or left behind.
7. orking out some suitable arrangement with other concerned teachers.
8. Providing insurance for long trips.
9. Arranging transport.

10. Arranging money.
11. Making suitable arrangement for accommodation.
12. Making adequate arrangement for eating.
13. Ensuring that no one is segregated because of his race or colour.
14. Calculating time while remembering that groups do not move as fast as individuals.
15. Informing students as to what to look for, to take notes and obtain materials.

Evaluation of Excursion and Field Work

Following points may be specially considered in the evaluation of historical excursions:

Was the time sufficient for the trip?
Was the group of a manageable size?
Were the arrangements satisfactory?
Did the group see what it wanted to see and expected to see?
Was the group interested and attentive?
Was the trip sufficiently correlated with the school work?
Were there any avoidable delays or wastage of time during the trip?
Were the specific educational objectives served by the trip?
Was it worthwhile to undertake the trip?
What were the most unsatisfactory things about the trip?
What were the most satisfactory things about the trip?
In case of repeating the trip, what changes should be made?

Suggestive List of Places for Field Trips

The following list is by no means exhaustive. It is only suggestive.

1. Airport, 2. Art gallery. 3. Bakery 4. Bank, 5. Brick yard, 6. Business college, 7. Candy factory, 8. Canning factory, 9. City hall, 10. City water plant, 11. Coal mine, 12. Court room, 13. Dairy, 14. Farm, 15. Fire department, 16. Flower garden, 17. Freight yard, 18. Historical sites, 19. Hydroelectric plant, 20. Ice-cream factory, 21. Iron mine, 22. Library, 23. Livestock farm, 24. Mill, 25. Monuments, 26. Museum, 27. Newspaper office, 28. Nuclear energy plant, 29. Oil well, 30. Packing plant, 31. Park, 32. Photographic studio, 33. Planetarium, 34. Police station, 35. Post office, 36. Quarry, 37. Railway station, 38. Rubber factory, 39. Steel plant, 40. Telephone exchange, 41. Television studio, 42. Theatre, 43. University, 44. Voting polls, 45. Zoo.

18.9 STORY TELLING

Educators are unanimously agreed that the bed-rock of Civics teaching is a series of suitable and well-chosen stories presented with care and liveliness. There is a 'vital nourishment' in the anecdotal approach to the teaching of Civics. Colourful, realistic and vivid stories stir the emotions and arouse the sympathy of the children.

Story telling can make Civics throb with life and interest.

A good story told in a proper manner goes a long way in firing the imagination of the students.

Stories of discoverers, heroes, sailors, soldiers, saints, scripts, etc. have a unique value of training the creative faculties of students.

Story telling is a very useful device in inculcating traits of character such as piety, truthfulness, valour, charity and the like.

Story Telling as an Art

Story telling is one of the most important methods of teaching Social Studies. It is an art which enables the teacher to come very close to the heart of the students and thereby he attracts their attention. Some teachers are born story tellers and they are very fortunate in this respect. This art of story telling aims at presenting to the pupils, through the medium of speech, clear, vivid, interesting, ordered sequences of events, in such a way as their minds reconstruct these happenings and they live in imagination through the experiences recounted either as spectators or possibly as participators. Story telling enables the teacher to make lessons lively and interesting to the pupils. Stories of great personalities, reformers, writers, saints, discoverers, statesmen and scientists, etc. must be told to the students. Story telling helps in enhancing the interests of the students in the subject. It goes a long way in firing the imagination of the students. Story telling can be relied upon by the teacher as the best companion for helping in developing in his pupils traits of character, such as, charity, piety, truthfulness and valour, etc.

The art of story telling can be cultivated by:

1. Observing skilful narrators.
2. Studying the work of successful story writers.
3. Practising story telling.
4. Critically evaluating one's own performance and bringing about necessary changes.

Guidelines for Effective Story Telling

In telling a story the teacher should be guided by the following points:

1. Suitable stories for the age of the students should be selected. A story that appeals and interests the seven years old child will not suit a four year old child.
2. The stories should be short and the plot easy.
3. The teachers must know well the story that he wants to narrate. If he stops in the middle it will detract charm from the story.
4. Language employed in telling a story should be very simple and easy.
5. A story should be told and not read. The story loses a great deal of its interest for the children if it is read.
6. The teacher himself should like the story and take interest in story telling.
7. There should be plenty of action in the stories. Key sentences and phrases should be repeated as the children enjoy this repetition. The stories should be loaded with activities and experiences familiar to the children. R. Strang has observed, "Stories for young children, therefore, should be told in terms of

action and sense impressions. Up to the age of six years, a child is most alive to moving things—engines, boats, horses and wagons, animals, boys and girls in action. Children lose interest when the action is interrupted by a long descriptive passage. In telling a story one can notice the drop in interest during descriptive and explanatory portion and the flare-up of interest again when the action is resumed. Since the young child's own activities and experiences are the ones most interesting to him, the first stories should be about experiences familiar to children."

8. Conversation, if any, in the story should be given in direct speech and not indirect.

9. The methods of introducing and developing the story should be thought out before-hand.

10. The story should be told in a natural way and very vividly.

11. Humour makes the story more interesting and should not be neglected.

12. To make the story more realistic, the teacher may use pictures and draw diagrams on the blackboard.

13. The story should suggest and inspire the students to action. Opportunities of 'playing the story' should be provided and utilised.

14. Ryburn suggests that well-known and familiar stories can be made fresh if they are told as though one of the characters in the story were telling it. He writes, "The story of Asoka and the Kalinga war could be told as if Asoka himself were telling it."

15. The story must have some aim beside mere enjoyment. The teacher must keep in mind the aim while narrating a story. It is all the more better if the students too know the aim.

19

Questioning and Answering

19.1 SIGNIFICANCE OF QUESTIONING

It is well said about the importance of questioning:

"I keep six honest serving men,
They taught me all I know,
There names are what and why and when,
And how and where and who".

The art of questioning is the most potent weapon in the educational armoury of the teacher. "Good questions" writes F. Theodore Struck, "by their very nature, are educative, and they have a very prominent place in all kinds of learning". Questioning plays an indispensable part in 'learning', 'teaching', and 'testing'. If used in the right way, at the proper time, questions led to new realms of understanding; they serve as means of organising knowledge, or correlating the results of educative experiences of tying together units of learning; and of integrating personality. One who questions faultlessly teaches effectively, is not without meaning. Salmon holds that a bad questioner is a bad teacher; he may be a good lecturer. In the words of Ryburn, "It is not exaggeration to say that the success of a teacher in any particular lesson, and in teaching in general, depends upon his ability to question well." According to Raymont, "The acquisition of a good style of questioning may be laid down definitely as one of the essential ambitions of a young teacher."

19.2 PURPOSES OF QUESTIONS

1. To test the previous knowledge of the students.
2. To enable them to recall something.
3. To enable them to recognise something.
4. To enable them to think over something.
5. To enable them to reason about something.
6. To elicit something from students.
7. To stimulate interest and effort on the part of students.
8. To keep the children mentally alert.
9. To promote initiative and originality.
10. To stimulate the curiosity of the students.
11. To ascertain whether they are following the lesson or not.
12. To link new knowledge with the old.
13. To revise the lesson and thus fix the facts in the minds of the students.

14. To secure the cooperation of the students.
15. To diagnose the weak points of the students.
16. To formulate general rules.
17. To synthesise.

19.3 CLASSIFICATION OF QUESTIONS

- Introductory or Preliminary Questions
- Developing Questions
- Recapitulatory Questions
- Evaluating or Testing Questions

Skills in Introductory Questions/Preliminary Questions

These questions are generally asked at the beginning of the lesson. These serve the following objectives:

(i) Test the previous knowledge of the students.
(ii) Link the new knowledge with the already learnt knowledge.

19.4 LEVELS OF CLASSROOM QUESTIONS

Questions are broadly divided into three levels as under:

1. Lower order questions
2. Middle order questions
3. Higher order questions

(See Fig. 19.1)

I. Examples of Lower Order Questions

Recall

1. When was Jawaharlal Nehru born? (Recall of fact)
2. What is the definition of force? (Recall of definition)
3. What are the laws of gravitation? (Recall of laws)

Recognition

1. What words in this sentence are adjectives? (Seeking recognition of certain words as adjectives)
2. What is this? (Showing a barometer in the class) (Seeking recognition of an object)

II. Examples of Middle Order Questions

Translation

1. What does this model represent? (Seeking the translation of an idea contained in a model into the verbal form)

2. How can we represent 'happiness' of the child in a picture? (Seeking the translation of an idea into a pictorial form)

3. Define 'state' in your own words. (Seeking a change in the mode of expression of a definition)

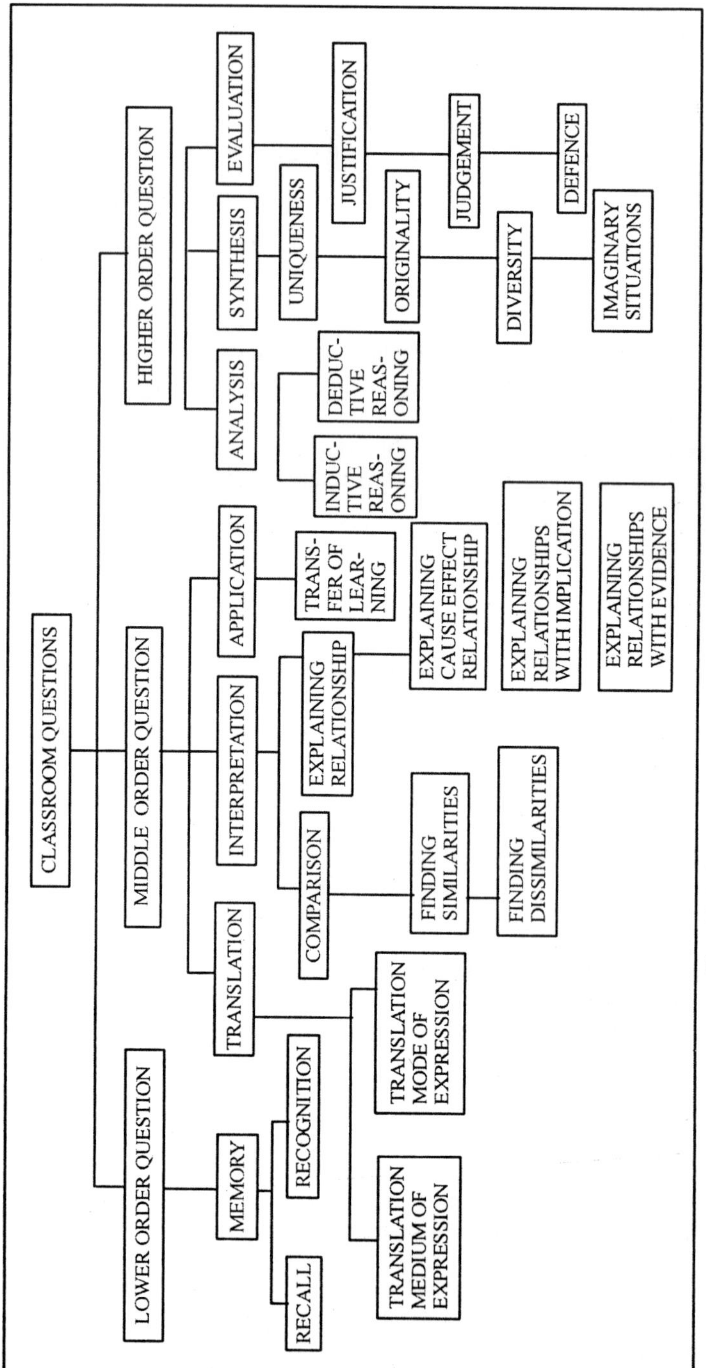

Fig. 19.1: Levels of Classroom Questions (NCERT, 1982)

Comparison

1. Compare the city life and the village life. (Seeking comparison to search for similarities and dissimilarities)

2. Compare the similarities between the powers of the Prime Minister and Chief Minister? (Seeking the comparison through pointing out similarities).

Explaining Relationships: How is price rise related to demand and supply?

Application: Considering natural resources and climatic conditions of this place, which industry can come up here?

These questions enable the teacher to test the readiness of the students' mind and their entering behaviour. Questioning at this stage enables the teacher to follow the maximum 'Form known to the unknown'.

Questions should be relevant to the topic. The number of questions should be very small, say three or four.

Skills in Developing Questions: These questions are said to be the backbone of the lesson. They are used:

(i) to develop a particular line of thought;
(ii) to lead to pupils to discover facts for themselves;
(iii) to formulate new generalisations in an inductive way;
(iv) to focus attention on important points;
(v) to develop knowledge step by step;
(vi) to enable the students to use their powers of observation, of comparison and concentration;
(vii) to break the narrative in order to ensure that the class is following; and
(viii) to make the inattentive students attentive ones.

A great skill is required on the part of the teacher to ask developing questions. The teacher has to lead the students to think and discover facts for themselves. While narrating a story, the teacher should not ask questions.

Recapitulatory Questions: Such questions are generally put at the end of a lesson or at the end of each section of the lesson.

Such questions serve two purposes:

1. To enable the teacher to know if the children have picked up the ideas he wanted them to learn.
2. To serve the purpose of revision and to give a good opportunity of practice.

Skills in Evaluating or Testing Questions: These questions relate to periodic internal as well as external evaluation.

Types of Questions

1. *Comparison or Contrast*: Example: What is the difference between wealth and capital?

2. *Decision far or Against*: Example: Do you consider it correct to call Chandragupta Maurya as the first Emperor in India?

3. *Application in New Situations*: Example: Suggest measures to remove illiteracy in your village or town.

4. *Classification*: Example: Are the following free goods or economic goods—air, sun-shine, machinery, gold, food?

5. *Relationship between Cause and Effect*: Example: What is the relation between population and economic prosperity?

6. *Example or Illustration*: Example: Describe cases when prices increase with the decrease in the supply of some commodities.

7. *Statement of Aim*: Example: Why is the author interested in the study of problem children?

8. *Criticism*: Example: Do you think Asoka was justified in following the policy of 'Non-violence'? Elucidate.

9. *Inference*: Example: From the data given, which place do you consider to be more hotter?

10. *Discussion*: Example: Discuss the most important proposals for bringing down the prices.

11. *Definition*: Example: Define elasticity of demand.

12. *Recall*: Example: What do you consider the three most important inventions of the last century?

13. *Summary*: Example: What were the causes of the downfall of Mughal Empire?

14. *Observation*: Example: Observe this experiment.

15. *Formation of New Questions*: Example: What questions did occur to your mind after listening to the exploits of Samudragupta?

III. Examples of Higher Order Questions

Analysis: Does the evidence support the generalisation that farmers in India are in debt?

Syntheses: What sort of life do you expect without printed material?

19.5 SKILLS IN QUESTIONING

The teacher should bear in mind the following in this connection.

1. The question should be asked first and then the student asked to answer it. The main advantage in asking the question first is to set the whole class thinking to find out the answer. On the other hand, if a particular student is asked to stand or sit, as the case may be, and then the question is put to him, other students may not show much interest.

2. Questions should be evenly distributed. No child should be neglected. At the same time questions should not be given in a regular order round the class. Generally there is a tendency to put either too many questions or too less to the students sitting at the back or in the front. Such a tendency should be avoided.

3. Plenty of time should be allowed for pupils to think of the answer. However, the time allowed will depend upon the nature of the question.

4. The inability of a child to answer a question should be accepted. The teacher should avoid wasting time in trying to get an answer out of a child who cannot answer.

5. A volley of questions asked in a rapid-fire manner is upsetting.

19.6 CHARACTERISTICS OF GOOD QUESTIONING

1. The language of the question should be simple.

2. Questions should not be ambiguous, lengthy and vague. They should be clear, brief and to the point.

3. They should be suited to the ability of the children to whom the questions are put.

4. Questions should be relevant to the topic.

5. Questions should be graded. They should neither be too easy nor too difficult; if the question is too easy, the child will not take any interest in it. If it is too difficult, he will get discouraged.

6. Question once asked should not be repeated unless the teacher is sure that the class has not followed it.

7. The teacher should try to vary the form of his questions.

8. Two questions should not be asked in one.

9. Questions should be interesting as far as possible.

10. Questions should be framed in such a way that these do not encourage guess work. The teacher should not generally admit answers like 'yes', 'no' or other single words.

11. Questions should be of developing nature. Every question should grow out of the response of the previous one. Questions should be in a sequence so that lesson may develop properly.

12. Suggestive questions such as "Was Sardar Patel an iron man?" should be avoided as they fail to encourage mental activity.

13. Leading questions such as "Do you know that Subhash Chandra Bose was the founder of the Indian National Army?" should not be asked.

14. Echo questions such as "Mahatma Buddha was born at Lumbini. Where was Mahatma Buddha born?" should not be asked.

15. Phrases like "Can anyone answer this questions" should be avoided.

16. Questions should be addressed to the entire class.

17. Questions should be asked in a pleasing manner.

19. Adequate time should be allowed to answer.

19.7 THE TEACHER'S ATTITUDE TO PUPILS' QUESTIONS

Following points should be kept in mind:

1. The students should be encouraged to ask questions.

2. Relevancy in questions should be insisted upon.

3. The teacher must insist on courtesy. Several pupils should not be allowed to ask questions at the same time. Everyone should be asked to listen to a question.

4. Pupils' questions may be made the starting point for a small project.

5. The teacher should be frank enough to admit his inability to answer question when he does not know the answer. However, in due course, he should be able to answer that question. For the sake of prestige in the eyes of the students, he should not give a wrong answer.

Judicious Blending of Talking and Questioning: Questioning is not a one-way traffic. There is an ample scope for the teacher as well as the students to put questions. The teaching-learning process is effective only when the teacher as well as the pupils are active and cooperative. The aim of the teaching-learning process is to enable the child learn in such a way that it enables him to adjust himself to the environment. As both the teachers and the pupils are attempting to realise the same goal, it is evident that they must be active and not passive.

19.8 SKILL IN ANSWERING

The same care and skill in dealing with pupils' answers, as in questioning them should be shown. After all, what for do we ask questions? Not for the sake of question! The aim is to motivate children, to create interest, to test what the child knows and what he does not know, to encourage and stimulate thinking and fact-finding and to clear ambiguities and doubts. The quality and the nature of the answer reveal whether the purposes of questioning are fulfilled or not. Rather it may be put that questioning is a means to teach something that is revealed through the answers. Questions and answers may be compared with the blades of scissors. Both are indispensable in the teaching-learning process as both the blades are required to cut a piece of cloth.

Answers reveal the deficiency of the students as well as the teachers. They are the touchstone to test the effectiveness of the teaching-learning process. If the answers are not satisfactory, it clearly indicates that either there is something wrong with the teaching process or with the learning process. Either the teacher has not taught in the proper manner or the students have not understood the subject-matter. Therefore, answers provide an important tool to make necessary changes in the teaching-learning process.

Classification of Answers

A close analysis of the various types of answers shows that these can be put under the following six categories:

(i) Right and correct answers.
(ii) Correct but incomplete.
(iii) Partially correct and partially wrong.
(iv) Wrong but intelligent.
(v) Ridiculously wrong.
(vi) Mischievous.

How to deal with answers. No hard and fast rule can be laid down for dealing with various categories of answers. *Ward and Rascore* write in this connection, "There are no rules. It is unwise to pass over all wrong answers as it is unwise to deal with all. Some are genuine misconceptions, which the teacher must clear up at that time or later on, others are imperfect and incomplete answers, genuine also, which must be rounded off, others are haphazard or stupid and should be treated with contempt or else with such brief but emphatic words of disapproval as the teacher may have a command". The following are the different ways of dealing with answers.

1. *Appreciation*: The teacher should in general appreciate the answers of the students as appreciation will encourage the students to think further. Even if the answers are wrong but teacher feels that the child is making genuine attempts, due appreciation should be given.

2. *Analysis of Wrong Answers*: When the answers given by most of the students are wrong, the teacher should try to analyse their causes. The causes may be as under:

(i) Defective or difficult language used by the teacher.
(ii) Defective explanation of the subject-matter taught.
(iii) Inattentiveness on the part of the students.
(iv) Lapses of memory.
(v) Toughness and complexity of the subject-matter.

In such cases, the teacher should accept the responsibility and should not feel shy of teaching the subject-matter again.

3. *Encouragement of Children*: When the answers are partly right and partly wrong, the students should be encouraged to analyse themselves the nature of their mistake. The teacher may ask further questions to analyse the nature of the mistake. When all the factors which are responsible for wrong answer, or answers are not clear to all the students, they may be asked to build up the real answers once again. It is unwise on the part of the teacher to be impatient and to make the necessary completion or correction himself.

4. *Treatment of Wrong Answers*: When a particular student gives a wrong answer, the teacher should not pass on till he gets the right answer without explaining why the first answer is wrong. The child must be made to understand why his answer is wrong. He is not likely to gain anything from the right answer if his doubts remain unexplained.

5. *Answers Carrying Some Version, Other than Expected by the Teacher*: The teacher should accept and appreciate correct and complete answer although it may differ from the answers as expected by the teacher. There are a few intelligent students in every class who believe in novelty and do a lot of extra-reading. The difference in approach should be explained by the teacher.

6. *The Form of the Answers According to the Nature of the Lesson*: Whether the answer should be in bits or incomplete sentences depends upon the nature of the lesson. Complete sentences may not be insisted upon in Arithmetic, Science and in some cases in History or Geography. But in a language lesson where the aim is to develop the power of expression, the teacher should insist upon complete sentences. No general rule can be laid down. It is up to the teacher to decide the form of the answer. But it must be stressed that whatever be the form answers should be in a clear, simple and concise language.

7. *Answers Based on Right Understanding*: The teacher must make sure that the answers as given by the students are really based on genuine mental activity. Parrot fashion words, though they may have sense, are not based on any thought or understanding on part of the child. The teacher must go deeper and ensure that the child really knows what he says.

8. *Answers Given in Unison*: Answer given in unison should be discouraged. Such answers lack educational value and, therefore, should be disallowed. Assertive students should not be allowed to usurp the right of others who are slower or are perhaps making a mistake. Students should not be allowed to interrupt others while they are answering questions.

9. *Observance of Courtesy*: The teacher should see that the ordinary

courtesy is observed in answering questions. The students should stand or sit and address in the proper way.

10. *Encouragement to Shy and Submissive Students*: There are always some students who feel shy and become nervous when questions are put to them. Though they know the answers quite alright, yet they remain mum. The teacher should, in all such cases, give more encouragement and appreciation.

11. *Repetition of Good Answers*: Good answers of the students should be referred to the class, got repeated, preferably by another pupil. The teacher should avoid to repeat a correct answer himself unless he wants it to be specially stressed.

12. *Discouragement to Irrelevant Answers*: The students should be made to realise the cause of the irrelevant answer. The teacher should analyse thoroughly whether the irrelevant answer is due to some mischief on the part of the student.

13. *Development of the Summary of the Lesson with the Help of the Answers*: The answers given by the students at the recapitulatory stage may be used to develop a summary of the lesson. All the answers in brief may be written on the blackboard and the students encouraged to develop an integrated summary with the help of these answers.

Conclusion: Correct, clear and thoughtful answers result from clear and thought-provoking questions. The better means of evoking responses from the students are sympathy, patience and encouragement rather than impatience, harshness or snubbing them. Right and correct answers imply that the teacher is using right and correct methods of teaching and the students are learning in an appropriate manner. It may, therefore, be concluded that the pupil's answers to the questions are equally important if not more than the questions of the teacher in teaching-learning process.

Questions properly planned, carefully worded, evenly distributed, scientifically, and psychologically asked, honestly answered and intelligently followed up are very profitable and in fact indispensable in the effective teaching-learning process. Colvin gave recognition to questioning in these words, "The efficiency of instruction is measured in a large degree by the nature of the questions that are asked and the care with which they are framed. No teacher of elementary or secondary school subjects can succeed in his instruction if he has not a fair mastery of the art of questioning."

19.9 SKILL OF PROBING QUESTIONS

The term probing implies going deep in the matter in hand. It is defined as the art of response management comprising a set of behaviours or techniques for going deep into student's responses with a view to elicit the desired responses. N.K. Jangira and his associates (1980) name the skill of probing questions as the skill of response management on account of its emphasis on the ways and means of response management.

The skill of probing questions comprises the following component behaviours or techniques:

1. Prompting.
2. Seeking further information.

3. Refocusing.
4. Redirection.
5. Increasing critical awareness.

Prompting

In the teaching-learning situation, prompting refers to the cues or hints provided by the teacher through well-defined questions to the students for arriving at the desired response from the undesired situations like no response, incorrect, partially correct or incomplete sentences. It may be noted that here the teacher himself does not provide the answer to the questions asked in the classroom by him or any student but tries to manage the situation by giving cues.

The selection of specific prompt (cues or hints or restructuring or phrasing of the question) in a particular situation depends upon factors like previous experience of the students, ability of the students to manipulate the relevant facts, concepts or principles, logical consistency of the response and the level of maturity etc. of the students.

Seeking Further Information

For seeking further information from the students, questions like 'give some examples', 'make it more clear', by giving some evidence, are often asked.

Refocusing

In refocusing, the teacher asks the responding student either to relate his response with something already studied by him or to consider implications of his response in a more complex and novel situation.

Redirection

This technique is generally used in a 'no response' or 'incomplete response' situation and requires putting or redirecting the same question to several students for eliciting the desired response.

Increasing Critical Awareness

This technique is applied in a correct response situation to increase critical awareness in the students. Questions like, How would you justify it? Why do you assume so? How does it happen? are helpful in asking the responding student to justify his response for the purpose of increasing critical awareness in him.

20

Audio-Visual Aids in the Teaching of Civics

20.1 MEANING OF AUDIO-VISUAL AIDS

Audio-visual aids, audio-visual material, 'audio-visual media', 'communication technology', 'educational or instructional media' and 'learning resources'—all these terms, broadly speaking, mean the same thing. Earlier the term used was audio-visual aids in education. With the advancement in the means of communication and that of technology, educators coined new terms. More specifically media refers to films, filmstrips, recordings etc. The use of newer terms Educational Technology or Instructional Technology is primarily due to the dynamic expansion of programmed learning, computer assisted instruction and educational T.V. This revolution in the field of audio-visual education is the outcome of the development in electronics, notably those involving the radio, tape recorder and computer.

The following definitions of audio-visual aids help to provide a comprehensive and vivid view of these terms:

Burton—Audio-visual aids are those sensory objects or images which initiate or stimulate and reinforce learning.

Carter V. Good—Audio-visual aids are those aids which help in completing the triangular process of learning, i.e., motivation, classification and stimulation.

Edgar Dale—Audio-visual are those devices by the use of which communication of ideas between persons and groups in various teaching and training situations is helped. These are also termed as multi-sensory materials.

Good's Dictionary of Education—Audio-visual aids are anything by means of which learning process may be encouraged or carried on through the sense of hearing or sense of sight.

Kinder, S. James—Audio-visual aids are any device which can be used to make the learning experience more concrete, more realistic and more dynamic.

Mckown and Roberts—Audio-visual aids are supplementary devices by which the teacher, through the utilisation of more than one sensory channels is able to clarify, establish and correlate concepts, interpretations and appreciations.

20.2 BRIEF HISTORY OF THE USE OF AUDIO-VISUAL AIDS

A Dutch humanist, theologian and writer Desiderious Erasmus (1466-1536) discouraged memorisation as a technique of learning and advocated that children should learn through the aid of pictures or other visuals. John Amos Comenius (1592-1670) prepared a book known as *Orbis Sensulium Pictus*. (The World of Sense Objects) which contained about 150 pictures on aspects of everyday life. The book is considered to be the first illustrated text-book for childhood education. This book gained wide publicity and was used in childhood education centres all over the world. Jean Jacus Rousseau (1712-1778) and other educators stressed the need of pictures and other play materials. Rosseau condemned the use of words by teachers and he stressed 'things'. He pleaded that the teaching process must be directed to the learner's natural curiosity. Pestalozzi (1756-1827) put Rousseau's theory into action in his 'object method'. He based instruction on sense perception.

Eric Ashby (1967) identified four revolutions in education: education from home to school, written words as tool of education, invention of printing and use of books and lastly the fourth revolution in the use of electronic media, i.e., radio, television, tape recorder and computer in education.

20.3 PSYCHOLOGY OF USING TEACHING AIDS/AUDIO-VISUAL AIDS

In addition to reading, vicarious experience can be gained from still pictures, films, filmstrips resource persons, simulations mock-ups television and the like. The more concrete and realistic the vicarious experience, the more nearly it approaches the learning effectiveness of the first level. Of course, unless the learner realizes that he is dealing with a substitute, his learning may not be comparable to that of real-life learning.

Interest in the role of the senses in learning was already there in educational circles when instructional media began their ascendancy. It has long been recognised that the various senses condition the reception of messages in the communications act. Research done by Cobun (1968) indicated that:

1 per cent of what is learned is from the sense of TASTE.
1.5 per cent of what is learned is from the sense of TOUCH.
3.5 per cent of what is learned is from the sense of SMELL.
11 per cent of what is learned is from the sense of HEARING.
83 per cent of what is learned is from the sense of SIGHT.

Retention of what is learned is likewise related to sense experience.

Observation and research by Cobun tended to show, holding time as nearly constant as possible, that people generally remember:

10 percent of what they READ.
20 percent of what they HEAR.
30 percent of what they SEE.
50 per cent of what they HEAR AND SEE.
70 per cent of what they SAY.
90 per cent of what they SAY as they do a thing.

Popular Saying on Audio-visual Aids

I hear, I forget.
I see, I remember
I do, I understand

20.4 SIGNIFICANCE AND USES OF AUDIO-VISUAL AIDS

The basic assumption underlying audio-visual aids is that learning—clear understanding—stems from sense experience. The teacher must 'show' as well as 'tell'. Audio-visual aids provide significant gains in informational learning, retention and recall, thinking and reasoning, activity, interest, imagination, better assimilation and personal growth and development. The aids are the stimuli for learning 'why', 'how', 'when' and 'where'. The 'hard to understand principles' are usually made clear by the intelligent use of skilfully designed instructional aids.

According to *Gandhiji*, "True education of the intellect can only come through a proper exercise and training of bodily organs—hands, feet, eyes, ears, nose, etc.".

Commenting on the use of audio-visual aids, the Kothari Commission 1964-66 observed that it should indeed bring about an 'educational revolution' in the country. It further stated that the supply of teaching aids to every school was essential for the improvement of the quality of teaching.

The National Policy of Education, 1986 and as modified in 1992 has laid a great stress on the use of teaching aids especially improvised aids, to make teaching-learning more effective and realistic.

In the words of Edgar Dale, "Because audio-visual materials supply concrete basis for conceptual thinking, they give rise to meaningful concept enriched by meaningful association, hence they offer the best antidote for the disease of verbalism".

Some of the important values of the proper use of audio-visual aids are given below:

1. *Clear Images*: Clear images are formed when we see, hear, touch, taste and smell as our experiences are direct, concrete and more or less permanent. Learning through the senses becomes the most natural and consequently the easiest and effective.

2. *Retentivity*: Audio-visual aids contribute to increased retentivity as they stimulate response of the whole organism to the situation in which learning takes place.

3. *Helpful in Fixing up New Learning*: What is gained in terms of learning, needs to be fixed up in the minds of students. Audio-visual aids help in achieving this objective by providing several activities, experiences and stimuli to the learners.

4. *Helpful in Attracting Attention*: Attention is the true factor in any process of teaching and learning. Audio-visual aids help the teacher in providing proper environment for capturing as well as sustaining the attention and interest of the students in the classroom work.

5. *Based on Maxims of Teaching*: The use of audio-visual aids enables the teacher to follow the maxims of teaching like 'concrete to abstract', 'known to unknown' and 'learning by doing'.

6. *Best Motivators*: They are the best motivators. The students work with more interest and zeal. They are more attentive.

7. *Vicarious Experience*: It is beyond doubt that the first-hand experience is the best type of educative experience. But it is practicable not to provide such experiences to pupils. Substituted experiences may be provided under such conditions. There are many inaccessible objects and phenomena. For example, it is not possible for the pupils living in India to see the Eskimoe.

Similarly, it is not possible for an average man to climb the Mount Everest. There are innumerable such things to which it is not possible to have direct access. So, in all such cases, these aids help us.

8. *Variety*: 'Mere chalk and talk' do not help. Audio-visual aids give variety and provide different tools in the hands of the teacher.

9. *Freedom*: When audio-visual aids are employed, there is great scope for children to move about, talk, laugh and comment upon. Under such an atmosphere the students work because they want to work and not because the teacher wants them to work.

10. *Opportunities to Handle and Manipulate*: Many visual aids offer opportunities to students to handle and manipulate things.

11. *Antidote to the Disease of Verbal Instruction*: They help to reduce verbalism. They help in giving clear concepts and thus help to bring accuracy in learning. As observed by Raymond Wyman (1957), "We (teacher) tell students, and we provide them with written material so much of the time. Words are wonderful. They are easily produced, reproduced, stored and transported. But the overuse or excessive use of words can result in serious problem, chiefly, the problem of verbalism (using or adopting words or phrases without considering what they mean) and forgetting."

12. *Vividness*: Audio-visual aids give vividness to the learning situation. A film on Buddha provides a vivid picture of his life and teachings.

13. *Realism*: The use of audio-visual aids provides a touch of reality to the learning situation. By seeing a film show exhibiting the life of the people of the Tundra region, students learn it more effectively in about 2 hours than by spending weeks by reading.

14. *Saving of Energy and Time*: A good deal of energy and time of both the teachers and students can be saved on account of the use of audio-visual aids as most of the concepts and phenomena may be easily clarified, understood and assimilated through their use.

15. *Positive Environment for Creative Discipline*: A balanced rational and scientific use of audio-visual aids develops motivation, attracts the attention and interests of the students and provides a variety of creative outlets for the utilisation of their tremendous energy and thus keeps them busy in the classroom work. In this way, the overall classroom environment becomes conducive to creative discipline.

16. *Reinforcement to Learners*: Audio-visual aids prove effective reinforcers by increasing the probability of re-occurrence of the responses associated with them and thus render valuable help in the teaching-learning process.

17. *Positive Transfer of Learning and Training*: Use of audio-visual aids helps in the learning of other concepts, principles and solving the real problems of life by making possible the appropriate positive transfer of learning and training received in the classroom.

18. *Development of Higher Faculties*: Verbalism promotes memorisation. Use of audio-visual aids stirs the imagination, thinking process and reasoning power of the students, and calls for creativity, and inventiveness and other higher mental activities on the parts of students and thus helps the development of higher faculties among the students.

19. *Promotion of Scientific Temper*: In place of listening to facts, students observe demonstrations and phenomena and thus cultivate scientific temper.

20. *Spread of Education on a Mass Scale*: Audio-visual aids like radio and television help in providing opportunities for education to people living in remote areas. They also help in promoting adult education.

21. *Encouragement to Healthy Classroom Interaction*: Audio-visual aids, through their wide variety of stimuli, provision of active participation of the students, and vicarious experiences encourage healthy classroom interaction for the effective realisation of teaching-learning objectives.

22. *Meeting Individual Differences*: There are wide individual differences among learners. Some are ear-oriented, some can be helped through visual demonstrations, while others learn better by doing. The use of a variety of audio-visual aids helps in meeting the needs of different types of students.

20.5 CHARACTERISTICS OF GOOD TEACHING TECHNOLOGICAL AIDS

1. They should be meaningful and purposeful.
2. They should be accurate in every respect.
3. They should be simple.
4. They should be cheap.
5. As far as possible, they should be improvised, i.e., teacher made or locally made.
6. They should be large enough to be properly seen by the students for whom they are meant.
7. They should be up to date.
8. They should be easily portable.
9. They should be according to the mental level of the students.
10. They should motivate the learners.

20.6 PRINCIPLES IN THE USE OF TEACHING TECHNOLOGICAL AIDS

1. *Principle of Selection*: Teaching aids prove effective only when they suit the teaching objectives and unique characteristics of the special group of learners. Following points may be kept in view in this regard:

   (i) They should suit the age-level, grade-level and other characteristics of the learners.
   (ii) They should have specific educational value besides being interesting and motivating.
   (iii) The should be the true representatives of the real things.
   (iv) They should help in the realisation of desired learning objectives.

2. *Principle of Preparation*: This principle requires that following points should be attended to:

   (a) As for as possible, locally available material should be used in the preparation of an aid.
   (b) The teachers should receive some training in the preparation of aids.
   (c) The teachers themselves should prepare some of the aids.
   (d) Students may be associated in the preparation of aids.

3. *Principle of Physical Control*: This relates to the arrangement of keeping aids safely and also to facilitate their lending to the teachers for use.

4. *Principle of Proper Presentation*: This principle implies the following points:

(i) Teachers should carefully visualise the uses of teaching aids before their actual presentation.

(ii) They should fully acquaint themselves with the use and manipulation of the aids to be shown in the classroom.

(iii) Adequate care should be taken to handle an aid in such a way as no damage is done to it.

(iv) The aid should be displayed properly so that all the students are able to see it, observe it and derive maximum benefit out of it.

(v) As far as possible, distraction of all kinds should be eliminated so that full attention may be paid to the aid.

5. *Principle of Response*: This principle demands that the teachers guide the students to respond actively to the audio-visual stimuli so that they derive the maximum benefits in learning.

6. *Principle of Evaluation*: This principle stipulates that there should be continuous evaluation of both the audio-visual material and accompanying techniques in the light of the realisation of the desired objectives.

20.7 PROBLEMS IN THE USE OF TEACHING TECHNOLOGICAL AIDS

While all these aids are becoming more and more popular day by day, there are still some problems to be faced and solved. These are:

(i) *Apathy of the Teacher*: Teachers in general are yet to be convinced that teaching with words alone is very tedious, wasteful and ineffective.

(ii) *Indifference of Students*: The judicious use of aids arouses interest but when used without a definite purpose they lose their significance and importance.

(iii) *Ineffectiveness of the Aids*: Due to the absence of proper planning and the lethargy of the teacher and without proper preparation, correct presentation, appropriate application and discussion and the essential follow-up work, the aids do not prove their full usefulness. A film like a good lesson has various steps—Preparation, Presentation, Application and Discussion.

(iv) *Financial Hurdles*: The Central and State Governments have set-up Boards of Audio-Visual Education and have chalked out interesting programmes for the popularisation of teaching aids but the lack of finances is not enabling them to do their best.

(v) *Absence of Electricity*: Most of the projectors, Radio and T.V. cannot work without the electricity current which is not available in a large number of schools.

(vi) *Lack of Facilities for Training*: Training colleges or specialised agencies should make special provision to train teachers and workers in the use of these aids.

(vii) *Coordination between Centre and States*: Good film libraries, museums of audio-visual education, fixed and mobile exhibitions and educational 'melas' should be organised both by Centre and the States.

(viii) *Language Difficulty*: Most educational films are in English. We should have these in Hindi and other important Indian languages.

(ix) *Not Catering to Local Needs*: Little attention is paid in the production of audio-visual aids to the local factors.

(x) *Improper Selection of Films*: Films are not selected according to the classroom needs.

20.8 FUTURE OF THE USE OF TEACHING TECHNOLOGICAL AIDS

Today, the problem is not whether visual aids should have a place in education. Their place has been recognised long ago. The problem, now, is that of extending the benefits of these aids to all teachers and all children. The future can be bright if there is proper planning on the part of the Government and coordination between producers, teachers and students. Useful and effective aids can be produced after getting the reaction of the audience and doing research work in the field. A great deal is being done already but a lot more still remains to be doe.

20.9 CLASSIFICATION OF TEACHING AIDS

Classification Number 1: Projected and Non-Projected Aids

Projected Aids	*Non-Projected Aids*				
	Activity Aids	*Audio Aids*	*Dimensional Aids*	*Display Boards*	*Graphic Aids*
1. Films 2. Filmstrips 3. Opaque Projector 4. Overhead 5. Slides	1. Computer Assisted Instruction 2. Demonstrations 3. Dramatics 4. Experimentation 5. Field Trips 6. Programmed Instruction 7. Teaching Machines	1. Radio 2. Recordings 3. Television	1. Diagrams 2. Models 3. Mockups 4. Objects 5. Puppets 6. Specimens	1. Black-boards 2. Bulletin 3. Flannel Board 4. Magnetic Board 5. Peg Board	1. Cartoons 2. Charts 3. Comics 4. Diagrams 5. Flash Cards 6. Graph 7. Maps 8. Photo-graphs 9. Pictures 10. Posters

Classification Number 2: Audio Aids, Visual Aids, and Audio-Visual Aids

Audio Aids	*Visual Aids*	*Audio-Visual Aids*
1. Language laboratories 2. Radio 3. Sound distribution system sets 4. Tape and disco recordings.	1. Bulletin boards 2. Chalk boards 3. Charts 4. Drawings etc. 5. Exhibits 6. Film strips 7. Flash cards 8. Flannel boards 9. Flip books	1. Demonstrations 2. Films 3. Printed materials with recorded sound 4. Sound filmstrips 5. Study trips 6. Television 7. Video-tapes

(*Contd.*)

Audio Aids	*Visual Aids*	*Audio-Visual Aids*
	10. Illustrated books	
	11. Magnetic boards	
	12. Maps	
	13. Models	
	14. Pictures	
	15. Posters	
	16. Photographs	
	17. Self-instructional	
	18. Silent films	
	19. Slides	

Classification Number 3: Big Media and Little Media

Big Media	*Little Media*
1. Computer	1. Audio Cassette
2. VCR	2. Graphics
3. T.V.	3. Film Strips
	4. Radio
	5. Various Visuals

Classification Number 4: Three Dimensional Aids

1. Models 2. Mock-up 3. Specimens

Three dimensional aids are the replica or substitute of real objects.

21

Description and Preparation of Audio-Visual Aids

21.1 SIGNIFICANCE OF RADIO AS AN EDUCATIONAL AIDS

R.G. Reynolds has expressed the significance of radio as an aid in teaching in these words, "Radio is the most significant medium for education in its broadest sense that has been introduced since the turn of the century. As a supplement to classroom teaching its possibilities are almost unlimited. Its teaching possibilities are not confined to the five or six hours of the school day. It is available from early morning till long after midnight. By utilising the rich educational and cultural offerings of the radio, children and adults in communities, however, remote, have access to the best of the world's stores of knowledge and art. Some day its use as an educational instrument will be as common place as text-books and blackboards".

The potential of radio as an instructional aid is given by Frederic as, "I like to think of education by radio as a timely, vital and dramatic thing, a system of learning or acquiring more information, a means of widening one's horizon or enriching one's life and breaking down prejudices through inspiration and not perspiration; an education by desire and not by discipline; a pattern or swiftly changing pictures, events with keen interpretations, not statistics and formula's; a moving panorama of the world in which we live—right now, while we are living in it—not a dreary drill of text-books and tests. In short, I feel that one of broadcasting's most helpful contributions to education and one of its real responsibilities to itself and its listeners is the popularising of education itself."

Merits of School Broadcasting

1. Using for regular class teaching.
2. Enrichment of school programme.
3. Furnishing up-to-date material.
4. Developing critical thinking.
5. Providing information about population education, energy conservation, preservation of wild life etc.
6. Promoting emotional and national integration.
7. Popularising science with a view to developing scientific outlook.
8. Imparting vocational skills.
9. Providing opportunities for student participation.

10. Providing an alternative approach to the education of out of school children.
11. Developing leisure time interest and appreciation.
12. Helping in the spread of elementary education.
13. Bringing the school into contact with the world around.
14. Serving as a training component for teachers.
15. Helping in the promotion of adult education.
16. Assisting in the spread of non-formal education.

Limitations and Shortcomings

1. Radio broadcast is a one-way communication. Students cannot put questions to the broadcaster.
2. The educational value of radio broadcasting depends primarily on the use of sense of hearing.
3. The students have little opportunities to participate in the instructional activity. They are passive listeners for most of the time.
4. In several cases, broadcasting time does not suit all educational institutions.
5. The number of receiving sets is not adequate in the case of several educational institutions.
6. It becomes very difficult to integrate school programmes with radio broadcasts.
7. A continuing listening on the part of the students may make them inattentive and uninterested in the task of gaining learning experiences.
8. Usually there is paucity of adequate pre-information, manual or guides regarding radio broadcasts with the result that the students and teachers both face difficulties in making necessary preparation for the utilisation of these programmes.

Suggestions for Effective School Broadcasting Programmes

1. The school broadcasts should not be merely course lessons but should have a wider horizon of application in day-to-day life.
2. The school broadcasts should be planned according to the needs of the syllabus, students and concerned teachers.
3. Teachers should occasionally meet, discuss and plan the type of assistance required on mass media instructional facilities.
4. The radio programmes should be intended to give supplementary information to the various topics in the syllabus.
5. Good planning and administration is highly needed so as to make the programmes effective and worthwhile.
6. Broadcasting time should be suitable to schools.
7. Adequate feedback should be provided.
8. There should be proper follow-up on school broadcasting programmes.
9. Adequate listening facilities should be provided in schools.
10. Broadcasts should be made in easy and simple language.
11. Broadcasts should be made in a pleasing style.

In short all the six main stages of a radio broadcast, namely, production, preparation, listening to the programme, feedback, consolidation of acquired knowledge and evaluation should be carefully attended to.

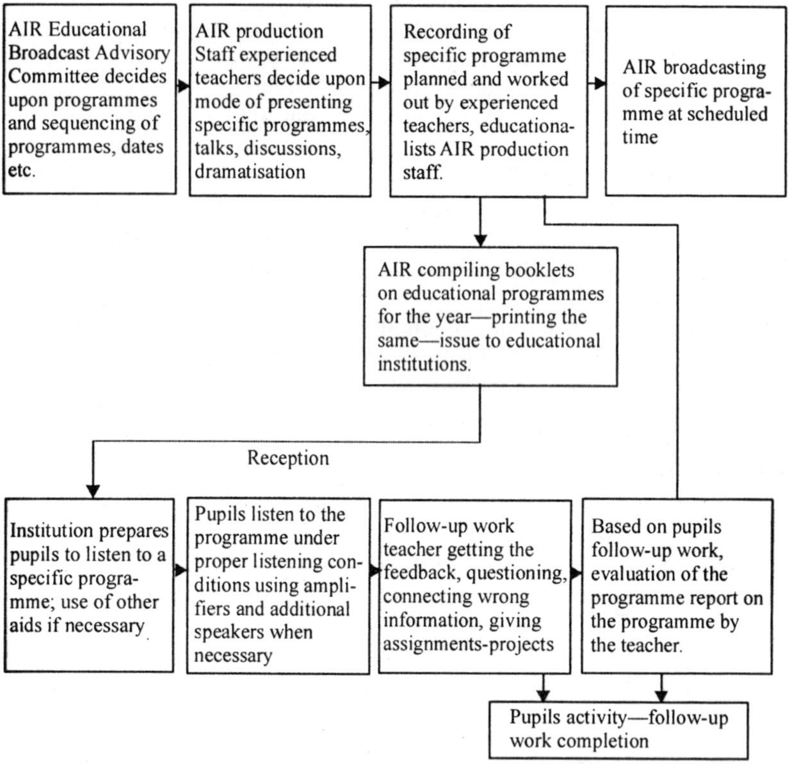

Fig. 21.1: Flow Chart of Educational Broadcast Programme in India

History of School Broadcasting

Ever since the start of school broadcasting by British Broadcasting Corporation (B.B.C.) in 1920, it has made rapid strides in making sound contribution to formal education. In the U.S.A., in 1923, there were programmes in accounting from New York; programmes in arithmetic and literature from Oakland in 1924; music appreciation lessons in 1925 from Cleveland By 1952, 20 States in U.S.A. had provision for educational broadcasting. Around the same time about 98% of the schools in U.K. were equipped with radio and there were regular daily programmes.

Bombay Station put out items of special interest to school children occasionally from January 1929. From April 30, the Corporation of Madras had regular school broadcasts for half an hour on all weekdays. Similar programmes were introduced by Calcutta Station in 1932.

The programmes for schools produced by Akashwani Stations are for the following categories of people:

(a) Children of primary classes; (b) Children of secondary and higher secondary classes; (c) Preparing lessons for secondary and higher secondary classes near examination time; (d) Teachers; (e) General enrichment programme for children.

21.2 TAPE RECORDER

A tape recorder is a portable electronic gadget to record, reproduce, erase and re-record sound on a magnetic tape (Figs. 21.2 and 21.3).

A tape recorder in its own can be very effective for classroom instruction. Pre-recorded tapes consisting of lessons by eminent teachers on any subject can be played in the class. Such instructions become impressive not only because of the novelty but also because of their being well-thought and planned.

The tape recorder has proved to be a boon in teaching foreign language like English. Pre-recorded tapes on English lessons can be played in the classroom to teach not only the contents of the lesson but also proper accent, pronunciation and intonation which an average English teacher very much lacks.

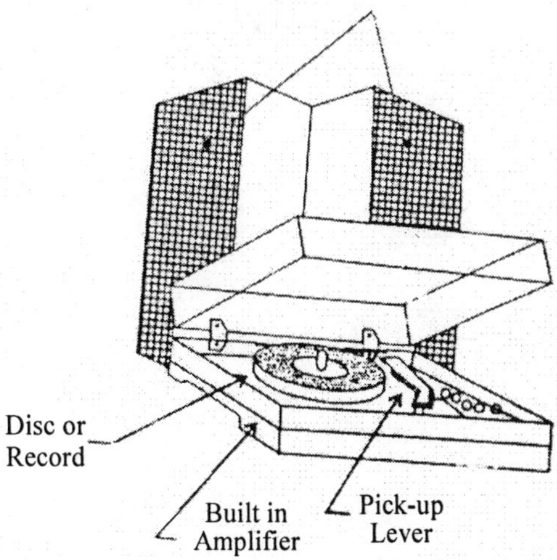

Fig. 21.2: Portable Tape Recorder

Examples of Matter for Tape Recording

(1)	(2)	(3)	(4)	(5)	(6)	(7)
Talks and Discussions	Historical documents	Literary products	Languages pronun- ciation etc.	Dramatics	Music performances	Interviews of great personalities

Educational Value of a Tape Recorder

The tape recorder as a teaching aid has the following advantages:

1. Tape recorder is the commonly available aid which is rather economical to use as recording can be erased and the tape reused.

2. Tape recorder, it being a common household equipment, is easy to operate as it has only a few controls.

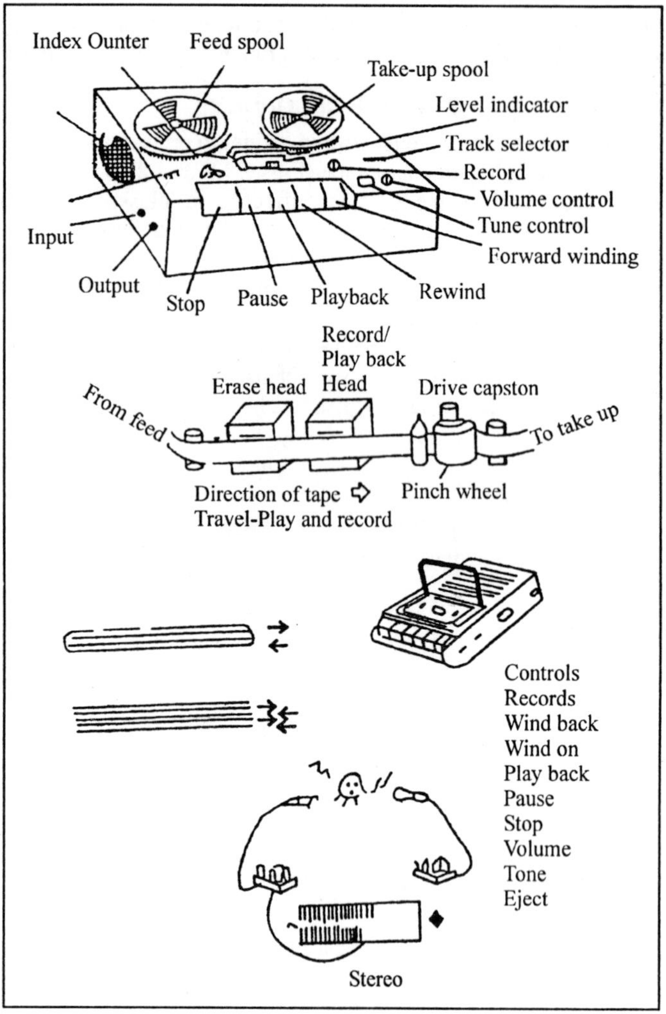

Fig. 21.3: Tape Recorder

3. Valuable recordings can be stored for re-use for mass instruction.

4. The speeches of well-known personalities can be recorded at a convenient place and brought to the school for replay to the students.

5. Tape recording provides flexibility for the teacher to edit and evaluate material.

6. On the spot events can be recorded and played at an appropriate time for classroom instruction.

7. Flexibility in use of tape recording provides the personal aspect of interest and convenience.

8. It is a fact that we want to listen to our own voice and this gives an added advantage of prompting children to participate in the learning programmes.

9. Being a kind of voice mirror, tape recorder can be used for improving spoken language and as a training or corrective tool for speech modulation and oral presentation of subject-matter.

10. Tape recording can make lesson enjoyable when used along with other visual aids.

11. Tape recorder is of immense value for teaching music, phonics, oral reading, poetry and recitation, etc.

12. Tape recording can be easily done from other sources like radio, television, movies etc. for use in the classroom.

13. The children may study and learn the sounds of different animals with a tape recorder. As each child is asked to imitate the sound of a goat, sheep, cow, hen, lion, etc. the teacher records the sound and tells the words specifying these sounds. This is a good exercise as for primary students. It combines learning with enjoyment.

14. The teacher records off-hand the voices of different children for a game of recognising students from their voices. After the game, correct pronunciation of generally mis-pronounced words can be taught through recordings.

15. A lesson in reading could be recorded and replayed for telling specific mistakes and their correction. Such a use of tape-recording creates a desire to improve on the part of student in areas of pausing, intonation, pronunciation etc.

16. Debates, discussions, seminars in history, economics, social sciences and sciences may be tape recorded for replaying them to review and evaluate.

17. Oral readings of students may be tape-recorded for criticism and remediation.

18. Dramatisation may be included in story telling and recitation through special background sound effects for arousing emotions.

A resourceful teacher can use a tape recorder in a variety of ways to make lessons inspirational, interesting and meaningful to children.

Suggestions for Using Tape Recorder Effectively

1. Choose a room with proper acoustics. A heavily curtained room in the school will be an ideal one. Special recording studies have the walls covered with sound absorbing materials like straw-boards.

2. Place the tape recorder on a steady table and insert the cassette. Plug in the power cord if the tape recorder is not to be run on the battery. Check the working of the tape recorder before recording the lesson.

3. Locate the microphone input socket and plug in the microphone. It is advisable to use external microphone placed 25 to 30 cm away from the person whose voice is recorded.

4. Press the record-button, speak into the microphone (do not blow in as it can damage the microphone), watch the sound level indicator or meter and appropriately adjust the volume control and tone control etc.

5. After testing and setting the tape recorder, rewind the cassette completely and the recorder on stop before actual recording.

6. Record the actual material spoken into the microphone by pressing the record and play buttons simultaneously.

7. After recording is over, rewind and play the tape recorder for editing, auditing and evaluation before it is used in the classroom.

Some Do's for Teachers in the Use of Tape Recorder

1. The teacher must practise the use of tape recorder to get familiar with various controls and techniques.
2. The teacher must prepare and practise tape recorded lessons before use in the classroom.
3. The teacher must prepare tape recorded material and catalogue it properly.
4. The teacher must record programmes from other sources such as radio programmes, T.V. programmes, performances in and out of the school etc.
5. The teacher must start a cassette library in his own subject area. He should use the tape recorder for speech training and corrective feedback.
6. The teacher should supplement tape recorder instruction by other teaching aids. For example, a story may be played back with the drawn pictures and diagrams illustrating various scenes.
7. The teacher should use the tape recorder for recording interviews, talks and discussions of experts.

21.3 VISUAL AIDS: OVERHEAD PROJECTOR, SLIDE PROJECTOR, MAPS, CHARTS, MODELS, FLASH CARDS, DISPLAY BOARD DIAGRAMS

Overhead Projector (OHP)

Overhead projector (Fig. 21.4) is a device that can project a chart, a diagram, a map, a table or for that matter, anything written on transparent plates, upon a screen or the white wall before students in a class. This makes teaching illuminative, illustrative and impressive. It also saves a great deal of the teacher time used in drawing or writing them. These transparencies can also be preserved by the teacher for future display while taking up the same topic. It is very simple to prepare such transparencies. All that a teacher has to do is to draw/or write, as the case may be, upon transparent plates with any dark ink with a fibre tipped pen. Any material meant for display before the class while teaching can also be typed on such transparencies using a good carbon paper. In case transparencies are to be washed out for use, washable water colour can also be used for writing on the transparencies.

Construction of an Overhead Projector

An overhead projector consists of a metal box with a 1000 watt bulb and a concave reflector. A condenser lens illuminates the transparency placed on the glass sheet on the top of the box. There is a vertical rod by the side of the box which carries an objective convex lens parallel to the transparency and plain mirror to reflect the image on the screen. The objective lens and mirror combination can be slided up and down the rod with rock and pinion arrangement operated by a knob. The movement of the objective lens and mirror focuses the image properly on the screen. There is also a small exhaust or cooling fan in the overhead projector to blow out the excess heat produced by the bulb.

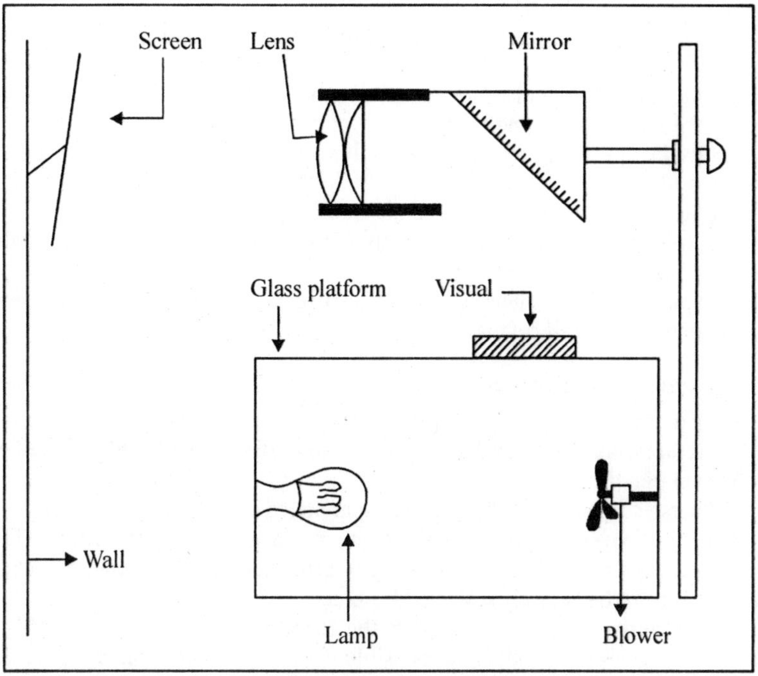

Fig. 21.4: Overhead Projector

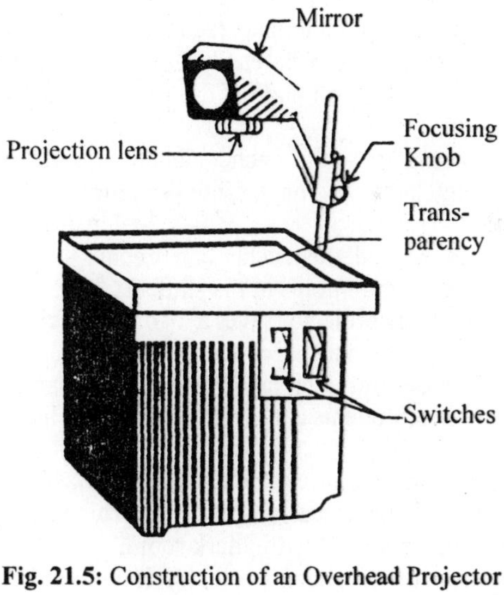

Fig. 21.5: Construction of an Overhead Projector

Operation of an Overhead Projector

While using an overhead projector, one should proceed in the following steps:

1. Place the overhead projector on a stable table with the objective lens facing the screen being the teacher.
2. Put the cord plug into a power wall-socket. Switch on the blower first and then the bulb.
3. Place the transparency on the glass top.
4. Move the objective lens and mirror assembly up and down to get the image in focus on the screen.
5. Explain about the material on the transparency sitting behind the overhead projector with a small pointer.

Advantages of an Overhead Projector

1. An overhead projector can project a large number of instructional material like diagrams, charts, maps, worksheets, graphs after those are transferred on the transparencies.
2. Its use can be quite cheap as transparencies can be used repeatedly.
3. In the overhead projector the teacher can write directly with a glass marking pencil and the writing is directly projected on the screen. After use the writing can be wiped off with cloth piece.
4. An overhead projector enables the teacher while facing the students keep an eye contact which is not possible with other projection equipments.
5. Unlike other projection equipment, it allow the teacher the psychological technique of progressive disclosure to build up his lesson in sequential learning.
6. An overhead projector can be used in a normally lighted room. The students can take down notes and the teacher facing the class can observe the student's reactions and strengthen his presentation.
7. An overhead projector can be easily used with other visual aids also without the fuss of switching on and off the room lights as in the case with other projection aids.
8. The verbal explanation of the teacher can be supported with illustrations as he can directly sketch the diagrams; write key points and main concepts on the transparency.
9. If an acetate roll is used, the teacher can prepare the whole study course beforehand and give accurate notes to his students.
10. The use of overhead projector saves a lot of teacher's time for utilisation for individual guidance and corrective feedback.
11. With the overhead projector, an enlarged image can be obtained with a less distance. Therefore, students can sit close to the teacher and this produces better rapport.
12. As an overhead projector can be used in the classroom, the difficulty of ventilation does not hamper teaching-learning which is the case with other projection equipments that are used in dark room.
13. The operation of overhead projector is convenient as it involves switching and focusing only.

Precautions to be Taken in the Use of an Overhead Projector

1. Cover the projector when it is not used so that no dust gets deposited on its lenses and bulb which will make image on screen dull.

2. Dust the projector before and after use and occasionally clean the lenses with soft tissue papers or flannel cloth available with the opticians.

3. Do not keep the bulb on for a long time as it can overheat the projector and damage the acetate transparencies as well as the bulb. Switch off the bulb after every 5 to 10 minutes of use of the projector keeping the blower on for some time.

4. Do not keep the overhead projector when the bulb is on as the filament of the bulb may break due to jerks during shifting.

5. Do not keep the overhead projector too low, as it will make the image distorted, i.e., image will get wider at the top and narrower at the bottom. This distortion is called 'keystoning'.

Slide Projector

With a slide projector photographic slides can be projected on the screen or on the wall before the class. Photographs of relevant matter meant for teaching in the class can be developed on celluloid slides and displayed with the help of such a projector. The teacher's lesson can also be recorded on an audio cassette and played with a tape recorder suitably synchronising with the slides by manipulating a remote control switch. Such an arrangement is called a tape-slide sequence. In case there are several slides to be shown in quick succession, the tape-slide sequence can bring as interesting an effect on the viewers as do the move films.

An ordinary slide projector has a frame containing two slits into which slides are put for focusing. They are manually and continuously replaced by other slides one after another.

An improved type of a slide projector (Fig. 21.6) consists of a circular disc with more slits where even a hundred or more slides can be inserted in a sequential order which can be projected on the screen with the help of a remote control switch to be suitable manipulated by the teacher as he delivers the lesson.

Maps

Significance of Map Study: In several subjects, especially social studies, the learning of many geographical, historical and economic concepts remains unreal, inadequate and incomplete without map media. A resourceful teacher by motivating the pupils will turn the fear of map into the genuine love for them. This, however, pre-supposes the invariable use of maps at every possible opportunity by the teacher in the classroom, and the possession of individual atlases by pupils. Every student should also know certain elementary aspects of map presentation, such as, copying, enlarging and reducing, symbolising, colouring, and preparation of key. Most of the students develop an aversion to maps because they do not know skills relating to maps preparation.

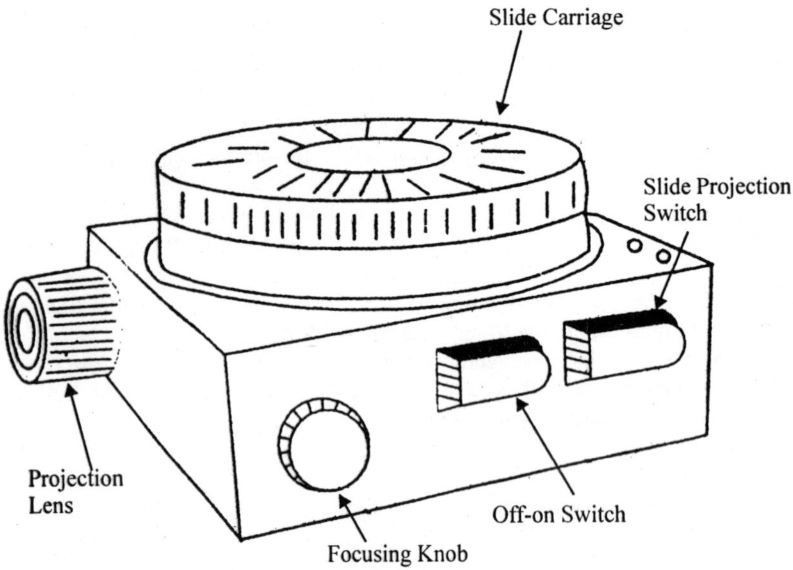

Fig. 21.6: Automatic Slide Projector

Meaning of Map: A map is an accurate representation plain surface in the form of a diagram drawn to scale, the details of boundaries of continents, countries etc. Geographical details like location of mountains, rivers, altitude of a place, contours of the earth surface and important locations can also be represented accurately with reference to a convenient scale with suitable colour scheme.

Identification of Various Aspects of Maps

1. Understanding and interpreting the key of index.
2. Understanding the lines—boundary lines, lines of communication, lines indicating the rivers, contours, meridians and parallels.
3. Understanding the colours, tints, shadows, symbols in a map or globe.
4. The top of every map is not north, but the direction of northern pole is north.
5. Distinction between the various types of maps such as relief, political, distribution maps, etc.

6 Understanding of the position of earth in the universe. Many students suffer from a notion that the earth leans in June towards Sun northwards and in December southwards and thus the seasons are formed. Earth never dances that way. The student shall understand that the inclination of earth is constant and the learning effect changes due to its rotation around the Sun.

Various Types of Maps

1. *Relief Maps* (*Regional and the World*): This requires the knowledge of colours, contours, symbols and the other connected ethics of map making.
2. *Historical Maps*: Maps in history reveals the changing times and the

growth and decline of various kingdoms. Knowledge of lines of boundaries and other symbols is necessary.

3. *Distribution Maps*: Generally, the student shall associate with the following types of distribution maps:

(1) Vegetation maps, (2) Population maps, (3) Economic maps, (4) Statistical maps, (5) Dot maps, (6) Pictorial maps, (7) Language, race and other human division maps, etc.

4. *Geographical Maps:* Colour maps, weather map, seismological map, archaeological maps, rainfall maps, geological maps, etc.

Charts

Meaning of Chart: A chart is a combination of pictorial, graphic, numerical or vertical material which presents a clear visual summary. The most commonly used types of charts include outline charts, tabular charts, flow charts and organisation charts. Other types of charts are technical diagrams and process diagrams. Flip charts and flow charts are also being used. Ready-made charts are available for use in teaching in almost all area in all subjects. But charts prepared by a teacher himself incorporating his own ideas and lines of approach of the specific topic are more useful.

Purposes of Charts: Charts serve the following purposes:

1. For showing relationship by means of facts, figures and statistics.
2. For presenting materials symbolically.
3. For summarising information.
4. For showing continuity in process.
5. For presenting abstract ideas in visual form.
6. For showing development of structure.
7. For creating problems and stimulating thinking.
8. For encouraging utilisation of other media of communication.
9. For motivating the students.

How to Use Charts Effectively

1. Teacher-made charts should be preferred.
2. Students should be involved in the preparation of charts.
3. Charts should be so large that every detail depicted should be visible to every pupil in the class wherever he is sitting.
4. Charts should display information only about one specific area in a subject.
5. A chart should not contain too much written material.
6. A chart should not contain too many details.
7. A chart should give a neat appearance.
8. When a chart is to be used in the classroom, the teacher should make sure that there is provision for hanging the chart at a vantage point.
9. The teacher should have a pointer to point out specific factors in the chart.
10. Straight pins, staples, pegboard, clips, gummed hangers, paper-clips, folded making tapes may all be used for fastening charts without damaging them.
11. Charts should be carefully stored and preserved for use in future.

Types of Charts

The following is a list of basic types of charts in terms of arrangements and the kinds of ideas which they may express:

1. *The narrative chart*, an extended left-to-right arrangement of facts and ideas for expressing: (a) the events in a process, such as, shoe making, oil cracking, or the like, (b) the events in the development of a significant issue to its point of resolution or to present status (sometimes a time limit). Example: the events leading to the separation of the Bangladesh from Pakistan, the events leading to the establishment of the idea that an individual should be free and that he should have a voice in his own government and the events leading to increased regulation of business by government, (c) technological improvement over a period of years such as improvement in transportation, communication, manufacturing, etc.

2. *The tabulation chart*, a left-to-right, top-to-bottom arrangement of facts and ideas for expression: (a) numerical data for making comparisons, (b) lists of products, mountains, rivers, or the like in selected areas.

3. *The cause and effect chart*, usually a limited left-to-right arrangement of facts and ideas for expressing: (a) relationship between standard of living and such factors as economic system, availability of natural resources, level of technological advancement, (b) relationship between a culture and neighbouring cultures, (c) relationship between rights and responsibilities, (d) relationship between a complex of conditions and change or conflict, (e) relationship between the elected and the electors, (f) relationship between community workers and the community which supports them.

4. *The chain charts,* a circular or semicircular arrangement of facts and ideas for expressing: (a) transitions, such as, the transitions from raw materials to useful products, (b) cycles, such as the water cycle.

5. *The evolution chart*, a left-to-right arrangement of facts and ideas for expressing: (a) changes in specific items from beginning to data, perhaps with projections into the future. Example: origin of the automobile and its subsequent development, early basic homes and changes in basic homes to date, (b) change in standard in food consumption, length of work, weak purchasing power of rupee or the like.

(Adapted from *Social Instruction in the Secondary School* by Richard E. Servey)

21.4 THREE DIMENSIONAL AIDS

Three dimensional aids serve as good substitutes for the real objects. There is no doubt that an encounter with real objects serves as an unmatchable source of learning. But on account of several reasons it may not be possible to bring the real objects in the classroom. The real objects may be too large to move or store in the classroom. It may be too small to be seen for a group of students. It can be too complicated in real form to be understood. Its movements may be too slow to be studied completely. It can be too expensive to be purchased by an educational institution. Being handicapped in such situations a teacher has to search for some good substitute for the real objects.

Models diagrams, mock-ups and specimens are the important three dimensional aids.

Models: Models are the replicas or copies of the real objects. Models are usually of three types: solid, cross-sectional and working. Models are concrete objects, some considerably larger than the real object. Sectional models explain clearly the structure or functions of the original. In some cases working models of the original are used where the specific function of the original is duplicated and could be explained easily.

Following are the important functions of models:

1 Models simplify reality.

2. Models concretise abstract concepts.

3. Models enable us to reduce or enlarge objects to an observable size.

4. A model provides the correct concept of an industrial unit or a bridge or a dam like, the Bhakra Dam etc.

5. A working model explains the various processes of objects and machines.

6. Preparation of models could form a topic for project work. This is very helpful to create interest in creative activity in pupils.

Cardboard, plastic, plaster of paris, wood thermocole, and metal etc. can be used in the preparation of a model.

Mock-ups: A mock-up refers to a specialised model or working replica of the object being depicted. In a mock-up, a certain element of the original reality is emphasised or highlighted to make it more meaningful for the purpose of instruction. While a model is recognisable limitation of an object (though larger or smaller that the original one), a mock-up may or may not be similar in appearance. Mock-ups of aeroplanes, automobile engines, bridges, ships and tunnels, etc. may be demonstrated for explaining their structure and actual working. Mock-ups are often used in technical institutions for training purposes.

Dioramas: A diorama is a three -dimensional scene in depth incorporating a group of modelled objects and figures in a natural setting. The diorama scene is set-up on a small stages with a group of modelled objects kept, on the foreground which is blended into a painted realistic background. Dioramas are very effective in the teaching of biological and social sciences.

21.5 FLASH CARDS

Meaning of Flash Cards

Flash cards are small cards of generally 25 cm × 30 cm size which are shown for a few minutes to the class to send across some message or to impart an idea. The message is written on the flash card.

Preparing a Flash Card

A simple type of flash card may be prepared by cutting a foolscap chart sheet and cutting it into four equal parts to get the flash card, the message or idea to be conveyed may be written either in the free hand or using lettering stencils and sketch pen. The height of writing on the flash card may be approximately 5 cm so that the entire class could see the flash cards properly.

It is advisable to make a rough card on the ordinary paper first and then transfer it on the chart paper or cardboard flash card.

Type of Lettering on the Flash Card

(1)	(2)	(3)	(4)	(5)	(6)
Written or script form	Free hand printing	Commercial printing	Printing by stencil	Stencil cutout letters	Rubber stamp sets

Some Guidelines for Preparing Flash Cards

1. First make a rough draft on ordinary paper.
2. Rule guidelines.
3. Layout blocks for each letter.
4. Draw lines lightly with pencils.
5. Trace with ink or crayon.
6. Use speedball pen with a thick point.
7. Use dark colours. Black and red are the most affective colours.
8. Use tracing paper to place more intricate material on flash cards.

Advantages for Using Flash Cards

1. Flash cards can be used for introducing a topic.
2. Flash cards can be used to review a topic.
3. Flash cards can be used for drill and practice in learning alphabets and numbers etc.
4. Flash cards can be used for developing the cognitive abilities of recognition and recall of students.
5. A series of flash cards can be used for playing educational games. This introduces an element of fun in learning.
6. Flash cards can serve as supplementary aid and can be effectively used with other aids.

Guidelines for Using Flash Cards Effectively

1. Before the use of flash cards a brief introduction about it may be given to students.
2. Flash card should be held high with both hands so that all the students can see it.
3. Sufficient time should be given to students to see the flash cards.
4. Responses of the students may be secured as per instructions already given.
5. Lesson may be reviewed by using flash cards selectively.

21.6 DISPLAY BOARDS

Display boards include bulletin board, flannel board, plastic graph board, magnetic board and pegboard.

Bulletin Board: A bulletin board commends itself as a valuable source of information for vitalising our day-to-day practical activities and aspects of modern life. News items of current importance can be put up along with other facts of importance like market trends.

Flannel Board: It is a rectangular board with flannel stretched over. Displays made of thin cardboard with coarse sand paper pasted in back may be shown on the flannel and changed with the progress of the lesson.

Plastic Graph Board: It is any smooth polished surface like plate glass rigid plastic sheet or laminated plastic sheet etc. with display material made of thin flexible sheets of different colours cut to required contours.

Magnetic Board: It is a thin mild steel sheet kept flat over a thin rigid wooden plank. Display are cut-outs made with cardboard or thin plastic sheets to the back of which are attached thin ceramic magnets.

Pegboard: It is a perforated painted hard board. Displays could be positioned at desired points by pegs.

21.7 DIAGRAMS

Diagrams are very helpful in supplementing vertical illustrations in teaching. Difficult operations may be explained with the help of diagrams. The parts of flower or leaf can be suitably explained by means of sketches drawn by the teachers in front of the class on the blackboard. Simple diagrams can be used to explain different phenomena in geography and science. The diagrams of battle plans and forts can be drawn on the blackboard. The area and volume etc. in mathematics can be illustrated through diagrams.

A teacher is expected to possess the skill of drawing diagrams easily, neatly, rapidly and readily on the blackboard.

21.8 AUDIO-VISUAL AIDS: TELEVISION

Significance of Educational Television (ETV)

Television is the most potential instrument in educating masses and thereby narrowing down the gap of progress between the developing and developed countries of the world. For a country like India which has vast and inaccessible areas, different climatic conditions, large and ever growing population, T.V. can be an important central media in providing functional, formal and non-formal education to the masses. It can also help in bringing about social and cultural changes bearing on art, music, drama and literature. It is through television that stimulating and thought-provoking views of renowned statesmen, scientists, artists and teachers can be shared by all. Television helps in enforcing the public understanding of social; political and scientific advancement of a country.

Brief History of ETV

The electronic age has come too fast and gone too far. T.V. has become child's third parent and a first teacher. The history of television shows that it is a very powerful, informative, socialising and mobilising force. Most of the countries of the world have gone for television to solve their difficulties and problems relating to education. Direct television instruction started decades back in progressive countries like U.K. and U.S.A. The regular programmes were sent on air in November 1936 by BBC. Remote areas were provided with television sets. By 1958 more than 98% of the population was covered by television transmission. By 1961 Moscow and U.K. shared the programmes with each other. By 1962 American Engineers, succeeded in bouncing television waves across the Atlantic on a Satellite-Telestor. In 1967 the first regular service of coloured television in Europe began on BBC-2.

For the first time, television for instructional purposes was used in the U.S.A. A large number of experiments in instructional television were conducted there. In 1958, a project entitled continental classroom started instructional television for the whole of U.S.A. It telecasted a programme 'Physics of the Atomic Age' for science teachers. About 40,000 teachers received instruction through this programme. Later on, several programmes such as modern chemistry, contemporary mathematics and new biology were also telecast by this project. In 1961, a project called "Mid-west Airborne Instructional Television" started instructional television. About 13,000 schools received the programmes benefiting about five million students, a cost of 7.5 million dollars or at an expenditure of 1.5 dollar per student. At present there are hundreds of instructional television programmes being telecast in U.S.A. and other countries.

Chief Merits of Educational Television

1. It permits the use of the best available teacher to teach a subject for a large number of student viewers. It preserves the expert teaching skills of such teachers on video tape or film for later use.
2. It provides a common experience to all students when they all see the same basic ideas or techniques on television.
3. It provides the teacher an opportunity to observe the instructional methods and ideas of their experts and to increase his own knowledge of teaching methods and stimulate new ideas.
4. It provides technical advantages not readily available in normal classrooms for illustration or demonstration.
   (a) It makes possible close-up magnification of small objects, components, intricate mechanisms, meters, diagrams, etc. giving student a "front-row seat".
   (b) It allows instantaneous change of perspection by switching from a wide camera angle to a close-up or by "zooming" in.
   (c) It permits relationships between two illustrations or time-lapse between two stages of a process by dissolving one picture into another.
   (d) It provides for comparison of two or more illustrations by superimposure or "split screen" effects.
5. It directs the attention of the student to the exact detail of object which he should see by eliminating distracting surrounding.
6. It makes quick and lasting visual and oral impressions which can often reduce the time necessary to teach an idea or technique.
7. It makes it possible to bring large, scarce, new or confined equipment "into the classroom" electronically.

8. It incorporates useful film sequences, slides, graphic art and makes available teaching aids within a television presentation, tailored to meet the needs of a particular course or subject.

9. It saves time, effort and cost of setting up classroom projection equipment.

10. It brings instructional films into classrooms as needed with no special classroom preparation, no darkening of rooms or use of special ventilation in the room.

11. It provides more "immediacy" than instructional films.

12. It brings live demonstrations, video-tape or film presentations to the classroom at the instant or immediately after they occur.

13. It permits inclusion of up-to-date information, modifications, new equipment or techniques into the classroom instruction.

14. It allows the teacher time to observe individual students or to assist them during the television presentation, or to determine what needs further application after the presentation.

Limitations and Shortcomings of ETV

1. The medium is limited to one-way communication from teacher to student.

2. The total cost of teaching by television is more than normal classroom instruction, unless television is used to reach large number of students at one time or sequentially over a period of time.

3. Television has special and unique techniques and requires occasional re-arrangement of subject sequence.

4. Individual differences of the students are not attended to in a T.V. lesson.

5. T.V. lessons may not suit the school timings.

6. T.V. lessons are not flexible.

7. Instruction through T.V. is not child or learner centred.

Kinds of Educational T.V. Programmes

1. Total T.V. teaching.
2. T.V. as a complementary basic resources.
3. T.V. as a supplementary environment.

Kinds of Educational T.V.

1. *Open Circuit Television*: It is the usual type of telecast by commercial or non-commercial stations.

2. *Closed Circuit Television* (*CCTV*): It is the selective telecast which can be used only by specially equipped receivers. Its range is limited to the length of the cable. CCTV can be used to great advantage in educational institutions. Its capabilities are as under:

- (i) It increases the range of instruction to one or more locations beyond the classroom.
- (ii) It enables institutions to present televised instruction in accordance with their specific needs and schedules.
- (iii) It provides opportunities for the exchange of professors and courses between one institution and another linked to a circuit.

(iv) In teacher training institutions CCTV with video-tape recorders can be used to record performance of the teacher trainee during micro-teaching lessons. Video-tape provides the necessary feedback.

(v) CCTV is used in many medical colleges in developed countries. The entire operation can be covered by using a single television camera or a battery of cameras located at vantage points.

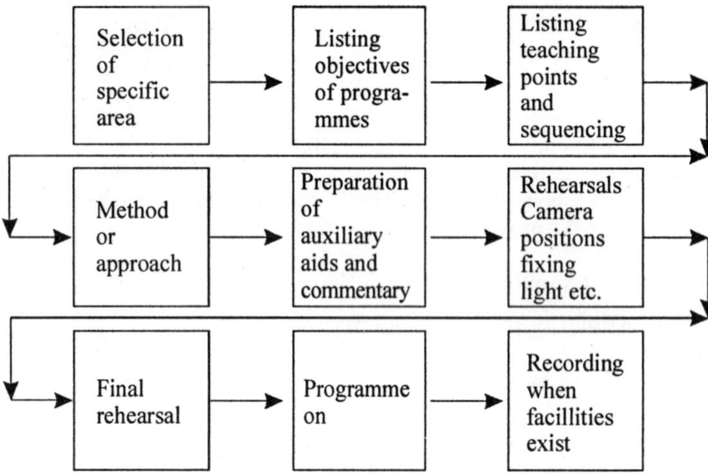

Fig. 21.7: Basic Procedures in Programming ETV

School T.V. programmes have five main stages and it is necessary that the teacher should be associated with each stage.

1. Planning and Preparation.
2. Presentation.
3. Production.
4. Utilisation.
5. Evaluation.

1. *Teacher in the Planning and Preparation of T.V. Programmes*: No T.V. programme for schools can be planned and prepared unless the classroom teacher is effectively associated with this work. To plan and prepare a good T.V. lesson, a thorough knowledge of the requirements of the students of different age levels, the suitability of the materials, the sequence and the contents are very vital and this can be met fully only by the classroom teacher. Experience tells that the classroom teacher can contribute effectively in this area if he has a good grounding and knows very well the mechanics of a good T.V. lessons.

2. *Teacher in the Production of T.V. Programmes*: Production is a technical thing but the knowledge about the mechanics of production must be known to the classroom teacher if he is to appreciate a good lesson, i.e., to locate its strong and weak points and suggest improvements.

3. *Teacher in the Presentation of T.V. Programme*: Again, in the presentation of a T.V. lesson it is only the classroom teacher who can deliver the goods—no doubt a teacher with initiative, imagination and subject competency.

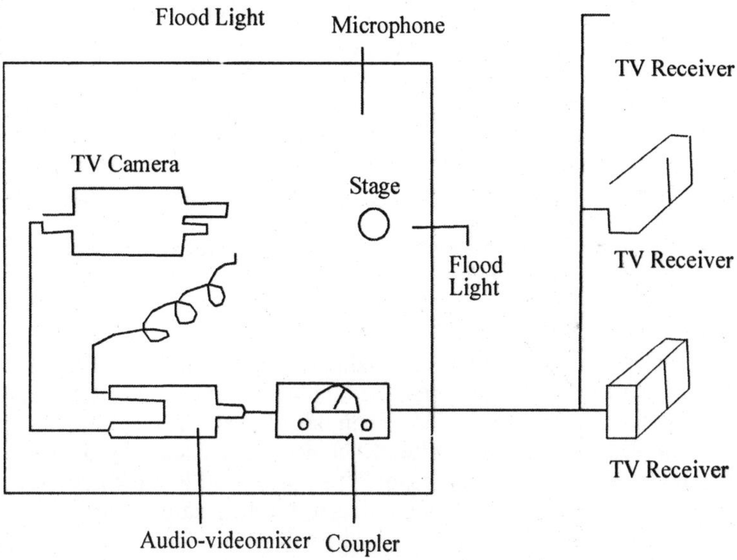

Fig. 21.8: Simple Closed Circuit T.V. System

The presentation involves only a selected number of teachers but the scope of selection involves all the teachers of a subject. A good selection can be possible only from a T.V. trained group. It is noted that without necessary training in this field even a very good and competent teacher in a school fumbles and stumbles in the studio.

4. *Utilisation of T.V. Programme and the Teacher: Pre-telecast Post-telecast:* Utilisation is the area where the teacher is the master of the situation. It may be emphasised that no T.V. lesson is complete without the introduction and follow-up exercises in the classroom by the subject teacher. An average lesson with proper and well-thought of introduction and follow-up can become a very effective lesson whereas a good lesson in the absence of one or both can go flat. The teacher has to inspire the students, prepare them and arouse their curiosity before the telecast of the lesson and afterwards has to clarify the doubts, if any, provide the missing links and reinforcement in the follow-up. He has also to integrate the T.V. lesson with his classroom teaching. He has also to take care of many other factors and provide congenial conditions to enable his students to really benefit from a T.V. lesson.

5. *Teacher in the Evaluation of T.V. Programme*: Evaluation is another important area. If tacked properly, it contributes considerably to the quality and usefulness of T.V. lessons. No evaluation is possible or worthwhile without the involvement of the classroom teacher. Moreover, simply involvement of the classroom teacher does not help much unless he is fully conversant and properly trained to evaluate and assess the T.V. lesson from all angles and has acquired competency to do the job well. Without proper training the teachers even fail to fill up the check-sheets properly—an exercise to be completed by the classroom teacher after every lesson.

Physical Facilities Needed for Effective Television Education

Once the television becomes an integral part of classroom teaching, the physical facilities available in the schools are as important as the quality of the programme, from the utilisation point of view. No matter how rich and valid the T.V. programmes are, they cannot reach the audience unless optimum physical facilities are available to the viewers. The availability of physical facilities appears to be quite simple yet it requires a constant vigil to keep them all in operational readiness.

Broadly speaking we can classify the physical facilities into three categories.

(a) Space and seating arrangements.
(b) T.V. sets, Antenna and other accessories.
(c) Literature.

(a) In each T.V. viewing school suitable space area must be earmarked for television viewing depending upon the number of viewers. Ideally speaking each class that has to view a T.V. lesson, should have T.V. set, fitted in the classroom itself but it is not possible. Therefore provision of a room, which can be converted into T.V. room should be made. Hall is another alternative for large number of viewers. Other points to be taken care of are:

(i) Placement of T.V. set and its adjustment.
(ii) Seating arrangement.
(iii) Lighting.
(iv) Ventilation.
(v) Space for demonstration, pre-telecast and post-telecast activities.

(b) It is needless to say that the T.V. sets should always be in operational condition so that these can be switched on at a very short notice. The various factors that put operating off are:

(i) Defective power points and plugs.
(ii) Defective Antenna.
(iii) Mis-adjustment of T.V. controls.
(iv) Major defect in the T.V.
(v) Voltage fluctuations.
(vi) Operational procedures like locked cupboards etc.

(c) The school television programmes by and large are syllabus based programmes and therefore the students must know the connecting links between their classroom teaching and the television programmes. These should reach the classroom teacher in the beginning of the session or term as the case may be.

Brief History of Television Education in India

The School T.V. Project was launched in Delhi by AIR on 2nd October 1961, with the collaboration of Directorate of Education, Delhi and the Ford Foundation of the U.S.A. Taking into consideration the specific needs and various other aspects, STY Project was introduced in Delhi Schools with the T.V. lesson, integrated with the school syllabus. To start with the project started in 140 schools with 360 sets, covering about 29,000 students. Today more than 4 lakhs students are viewing the programmes in more than 600 middle and secondary schools using about 900 T.V. sets.

To meet the requirements of the expansion of the project and the increased coverage, a separate T.V. Branch was created in the Directorate of Education in 1976. The main assignments of the T.V. Branch are:

1. to provide liaison between the Department of Education and Doordarshan Kendra formerly AIR.
2. to supervise and organise work pertaining to planning, preparation, utilisation and evaluation of the T.V. lessons.
3. to orient the classroom teachers to use educational T.V. effectively and also to supply and maintain T.V. sets in schools.

Changes in subjects and programmes have been taking place according to the needs.

The Satellite Instructional Television Programme

The Satellite Instructional Television Experiments (SITE) was a large scale experiment conducted by Government of India in the use of satellite for instructional purpose. During August 1, 1975 and July 30, 1976 the Indian Space Research Organisation jointly with Doordarshan, the Indian Television authority, broadcast instructional television programmes through a satellite. The Satellite—Applications Technology Satellite (ATS-F) was made available to India by United States National Aeronautics and Space Administration under a Memorandum of Understanding signed by India and the United States.

The responsibilities for the entire ground segment including the television programmers was that of India. The experiment was designed to expose people of far-flung rural areas particularly those poorly served by other means of communication to educational television programmes. The Experiment covered 2,400 villages in six States of India. The daily broadcast time of four hours was divided between primary school children in the morning and general audiences in the evening.

The SITE covered Andhra Pradesh, Bihar, Karnataka, Madhya Pradesh, Orissa, and Rajasthan. The SITE programmers were expected to transform rural communities by educating them about various socio-economic schemes and enlarging the base of people's involvement in development plans.

The programmes telecast for adult viewers were of three types: (i) news relating to the incidents of national importance, (ii) instruction-oriented programmes or dissemination of up-to-date knowledge relating to improved practice in agriculture, health, hygiene, family planning, nutrition, and (iii) some recreational programme interspersed with instructional ores.

INSAT (Indian National Satellite)

With the coming into operation of INSAT in 1983, live television programmes are available simultaneously in all parts of country. A microwave network has been installed throughout the country to relay television programmes.

The overall contribution of INSAT programmes expected to be instrumental in identifying the areas which could be developed faster by making people sufficiently receptive to new ideas and technologies evolved for rural development and increasing agricultural production.

Gyan Darshan

Gyan Darshan is being run as a T.V. cooperative between IGNOU, UGC, CIET-NCERT, NOS, IIT-Delhi. Technical Teachers Training Institute, National Literacy Missions etc. Launched as a joint venture between Prasar Bharti and IGNOU its unprecedented success has laid to rest earlier apprehensions that they would probably not be able to produce good quality T.V. software to run a 24-hours dedicated channel on education. Today, Gyan Darshan is beaming 23-hours of Indian software which 12 hours are curriculum based and the rest cover topics, such as, health, AIDS awareness, energy crisis, environment etc. They also give a 3-hour DD National hook up from 5.45 a.m. to 7 a.m. and from 9.30 a.m. to 11 a.m.

21.9 EDUCATIONAL FILMS

Significance of Educational Films

An educational film has been described as a teacher of great significance because it teaches through the whole body. The main aim of educational films is to elevate and educate them according to the patterns and principles set by the society. A good educational film should help the students to develop a sense of citizenship. A film on national integration can be prepared to help inculcate ideas of oneness and unity. 'Live and Let Live' can be the theme. A variety of topics—historical, biographical and of current interest can be covered.

Broadly speaking, a film is a multiple media of communication. It presents facts in a realistic way, dramatises human relations, arouses emotions and transmits attitudes. It may be used for the communication of ideas, attitudes and experiences to the masses of people. It is very effective in adult education. It has a very powerful influence on the minds of children and in shaping their personality.

Uses of Educational Films

Some of the main advantages of motion pictures are given below:

1. *Real Learning Situations*: The film puts before us the learning situations which look to the quite real and actual. The child sees something happening and his experience is direct. Therefore, he is deeply impressed.

2. *Increased Reading Interests of the Students*: Various investigations conducted in U.S.A. show that film producers arouse increased reading interest in children. They are stimulated to get more information about the fact they have observed in a film show.

3. *Motivation*: The film motivates teaching. The child takes a great interest. A long study of many weeks may not be able to bring home the facts of the French Revolution to a child but he will at once understand and learn everything about the movement if he is shown a film of the events.

4. *Quickness of Movement*: The events in a film show run very swiftly but without losing continuity and essence of development. Therefore, the effects are also received swiftly in a concentrated form.

5. *Vividness*: The learning situation is quite vivid. Everything is happening in such a way as if it is more than living and actual. All the activities are quite vivid.

6. *Selected Learning Situations*: A child learn from his actual life experience more than he learns from the lessons which he gets passively in the school. But life experience comes as a routine. Sometimes it has no educative value. Sometimes it may have adverse influence. But in an educational film, all the learning situations are selected ones. They have a great educational value.

7. *Recreation*: A film shown is recreational also. It is a play for the child and not work. Thus he learns through play-way. He feels light and happy after the show.

8. *Development of Study Habits*: Educational films develop study habits as children like to know more about the facts they have learnt in the show.

9. *Illustration of all the Learning Situations*: We cannot give an adequate idea of an ocean to a child who has never seen a lake even. A child cannot understand what a mountain is like if he has never come across a hill even in his life. But it is not possible for us to take every child to the ocean and mountains, to the deserts and valleys, to the Tundras and the Tropics. The film serves us here wonderfully. It brings the ocean, the mountains, the deserts, the valleys, the Tundras and the Tropics, all in their form and with all their grandeur into the school hall.

Charles F. Hoban and *E.B. Ormer* summarise the educational advantages of films as: means of imparting information, development of skills, development of attitudes, enlarging interests and development of the will to solve problems.

Limitations

1. Educational films sometimes include an element of fiction in historical events.
2. Recapitulation is not possible on the spot. Sometimes the teacher likes and the pupils too wish to dwell longer on a particular shot in the show. But the film does not wait. It goes on.
3. Really good educational films are not available in our country.
4. The whole process is very costly. All the schools cannot afford to have good halls, the projectors and other equipment for the purpose.
5. It may have some bad effect on eyesight.
6. Generally teachers are not trained to handle the projector and organise the show.
7. It needs electricity. Many village schools have no electricity.

Suggestions for Making the Optimum Use of Educational Films

The most important point to be taken into consideration is that the film must be relevant and purposeful.

When a film show is going to be arranged, the teacher should see that it is really needed in connection with the studies which are going on. He must discuss the background of the learning situations to be presented in the film show, previous to presentation. It should serve the purpose of recapitulation. The whole process may be arranged in the following steps:

1. Preliminary talk about the film.
2. Presentation of the film.
3. Discussion and follow-up on the film.
4. Recapitulation and recording of salient features.

Children's Film Society

The Children's Film Society India (CFSI) was established in 1955 as an autonomous body with the objectives of promoting and encouraging the Children Film Movement in the country. It also aims at providing children and the young people, films with clean and healthy entertainment. The organisation is engaged in production, acquisition, distribution and exhibition of the films suitable for the children and young people. The main office of the Society is at Mumbai and Zonal offices are at New Delhi, Chennai and Kolkata.

The society has set-up a National Centre of Films for Children affiliated to the International Centre of Films set-up at Brussels under the sponsorship of UNESCO. Some of the important films a teacher can make use are:

(1) Scout Camp,
(2) Guru Bhakti,
(3) Ganga Ki Lahren,
(4) Bachon se Batten,
(5) Gulab Ka Phool,
(6) Ekata,
(7) 26 January,
(8) Chaar Dost,
(9) Jaldeep

Important Sources of Educational Films

These sources are:

1. Children's Film Society, New Delhi

2. Central Film Library, National Institute of Audio-Visual Education, Indraprastha Estate, New Delhi

3. British Council in India, Rafi Marg, New Delhi

4. Burmah Shell Film Library, New Delhi

5. Ministry of Information and Broadcasting, Parliament Street, New Delhi

6. Indian National Commission for Cooperation with UNESCO, Ministry of Education, Government of India, Shastri Bhavan, New Delhi

7. United Information Centre, New Delhi.

21.10 EDGAR DALE'S CONE OF EXPERIENCE

Edgar Dale, the chief exponent of audio-visual aids in teaching is the originator of the 'Cone of Experience'. The diagram appears in his book *Audio-Visual Methods in Teaching* (1964).

All the learning experiences which can be utilised for classroom teaching are shown by Edgar Dale in a pictorial device—'pinnacle form'—which he called the 'Cone of Experience'. If we go up the pinnacle from its base, we find that every aid has been arranged in the order of increasing abstractness or decreasing directness. In a simple language, it may be stated that the 'cone' classifies the audio-visual aids according to their effectiveness in communication—aid at the base of the cone as 'most effective'—relative effect gradually decreases.

At the pinnacle of the 'Cone', the direct, purposeful experiences are represented. At the pinnacle of the 'Cone', the verbal symbols are represented.

Audio-Visual Experiences Shown in the Cone

The experiences included in the Cone are as indicated below:

1. *Direct, Purposeful Experiences*: The experiences gained through the senses are direct and purposeful. It has been amply observed, "An ounce of experience is better than a tonne of theory, simply because it is only as an experience that any theory has vital and verifiable significance." This, direct experience is gained through the aids mentioned at the base of the cone.

2. *Contrived Experience*: When the real thing cannot be perceived directly, its simplification becomes necessary. Contrived experience is like a working model which is an editing of reality and differs from the original either in size or in complexity. The real object may be too small or too big, may be confused or concealed. In such a situation, limitation is preferred for better and easier understanding.

3. *Dramatic Participation*: In dramatics, certain real events are presented through the play, the pageant (kind of community drama, usually based on local history), pantomine (actors do not speak, make movements) tableau (pictureline scene in which all the characteristics stand still, silently), and the puppets.

4. *Demonstration*: The teacher demonstrates or shows how things can be done. Examples: (i) shows by an experiment that the air exerts pressure, (ii) shows how to pronounce a word, (iii) shows how to draw a map.

5. *Field Trips*: The teacher takes students to visit business, industrial and historical places, etc.

6. *Exhibits*: Examples are: playing objects and models, etc.

7. *Motion Pictures*: Examples are: (i) Doordarshan programmes on various educational programmes, (ii) NCERT's programmes, UGC's and Indira Gandhi National Open University's several programmes, (iii) Documentary films shown on theatres.

8. *Radio Recordings and Still Pictures*: These provide visual experiences through slides and audio-experiences through radio-set, tapes and discs.

9. *Visual Symbols*: These include using cartoons, charts, diagrams, maps, etc.

10. *Verbal Symbols*: Verbal symbols constitute the most abstract learning experiences. Examples are: Verbal discourses, lecturing, land reading, recitation, etc.

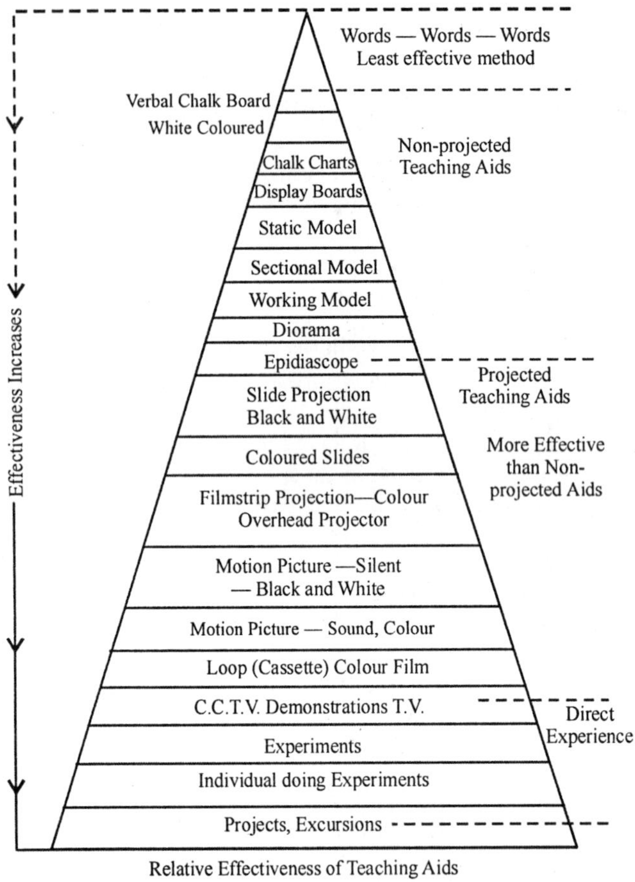

Fig. 21.9: Cone of Experience

21.11 BLACKBOARD

Significance of Blackboard

Blackboard is a unique device which in spite of newer and better devices in vogue, is irreplaceable as well as indispensable. It is the oldest and the best friend of a teacher. It is a mirror through which students visualise all about the teacher's mind, his way of explaining, illustrating and teaching as a whole. It is the cheapest and the most valuable teaching device and continues to be the '*sine qua non*' of our educational system. It is the most universally used aid. Writing on sand and clay was the ancient form of blackboard writing.

The use of blackboard in class teaching creates an informal environment and motivates learning. Teaching is no longer confined to any one instructional device. It is a help to 'planning', to 'crystallising' main points and to 'summarising' and 'reviewing' the main point of the lesson. Blackboard being a simple means of dealing with the whole class as a unit, it is extensively used during the course of a lesson.

Uses of the blackboard

Following are the uses:

1. The teacher can illustrate his lesson on the blackboard and draw the attention of the class to the salient features in the lesson.
2. The lesson can be phased and summarised in the right manner. Abstract statements can be clarified in the exposition stage and a summary containing important points can be given in the recapitulatory stage.
3. Questions and problems when planning class work or approaching a new subject can be listed by the teacher on the blackboard.
4. Pupils' interest in class work can be stimulated by blackboard writings and drawings.
5. It can be put to wide and varied uses. A teacher can use it for graphs, maps, graphic, statistics, sketches and various types of drawings.
6. It provides a lot of space for decorative and creative work.
7. The teacher can erase writings and drawings and start afresh.
8. It helps the teacher to focus the attention of his students on the lesson. It takes heed of varying capacities and rates of grasp of the students.
9. Ateacher can review the whole lesson for the benefit of the class with the help of the blackboard.

Types of Blackboards

1. *Fixed blackboard.* Fixed in the wall facing the class and normally made of wood or concrete cement.
2. *Blackboard on easel.* A portable and adjustable blackboard put on a wooden easel can be taken out of the classroom while taking classes in the open.
3. *Roller blackboard.* Made of thick canvas wrapped on a roller mostly used for teaching higher classes.
4. *Graphic board.* It has graphic lines and is used for teaching Mathematics, Science and Statistics.
5. *Magna board.* A board which enables teachers to make three-dimensional demonstrations with objects on a vertical surface. Small magnets are used to hold suitable objects fixed wherever they are put on this vertical surface.

Chalk Boards of Different Types of Surfaces

1. Point-coated pressed wood.
2. Dull finished plastic surface.
3. Vitreous coated steel surface.
4. Ground glass board.

Chalk Boards of Different Colours and Colour Chalks

Colour of the Blackboard	*Colour of the Chalk*
Green chalk board	White or yellow chalk
Grey board	Yellow
Red chalk board	Green, yellow

(*Contd.*)

Colour of the Blackboard	*Colour of the Chalk*
Orange chalk board	Blue or light green
Yellow chalk board	Blue
Rose chalk board	Purple, dark blue
Black chalk board	Any colour

Effective Use of Black-boards

Following points may be kept in view while using the blackboards:

1. Blackboard should be kept dean so that writing on it could be easily read by the students from all parts of the room.
2. Writing on the blackboard should be legible.
3. Letters and drawings should be large enough to be seen from all parts of the room.
4. Writing should be started from the top left corner.
5. Writing should be in straight rows.
6. Extreme lower corner of the blackboards should not be made use of as writing on it cannot be seen easily.
7. Material on the blackboard should not be covered by standing in front of it.
8. Only salient points of the subject matter should be written on the blackboard.
9. Diagrammatic visual presentation involving many processes should be prepared before the beginning of the lesson.
10. It should be ensured that the blackboard is well-lighted by natural or artificial means.
11. Everything needed for the blackboard should be got together before the class begins, i.e., collection of chalk rulers, T, square, compass, protractor, etc.
12. While writing on the blackboard, the teacher should ensure that the class is attentive.
13. Duster, and not hand or handkerchief, should be used in cleaning the blackboard.
14. Occasionally students may be asked to write or draw diagrams on the blackboard.
15. Teachers should develop the ability to draw freely on the blackboard. The map or chart or diagram that grows before the very eyes of the students is much more useful and valuable than a well-finished map, chart or diagram.
16. It should be ensured that the blackboard is periodically serviced.

21.12 PICTURES

Significance of Pictures

McKown and Roberts describe the significance of pictures as "From the time when he first drew pictures in the sand or scratched symbols on rocks, through the many developments and uses of papyrus, paper, canvas, marble, pen, ink, brush, paint and chisel, to the present when he utilises it in a wide variety of startling photographic representations, man has always found picturisation an indispensable tool for expressing ideas conveying information of others."

Presentation of Facts Through Pictures

The essential facts that could be presented through pictures are as follows:

1. ***Political History***

(a) Pictures of sources of Indian history.
(b) Pictures of great emperors and rulers.
(c) Pictures of significant events and battles.

2. ***Social History***

(a) Pictures illustrating the houses; dress, food, weapons, utensils, languages, etc. of various periods like the Mohen-jo-daro period, Vedic and Epic period, Buddhist, etc.
(b) Pictures showing societies in Modern India; houses, dress, food. etc.

3. ***Religious History***

(a) Pictures showing lives of religious leaders like Mahavira, Buddha, Christ, Mohammad, Guru Nanak, etc.
(b) Pictures depicting social movements and their leaders like Raja Ram Mohan Roy, Rama Krishna, Dayananda, etc.

4. ***Cultural History***

(a) Pictures showing architecture and sculpture of different ages—the Maurya period, the Indo-Scythian, the Gupta period, the Turko-Afghan period, the Mughal period, the British period.
(b) Paintings of the Guptas, Rajputs, Mughals and Modern Indians.
(d) Pictures of monuments.
(e) Pictures of architecture and sculpture in Southern India.

5. ***Economic History***

(a) Pictures of coins through the ages.
(b) Pictures of industries through the ages.
(c) Pictures of agricultural development.
(d) Pictures of electrical instalments.
(e) Pictures of transport through the ages.

20.13 SCRAP BOOKS

How to Maintain Scrap Books

The following principles may be followed in maintaining scrap books:

(i) The scrap book in which the collections are to be preserved should be of a good size, so as to be able to contain pictures, etc. of moderate size. A laboratory notebook type of exercise book should be selected for the purpose. The scrap book should have a strong binding so that it may last for some years; it should also have an attractive get-up. One should be proud to possess such a book.

(ii) Anything of interest to the pupils may find a place in that scrap book; it may or may not have relation to the course of study being pursued by the pupil. Generally the collections may fall under the following heads:

(a) pictures, (b) quotations, (c) information.

(iii) There should be some system in preserving the collections in the scrap book. The collections should be classified and each type of collection may be placed under the same section. The pupil may himself decide upon his principle of classification, but the teacher may give him broad guidance. For example, the scrap book may have a section on portraits. Quotations from important personalities may be placed under the portraits. Another section of the scrap book may concern itself with original sources. Information on sculptures, architecture, transport, etc. may be the other sectional heads for the scrap book. It may be mentioned that the principles which should be followed for classification of collections would depend upon the class in which the pupil reads. The scrap book may also have a list of contents at the beginning.

(iv) Every collection in the scrap book should be aesthetically arranged in it. It should also have proper titles. The pupil may put his own observations below it if he desires to do so.

22

Lesson Planning in Civics

22.1 IMPORTANCE OF LESSON PLANNING IN CIVICS

To be effective, every intelligent person plans out his work before undertaking its implementation. A surgeon diagnoses the case, prepares his surgical instruments before he puts the patient on the operation table; a lawyer makes attempts to anticipate and prepares for every move in the court; and engineer prepares his blue print before he actually starts the construction work of a bridge or a building; the house mistress plans the details of the daily meals; the sales manager gives careful attention to every step in a proposed selling campaign. So must a teacher plans and prepares his teaching lesson.

R.L. Stevenson has very aptly emphasised the importance of lesson planning in these words "To every teacher I would say, "Always plan out your lesson beforehand but do not be slave to it." *Begley* has put it thus, "However, able and experienced the teacher, he could do never without his preliminary preparation." *I.K. Davis* is perfectly right when he says, "Lesson must be prepared for there is nothing so fatal to a teacher's progress as unpreparedness."

22.2 MEANING AND DEFINITION OF LESSON PLANNING

A lesson plan is the blue print of the teaching-learning programme of the teacher which he is expected to follow in his classroom teaching in his daily work. It is prepared by him and indicates the aims to be realised by teaching a lesson, the methods to be employed and the activities to be undertaken in the class so that it is kept engaged for the realisation of the aim. A lesson plan is actually a plan of action. It indicates:

(i) The working philosophy of the teacher.
(ii) His information and understanding of his pupils.
(iii) His comprehension of the objectives of education.
(iv) His knowledge of the material to be taught.
(v) His ability to use effective methods of education.

Following definitions deserve careful attention for understanding the broad meaning of a lesson plan:

Bining and Bining—Daily lesson planning involves defining the objectives, selecting and arranging the subject matter and determining the method and procedure.

Lester B. Stands—A lesson plan is actually a plan of action. It, therefore, includes the working philosophy of the teacher, his knowledge of philosophy, his information about and understanding of his pupils, his comprehension of the objective of education, his knowledge of the materials to be taught, and his ability to utilise effective methods.

N.L Bossing—Lesson plan is the title given to a statement of the achievements to be realised and the specific means by which these are to be attained as a result of the activities engaged in day-to-day under the guidance of the teacher." This definition tends to focus the teacher's attention upon:

1. Outcomes or results in terms of the pupil.
2. Definite processes and procedures with a recognition of activity as the basis of learning.
3. The pupil in the foreground and the teacher in the background as guide and director only of the learning activity.

Nature of Lesson Planning

According to *Bossing*, "Lesson planning is essentially an experience in anticipatory teaching. It is living through in advance, mentally and emotionally, the classroom experience as the teacher visualizes it. The eager faces, the questions that will arise, the difficulties the pupils will encounter, the way these difficulties are to be met—all these the teacher will experience in imagination. This is the first essential of good planning. It is here that the teacher can bring into play to subtle power of well-developed imagination. The more vivid, the better, so long as it is fully tinged with realism."

22.3 FUNCTIONS OF LESSON PLANNING

Planning is essential not only in teaching but in all aspects of human activity. Probably, there is no type of work where the results of poor planning are so devastating as in teaching. R.L. Stevenson said, "To every teacher I would say, 'Always plan out your lesson beforehand but do not be slave to it'." Bagley has put it thus, "However, able and experienced the teacher, he could do never without his preliminary preparation." To be effective, every intelligent worker plans out his work. A surgeon diagnoses the case, prepares his surgical instruments before he puts the patient on the operation table; a lawyer makes attempts to anticipate and prepare for every move in the court, an engineer prepares his blue print before he actually starts the construction work of a bridge or a building; the house mistress plans the details of the daily meals; the sales manager gives careful attention to every step in a proposed selling campaign. So must a teacher plan and prepare his work.

A lesson plan indicates the aims to be realised by teaching a lesson, the methods to be employed and the activities to be undertaken in the class so that it is kept engaged for the realisation of the aim.

The lesson plan affects the teacher skill, intelligence ability and his personality. Following are the chief functions of planning:

1. It delimits the field of work of the teacher as well as of the students and provides a definite objective for each day's work.

2. As the goal is determined the teacher gets impetus to realise his goal.

3. It tends to prevent wandering from the subject and going off the way. It serves as a check on the possible wastage of time and energy of the teachers and students. It makes teaching systematic, orderly and economical.

4. Planning helps the teacher, to organise and the systemise the learning process. The activities in the lesson are well-knit, inter-connected and associated. The continuity of the educative process is ensured.

5. Planning helps in avoiding needless repetition.

6. Planning helps the beginning teacher to overcome the feeling of nervousness and insecurity. It gives him confidence to face the class.

7. Lesson planning gives opportunities to the teacher to think out new ways and means of making the lesson interesting and to introduce thought-provoking questions.

8. Lesson planning ensures a definite assignment for class and availability of adequate materials for the lesson.

Four Types of Planning

These are given as under:

(a) Planning of the work of the year in a definite manner and in units.
(b) Planning of each unit.
(c) Daily lesson planning.
(d) Planning shared with pupils.

22.4 LESSON PLANNING—OLD AND NEW

The modern emphasis is on providing learning experiences. We have repeatedly emphasised that good and effective teaching is 'causing students to learn'. It must stimulate the child to think and motivate him to learn further. The teacher is there to create learning situations and organise them in such a way that the child feels the inner urge to know, to think and to do. Therefore, the modern education makes the work of planning all the more important. Planning is not so elaborate and difficult in the traditional system of education which simply glorifies the subject-matter and fails to develop desirable habits, attitudes and skills. The present stress is on development of the abilities of the students, their attitudes, their experience and capacities. It is, therefore, inevitable for the modern teacher to plan his lessons very skilfully and carefully.

22.5 MERITS/ADVANTAGES OF LESSON PLANNING

1. *Development of Confidence in the Teacher*: The preparation of the lesson plan arouses self-confidence in the teacher as he is able to forecast problems and their probable solutions.

2. *Delimitation of the Subject-Matter*: The teacher is well aware of the definite subject-matter that he is going to cover in the allotted period.

3. *Systematic Management of Teaching-learning*: Lesson planning brings about system in the teaching-learning process. The teacher is able to present the proper material at the proper time and in the proper manner.

4. *Suitable Environment*: Objectives are fixed. Teaching techniques and devices are decided beforehand. Teaching aids are also predetermined. All these elements help the teacher to create a suitable environment in the class.

5. *Linking Previous Knowledge*: The teacher presents the subject matter on the basis of the previous knowledge of the students. This cements the new knowledge.

6. *Pre-determination of Learning Experiences and Activities*: Pre-determination of learning experiences to be provided to the students in the class enables the teacher to make the lesson effective.

7. *Orderliness in the Teaching*: Planning ensures clear-cut programmes and activities in the classroom.

8. *Procurement of Teaching Aids*: The teacher prepares/collects the teaching aids to be used in the class.

9. *Scientific Management of Teaching-learning*: It tends to prevent wandering from the subject and going off the way. It serves as a check on the possible wastage of time and energy of teachers and students. It makes teaching systematic, orderly and economical.

10. *Thought-provoking Questions*: Lesson planning provides opportunities to the teacher to think of new ways and means of making the lesson interesting and to introduce thought-provoking questions.

11. *Selection of Material*: Lesson planning enables the teacher to prepare a suitable scheme of selection and organisation of subject-matter, materials and activities.

12. *Avoidance of Repetition*: It enables the teacher to avoid repetition of activities, aids and devices.

13. *Well-knit Lesson*: Planning helps the teacher to organise the activities in the lesson into a welt-knit unit. Activities are also inter-related.

14. *Individual Differences of the Students*: Lesson planning enables the teacher to prepare a variety of material suitable to different needs of the students.

15. *Suitable Use of the Blackboard*: A planned lesson enables the teacher to think of way and means of making the best use of the blackboard.

16. *Suitable Recapitulation*: The teacher prepares recapitulatory questions beforehand.

17. *Appropriate Summary*: The teacher prepares beforehand an appropriate summary.

22.6 GENERAL PRINCIPLES AND STEPS IN PLANNING A GOOD LESSON PLAN

R. Schorling in *Student Teaching* suggests the following principles and steps in planning a good lesson plan:

1. Select the most appropriate aims.
2. Provide the illustrative materials available.
3. Include crucial questions.
4. Consider the level of the ability and interests of the pupils.
5. Consult course of study and grade requirement.
6. Select the best procedures.
7. Tie the lesson with previous ones.
8. Take into consideration the knowledge already possessed by pupils.
9. Include an appropriate assignment.
10. Consider supplementary materials in making the assignment.
11. Emphasise the main points of interest.
12. Give a logical order to activities that would lead towards a realisation of the aim of the lesson.

13. Provide for adequate summaries.
14. Make the plan flexible enough to allow teacher to leave it temporarily and follow pupil interests.
15. Budget the time devoted to phases of the lesson.
16. Provide a means for evaluating the results of the lesson and the teaching.

22.7 ESSENTIALS OF A GOOD LESSON PLAN

Generally speaking the following are the important characteristics of a good lesson plan:

1. *It should have Clear Aims*: The lesson plan should clearly state the objectives, general and specific, to be achieved.

2. *It should be Linked with the Previous Knowledge*: The plan should not let the lesson remain as isolated one. It should have its basis on the background of the class. It should grow out of what the pupils have already learnt.

3. *It should Show Techniques of Teaching*: It should state clearly indicate the various steps that the teacher is going to take, and also various questions that he will ask.

4. *It should be Written*: A lesson plan preferably be written and should not remain at the oral or mental stage. Panton writes, "The teacher is strongly advised, at least in the early stages, to make a written note of his preparation. Memory sometimes proves a treacherous servant, especially when his attention is divided." It is advisable, however, not to teach from notes. Excessive reliance upon these may undermine the teacher's confidence so that he can never do without them. If, however, the teacher has occasion while teaching to refer to his notes, it is better for him to do so openly than to take a suspicious look at them. He loses nothing in the eye of the children by the former method whereas by the second he is likely to be misjudge by his pupils. Writing helps in clarifying thoughts with concentration.

5. *It should Contain Suitable Subject Matter*: The materials of instruction or subject matter should be carefully selected or organised.

6. *It should be Divided into Suitable Sections or Units*: The plan should be divided into units, but care should be taken to see that the lesson remains an integrated whole and every unit develops from the previous and submerges into the next one.

7. *It should Provide for Activity*: The children must be given enough scope to be active. It should not make them mere passive listeners.

8. *It should Provide for Individual Differences*: The plan should be prepared in such a way as it does full justice to all the students of varied abilities.

9. *It should Show Certain Routine Things*: The plan should indicate the duration of the period, the period itself, average age of the students, subject and the class.

10. *It should Show the Illustrative Aids*: The illustrative aids to be used should be shown in the lesson plan.

11. *It should be Flexible*: The plan is a means and not an end. It is wrong to follow it slavishly. It is an instrument and should be used as such. The teacher

should be prepared to change his teaching methods from those as referred to in the plan, if need be.

12. *It should Refer to Reference Materials:* The plan becomes more useful if it refers to other reading materials. This, will motivate the bright students to do extra reading. Care should be taken to suggest only that material which is available in the school library.

13. *It should Include Assignment for Students:* A good lesson plan cannot be thought of without appropriate assignments for the students. Assignments can take different forms.

14. *It should Provide for Self-Evaluation:* A good lesson plan must have a suitable plan for self-criticism. The teacher should put some questions to himself and find out the answer and thereby judge the effectiveness of the lesson or otherwise.

15. *It should include the summary:* The lesson plan should include the summary of the whole lesson which is to be developed on the blackboard with the help of students.

22.8 APPROACHES TO LESSON PLANNING

Following are the main approaches to lesson planning:

1. The Herbartian Approach or Five Steps Approach.
2. Gloverian Approach.
3. The Evaluation Approach.
4. Unit Approach or Morrisonian Approach.
5. Project Approach.
6. RCEM Approach.

22.9 HERBARTIAN APPROACH

J.F. Herbart (1776-1841) and his followers developed the Five Steps Approach to lesson planning. To a great extent these steps are being followed with some modifications even today. Herbart propounded four steps: (1) Clearness, (2) Association, (3) System, (4) Method.

These names were changed by his disciples as given below:

1. Clearness to Preparation
2. Association to Presentation
3. System to Abstract (Comparison and generalisation)
4. Method to Application

These were further modified as—

1. Preparation
2. Presentation
3. Association and Comparison
4. Generalisation
5. Application

Preparation/Introduction

This step is concerned with the preparation of the mind of the students so that they may receive new knowledge. This is very essential both for the teachers as well as the children. The teachers must know what the children have already learnt and assimilated. He must have an accurate idea of what the children already know. The children must be made to realise what they do not know so that they may have a desire to know more. Preparation is just like 'preparing the ground before sowing the seed in it'. Nothing is to be imparted in vacuum. The 'Apperceptive masses' must be brought to the forefront. *J. Welton writes*, "Let the teacher then—as briefly and concisely as possible, pick up the thread of knowledge and get the pupils into the line of thought which leads from their present requirement to the new end. The better the teacher knows his class, the more accurately and quickly can he do this. This starting point must be known before the planning of the lesson can be profitably begun. It is this determination of the starting point, this power of putting oneself in the mental place and attitude of the pupils, that marks off the true artist in teaching from the mere mechanical grinder of facts and formulae. To know where the pupils are and where they should try to be are the two essentials of good teaching."

This step of preparation is also known as introduction.

Preparation means preparation on the part of the teacher as well as on the art of the students.

In preparation the 'will to learn' is aroused to some extent, whereas in motivation it is reinforced to a high degree.

Main Features of Preparation

1. It should contain no new knowledge.
2. It should stimulate curiosity.
3. It should be as brief as possible.
4. Much time should not be devoted to this step.

How to Start a Lesson

(a) The teacher may start his lesson with the help of two or three interesting questions.

(b) The teacher may start with the help of some aids, i.e., pictures, charts or models.

(c) He may put some questions on the subject-matter previously taught.

(d) He may start with the help of a situation. For example, in some topics he may take the situation of a cooperative store for profit and loss.

(e) He may start with the help of a relevant story.

Statement of the Aim

Announcement of the statement of the aim of the lesson in a clear, concise and specific form is very essential. It is necessary both for the teacher and pupil to know the general and specific aims of the lesson.

The form of the statement of the aim may be a brief question or a statement like this: "Today we shall study the role of the Reserve Bank of India."

Presentation or Development

It is here that the actual lesson is commenced. This step should involve a good deal of activity on the part of the students. The teacher will take the aid of various devices, e.g., questions, illustrations, explanation, expositions, demonstration and sensory aid, etc. Information and knowledge may be given, explained, revealed or suggested.

The teacher should bear in mind the following principles at the presentation stage:

(i) *Principle of Selection and Division*: The material to be presented should be wisely and judiciously selected. It should be divided into different sections. The teacher should also decides as to how much he is to tell and how much the pupils are to find out for themselves.

(ii) *Principle of Successive Sequence*: The different sections should be well-connected and should maintain a proper sequence. The teacher should ensure that the succeeding as well as the preceding knowledge is clear to the students.

(iii) *Principle of Absorption and Integration*: In the end separation of parts must be followed by the combination of the understanding of the whole.

Sometimes the word development is used in place of presentation as the term presentation smells of passivity. The term development of the lesson indicates the facts that there is pupil-teacher activity.

Association and Comparison

This step is related to the task of strengthening the acquisition of new material. New knowledge is to be presented to the children in such a way as it becomes associated with their previous knowledge or facts. The students are presented with new knowledge and are asked to observe it very carefully and to compare it with another set of facts and knowledge they already know. This helps to associate it with the old and thus to turn it into something new.

Generalisation

This step is concerned with the systematising of the knowledge learnt. Comparison and contrast lead to generalisation. In the inductive type of lessons the students are often required to establish some generalisations, rules or formulae. As far as possible, the teacher should see that the students draw out the conclusion themselves. If the generalisation is not the product of the student's own thinking, reflection or experience, it is of little value to them. The teacher should remain in the background. In the words of Ryburn, "It is bad teaching to give children ready-made general conclusions, concepts as we call them in psychology, which are founded on experience of the child himself, on his own precepts..... The child, with the teacher's help and guidance must be led to make his generalisations for himself."

Application

Knowledge is power only when it is used and tested. *T. Raymont* writes, "The mere acquisition of rules, precepts, principles, definitions and laws makes directly for pedantry rather than for healthy mental development." The fundamental law of psychology regarding learning is that the consolidation of knowledge takes place only when the knowledge learnt is applied to similar situations. Knowledge when it is put to use and verified becomes clear and a part and parcel of the mental make up.

The application also serves the purpose of revision and recapitulation of the principles learnt.

There is a difference between application and recapitulation. Recapitulation merely denotes revision or repetition of the knowledge learnt in the lesson whereas application requires a good deal of mental activity to think and apply the principles learnt to new situations.

Forms of Application

Following are the important forms of application:

1. Solving problems.
2. Drawing maps, charts or models.
3. Writing an essay.
4. Doing some practical work.
5. Setting new type tests.

Evaluation of the Concept of Herbartian Steps

Merits

1. It assists in making teaching systematic. The teacher proceeds on well-thought-out and definite lines.
2. It helps in avoiding unnecessary repetition in teaching.
3. It is useful in achieving the cognitive objective of teaching.
4. It makes use of the previous knowledge of the students for imparting new knowledge.
5. It employs the deductive and inductive methods of teaching.
6. It provides a useful framework confidence and self-reliance by following these steps and thus makes teaching effective.

Limitations

1. The scheme being very much intellectual in character is suited to knowledge lesson only. The scheme is not so useful in the case of skill and appreciation lesson.

2. There is more stress on teaching rather than learning.

3. The term preparation has been used in a vague manner. Preparation may be concerned with both teachers as well as learners.

4. Generalisation is not so simple a process as is envisaged by Herbart. It is not possible to have step in many cases.

5. The plan is rigid, stereotyped and mechanical in nature. This scheme does not provide for much thinking on the part of the students.

6. The term presentation has also been criticised as it speaks of inactivity on the part of the pupils.

7. Herbart was wrong to think that association was a distinct phase of the learning process. The fact is that this process of association and comparison is present from the very start of presentation.

Summing up: After considering both pros and cons of the Herbartian steps, one tends to conclude that there is no doubt that the steps as suggested by Herbart are of great value. They present us an attempt to point out the need of an orderly and systematic arrangement of instruction based on sound psychological laws. Steps or preparation and application have been recognised as universally valid. Regarding the value of general rules relating to the teaching process, T. Raymont writes, "The young teacher cannot be too earnestly warned that for him the great thing is to appreciate the 'spirit' of the formal steps and how much does this mean. It means that, though all the steps are not necessarily gone through in the treatment of any one section or unit of teaching, yet the 'order' in which steps occur cannot be departed from without disadvantage. That the acquisition of knowledge or of skill is a process of assimilation of new matter in the context of the old, that the relevant parts of the pupil's previously acquired stock of ideas should, therefore, first be recalled, that there should be a progress from the concrete and particular to the abstract and general, that ideas must be possessed before they can be applied, and that application in its turn makes for effective and permanent possession—these are truths as sure as the law of gravitation because they embody the plain facts of the working of a child's mind."

At another place Raymont writes, "Like the rules of any other art, however, the rules of the teaching art will not always be overtly employed. As soon as the teacher has thoroughly imbibed their spirit he may be left quite free to dispense with a formal array of preparation, presentation and the rest. Though the steps may no longer be explicitly stated or even thought of, they will always remain implicit in his best efforts, and he will be wise enough not to despise them because he has learnt to practise his art without conscious need of their help."

22.10 GLOVERIAN APPROACH

A.H.T. Glover in his book *New Teaching for a New Age* criticised Herbartian steps on the ground that these are stereotyped, gives less scope for pupil activity and fail to motivate students. If at all suitable the Herbartian pattern is suitable in the case of 'academic subjects' and the 'verbal child'.

Glover's scheme is based on four points:

(a) Questioning.
(b) Discussion.
(c) Investigation.
(d) Pupil-activity.

(a) *Questioning*: By a conscious process of good questioning, an intelligent teacher can lead his pupils through unfamiliar regions to a desired destination. The teacher should ask questions at different stages of the lesson. He should also encourage students to ask questions.

(b) *Discussion*: The next step is discussion. For this purpose it is better to divide the class into groups. The discussions should be directed in such a way as students are encouraged to express their ideas freely. Discussion should help the students to remove their difficulties.

(c) *Investigation*: Investigation may be individual or group investigation. The students are required to investigate on the topics selected.

(d) *Pupil-Expression*: This will be the last step. This should be in the form of practical activities. Glover classifies these as:

1. *Passive*: Here emphasis is on observing and listening.
2. *Active*: Activities may take the form of handwork, craftwork, gardening, drawing etc.
3. *Artistic or Recreative*: This includes activities like dancing, music and acting.
4. *Organisational*: This aspect may be present in the above activities.

22.11 MORRISON'S APPROACH OR UNIT APPROACH

This approach is associated with the name of Professor *H.C. Morrison* (1871-1945) of the University of Chicago. *Morrison* has explained the Unit Method in detail in his book *The Practice of Teaching in Secondary Schools* (1926). The unit method is very popular and frequently used in the U.S.A. The unit approach is based on the growing acceptance of the Gestalt-Organismic-Field Theories of learning which emphasise the 'wholeness' nature of learning. This approach is contrary to the older atomistic conception of learning according to which learning was a matter of adding one small item of knowledge to another bit by bit. The new approach is based upon the assumption that effective learning takes place in an environment in which the goals are clearly perceived and every phase of the operational procedure is viewed as a relational part of the total learner situation. The underlying assumption is that the learner reacts to the situation as a whole and not to parts in isolation.

(Already discussed in detail)

22.12 LIMITATIONS OF BLOOM'S EVALUATION APPROACH

The task of integration among behavioural objectives, learning experiences and evaluation devices puts heavy demands on teachers and the students.

This approach does not take into account the mental processes or mental abilities for writing out the educational objectives.

This is a highly structured approach and dominated by the role of the teacher in the teaching-learning process.

This approach makes the task of lesson planning quite rigid and mechanical.

Project Approach to Lesson Planning

This approach developed by *John Dewey* and *W.H. Kilpatrick* stresses self-activity, social activities and real life activities. (Discussed separately)

22.13 RCEM APPROACH

This approach to lesson planning has been developed at the Regional College of Education, Mysore and accordingly it is known as RECM Approach.

This approach makes use of the concept of system approach to education. The three main steps involved in this approach are: Input, Process and Output. The three aspects are as under:

1. Expected Behaviour Outcomes—EBOs
2. Communication Strategy—CS
3. Real Learning Outcomes—RLOs

Input step is concerned with the identification and specification of the educational objectives. It also includes the identification of the entering behaviour of the students. The objectives are written in behaviour terms. Input step resembles the 'introduction' step.

Process resembles the 'presentation' step of Herbartian approach. It represents the interaction process of the classroom. It includes activities of the teachers as well as students and teaching strategies.

Output is concerned with the evaluation phase of the lesson.

Merits of RCEM Approach

1. It is more suitable to Indian schools as it has been developed in this country.
2. Objectives are stated in terms of measurable abilities and mental process.
3. Teaching-learning situations, strategies, aids and materials are properly stated.
4. Evaluation aspect is properly taken care of.

Limitations of RCEM Approach

1. It is very tedious to write lesson plan of this type.
2. It is time consuming.
3. Very little literature is available on this approach.

Eclectic Approach to Lesson Planning: Summing Up

Herbartian approach is limited to the realisation of the cognitive objective and is hardly feasible in skill and appreciation lesson. Evaluation approach has a wider scope. Both approaches are highly structured, and teacher-dominated.

Evaluation approach is based upon sound psychological principles of learning but it is very difficult to follow in the normal classroom set-up. It needs more expertise on the part of the teachers. Herbartian approach on the other hand, is simple and can be easily followed.

We should be practical in our approach and try to pickup the good points of every approach and apply them suiting our classroom environment. We need a harmonious blending of all the approaches, as far as possible. The crucial point is that we follow an approach process and makes it effective and meaningful.

Notes

1. Student-teachers are advised to follow the guidelines and the format of the lesson plan recommended by their supervisors and teachers.

2. In very rare circumstances, to meet the extraordinary situation in the pupil-teacher may make a total departure from the lesson plan.

3. A lesson plan based on instructional behavioural objectives will be quite different.

4. A revision lesson will have a different lesson plan.

5. As far as possible, at the presentation or development stage of the lesson, it should be avoided to ask questions from the students from the subject-matter which is yet to be taught.

22.14 SUMMARY

Steps in Daily Lesson Plan and Their Significance

Steps	*Significance*
1. Title of the topic	For taking up the lesson in a definite framework.
2. Objectives of the lesson	For pin-pointing the learning outcomes so that these could be measured after teaching the lesson.
3. Teaching aids	For making teaching-learning more effective and at the same time making enjoyable. For serving as a base for the lesson.
4. Previous knowledge	For serving as a base for the lesson.
5. Statement of the aim (Preparation)	For preparing students for new learning and focusing their attention on a specific aim.
6. Presentation	For teaching the topic and giving new knowledge and understanding. It is in fact the heart of the lesson.
7. Application	For providing opportunities to apply the newly acquired knowledge and understanding.
8. Recapitulation	For finding out whether learning has taken place or not. This is also necessary for feedback.
9. Blackboard summary	For focusing attention on fundamentals of the lesson.
10. Home assignment	For reinforcement, practice and evaluation.

23

Civics Text-book and Supplementary Material

23.1 INDISPENSABILITY OF TEXT-BOOKS

Cronback in an introductory Chapter to "*Text Materials in Modern Education*" states "At the centre of the present-day education scene in America is the text-book. It takes a dominant place in the typical school from the first grade to college." The text-book is firmly entrenched in our schools. Its influence has been powerful in the past, is powerful now, and meets gradually with public approval. Evidence is available to prove that text-books are major factor in the formation of the curriculum. They tend to set the standards of the curriculum and the methods of teaching on all school levels. Most of the evidence points also to the fact that for a long time to come the text-book will be one of the primary tools of use by teachers in curriculum work. Regardless of whether some school systems or some teachers supplement the text-book with inner texts, with library materials and visual aids, or dispense with the text-book in favour of the use of specific references by students of various ages, the text-book is still the main tool employed by most teachers.

In ancient times mankind preserved its heritage of knowledge and culture primarirly through oral traditions, and transmitted it to its younger generation orally, too. Knowledge, then being limited in scope and quantum, and being relatively simple in nature, could be easily preserved and transmitted through the oral medium from generation to generation without much trouble.

However, the passage of time brought about a change in the life of a man. The frontiers of knowledge got considerably expanded with renaissance, and subsequently with the industrial revolution. Science and technology, and the movement of research supported by both cumulatively gave a great fillip to man's search for knowledge. Consequently, the oral tradition was found not only in adequate and incapable of doing the job but also less reliable and less objective in respect of preserving and transmitting the new expanding knowledge. Hence, the entry of the printed word in education, and its continued sway even now in the information age which is increasingly getting dominated by a motley of hardware and software. The increasing number of books and journals published in Countries all over the world, particularly the developed countries of the first and the second worlds, are an evidence to prove the indispensability of the printed word as a medium of education.

In fact, ever since the invention of the printing press, mankind has got itself so thoroughly used, even addicted to this medium that its education and acculturation cannot be conceived of in the absence of books. In a developing country like India, where literacy is to be spread among the masses on a massively wide scale, books will be more important than oral and other visual media of education.

We know that the education system in modern India has basically departed from the oral tradition of the system in ancient time so much so that it has now come to be virtually dominated by books, mostly text-books as a tool of both teaching and learning. It is so right from the primary school stage to the university.

In a way, this change from the oral tool to the printed one has many benefits. Philosophically, the teaching process has become more objective and unbiased. Intellectually, it has become more consistent and logical. Pedagogically, it has offered a systematically well-organised body of knowledge that can be easily taught and learnt. Economically, it has resulted in greater saving of effort and resources. Socially, it has, through a uniform structure and content, provided for an opportunity to learn the same body of knowledge to all sections of population. For a country like India all these benefits are no mean gain viewed in the context of her people's poverty, illiteracy and bewildering diversity.

23.2 TEXT-BOOK NOT THE END AND BE-ALL OF EDUCATION

The text-book is not the be-all and end-all of the enterprise of education. It represents but a segment of the curriculum as it embodies in itself only a sample of the formal, cognitive part leaning out the vast hidden effective conative and social part of the school curriculum. Its inadequacies even in respect of the component are too obvious to be ignored by the teacher and the learner. It has to be treated like that, and, therefore, supplemented and reinforced by a number of other tools and means to carry to its logical end the process of education initiated by it. These tools and means include library resources, instructional materials, learning aids, field experience, mass media, etc.

23.3 MEANING OF A TEXT-BOOK

Authors have given different definitions of a text-book. "A true text-book", according to the American Text-book Publishers Institute... "is one especially prepared for the use of pupil and teacher in a school or a class, presenting a course of study in a single subject, or closely related subject."

Webster's Dictionary defines text-book as, "a manual of instruction, a book containing a presentation of the principles of the subject used as a basis of instruction...."

Becon defines text-book as, "a book designed for classroom use, carefully prepared by experts in the field and equipped with the usual teaching devices."

To Hall-quest a text-book is, "a record of racial thinking organised for instructional purposes."

To Lange it is "a standard book for any particular branch of study."

A more comprehensive definition is given in the third edition of *Encyclopaedia of Educational Research.* It states, "In the modern sense and as commonly understood, the text-book is a learning instrument usually employed in school and colleges to support a programme of instruction. In ordinary usage, the text-book is printed, it is non-consumable, it is hardbound, it serves an avowed instructional purpose, and it is placed in the hands of the learner."

23.4 MAIN FUNCTIONS OF A TEXT-BOOK

1. *Text-book is an 'Assistant Master in Print'*: A text-book is content plus instructional technique. This technique is aimed at enabling the content understandable to the pupils even in situations where they are not helped by the teacher.

2. *A Text-book has a Structured Framework*: A text-book is essentially based on some pre-determined syllabi which circumscribe the limits of a text-book besides setting the standard at which it has to be written. It clearly spells out and interprets the syllabus both for the students and teachers.

3. *A Text-book is an Instrument of Instructional Objectives*: As an important tool of instruction, a text-book is an instrument for the achievement of pre-determined objectives.

4. *A Text-book is an Important Tool for the Teacher*: A text-book assists the teacher to plan his daily lesson, prepare assignments and organise class activities.

5. *A Text-book is a Constant Companion of a Student*: A text-book guides the students in learning—in the school and at home. A student uses it continuously and constantly. This feature distinguishes it from a general and reference book which a student consults once a while. Each word of the text-book has not only to be read by every student but is also expected to be understood.

6. *A Text-book is a Self-teaching Device*: A text-book enables a student to learn through his own efforts. A text-book provides an opportunity to a student to reflect and evaluate. A student can find the specific information he needs in a book. He can review material he has read from time to time to clear up uncertainties. He can move ahead as quickly or as methodically as his individual capacities for comprehension permit.

7. *A Text-book Provides Logical and Comprehensive Material*: A good text-book by providing material in a systematic and comprehensive form, sets a standard of minimum essential to be achieved by students of all categories. For a teacher, it provides essential knowledge at one place. All teachers are not in a position to dig up facts. A text-book, therefore, can be a constant standby of the teacher.

8. *A Text-book is a Transmitter of a Culture*: It serves as potential media of mass communication. It has a positive role to play in bringing about desirable cultural change by discarding certain out-dated values and customs and introducing radical changes.

9. *A Text-book Helps to Revolutionise Society*: A text-book is used not only for preserving the cultural heritage but also revolutionising a society, its values, beliefs and social systems.

10. *A Text-book Serves as a Rallying Point*: By providing a common ground for both the teachers and the students, it focuses attention on the same issues, events, sequences and circumstances.

11. *A Text-book Serves as a Laboratory*: A text-book enables a student to reinforce the learning, to do assignments at home, to prepare for the examination and to seek guidance and reference for further studies. It provides a common basis on which the process of reading, analysing, outlining and summarising can be mastered.

12. *A Text-book Serves as a Basis for Almost all the Methods*: Almost all the methods of teaching like the assignment, unit method, discussion and the project method can be used with advantage with the help of a text-book.

13. *A Text-book Gives Definite Information*: A text-book is a storehouse of basic and definite information needed for learning experiences of different kinds. The use of the text-book can help the pupils to sum up all the ideas of the unit, acquaint them with the vocabulary, help them learn enough about the topic to be able to proceed intelligently.

14. *A Text-book Generates Educational Interaction*: A text-book plays a crucial role in generating educational interaction in the classroom between the teacher and the learner, and also between the learner and other co-learners as a result of which learning occurs in a group.

15. *A Text-book Serves as a Syllabus 'De facto'*: A teacher defines and delimits his content of teaching. He uses the text-book as a prime instructional aid to generate a variety of educative experiences through group-work and individual assignments.

23.5 DEMERITS OF TEXT-BOOKS

Demerits of text-books are stated below:

1. They tend to dominate the educative process. They have influenced the purpose, character and scope of the curriculum. They have dominated the method of instruction and the evaluating process. They have narrowed down the scope of the curriculum.

2. They do not provide for direct experience. The students get ready-made knowledge and, therefore, fail to assimilate it properly.

3. They introduce uniformity and rigidity for definite achievements and skill all initiative and spirit of both the pupil and the teacher.

4. Text-books are a great hindrance in the new methods of teaching like the heuristic and the inductive. The students get ready-made answers and this defeats the very purpose of introducing new methods.

5. There is every danger that the text-books may be used for the purpose of indoctrination of the ideas and beliefs of the party in power. In fact, text-books have been used in many countries for the propagation of Fascist and Communistic ideas. They are a potent instrument in the hands of the party in power to inculcate narrow nationalism and racial prejudices.

23.6 HOW TO USE TEXT-BOOKS

A text-book should be treated as a means and not an end in itself. It should be borne in mind that it is a useful means to help him in his study. The students should never have the impression that a text-book constitutes a boundary and his task is simply to learn what it contains and no more. A text-book should serve as a basis of his learning. A text-book does not provide the last word on the subject. A text-book is not to usurp the functions of a teacher. It is to supplement his work and not supplant it.

23.7 CAN WE DO AWAY WITH TEXT-BOOKS?

We may not accept the sovereignty of a text-book but it must be admitted that the text-book is an indispensable means or tool in the teaching-learning process, whatever scheme is adopted. It is neither desirable nor feasible for most of the teachers to do without text-books. The only point is that a text-book should be used very skilfully and intelligently. It should be treated as 'an obedient slave' and not 'a commanding master'.

The Education Commission 1964-66 described the value of the text-book as an effective tool of learning and of diffusion of improved teaching methods in these words, "A good text-book written by a qualified and competent specialised in the subject, and produced with due regard to quality of printing illustrations and general get-up, stimulates the pupil's interest and helps the teacher considerably in his work. The provision of quality text-books, and other teaching and learning materials, can thus be an effective programme for raising standards.

23.8 MAIN CHARACTERISTICS OF CIVICS TEXT-BOOKS

1. Selection of content.
2. Organisation of content.
3. Presentation of content.
4. Verbal communication (Language).
5. Visual communication (Illustration).
6. Learning assignments (Exercises and projects).
7. Prelims and back pages.
8. Size of the book.
9. Printing layout.
10. Durability.
11. Price.

I. Selection of Content

1. Relevant content	The content should be relevant to the instructional objectives.
2. Coverage of course	The content should cover the topics given in the syllabus.
3. Adequate content	The content should be adequate in respect of each topic.
4. Authentic content	The content should be accurate and authentic.
5. Up-to-date content	The content should be up-to-date
6. Continuity and balance	The continuity and balance among the various topics covered in the books should be maintained.
7. Integrated content	The selected topics should be properly integrated from the preceding to the succeeding class or stage.

(Contd.)

8. Linking with life	Considerable material drawn from practical life situations and day-to-day life of the community should be incorporated.

II. Organisation of Content

1. Division into units	The subject-matter should be divided into proper chapters.
2. Division into sections	The matter should be properly divided into sections and paragraphs.
3. Psychological approach	The approach followed in the book should be suitable to the needs of the students.
4. Coherence in the subject matter	There should be sufficient coherence and sequence in the organisation of the subject matter.
5. Flexible organisation	The organisation should be flexible enough to submit to changes in accordance with the change in the instructional plans

III. Presentation of Content

1. Attractive and appropriate title	The titles of the chapters should be appropriate.
2. Motivating presentation	The presentation should motivate children for further study.
3. Interesting and creative matter	The matter should be presented in a creative and interesting manner to sustain interest.
4. Adequate terminology	The presentation should provide an adequate coverage of the terminology relevant to the syllabus.
5. Adequate provision for replication	It should provide adequate reinforcement of new items of learning through replication and application.
6. Provision for suitable suggestions for teachers	The presentation should provide some suggestions and implications for adoption of effective teaching methods and instructional strategies by the classroom teacher.

IV. Verbal Communication (Language)

1. Appropriate vocabulary	The vocabulary should be appropriate for the class level.
2. Short and simple sentences	The sentences should be simple and short.

(*Contd.*)

3. Correct spellings	The spellings should be correct.
4. Correct punctuations	Punctuation should be done correctly.
5. Grammatically correct language	The language used should be grammatically correct.
6. Proper use of technical terms	The technical terms should be used properly, and suitably explained wherever necessary.

V. Visual Communication (Illustrations)

1. Clear illustrations	The illustrations should be clear, correct and authentic.
2. Purposeful presentation of illustrations	The illustrations should be purposeful and appropriately placed in the text-books.
3. Adequate illustrations	The illustrations should be adequate, proper in size and suitably captioned.
4. Supplementation of text	The illustrations should supplement the text.
5. Variety of illustration	There should be variety in illustrations.

VI. Learning Assignments (Exercises and Projects)

1. Adequate exercises	The exercises should be adequate to test the various purposes like recapitulation, consolidation etc.
2. Wide coverage	The exercises should cover the significant content.
3. Variety in exercises	The exercises should provide variety.
4. Scope for projects	The projects should help in achieving various purposes of teaching of civics.
5. Real projects	The projects should have a close resemblance to actual life situations.
6. Challenging exercise books	The exercises should promote the spirit of enquiry and motivate the students for further study.
7. Graded exercises	These exercises should suit the special needs of the gifted as well as slow learners.

VII. Prelims and Backpages

1. Appropriate title page	The title page should give the necessary information. It means suitable title, author's name, publisher, place of publication and year of publication, etc.

(*Contd.*)

2. Suitable preface	Preface should give an idea about the scope and central theme of the book.
3. Effective introduction	Introduction should explain the scheme and purpose of the book.
4. Correct table of contents	The table of contents should be given correctly.
5. Bibliography	Bibliography should be given correctly and according to the uniform system.
6. Suitable glossary	Glossary should be given in adequate language.
7. Index	Index should be given where possible.

VIII. Size of the Book

1. Suitable size	The size should be suitable from the view-point of age group of students.
2. Suitable volume	The size should be suitable in relation to the volume of the book.

IX. Printing Layout

1. Suitable length and lines	The length of the line should be such as can be conveniently read by the students.
2. Suitable type	The type size used for chapter title, subtitles, footnotes, exercises, etc. should be suitable for the age group of the students.
3. Appropriate margin	The left hand, right hand, top and bottom margins should be appropriate.
4. Aesthetic outlook	The margins should provide an aesthetic look to the page of the book.
5. Appropriate spacing	Spacing between lines, and paragraphs should be appropriate.

X. Durability

1. Durable paper	The paper should be durable enough in view of the age group.
2. Life of the book	The paper should be durable enough in accordance with the cost of the book.
3. Suitable price	The quality of the paper should be in accordance with the cost of the book.

(*Contd.*)

4. Suitable building	The binding should be durable keeping in view the volume and functional life of the book.
5. Attractive binding	The binding should be attractive.

XI. Price

1. Price suited to the economic background	The price should be suitable in view of the economic background of the students.
2. Reasonable price	The price should be suitable keeping in view the printing layout, size and durability of the book.

23.9 RECOMMENDATIONS OF THE ISHWARBHAI PATEL COMMITTEE (1977-78) ON TEXT-BOOKS

Class I-IV/V

Text-books: We have referred earlier to the obsession with literacy resulting in the dominant position of text-books in our system of education. this has assumed serious proportions in that we have the not uncommon spectacle in cities, at least, of young children carrying loads of books to and from school because of the emphasis given to book learning by parents and teachers.

We are of the view that except in the case of language there is no need for text-books in Class I-II; in Class III-IV/V there should be one text-book for language; one book in mathematics and one for environmental studies.

Teacher's Guide Books and Teaching Aids: Teacher's guide books and teaching aids, we believe, are necessary and these should cover the whole range of activities for all classes and that in the preparation of guide books the principle of correlation should be the basis.

Class VI to VII

Text-books: We realise that there will have to be text-books, for each of the areas of study, but the number of these can be reduced by having one book for Science and one in which Civics and History are combined.

We are of the view that the number of pages in each text-book should be reduced to the minimum and that the language used should be easily understood by children of this age-group.

Class IX and X

History, Civics and Geography: We are of the view that the one area in which the present scheme is overloaded is in 'social studies' or 'social science'. In some of the courses prescribed by examining bodies under one or other of these headings the subjects included are History, Civics, Geography, Economics, Commerce and Psychology.

We agree with the conclusions of the Kothari Commission that History, Civics and Geography only should be taught in the area of the curriculum and that such correlation as is natural and possible should be introduced.

We have, therefore, recommended definitely that a course in History, Civics and Geography should be included in the scheme as, we believe, that such a course will, with the other areas of study, be sufficient to provide a broad-based general education.

Syllabus Frames

The Ishwarbhai Patel Committee have given syllabus frames in most subjects and not detailed syllabus. The frames give the main topics in each subject and it will be for the states, local authorities, education examination boards and schools to plan and fill in the details.

The Committee observed, "We believe that uniform courses of study designed to serve the needs of average schools cease to be meaningful as there is a large variety of schools in each state and there are many variable factors, such as, the quality of teachers, facilities available and the needs of children to be taken into consideration.

A single rigid scheme of studies for all schools may prove to be beyond the competence of some schools and may not provide a sufficient challenge to other schools.

The content of the courses, finally framed, must be capable of being taught or studied within the time allotted per week as given in the scheme. We believe that in each subject, only the main ideas should be introduced; these should be few and important and that in teaching they should be thrown into every possible combination so that the children will make these ideas their own and understand their application. In the words of a distinguished educationist, "We enunciate two educational commandments: "Do not teach too many subjects" and again "What you teach, teach thoroughly".

We believe that the main concepts in each subject should be studied and that unnecessary details, which overload the syllabus, instead of developing knowledge, inevitably lead to the memorising of scraps of information, never interconnected, never utilised.

Another value of providing syllabus frames only lies in the fact that the limits of knowledge to be expected at the end of the ten-year period will be clear to those responsible for framing courses at the higher secondary stage.

Freedom to Develop Text-books

We are also of the view that by not giving details of the courses, but only the main topics, it will be possible for education authorities to prepare text-book material to suit the needs of schools under their control.

We recommend that NCERT should concentrate on the production of instructional material and that state governments, education/examination boards, schools and other educational agencies should be free to adapt and develop this material to suit their particular needs.

23.10 SUPPLEMENTARY MATERIAL

Importance of Supplementary Material

Supplementary material is of potential value for teaching. Text-books cannot satisfy all aspects of critical and inspirational knowledge and may be even lacking details with regard to current contemporary affairs. Text-books cannot cope with the material of fast changing social events. Text-books, with rare exceptions, are not self-explanatory and the students stand in need of elaboration. Elaboration is possible through advanced works, reference books and source books, etc. Similarly autobiographies and biographies serve as inspirational sources. Well-written historical plays, short stories and speeches on related subjects are very helpful. Pamphlets prepared by local, state and national societies provide admirable material for students.

Supplementary material should be a vital factor in all the work of Political Science and Civics. Following advantages are gained from the proper use of collateral supplementary source and fiction reading:

1. Development of good reading habits.
2. Colourful understanding of the past.
3. Development of an intelligent and critical attitude.
4. Stimulating independent judgement.
5. Training in independent reading and thinking.

Bining and Bining point out the merit of supplementary material as, "During the period of adolescence, when interest can readily be aroused, when good habits can be developed, when attitude can easily be built up, when the capacity for forming ideals is strong, and when the mind is wide open to impressions, the natural desire for reading should be skilfully directed and the foundations laid for the wise use of books".

Five Types of Reading

These are as given below:

1. Reading for understanding.
2. Reading for memorisation.
3. Reading for the purpose of locating specific information.
4. Rapid reading for expanding general knowledge.
5. Reading for pleasure.

Most supplementary reading can be classified under the last three categories; major share going to fourth category of rapid reading.

Various Types of Supplementary Material

1. Autobiographies and biographies.
2. Historical fiction.
3. Magazines.
4. Newspapers.
5. Plays.
6. Poetry.
7. Travel and other stories.
8. Work books.

1. *Autobiographies and Biographies*: Autobiographies and biographies of great persons throw a flood of light on the social, economic and political conditions prevailing in their period. They also serve as source of great information.

2. *Historical Fiction*: It has been observed that historical fiction, by recreating the past, serves as a stimulus to the imagination, provides opportunities for the exercise of critical faculties and offers endless opportunities of extending human sympathy.

Historical fiction also serves as a source of entertainment. It also provides inspiration. Anand Math of Bankim Chandra Chatterji is very useful for creating a sense of unity and national pride in the people. Bande Matram of Rabindra Nath Tagore, which became the anthem of the struggle for national freedom is enshrined in this very novel. Historical novels in different languages are very helpful as supplementary material for creating interest in the past and widening the horizons of the understandings of the students.

3. *Magazines*: Many magazines contain interesting and latest material on different matters which can supplement classroom information. They enable the students to keep themselves abreast of the latest developments in various fields.

4. *Newspapers*: Newspapers help in bridging the gap between information contained in the books and changing developments in movements, trends, ideas and changes in politics, international relations and economic and civil life. Sunday and special issues such as Republic Day and Independence Day are full of important events. Articles on new researches in various fields can enlighten the students. It is, therefore, very essential that from the very beginning of their school career, students are made newspaper-minded.

5. *Travel Stories*: Travel accounts of the Buddhist Chinese travellers like Fahien, Hieun Tsang and Itsing who visited India provide a comprehensive account of the social and cultural life of the people living during that period. Their accounts are considered a great valuable source of information as they spent a few years in India and travelled widely. Similarly, travel accounts of the Arab sailors, merchants and the visitors who visited India during the medieval period provide interesting accounts. Alberuni and Ibn Batuta have furnished valuable descriptions of the period. Achievements of the rulers of the Vijay Nagar Empire have found an important place in the travel accounts given by the Portuguese and the Indian travellers.

6. *Work Books*: Work books are based on the principle of 'learning by doing'. They play a vital role in leading to the concretisation of the concepts presented in text-books. Work books provide opportunities to the students to apply knowledge gained through text-books. Pictures of the different scripts of different countries and of the tools and weapons motivate the students to learn more. Projects in social studies which have as part of their fulfilment the construction and manipulation of things are sometimes very valuable.

Supplementary material is intended to achieve the following objectives:

1. It aims at helping the students acquire additional information.
2. It aims at widening the horizons of the students.

3. It aims at enriching the knowledge already acquired through the text-book.
4. It aims at enabling the students develop study habits.
5. It aims at motivating them to write articles and speeches, etc.
6. It aims at serving as a means of bringing out the relationship between the present and the past.
7. It aims at enabling the students form an acquaintance with historical literature.
8. It aims at making the teaching of social sciences more inspiring and interesting.
9. It aims at enabling the students make the best use of their leisure time.
10. It incidentally helps the students form the conception of how social sciences material is built up. If used effectively, it not only vitalises instruction but also provides a new meaning to teaching and learning.

23.11 GUIDELINES FOR THE USE OF SUPPLEMENTARY MATERIALS

1. While suggesting supplementary material, the teacher should bear in mind the mental capacity of his students. Only those materials should be suggested which the students can grasp.
2. As far as possible, only those materials should be suggested which the students can get easily from the school library or local sources.
3. Suggested supplementary material should be within the easy reach of the pocket of the students if it is not available in the school library.
4. There should be no element of compulsion in supplementary reading. The teacher would do well to keep in mind the suggestion of Johnson in this regard, "there should be no set questions to answers, no problems to solve, no looking forward to any report, but complete freedom to read because he likes it or to stop reading because he dislikes it."
5. Language of the supplementary material should be simple so that it may maintain the interest of the students.
6. For motivating the students, the teacher should maintain a small library in the classroom or a reserved shelf in the library or hall so as to make it easily available to students.
7. The students may be motivated to keep their own record of supplementary reading done as: (a) Name of the book; (b) Author's name; (c) Publisher's name; (d) Newspaper or the magazine read by them; (e) Extracts taken.
8. Supplementary material should be well-illustrated.
9. Supplementary material as the name implies should only supplement the text-book and not replace it.
10. Supplementary material should be scientifically and systematically classified and arranged in a proper sequence.
11. Supplementary material should be authentic and not a distortion of facts or politically motivated.

24

Civics Room and Museum

24.1 NEED FOR SPECIAL ROOM OR LABORATORY

A modern teacher has come a long way from those old days when 'chalk' and 'talk' were the only aids of teaching. Modern technology has placed different types of instructional aids at his disposal. Apart from text-books, there are different types of reference books, pamphlets, magazines, maps, globes, charts, projects, etc. which must be used to make the teaching-learning process effective.

A special room or what a few subject specialists would like to term as laboratory, fully equipped with modern aids, will provide a pleasant social and cooperative environment where the teachers and the learners feel homely. It is a must for every school. It has been observed by M.P. Moffatt, "Classroom furnishings and their arrangements have direct bearing upon the quality of results obtained. Satisfactory outcomes can be expected from any classroom situation only when adequate facilities are provided. It should be furnished to provide a suitable environment for acquiring and practising social studies skills".

It has been recognised that like sciences, social sciences also require a specially equipped room or laboratory. This alone can facilitate the use of modern methods and techniques like play-way method, problem method, project method and the socialised recitation method, etc. Special setting and equipment are needed for utilising these methods.

A special room should serve the purpose of a classroom, a library workshop, an amateur theatre, a student's club, a stock room, all combined into one. It may grow steadily and constantly as regards equipment. It should become the exciting 'hub' of activity for the students and teachers. It should be so planned and arranged that it provides an inviting and stimulating environment. It should be a place of 'doing' rather than of 'talking'. The subject library is an integral part of social sciences programme and it helps in making it as living and vital discipline. The library is the treasure vault of the store house of ideas. In fact, it is the flowing stream of living thought. The subject library provides suitable opportunities to the student to use facts in a creative and productive way to arrive at their own independent conclusions and enable them to grow in enriched knowledge, abilities, skills and interests.

Following are some of the considerations which necessitate the provision of a special room or laboratory for political science and civics:

1. Providing 'home of their own' to teachers for developing enthusiasm for the subject and faith in themselves and the students.

2. Creating and maintaining an effective teaching-learning environment.
3. Providing a quick and ready functional environment by making available work room for the students.
4. Introducing variety in teaching methods and facilitating the use of teaching aids readily and conveniently.
5. Saving energy and time in carrying round equipment like charts, maps, models, pictures and projects, etc.

24.2 EQUIPMENT OF THE ROOM

The room should be well-equipped so that functional environment is created and the teacher and the students are motivated to work. It should have the following equipments:

1. Audio-visual material which includes epidiascope, film strip, magic lantern, projector, tape recorder, etc.
2. Bulletin boards.
3. Charts and graphs.
4. Flags.
5. Globes.
6. Maps and atlases.
7. Models.
8. Meteorological instruments—barometer.
9. Rocks-stones and minerals.
10. Slide album containing slides showing architecture, dancing, painting, sculpture, etc.
11. Stamps of different kinds.
12. Survey instruments—Box compass, compass, chain and arrows, divider, foot rule of scale, flags, plane table, prismatic compass, protector, spirit level, survey field book, tape, tripod.
13. Time charts and graphs.
14. Text-books.
15. Reference books.
16. Unit booklets dealing with a variety of topics, ranging from family life and neighbourhood to people of other lands and places.
17. Literary materials which include tales of adventure, easy biographies, historical series, travel stories, animal stories, historical novels, etc.
18. Periodicals and magazines dealing with current events and various aspects of life showing art, literature, music, dance, etc.
19. Pamphlets published by various agencies including Central and State Governments and specialised agencies and also by international agencies like the UNO and UNESCO, etc.
20. Newspapers.

24.3 MUSEUM

Role of the Museum

The Secondary Education Commission, on the role of school museums observed, "Museums play a great part in the education of school children as they bring home to them much more vividly than any prosaic lectures, the discoveries of the past and the various developments that have taken place in many fields of science and technology." Again the Commission observes, "We believe it is necessary from the educational point of view to establish such museums in important centres at least wherein both ancient and modern collections will be exhibited and in some cases even demonstrations given of the actual process of development of various scientific discoveries. Nothing can impress students in the formative age so much as the actual visualising of these experiments in a graphic manner."

These museums are made up of materials used in classroom teaching which, in many cases, are collected, classified and exhibited by students, with or without the help of a teacher. The museum activities may be an extra-curricular function of the class or the school or they may be incorporated into a scientific-experimental method of teaching.

Objectives of a Museum

Following are the main objectives of a museum:

(a) to form within the school or the classroom an embryonic community dedicated to the usual occupations reflected in the school life of adults;

(b) to permit visual instruction and experimentation with actual museum specimens;

(c) to stimulate enthusiasm for study and research among both teachers and students;

(d) to stimulate interest, cooperation and participation in the cultural activities and scientific research conducted by the larger museums;

(e) to instruct students in proper scientific methods of laboratory research and museum conservation and exhibition techniques;

(f) to form, in the absence of larger museums in the community, a nucleus from which the classroom museum can grow beyond the limits of the school to serve ultimately the community and the region as a whole.

New exhibit programmes, interpretation, visual communication: What then are some of the ways in which museums as cultural and educational centres of the community can communicate successfully with their transitory visitors of heterogeneous composition? Based on various audience-testing experiments the following media can be used to heighten the effectiveness of visual communication:

(a) *Dramatic Labels*: Experiments suggest that large letters placed at the focal point of the case or exhibit area will successfully headline the exhibit and catch the visitor's attention.

(b) *Dramatic Lighting*: Light is a means of visual communication as well as an attention getter. Coloured lights that change, fade or highlight an exhibit can be used with great dramatic effect. Light can also be used to tell a story and to convey a sense of passing time. Light is particularly important in art museums.

(c) *Dramatic Utilisation*: Again experiments suggest that museum visitors should be given a chance to feel exhibits as well as to see them. Of course, much depends on the nature and expendability of the object involved but certain types of material—objects of wood, stone and metal and special "touch me" samples of animal skins and fabrics—can be used with great success to satisfy the visitor's urge to touch while permitting a minimum of danger.

(d) *Dramatic Sound Effects*: Sound, like light, can be used to heighten the dramatic effect of visual communication. For example, an Amazon rain forest exhibition can be made vastly more effective by adding the sound of tropical rain, the croaking of frogs, the chattering of monkeys, and the beat of drums. An exhibit of mediaeval art can be made more meaningful if it is accompanied by music of the same period.

Visits to Museums

Whenever possible, students may be taken to museums. It is important to remember that these visits may be well-organised and necessary preparation made. Important points to be noted should be told to the students before the actual visit. It is preferable if the teacher himself acquaints himself with the contents of the museums before arranging student's visit. Necessary permission of the museum authorities may also be obtained. Students may be asked to observe the contents of exhibits very minutely. A follow-up session may also be arranged for discussing important points after the visit.

24.4 FIELD WORK OR SURVEY

Meaning of Survey

The word 'Survey' is derived from the words 'sur' or 'sor', and 'veeir' or 'vieor' which mean 'over' and 'see' respectively. According to *Webster's New Collegiate Dictionary*, a survey is a 'critical inspection, often official, to provide exact information'. A survey deals with 'What is'. It describes and interprets what exists at present.

Survey Defined

Whitney, F.L.—"The Survey, according to recent social science terminology, is an organised attempt to analyse, interpret and report the present status of a social institution, group or area."

Yang Psin Pao—"A social survey is usually an inquiry into the composition, activities and living conditions of a group of people."

A survey is often conducted by collecting samples. Samples represent the entire population. For example, out of 10,000 families of a locality (population) we may select only 1,000 families. Thus, 1,000 families will represent the characteristics of the 10,000 families. This is known as 'sampling'.

Significance of Survey, Outdoor Work and Field Work

Teaching and learning in the outdoors implies teaching and learning outside the four walls of the classroom. It may also imply teaching and learning outside the school premises, i.e., from natural surroundings and from various community resources. This approach to education is based on the well-established principle of 'learning by doing'.

The principal premises underlying the implication of outdoor education for all subjects add at all levels are:

1. That which can be learnt inside the classroom, should be supplemented by outdoor learning.
2. That which can be learnt in the outdoors through direct experience is more durable and effective.
3. That people and things are seen in their true relationships in the outdoor learning.
4. That school is not the only place of teaching-learning.
5. That the hidden curriculum outside the school should be taken note of.

Over the years, educator-philosophers like Comenius (1592-1670), Rousseau (1782-1852), Pestalozzi (1746-1827), Herbart (1746-1841), Froebel (1782-1852), Spencer (1820-1903), Dewey (1859-1952), Tagore (1861-1941) and Gandhiji (1869-1948) have pointed out the need for reinforcing abstract learning with concrete experiences. Going back to the Vedic and Epic periods, we find that Ashrams, mostly located at pleasing surroundings in the countryside/forests were the most important places of teaching-learning.

Lord Chesterfield (1694-1773) in a letter to his son away at school, aptly advised him, "The knowledge of the world can only be acquired in the world and not in a closet. Books will never teach you but they will suggest many things to your observation."

Gandhiji observed, "It is gross superstition to suppose that knowledge can be obtained only by going to schools and colleges. The world produced brilliant students before schools and colleges came into being."

Outdoor education aims at enriching, vitalising and complementing content areas of social studies by means of first hand observation and direct experience outside the classroom. By extending the classroom into the out of the doors, a setting can be provided for bringing deeper, insight, greater understanding and real meaning to those areas of knowledge which ordinarily, are merely read and sometimes discussed but seldom experienced.

Merits of a Survey

A survey:

1. Provides the student a reliable evidence about the existing situation.
2. Motivates student through participation.
3. Makes the learning effective.
4. Helps the students to correlate their knowledge.
5. Develops practical skills of interpretation and presentation of data among the students.
6. Provides opportunities for human interaction leading to social growth.
7. Tends to develop initiative and responsibility among the students.
8. Provides an opportunity to the students to react to unexpected events, conditions or the actions of others.
9. Provides for a logical and psychological procedure.
10. Makes the student research minded.

Limitations of the Survey Method

The main limitations of survey method are as follows:

1. Requires good deal of time.
2. Is expensive.
3. If excessively used, it overburdens both the teacher and the students.
4. If data is insufficient, it leads to drawing of wrong generalisations.

Scope of Outdoor or Field Work or Survey in Civics

There is a great scope for field activities in the teaching of Civics. Following are some of the activities that can be organised in this regard:

1. Survey of economic needs of a community.
2. Land used survey.
3. Household survey.
4. Survey of sources of irrigation for farming in the neighbourhood.
5. Survey regarding means of personal transport.
6. Survey of agricultural implements used by farmers.
7. Survey of manures and fertilizers used by farmers in a village.
8. Traffic flow survey.
9. Working of a bank.
10. Working of a cottage industry.
11. Visit to a market.
12. Visit to stock exchange market.
13. Visit to a factory.
14. Visit to an industrial area.
15. Survey of economic and social amenities available in two different areas.
16. Working of an employment exchange.

Guidelines for Conducting a Survey and Illustrated Examples of Conducting Survey

The following instructions should be given to the students:

(i) They should establish proper rapport with the inhabitants of the area.
(ii) They should explain the objective of the survey.
(iii) Their questions should be simple and brief and should be of concern with their survey.
(iv) Such formalities as enquiring about the well-being of the person from whom the questions are to be asked will make the job easy.
(v) Questions should not be asked to a person when he is busy in work.
(vi) The answers should be noted down immediate in record book so that they do not forget it later on.

Stages of the Survey Process

The entire survey is divided into following five stages:

1. *Preliminary Stage*: At this stage, the surveyor prepares the plan of the field work. This is also known as planning stage.

2. *Operational Stage*: This stage comes when the surveyor completes his survey in the field according to the plan.

3. *Tabulation Stage*: After completing the survey the data collection are arranged in tabular form.

4. *Mapping Stage*: At this stage, maps of the concerned area are drawn on the basis of data collected during the survey.

5. *Reporting Stage*: Report is prepared after completing the entire survey process. Conclusions are presented in the report. Remedies to the problem are also suggested.

25

Civics Teacher and His Qualities

25.1 IMPORTANT ROLE OF THE TEACHER OF CIVICS

Independent India has by common consent adopted democracy as the best form of government. Democracy, however, needs a body of citizens who are ever prepared to shoulder the responsibilities that go with freedom. To have such citizens tomorrow, we must develop in our children and youth of today the knowledge competence and sense of values that would make them effective members of the nation. The home, the neighbourhood and the social and political institutions contribute to the development of good citizenship in growing children, but the greatest responsibility falls on the educational institutions and the school must lay a film foundation of these qualities and values.

Every society expects its educational institutions to help in developing competent citizens who would at the same time maintain the existing values and adopt fresh ones. Every school subject must, either through the matter taught or through the ways of learning it, contribute to growth of knowledge and competence in learners. Perhaps, of all the subjects Civics can contribute the most. A great responsibility, therefore, devolves upon the teacher of Civics. He must thoroughly prepare himself to meet that challenge.

25.2 ROLE OF THE CIVICS TEACHER IN THE SCHOOL

Following are the important roles which a teacher of Civics is expected to play:

1. Serving on school committees.
2. Working with parents.
3. Counselling students.
4. Filling out reports.
5. Acting as a home room teacher or house master.
6. Having contacts with school officials.
7. Issuing grades and reports.
8. Taking part in co-curricular activities.
9. Working with clerical staff of the school.
10. Taking part in social affairs involving teachers and students.
11. Taking part in community activities.
12. Assisting student teachers.
13. Participating in professional activities.
14. Performing miscellaneous duties in the total life of the school.

15. Organising UNESCO clubs.
16. Organising educational tours and excursions.

25.3 EIGHT C'S OF AN EFFECTIVE CIVIC TEACHER

1. Content mastery.
2. Confidence.
3. Caring of the pupils.
4. Communication skill.
5. Creativity.
6. Curiosity.
7. Commitment.
8. Catalytic power.

25.4 ESSENTIALS OF A CIVICS TEACHER

These may be categorised as: (i) Scholarship; (ii) Professional Training; (iii) Personality; (iv) Human Relations; (v) Teaching Skills.

I. Scholarship

This includes: acquaintance with problems of day-to-day life; background of a liberal education; reading of magazines and newspapers; an extensive and intensive study of books on the subject taught; sound knowledge of the subject taught.

II. Professional Training

This incorporates: desire for improvement; professional attitude; study of professional books; study of educational magazines; sound professional training.

III. Personality

It has three aspects: physical virtues; passive virtues; executive virtues.

(a) *Physical Aspects*: These include: personal appearance including dress, carriage, social expression, mannerism and personal cleanliness; etiquette including good manners, observance of social forms, courtesy and refinement; voice, rich and mellow; good language command including pronunciation, enunciation and grammar; health.

(b) *Passive Virtues*: These include: enthusiasm; fairness; friendliness; optimism; patience; self-control; sincerity; sympathy; tact; understanding.

(c) *Executive Abilities*: These include: adaptability; directive ability; industry; initiative; organising ability; resourcefulness; self-confidence; self-reliance.

IV. Human Relations

This comprises amicable relations; relations with students; relations with colleagues; relations with parents; relations with school personnel; relations with administrators, inspectors, supervisors, etc.; relations with the community; relations with publishers, stationers, sports dealers, etc.; relations with professional organisations and workers.

V. Teaching Skills

The Core Training Programme Package (CTPP) of the NCERT (1979) aiming at enabling the teachers to acquire mastery of manipulative skills for making their teaching effective includes the following skills:

(A) Skill of class management.
(B) Skill of communication (Teacher's Acts).
(C) Skill of interaction (Teacher-Pupil Acts).
(D) Skills of the use of teaching aids.
(E) Skills of attitude and behaviour.

A. Skills of Class Management

This includes:

1. *Control and Modification of Facial Expression*: The teacher should enter the class as a balanced person. It is necessary to emphasise the need for neatness and simplicity in his dress and appearance. Gaudy dress and shabby appearances should be avoided. The teacher must maintain his calm and confidence in the face of gesticulation and mimicking of the group.

2. *Greetings and Taking up Proper Positions in the Class*: The teacher is expected to offer the greetings while entering the class and then take the central place facing the class. He is also required to keep moving to the central place when students are offering greetings orally or by standing up in their seats and then face the class and respond to the greetings.

3. *Movements (Locomotion in the Classroom)*: Appropriateness of movements lies in providing a balanced supervision to the class and in being available at the right time to the student who needs help.

4. *Use of Appropriate Gestures in Various Situations and Various Stages*: Expressions of gestures of approval, appreciation and disapproval also have a great bearing on learning. The tendency of offering undue smile or encouragement or displeasure would form the negative points. Praise like gold and silver owes its utility to scarcity.

B. Skills of Communication (Teacher's Acts)

This comprises five skills: narration, recitation, dramatisation, explanation and demonstration. These skills are teacher-dominated.

(1) *Narration*: It involves the art of articulated speech making. It is of the following types:

(i) Event centred read out from a written text.
(ii) Event centred delivered with the help of notes.
(iii) Event centred spoken extempore.
(iv) Theme centred read out from a written text.
(v) Theme centred delivered with the help of notes.
(vi) Theme centred spoken extempore.

(2) *Recitation*: This includes:

(i) Reciting poems with a written script.
(ii) Reciting poems without a written script.
(iii) Reciting songs and rhymes with a written script.
(iv) Reciting songs and rhymes without a written script.

(3) *Dramatisation*: Dramatisation involves creation of both visual and audio environment appropriate to the event. Facial expressions appropriate to the occasion, modulation of voice, movements, pauses, creation of appropriate environment and proper sequence of presentation are very important. Dramatisation may be done in the following cases:

(i) Short events with the help of a written script.
(ii) Short events without the help of a written script.
(iii) Full story with the help of a written script.
(iv) Full story without the help of a written script.

(4) *Explanation*: This involves:

(i) Paraphrasing and correlating a given passage.
(ii) Elaborating and correlating a given passage.

(5) *Demonstration*: Following are the main steps:

(i) Preparing for a demonstration.
(ii) Explaining and demonstrating each step while performing.
(iii) Winding up a demonstration.

C. Skills of Interaction (Teacher-pupil acts)

This includes:

1. *Questions and Feedback*:
   (a) Framing various types of questions.
   (b) Framing questions pertaining to hierarchical objectives.
   (c) Presentation and distribution of questions to the whole class and feedback by verbal and non-verbal cues.
2. *Discussion*: This relates to
   (i) Selecting a suitable topic for discussion.
   (ii) Collecting and systematising information.
   (iii) Initiating, sustaining and guiding a discussion.
   (iv) Concluding a discussion.
3. *Problem Solving*: This pertains to:
   (i) Presentation of a problem.
   (ii) Analysis of the problem.
   (iii) Initiating and sustaining the process of problem solving.
   (iv) Guiding problem solving activities.

D. Skills in the Use of Teaching Aids

This consists of:

(a) Selection of teaching aids as per needs.
(b) Preparation of charts, models, maps and diagrams.
(c) Operation of mechanical aids visual aids.
(d) Positioning while writing on and explaining from the blackboard.
(e) Writing on the blackboard with reference to size, shape, boldness and colour of letters.
(f) Drawing, sketching, preparing tables and graphs on the blackboard.

E. Skills for attitude and behaviour

This comprises:

(a) Patient Listening.
(b) Suggesting.
(c) Guiding.
(d) Counselling.

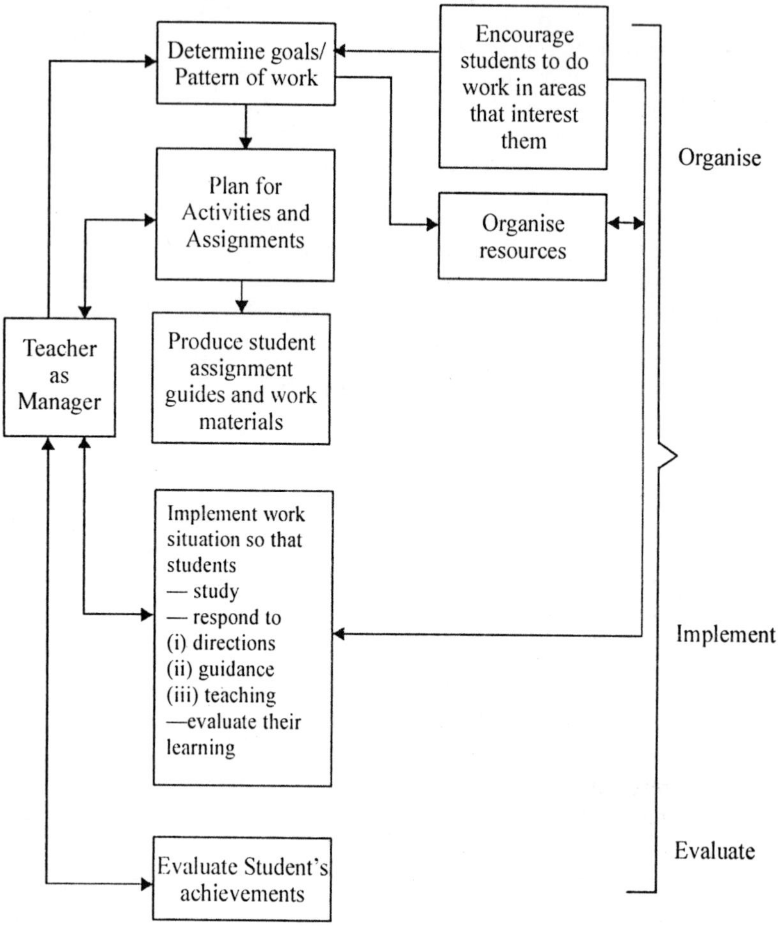

Fig. 25.1: Role of the Teacher (Davies 1978)

25.5 NINE SPECIAL QUALITIES OF A CIVICS TEACHER

1. Art of Development of Human Relations

Civics has always been the 'proper study of mankind', meaning, the study of human relationships. Such studies have a special broad emphasis because they are clustered around problems of social behaviour involving much diverse information drawn from many standard disciplines of knowledge. A Civics teacher, therefore, has to be very much concerned with this aspect. I.B. Berkson has observed, "As a specialist in human relations, he is called upon more often than many of his colleagues for public appearances and as a moderator of discussion of current and public interest."

2. Objectivity

Another responsibility of the teacher lies in the recognition and acceptance of objectivity as a continual criterion. The teacher's job is not to indoctrinate but to equip students to make decisions based on sound and objective knowledge. The teacher's objective duty is not to select for the student but to point out to him the choices which he may make himself and the method by which such choices may be made. The teacher of Civics is perhaps always the focus of public eye more than others because of the very nature of his subject matter, dealing as it does with people and with the contemporary scene. He must discuss issues that are considered controversial and, therefore, he must be doubly careful to pursue his investigations and teaching with objectivity.

3. Deep Knowledge of the Subject

The primary task of any teacher is a thorough knowledge of the subject matter which the teacher will attempt to get his students to learn. It is very necessary to bear in mind that 'lack of subject preparation stands near the top of virtually every list of causes of teacher failure'. This certainly does not mean that every school teacher must be a specialist in some branch of study. This is the function of doctors of philosophy in colleges and universities. The teacher, however, must know, broadly and deeply, the subject matter which he teaches.

4. Application of Field Study Theory

Teachers of Civics should early get into the habit of "field study" i.e. an application of a field theory to the process of learning, both for themselves and for their students. Each problem that comes up for investigation and learning is a field of inquiry which can be examined from many different points of view and by drawing upon the knowledge of many different disciplines.

5. A Well-informed Teacher

The contents of Civics change as rapidly as the world changes. The children of today grow up in a rapidly changing, moving and accelerated universe. They want latest and up-to-date knowledge. It is, therefore, very imperative that the teacher of Civics should be keenly interested in the latest developments in economics, social, political and cultural life not only of his own country but also of the world at large. The teacher of Civics should also acquire a broad understanding of the family, community, state, nation and the world at large.

6. Widely Travelled Person

First hand information of the important and significant cultural, geographical and historical buildings and places, art galleries, museums, dams, factories and projects, etc. will greatly help the teacher to enrich and vitalise teaching. Educational tours will also enable him to develop breadth of outlook and width of understanding which will assist him to interpret the culture of different parts of the country and the world to his pupils and thus promote emotional, national and international understanding.

7. A Good Communicator

Only a good communicator can guide discussion, stimulate interest and create in the classroom an environment which is rich in materials and where pupils are challenged to work and learn together. He should also be a good story teller and a man of imagination.

8. Skill in the Use of Technological Aids

A teacher is expected to possess adequate skill in the use of various aids which enables him to bring vividness and attractiveness in the lesson. Skill in map drawing and preparation of charts is also very essential.

9. An Interpreter of Various Experiences

M.L. Jacks has observed, "Above all he is an interpreter—interpreting not only the experience of his pupils but also the community to which they belong, its past no less than its present, its purposes and efforts to achieve those purposes, its cultural and technical achievements, its opportunities and possibilities, the invitation for service which it extends and the rewards, glittering or dimly discovered which it offers". A teacher of Civics is in a very advantageous position to bring together the past and the present, the new and the old, the alien and the native, the near and the distant.

25.6 SELF-APPRAISAL BY CIVICS TEACHER

A teacher may like to evaluate himself on the following points:

A. Attitude Towards the Subject

1. Does my attitude towards the teaching of Civics stress facts to the neglect of ideas?
2. Do I obtain most of my social knowledge from books?
3. Do I observe events and trends in my community with a reasonable degree of insight and critical judgement?
4. Do my assignments emphasise facts at the expense of interpretation and critical judgement?
5. Do my tests give students an opportunity to show that they have passed from memorisation stage to such procedure as comparison, contrast, selection, evaluation, deduction and judgment?
6. Do I help my students to interpret successfully the meaning of factual material?
7. Do I help students to use terms with precision?
8. Do I try to restrain excessive use of emotion to the thought processes of students?
9. Do I encourage the students to ask questions that show the development of capacities higher than that of memory alone?

10. Do students show a capacity to apply in Civics those procedures that are expected in sciences—collecting and cataloguing the facts and drawing conclusions from them?

11. Are students becoming increasingly aware of the importance of relevancy in the discussion of a subject?

12. Am I constantly relating Civics to the live the experiences of students?

13. Am I assisting students to work out a satisfactory compromise between the rigorous of abstract thinking and the human need for satisfying emotional loyalties?

14. Am I assisting students to adjust their thought processes and attitudes to the changes in the social world about them?

15. Do I arouse students' interest in my subject and acquaint them with its cultural and vocational values?

16. Do I set-up a provocative environment for the subject construction of experience, utilising many school and community resources?

17. Do I use community resources to link the subject with life?

18. Do I seek professional growth continuously by such procedures as study, travels, meetings, professional conferences, etc.?

B. Attitude of the Civics Teacher Towards Students

1. Do I provide every student in my classwork so suited to his abilities and needs that he can succeed with reasonable effort?

2. Do I treat my students with reasonable consideration?

3. Do I respect each individual's personality?

4. Do I have faith in the realisation of the best potentialities of each individual?

5. Do I keep my classroom atmosphere free from an intensely competitive atmosphere?

6. Do I stimulate students to discover and evaluate their own abilities, strengths and weaknesses and to meet difficulty or criticism in a constructive way?

7. Do I try to understand my students rather than to judge them?

8. Do I watch the trend of the developing interests and attitude of my students?

9. Do I respect the right of every student to have confidential information about himself withheld except when its release is authorised in his or public interest?

10. Do I avoid disparaging remarks about child which might undermine his confidence?

C. Attitude of the Teacher Towards Democratic Principles

1. Am I an example of democratic values?

2. Do I act as a democratic group leader?

3. Do I organise democratic groups which widen the area of common concern and encourage social interaction?

4. Do I provide conditions by which social control will come out of the group situation?

5. Do I arrange learning experiences which are based on the interests, capacities and needs of the children and which have continuity with life?

6. Do I provide conditions out of which arise opportunities for cooperatively solving a wide variety of problems and evaluating outcomes?
7. Do I share in formulating the purposes, policies and methods of the school?
8. Do I try to become integrated into the community through active participation in the social life of the group?
9. Do I aid in the achievement of new cultural patterns which extend freedom?
10. Do I discuss controversial issues from an objective point of view thereby keeping the class free from partisan opinion?

D. Attitude of the Civics Teacher Towards Parents and Colleagues, etc.

1. Do I provide parents with information that will serve the best interests of children?
2. Am I discreet with information received from parents?
3. Do I adhere to any reasonable pattern of behaviour accepted by the community for a professional person?
4. Do I refrain from discussing confidential and official information with unauthorised persons?
5. Do I deal with other members of the profession in the same manner as I myself wish to be treated?
6. Do I speak constructively of other teachers?
7. Do I honestly report to responsible persons in matters involving the welfare of the students, the school system and the profession?
8. Do I accept no compensation from producers of instructional materials when my recommendations effect the local purchase or use of such teaching aids?
9. Do I recognise that everyone has some strength and weakness?
10. Do I keep quiet when I see fault in others?
11. Do I pick appropriate time and opportunity to ask for help or advise from others?
12. Do I expect everything to go my own way?

26

Utilising Community Resources and Current Affairs in Civics

26.1 SIGNIFICANCE OF COMMUNITY RESOURCES

A Community is a child's laboratory for providing 'concrete', 'seeable' and 'tangible' resources for the teaching and learning of Civics. Every community possesses varied resources that greatly help in supplementing and enriching classroom teaching of Civics. It is not enough for a child to have a more 'knowledge' of the factories, farms, council sessions, museums and social agencies and institutions, etc. He must have the 'acquaintance with' all these. A school cannot remain an 'ivory tower'. A well-planned and thoughtfully and scientifically carried out programme of utilising community resources brings the school and the community quite closer to each other.

Important Community Resources

Ordinarily we include only those community resources which are within the 'walking distance'. Following are the important community resources:

1. *Places of Civic Interest*: These include the village panchayat, state legislature, etc.
2. *Places of Cultural Interest*: These include art theatres, clubs, emporium galleries, kala kendras, museums, radio stations, T.V. stations, zoos, etc.
3. *Places of Economic Interest*: These include agricultural farms, banks, commercial centres, telephone exchange, etc.
4. *Places of Geographical Interest*: These comprise dams, hills, lakes, rivers, river valley, projects, rocks, springs, tea garden, waterfalls, etc.
5. *Places of Historical Interest*: These include caves, churches, excavations, forts, gurdwaras, inscriptions, mosques, pillars and temples, etc.
6. *Places of Scientific Interest*: These consist of broadcasting stations, engineering institutes, thermal and hydro-power generating stations, television centres, etc.
7. *Government buildings*. These include fire stations, law courts, military installations, police stations, public libraries, etc.
8. *Forms of social control*. These comprise attitudes, beliefs, customs, ceremonies, rituals, traditions, etc.

26.2 METHODS OF UTILISING COMMUNITY RESOURCES

There are basically two ways:

I. Taking the school to the community.
II. Bringing the community to the school.

26.3 TAKING THE SCHOOL TO THE COMMUNITY

This includes:

(1) *Fields trips* to places of civic, cultural, geographical, social and scientific places. These trips are very helpful in integrating classroom instruction, stimulating imagination and learning providing sensory perceptions, seeing life vividly, learning in the art of living with others and expanding emotional intellectual horizons.

(2) *Community service* includes cleanliness of the community, attending on the sick, social service in fairs, planting of trees, digging of manure pits, making of drains, etc. All these activities help in developing a sense of dignity of labour, fellow-feeling, etc.

(3) *Social survey clubs* should be organised in schools which could undertake to investigate some of the crying needs and problems of the surrounding areas, e.g., the condition of roads, the percentage of literacy, the drainage of the village street or town, etc.

The study of the community will help the child:

(a) to have a keener knowledge and understanding of social facts.
(b) to develop a more sympathetic attitude towards other people.
(c) to develop a desire to take more active part in community affairs.
(d) to have a recognition of certain forces that shape personal and social living.
(e) to have a greater sensitivity to the need for accepting social responsibility.
(f) to have a more intelligent concern for democratic institutions, their functions and contributions.
(g) to develop new interests in occupational fields.
(h) to understand the problems of the community in a better way.
(i) to appreciate that the individual must play an important role for the welfare of the community.

The study of the community will help the teacher:

(i) to correlate his teaching with the life of the community.
(ii) to utilise a rich source of instructional aids and material.
(iii) to fit the curriculum to the personal and social needs of pupils.
(iv) to develop better public relations.
(v) to cooperate with all other agencies engaged in school and community improvement.

26.4 BRINGING THE COMMUNITY TO THE SCHOOL

Following are the important means of bringing the community to the school:

1. Celebration of Festivals

Our festivals are the 'visible' embodiments of our culture. They form an integral part of community life. They can be exploited for purposes of education in schools. To quote T.S. Avinashilingam, "These days, far from being declared holidays with schools closed, should be the days when school works in full strength not for the usual routine work, but for understanding the implications of the festivals and reliving them in the lives of children". Broadly speaking, we have six types of festivals:

(i) Religious festivals such as Shivaratri, Ganesh Chaudas, Durga Ashtmi, Anant Chaudas, Moharram, Easter, Christmas, etc.

(ii) Seasonal festivals, such as, Basant Panchmi, Lohri, Baisakhi, Nirjala Ekadasi.

(iii) Days of national rejoicinig accompanied by all kinds of fun, frolic, art and music, such as, Holi, Deepawali, Dussehra.

(iv) National festivals, e.g., Independence Day, Republic Day, Mahatmaji's Birthday.

(v) Celebrations of the birthdays of national heroes, e.g., Buddha, Shanker, Guru Govind Singh, Guru Nanak, Guru Ravi Dass, Lala Lajpat Rai, Guru Teg Bahadur, etc.

(vi) Literary festivals, e.g., The Days of Tulsidas, Surdas, Tagore, Kalidas.

By organising the birthdays of the national heroes, the students may be inspired by high ideals by re-telling the stories of their lives, the dangers they faced, the tremendous odds they had to overcome and the efforts they had to make before attaining their objectives. It must be stressed upon the students that they must dedicate themselves to the service of the nation to which they belong.

National celebrations, such as, Independence Day may be used as occasions to focus attention on the various problems to be solved.

Celebration of the literary festivals like the days of Kalidas and Tulsidas help us to remember them and study their great works.

Seasonal festivals help the children to understand the exhilarating effect of the change of seasons which the festivals indicate.

Attempt should be made to celebrate these festivals in the school premises so that the parents may also be brought into close contact with the activities of the school. Some of the festivals at which many people gather provide opportunities of social service to the students and teachers and thereby help in establishing a good relationship between the schools and community.

2. The School as a Social, Recreational and Cultural Centre

As most of the village schools are the only common meeting place in the villages, the cultural, physical and social activities in the villages should be planned, organised and held in the school with the joint cooperation of the public, the staff and the pupils. In this way, social service activities, such as, health and education weeks should be organised in the schools. Spiritual discourses, national celebrations, etc. attract members of the community to the school.

School grounds should also be made use of by village people for play as they have no other properly maintained and marked grounds available for them. They may play after the regular scheduled games for the pupils of the school are played.

The older sections of the community may also use the school ground to spend their evenings and discuss problems of the day. Evening programme involving entertainment by magic lanterns, projectors or shows, radio programmes can be organised with no prejudice to school work.

District tournaments may be conducted in the schools where thousands of people meet on these occasions.

3. Adult Education Centre

The schools should become centres of adult education both in rural and in urban areas. They should conduct regular campaigns against illiteracy and educate the adults of the locality. Students should also be associated in this work.

4. School Library

Efforts should be made to extend the services of the library to the community and this may take many forms:

(i) Issuing of books to parents and others in the name and responsibility of the pupils.

(ii) Opening of school library for public use before and after school hours on holidays and during vacation.

(iii) Giving a room to a social service organisation for keeping books and serving as a library for the community.

(iv) Issuing of books to the Secretary of Old Students Association who may act as librarian to the old students and may be responsible for returning the books to the school.

5. Experience of the Members of the Public

Various "resource visitors" may be invited to the school to give out their life experience in various walks of life and increase the general knowledge of the pupils. "What we would like to see is a two-way traffic", thus observed the Secondary Education Commission. "Interested members of the community engaged in various useful vocations and professions, will be invited to the school from time to time to talk about their particular work, to show its place and significance in the life of the community, to discuss its difficulties as well as its rewards. In this way, outside life will flow into the school and lower, if not knock down, the wall which at present isolates it from the currents of life operating outside."

6. Parent-teachers Association

There should be a parent-teachers association in the school which will help them to understand each other's point of view and will enable them to learn to cooperate in the common task for giving a better, more rational and more sympathetic deal to the children.

7. Exhibition

On occasions like the 'school day', an exhibition may be arranged for the benefit of the students and the public. This school exhibition may consist of three sections:

(i) A United Nations Posters and Charts Exhibition consisting of UN posters and charts collected by the school UN Association.
(ii) An arts and crafts exhibition consisting of paintings, drawings, collections of curious articles, stamps and coin collections, etc. In this exhibition, the collections of parents may also be included.

8. Meeting with the Parents of Children of a Particular Class

The parents of children of one particular class at a time may be invited to have a general discussion with the teachers in-charge of various subjects in that class. Discussion may centre around medical examination, projects undertaken by the class, progress of children and various other matters directly pertaining to the welfare of the children.

9. Inviting Parents to Witness Training Displayed by Children in Various Fields

Proficiency gained by a child at a particular game, or special aptitude shown at particular co-curricular activity may be brought to the notice of the parent.

10. Participation by the Parents in School Programmes

(a) Some parents can lend a helping hand in raising funds for the school. Their help should be secured. This will develop in them 'a sense of belongingness' to the school. These are the many ways through which the parents can help the school authorities, i.e., by donating or lending books, giving stipends to the poor students, arranging mid-day meals for the poor, etc.
(b) The school authorities should not hesitate to utilise the knowledge, skill and experience of the parents in supplementing class teaching. A doctor may be requested to give lectures on hygiene and physiology. Similarly the services of the parents in other fields may be utilised.

11. Career Conferences

Career conferences may be organised and the parents asked to attend them. Specialists in different fields may be selected from amongst the parents and their talks arranged on the various aspects of their occupations.

12. Association of the Parents in the Management of the School

Parents may be associated with the managing committees of the school. There can be no other person more interested in the school than the parents of the pupils.

13. Educational Conferences

Educational conferences should be organised in which parents, teachers and representatives of the education department participate. These conferences help exchange of thoughts, opinions, experiences, stock taking of the past and plan for the future.

14. Making the School as a Centre of Community Service

National, social and cultural functions should be organised in the school and the parents invited to attend them. School library may be thrown open to the parents. Labour weeks may be organised wherein students render them some social service to the community.

15. Celebration of Parents' Days

It may be a full working day. The parents may be taken round the school so that they may see how the classes are held and where their children sit. Actual teaching done in the class may be shown to them. On the parents day, activities, such as, debates, dramatics etc. may be organised. Children's work like calligraphy, models, charts etc. may be organised in the school.

The parents may be taken to special rooms like the geography, history, science, craft, etc. School sports may be organised on this day. It may take the form of Annual Prize Distribution or School Annual Day. Adequate preparation should be made so as to give a good show of school activities. A light refreshment to the parents may be served if the funds permit.

26.5 ROLE OF A TEACHER IN ENLISTING PARENT-TEACHER COOPERATION AND UTILISING COMMUNITY RESOURCES

1. The teacher should show considerable patience and tact in dealing with parents.
2. He should not mind facing a rebuff or two at the hands of some hostile parents.
3. He should allow the parents to talk freely.
4. He should make a thorough study of the child's problems, his abilities, limitations and assets and discuss these with his parents.
5. He should not let the parent have the idea that the teacher is prejudiced against his child.
6. He should offer suggestions to the parents in a polite and convincing manner.
7. He should make the parents realise that he is sincerely interested in the welfare of the child.
8. He should impress upon the parents that he is also an active partner in the education of the child.
9. He should convince the parents that the school has the atmosphere and the apparatus to give the child an all-round instruction, make his life at school a profitable period and make him fit for life after school.

In view of the mass illiteracy in our country, the initiative for the home school cooperation rests upon the teachers. To quote S. Bala Krishna Joshi, "Parental cooperation cannot be had by learned disquisitions on the subject, or by periodical pamphlets posted to the parties. It cannot be created overnight. We cannot wake up one fine morning and find the parents pitch forked into cooperation. It is based on series of silent acts of sincere service to children. It is the natural consummation of devoted deeds of dedication at the shrine of duty." All possible avenues should be explored to establish contacts with the parents.

In the end we may stress the importance of making the parents and the community interested in school work in these words. "The ordinary machinery for good school life," writes Thring, "is a thing of calculation and measurement but all discussion is in vain unless parents are interested."

26.6 SIGNIFICANCE OF CURRENT AFFAIRS

Teaching of current affairs makes the subject lively and interesting. Current affairs increase the power of discrimination, comprehension, critical and constructive analysis qualities needed for enlightened citizenship. Current affairs are a living history of civic and social events and form an important part of the learning activities of 'social living' for the child.

26.7 MEANING OF CURRENT AFFAIRS

It has been stated by *R.S. Kimbal*, "It is a field, which is concerned with all those happenings, both, domestic and international, social, political or economic a knowledge and understanding of which is necessary as a basis for a citizenship, of loyalty and service." Current affairs represent an 'extension' and 'exemplification' of the major topics of the curriculum in social sciences.

26.8 MAIN OBJECTIVES OF TEACHING-LEARNING OF CURRENT AFFAIRS

1. Expanding popular information.
2. Helping pupils identify important problems and issues to see how these affect their lives and to sense what they can do about them.
3. Helping pupils recognise democratic values in reacting to problems and issues.
4. Encouraging pupils develop habits of continued reading, listening, enquiring and observing ways of keeping well-informed about current affairs.
5. Helping pupils acquire proficiency in locating, organising and evaluating information on important issues and in evaluating and analysing the judgement of others on these issues.
6. Helping pupils acquire the greatest possible proficiency in the skills needed for obtaining and using social information.
7. Helping pupils develop facility in the democratic discussion of issues, orally and in writing.
8. Helping pupils see the importance of revising judgement in the light of new evidence.
9. Affording pupils a variety of opportunities for action to implement conclusions reached on important issues.
10. Promoting the ability of pupils to distinguish between more important and less important news items.
11. Promoting the ability of the pupils to take a position on controversial issues.

12. Developing the ability of the pupils to foretell the likely consequences in terms of present developments.

13. Helping the pupils relate school learning to life outside the school.

14. Promoting the critical appraisal of information obtained from the newspapers, magazine, radio, television, etc.

15. Promoting discrimination in the choice of authors and sources of information.

16. Promoting understanding and tolerance.

17. Promoting national oneness and unity.

18. Promoting the cause of international understanding and world peace.

26.9 SCOPE OF CURRENT AFFAIRS

Current affairs in social studies include ideas, changes, movements and trends in parties and politics, election results, change in governments and government policies, defence, international relations and foreign policies, etc. Reforms—cultural, economic, educational and social, etc. amendments in the constitution, court discussions on election petitions and interpretations, etc., all constitute current affairs in social studies.

26.10 NATURE OF CURRENT AFFAIRS

There are broadly speaking four methods to use current affairs in social studies:

1. *Current Affairs as a Subject*: This implies including current affairs as a separate discipline of school curriculum. This approach is not very conducive as it will unnecessary entail the study of additional subject and the students will treat it as an examination subject.

2. *Current Affairs as a Resource*: This view considers current affairs as a reservoir of illustrations which may be utilised to clarify the events, movements and topics described in the text-books. Here, it is not obligatory on the part of the teacher to devote definite time from his daily schedule to the study of current affairs. He may do so occasionally.

3. *Current Affairs as a Method*: According to this view, current affairs should be used as a method or as a means or approach or procedure of simplifying difficult portions of the text-book and linking the present with the past. Elections to Parliament or State legislatures, etc. may serve as starting points of a unit or a topic.

4. *Current Affairs as a Means of Motivation*: Children by nature are interested in what is happening now. They are interested in new inventions, new discoveries, elections, electricity, projects etc. These topics can serve as motivation as this is the natural procedure of going from known to unknown, concrete to abstract, definite to indefinite and from immediate to distant.

Criteria for the Selection of Current Events

1. *Continuity* of the process of any cultural, economic, political and social event.

2. *Consequence* of the effects or results of a particular news or report in the press.

3. *Nationality* regarding the countries, groups and persons influencing events.
4. *Recency* of discoveries and inventions, etc. affecting changes in different areas and especially social ones.
5. *Reliability* of sources, distinction between rumour and truth, fact and fiction.
6. *Scope* regarding the impact of an event—local, national or international.
7. *Suitability* regarding the age, ability, aptitude and interest of the students.
8. *Utility* of events for students.

Major Sources of Current Problems for Students

1. Radio and television.
2. Current newspapers.
3. Current magazines.
4. Newsreels in theatres.
5. Current events papers in schools.
6. Discussions with adults.
7. Assembly programme.
8. Youth forums in the community, sponsored by the school, community centres, youth groups, civic organisations.
9. School and local libraries.

Difficulties Encounters in the Teaching of the Current Events

1. Biased sources of information.
2. Limited sources of information.
3. Highly controversial issues to discuss.
4. Reading difficulties of some students.
5. Superficial coverage.
6. Inadequate methods of teaching current events.
7. Inadequate background of teachers.

26.11 ILLUSTRATIONS OF CURRENT AFFAIRS

Illustrations can be given as:

1. General elections in democratic countries.
2. General elections in non-democratic countries.
3. Elections to the President.
4. Space travels.
5. Breaking out of hostilities between two countries.
6. International conference and meetings and conferences sponsored by the UNO and other agencies.
7. International years like the child, women, etc.
8. Interesting court cases and judgements.
9. Visits of a foreign dignitary.
10. Celebration of national or international day.
11. Special campaigns like literacy, van mahotsav, prohibition, cleanliness drive, family welfare, etc.
12. Inauguration of special projects.

13. Budget.
14. Defence.
15. Price index.
16. Taxation.
17. Population census.

Methods of Teaching Current Events

1. Chart making.
2. Debates or broadcasting and T.V. programmes.
3. Dramatising news events.
4. Drawing cartoons to illustrate events.
6. Map drawing.
7. Mock Parliament.
8. Morning assembly talks.
9. News bulletin board and pinning clippings on it, pinning strips of yarn from each clipping to the place on the map where the event occurred, etc.
10. Preparation of notebooks and files.
11. Quiz competitions.
12. Round table discussion.
13. Talks of experts.
14. Visits to gram panchayat, state legislature and parliament.
15. Wall of the world—depiction of current events on the wall of the social studies room through various types of visual material.

26.12 ROLE OF THE TEACHER

The role of a teacher is that of a successful guide and a leader. For playing this role he must be wide awake, an active, enlightened and well-informed person. He must listen to news broadcasts and telecast, read current events, attend lectures and discussions, study and analyse reports and editorials, participate in school and community relations and see good news reels and documentaries. *R.S. Kimball* has observed, "Current affairs can be taught successfully when a teacher is sufficiently interested himself. The varying degrees of success, however, seem to indicate that the ability of the teacher, rather than the quality of the medium or the method is the determining factor. Almost any device can be used effectively. The teacher's own interest, his own enthusiasm, his own understanding of what should be accomplished, are the matters which determine the failure or success of current events teaching. The best available media fail in their purpose when used by a class guided by a teacher unskilled in methods of current events instruction."

26.13 CONTROVERSIAL TOPICS AND CIVICS TEACHERS

Teachers are under close scrutiny of the public as they form the core of the democratic action. It is widely believed that the standard of behaviour set by them in and out of the school stands examination and can be worthy of emulation by the impressionable youngsters who make up the student body. The teachers should have opinions but opinions derived in an objective manner from a weighing of evidence. The teacher is expected to discuss issues that are considered controversial. Most of the current issues are controversial since they demand choice. If there is no ground for choice and, therefore, no problem of controversial treatment, the teacher must be very careful to pursue his investigations with objectivity. The teacher must operate within the limits set by his profession and the pursuit of truth. He should not air his without any proportion.

Academic freedom implies that the teachers should be willing to exercise good judgement, hold objectivity in high esteem and encourage reflective thought in themselves.

The teachers must also bear in mind that just as they are involved in academic freedom, students too equally and more importantly hope to learn to evaluate facts and human relationship for which they must have academic freedom to learn. Freedom of enquiry must be followed by free and objective instruction.

Academic freedom does not imply the right of indoctrination. James High of the University of California has explained this as, "An opinion, derived by any means, if made the sole content of teaching and set-up as the 'right' answer, constitutes indoctrination and cannot be countenanced under the guise of academic freedom". Schools are for the purpose of broadening the horizons of the students. Means employed must be objective and honest differences of opinion accepted. It is the duty of the school system to encourage reflective thought. Continued interest in the preservation of academic freedom throughout all ranks of society must stem originally from the schools. Reflection is the only unique and original tool man has reflected thought concentrated on the records of the human past results in wisdom of the exercise of human choice in the future. After reflecting, man does not always make the best choices, but without it any good choice would be totally accidental. Critical, constructive and tolerant attitude is a great part of adequate citizenship and all efforts have to be made in teaching to realise this objective. A teacher has to perform this task very intelligently and skilfully.

One school of thought tends to hold the view that school is a temple of learning and its devotees, i.e., children should be kept away from controversial issues. They point out that the conflicts of the real world must not enter into the portals of this temple and conflicting issues must not find their way in it. If they enter, they are likely to vitiate to the classroom environment.

Richard E. Servey points out that basically teaching acts comprise the following:

(1) Clarifying with the children the issue that lies at the heart of their concern.

(2) Guiding them in identifying the different choices possible for deciding the issues.

(3) Encouraging them to explore the facts and ideas which support the issues.

(4) Guiding them in an analysis of the facts and ideas to determine bases for opinions.

(5) Guiding them towards suspended judgement.

The teacher should encourage the students to make their own choice of the moment, but to think more about it and to be on the alert for more pertinent information. The teacher should feel free to express his own favoured choice for action and to substantiate it but should point out that he too is limited in what he can do about making the final decision. He can somewhat assuage fears by suggesting that the other choices for action have strengths to be considered.

Regarding older pupils bringing up an issue unexpectedly not because they are particularly curious or frightened but because they are keen to know the reaction of the teacher, it may be observed that it will be advisable if the teacher responds by turning the issue addressing back to the questioner or by having the entire class respond to it. When the students have given their points of view, he should present his own in a most matter-of-fact way'. The teacher in no case should make provocative statements or make derogatory remarks directly or indirectly.

26.14 SOME SUGGESTIVE ACTIVITIES FOR THE TEACHING OF CURRENT EVENTS

1. Make a collection of clippings on a current issue or hill and mount them for the class or school to see, taking care to have several view-points represented.
2. Make a similar collection of cartoons on an issue, again presenting at least two major points of view.
3. Listen to a radio or television programme on an issue or current importance.
4. Develop a large chart showing how a bill is written, introduced, and developed in a state of national legislative body. Or make a flannelgram to show how a bill develops into a law or is finally rejected.
5. Present a panel before a class, school assembly, local club, or other organisation in your community.
6. Draw a world map showing the different types of government now existing.
7. Study the life of a political leader, past or present.
8. Study the life of a champion of democracy in the economic or social or educational areas of life.
9. Interview local officials on their duties and problems.
10. Interview an older citizen about the change in township governments in his or her lifetime.
11. Examine the local budget for the current year and compare it with similar budgets in other year.
12. Do the same with the state or federal government budgets.
13. Examine your student government and try to suggest ways in which it might be improved.
14. Read about presidents of Local Bodies and explain why they have increased in numbers in recent years.

16. Organise a library squad, audio-visual squad, or some other service activity or join one if it is already in existence.
17. Plan a survey of school traffic or traffic hazards, or make some similar survey that will benefit your school and/or community.

18. Suggest improvement in the ways of holding school elections.

19. Interview local officials on planning activities.

20. Make a list of the services rendered by your local government and check the ones that help you as an individual directly or indirectly.

21. Do the same for the state and/or federal government.

22. Take pictures of local government activities and mount them in your classroom or school.

23. Arrange a debate on some current issue, such as, the raising of the sales tax, the lowering of the voting age, etc.

24. Visit the local employment agency and find out about its activities.

25. Investigate the growth of the movement of towns.

26. Prepare an exhibit of the UN and/or its agencies.

27. Start a campaign to collect books and magazines for your school library.

28. Visit a local court and talk with the judge.

29. Attend the meetings of political parties in your community.

30. Arrange for a trip to the state assembly while it is in session.

31. Suggest the holding of a model Parliament or a model UN Assembly to the proper persons in your school or community.

32. Conduct a poll of citizens on a current issue, being sure to word your topics without bias and to protect the answers of the persons interviewed.

33. Obtain and use in class the income-tax forms prepared by the income-tax department.

27

Role of Teaching of Civics in Emotional and National Integration

27.1 MEANING OF NATIONAL AND EMOTIONAL INTEGRATION

National and emotional integration implies a feeling of oneness which may transcend all groups or cultural differences and synthesise the different religions, castes, linguistic communities emotionally into a compact whole. It implies a feeling among citizens of India that India is 'One' and we belong to it culturally and emotionally. "What is in the interest of India, it is in our interest. Country comes first and other loyalties are subservient to it. We must share and respect common objectives, purposes or ideas and give them a higher place over sectional, linguistic, racial and other loyalties.

The Kothari Commission defines it as, "National integration includes a confidence in nation's future development of feeling of values and duties."

Generally national and emotional integration is treated as a single term and not taken as two terms, i.e., national integration and emotional integration. Sometimes only the term 'national integration' is used.

Emotional integration may imply several things, i.e., individual emotional integration or emotional integration of personality of an individual, family emotional integration, i.e., integration with the family, caste, emotional integration, linguistic emotional integration, regional emotional integration and national emotional integration.

The term emotional integration in educational psychology is used with reference to the integration of the personality of an individual.

27.2 WHY NATIONAL AND EMOTIONAL INTEGRATION! NEED FOR NATIONAL AND EMOTIONAL INTEGRATION

India is a land of so many faiths, creeds, castes, languages, etc. It is very essential that people of different faiths and creeds, etc. think in terms of nationalism and place the welfare of the country above such narrow considerations. In the words of the Emotional Integration Committee, "One of the hardest problems before us today is the building up a national mind by curbing the religious, linguistic and communal conflicts which tend to disunite us". Jawaharlal Nehru observed that national integration would weld Indian people into one and make India into "one strong national unit maintaining at the same time all our wonderful diversity".

Jawaharlal Nehru stressed four aspects of National and Emotional Integration:

1. National Integration for the Creation of a Mighty Nation

The main thing we have to keep in mind is the emotional integration of India. We must guard against being swept away by momentary passion, whether it is religion misapplied to politics or communalism or provincialism or casteism. We have to build up this great country into a mighty nation, mighty not in the ordinary sense of the world, that is, having great armies and all that, but mighty in thought, mighty in action, mighty in culture and mighty in its peaceful service of humanity.

We should not become parochial, narrow-minded, provincial, communal and caste-minded, because we have a great mission to perform. Let us, the citizens of the Republic of India, stand up straight, with straight backs, and look up at the skies, keeping our feet firmly planted on the ground and bring about this synthesis, this integration of the Indian people. Political integration has already taken place to some extent, but what I am after is something much deeper than that of an emotional integration of the Indian people so that we might be welded into one, and made into one strong national unit, maintaining at the same time all our wonderful diversity.

2. National Integration for the Success of Democracy and Socialism

Democracy, while it ensures free expression, and freedom of thinking, also demands something else. It demands unified action afterwards. It demands acceptance of decisions taken. Otherwise, there is a break up. It has been our misfortune through long periods of history to be very fictitious, to be liable to separatism, with the result that the great strength of India has been wasted in inner conflict, in inner argument and in fissiparous and separatist tendencies. Surely, we should learn something from the history of India. We have produced great men in every field of human endeavour, in thought, in action, in, art, in literature, in music. Yet we have failed to take advantage of this greatness because of the tendency amongst us to disrupt, to go our individual ways.

3. National Integration by Ending the Curse of Caste System

What will emerge from the labour and the tumults of the present generation? I cannot say what will tomorrow's India be like. I can only express my hopes and wishes. I want India to advance on the material plane to raise the standards of living of her vast population; I want the narrow conflicts of today in the name of religion or caste, language or province, to cease, and a classless and casteless society to be built up where every individual has full opportunity to grow according to his worth, and ability. In particular, I hope that the curse of caste will be ended, for there cannot be either democracy or socialism on the basis of caste.

4. National Integration through Synthesising Religious Values

Four great religions have influenced India, two emerging from her own thought, Hinduism and Buddhism, and two coming from abroad but establishing themselves firmly in India, Christianity and Islam. Science today challenges the old concept of religion. But if religion deals not with dogmas and ceremonials, but rather with the higher things of life, there should be no conflict with science or *inter-se* between religions. It might be the high privilege of India to help in bringing about this synthesis. That would be in India's ancient tradition inscribed on Asoka's Edicts.

Following are the main reasons for bringing about national and emotional integration of India:

1. Developing broadmindedness among the people.
2. Economic development of India.
3. Raising the standard of living and life of the people.
4. Developing patriotism and national spirit among the people.
5. Safeguarding the unity and integrity of India.
6. Making democracy successful.
7. Safeguarding national defence.
8. Developing spirit of mutual tolerance and understanding.
9. Bringing harmony among people of diverse outlooks.

27.3 CONSEQUENCES OF LACK OF NATIONAL AND EMOTIONAL INTEGRATION

1. Rise of communal tendencies resulting in communal riots.
2. Spread of the cult of casteism.
3. Narrow regional outlook.
4. Growth of separatist tendencies.
5. Rise of terrorism.
6. Danger to national unity.
7. Hurdles in law and order.

27.4 FAVOURABLE FACTORS FOR NATIONAL AND EMOTIONAL INTEGRATION

1. Constitutional provisions regarding equality of opportunity.
2. Declaring India as a secular state and freedom of worship etc.
3. Provision of special facilities for the disadvantaged sections.
4. Constitution of All-India Services.
5. Division of powers between the Union and State Governments.
6. National symbols.
7. Special financial help to backward regions.
8. Cultural unity and teachings of great saints.
9. Network of means of communication and transport.

27.5 BARRIERS TO NATIONAL AND EMOTIONAL INTEGRATION

Major barriers to national and emotional integration in India are as under:

- **Casteism**
- Classism
- Communalism
- Ignorance

- Illiteracy
- Linguism – Narrow mindedness
- Provincialism – Political ambitions
- Regionalism
- Religious fundamentalism
- Sectarianism
- Selfishness of leaders
- Uneven regional development

27.6 ROLE OF EDUCATION IN DEVELOPING NATIONAL INTEGRATION

In the words of *Dr. Radhakrishnan*, "National integration cannot be built by brick and mortar, it cannot be built by chisel or hammer. It has to grow silently in the minds and hearts of men. The only process is the process of education."

The Emotional Integration Committee (1961) highlighted the role of education as "Education can play a vital role in strengthening emotional integration. It is felt that education should not only aim at imparting knowledge but should develop all aspects of a student's personality. It should broaden the outlook, foster a feeling of oneness and nationalism and a spirit of sacrifice and tolerance so that narrow group interests and submerged in the larger interests of the country."

27.7 EMOTIONAL INTEGRATION COMMITTEE (1961) ON THE ROLE OF CIVICS AND SOCIAL STUDIES IN EMOTIONAL INTEGRATION

The Ministry of Education, Government of India, appointed the Committee on Emotional Integration under the Chairmanship of Dr. Sampurnanand in 1961. The Committee made valuable recommendations on the role of education in promoting the process of emotional integration programmes for youth in schools and colleges. The Committee laid special stress on the role of Civics and Social Studies. It observed, "The teaching of Civics and Social Studies at all levels, i.e., the primary, secondary and university stages would impart knowledge of the geographical, historical and cultural background of the country and the world as a whole."

The Committee gave the following suggestions:

1. *Reorientation of the Curriculum*: It is felt that the school and college curriculum should be reoriented to suit the needs of a secular state.

At the primary stage, stories, poems, folklore and teaching of social studies, national anthem and other national songs, should find an important place.

At the secondary stage the curriculum should include, among other things, the study of language and literature, social studies, moral and religious instruction and co-curricular activities.

At the university level the study of different social sciences, languages and literature, culture and art and also the exchange of teachers and students should place in the curriculum.

2. *Co-curricular Activities*: The pslace of co-curricular activities in the curriculum is considered to be very important. It is felt that participation in co-curricular activities helps in the growth of a well-balanced and well-adjusted personality. It creates a group feeling of oneness and brotherhood, broadens

the outlook and develops a catholicity of spirit and tolerance which are necessary for good citizenship. These activities include common observance and celebration of festivals and events of national importance, sports, educational excursions, tours, and picnics, military training like the NCC, ACC, scouts and guides, student camps, debates, symposia, dramatics, and youth festivals. The use of audio-visual aids like films, pictures, radio and T.V. is very necessary.

3. *Text-books*: In order that the text-books play their legitimate role in strengthening of emotional integration, it is necessary that they be reoriented and improved. In the preparation of text-books special care needs to be taken to see that facts are not misrepresented, distorted or exaggerated to create prejudice. The get-up as well as the content of text-books require a change. At the primary level, the text-books writers should make a liberal use of pictures and illustrations so as to create interest in the child at the very outset.

4. *Singing of National Anthem*: Children should be taught to sing the National Anthem in unison and behave in a disciplined way when it is sung. They should also be taught the meaning of the verses.

5. *Reverence for the National Flag*: Students should be told the history of the National Flag and taught at the earliest stage to show reverence for the National Flag.

6. *Celebrations of National Days*: January 26, August 15 and October 2 should be celebrated in schools with the full participation of the teachers, the students and the community.

7. *Special Talks on the Unity and Oneness of the Country*: Special meetings of the school assembly should be held from time to time and the speakers speak to the children on topics dealing with the unity and oneness of the country.

8. *Taking Pledge*: Students may be asked to repeat a pledge twice a year dedicating themselves to the service of their country. A draft of such a pledge in English is given below:

> "India is my country, all Indians are brothers and sisters.
>
> I love my country, and I am proud of its rich and varied heritage. I shall always strive to be worthy of it.
>
> I shall give my parents, teachers and all elders respect and treat everyone with courtesy. I shall be kind to animals.
>
> To my country and my people, I pledge my devotion. In their well-being and prosperity alone lies my happiness."

9. *Open-Air Dramas*: Open-air dramas may be staged four times a year by every school. At least one play should be based upon a theme derived from the classics or from the history of ancient India. In predominant Hindu areas there should be some plays dealing with non-Hindu lives and vice versa.

10. *Students Exchange and Tours*: Such tours should be conducted from one state to another. The inter-state visits, if properly organised, should do much to acquaint both teachers and children with different parts of the country.

A network of youth hostels should be set-up by all the states in selected places.

11. *School Improvement*: Students should be associated with the cleanliness of the school premises. This would not only increase their pride in it, and loyalty to the school but would also help in improving the school for future students.

12. *Suitable Handbooks for Teachers*: Suitable handbooks for teachers in the social studies and languages should be published.

13. *All-India Award*: An annual all-India award for the best general essay on different States in India should be instituted.

14. *Educational and Travel Documentaries*: Educational and travel documentaries with particular emphasis on various aspects of Indian scenery, flora and fauna, on various developmental and reconstruction programmes should be produced for use in schools and these should form a regular feature of the schools.

15. *School Projects*: Schools may conduct several projects which improve their general knowledge of the country. For instance a 'Know Your Country' project can be undertaken during which children may share in your collection of information about a State in the Indian Union other than their own.

16. *Exchange of Professors*: Distinguished professors should also be deputed periodically to different universities so that a large range of students can benefit from their experience.

17. *All-India Youth Council*: An all-India youth council should be set-up to coordinate all the youth programmes taken up by the Central and State Governments and also to help various agencies to extend their efforts.

National Policy on Education (1986 and Modified in 1992) on National Integration

Common Core Curriculum: The NPE provides for a common core curriculum including the History of Indian Freedom Movement, the constitutional obligations and other content essential to national identity. These contents are expected to cut across subject areas and designed to promote values such as India's common cultural heritage, egalitarianism, democracy and secularism, equality of the sexes, protection of the environment, removal of social barriers, etc.

Uniform Educational Structure: A uniform educational structure should be established all over the country.

Equality of Opportunity: Equal educational opportunities should be provided to all.

Educational Opportunities in All Parts: All parts of the country should be provided with suitable educational institutions.

Social and National Service: Social and national service should be made an integral part of education as its absence is also responsible for increasing the gulf between the educated and the uneducated classes.

Role of the Civics Teacher in National and Emotional Integration

(See the Role of Civics Teacher in Chapters on 'Civics Teacher and Current Affairs' and 'Civics Teacher and His Qualities')

Emotional Integration—A Challenge

The emotional integration of the Indian people is a challenge that cannot be ignored. Charity and compassion must be practised if they are not to remain catchwords and empty phrases. Integration touches all points of national life and depends in the final analysis on our young people in schools and colleges. Teachers of Political Science and Civics can play an important role in the field of national and emotional integration.

28

Salient Features of Indian Constitution

28.1 THE CONSTITUTION OF INDIA AS A GUIDING FORCE AND SOURCE OF INSPIRATION

The Constitution of India and in fact of every nation in the world sets out its cultural, economic, educational, political, secular and social ideals and values. It also provides broader outlines for their fulfilment.

The Constitution of India was adopted by the Constituent Assembly on November 26, 1949 and it came into force on January 26, 1950.

Notwithstanding certain constraints, the Constitution of India has worked well when we compare the political state of affairs of some countries of the Third World. As envisaged by the founding fathers of the Constitution, democracy is firmly established in India. In our neighbouring countries like Myanmar, Pakistan and Sri Lanka, several political upheavals have taken place. In India, elections to the Parliament and State Legislatures have taken place, by and large, on time. Changes in government of different political parties have occurred in a peaceful manner at the Central and State levels. Unity and integrity of the country has remained intact.

Integration of some 600-odd states was a marvellous feat.

Judiciary has been working independently and in an impartial manner.

However, there is a negative side also. It appears there has been a loss of appropriate ethical and moral values. The concept of national character has not taken roots.

Some of the terms like 'Socialist' and 'Secular' have been used without explaining their meanings. On account of this Sir Ivor Jennings has described the Indian Constitution as a "Lawyers' Paradise." The Constitution has provided a vast scope for litigation.

28.2 CONSTITUTION OF INDIA AT A GLANCE

The Constitution of India covers all fields of national life and is very comprehensive. It is the lengthiest constitution in the world. It contains the Preamble, 395 Articles incorporated in 22 parts. Besides, there are 12 Schedules which furnish details and explanations of the Articles. Following chart provides the broad contents of the Articles and Schedules:

Parts: Subjects, Articles and Number of Articles in the Constitution

Sl.No.	*Subject*	*Articles*	*Number of Articles*
1.	Union and Its Territories	1 to 4	4
2.	Citizenship	5 to 11	7
3.	Fundamental Rights	12 to 51	40
4.	Fundamental Duties	51A	(included in 51)
5.	Union	52 to 151	100
6.	States	152 to 237	86
7.	States in Part B of the First Schedule	238	Repealed
8.	Union Territories	239 to 242	3 (242 repealed)
9.	Panchayats	243	1
9A	Municipalities	243	
10.	Scheduled and Tribal Areas	244	
11.	Relations between the Union and the States	245 to 263	19
12.	Finance, Property, Contracts and Suits	264 to 300	37
13.	Trade, Commerce and Intercourse within the Territories of India	301 to 307	7
14.	Service under the Union and States	308 to 323	16
14A.	Tribunals	323	1
15.	Elections	324 to 329	6
16.	Special provisions relating to certain classes	330 to 342	13
17.	Official Language	343 to 351	9
18.	Emergency Provisions	352 to 360	9
19.	Miscellaneous	361 to 367	7
20.	Amendment of the Constitution	368	1
21.	Temporary, Transitional and Special Provisions	369 to 392	24
22.	Short Title, Commencement, Authoritative Text in Hindi and Repeals	393 to 395	3

28.3 CHIEF FEATURES OF THE CONSTITUTION OF INDIA

1. Appropriate Sources of the Constitution

The Constitution of India derives its sources from the following:

(1) Heritage of India.

(2) Ideals and Values as motivated the freedom fighters.

(3) Purna Swaraj Resolution.
(4) Study of Constitution of Other Countries.

2. Representative Nature of the Constitution Makers

The Constituent Assembly was a representative body of nearly all communities and regions of India. It included some of the foremost men and women in India who had distinguished themselves in various walks of life. The best available legal talent in the country was associated with the framing of the constitution. The Assembly had in it several political leaders who had fought for the freedom of the country. Dr. Rajendra Prasad, Jawaharlal Nehru, Sardar Patel and Maulana Azad were the acknowledged leaders of the Indian National Congress. Competent persons like Dr. Shyama Prasad Mookerjee, Sardar Baldev Singh, Frank Anthony and H.P. Modi were associated with the framing of the constitution even though they were not members of the Indian National Congress. Frank Anthony and H.P. Modi represented the Anglo-Indians and Parsees respectively. Constitutional experts like Alladi Krishnaswamy Ayyar, B.R. Ambedkar and K.M. Munshi were also members of the Constituent Assembly. Mrs. Sarojini Naidu and Mrs Vijaya Laxmi Pandit deserve special mention.

B.N. Rao, an eminent jurists was the Constitutional Adviser.

3. The Preamble as the Soul of Our Constituent

In the words of Gajendragadkar, a former Chief Justice of India, "The basic philosophy can be found in the Preamble to the Constitution".

The preamble serves as the 'light house' which throws lights on the aspirations, ideals and values of the people for which a constitution is framed. Accordingly, the Preamble to the Indian Constitution sets out the national objectives of the Indian State. It indicates the manner in which the Government of India is to be carried on. It also states that the people of India are determined to realise their objectives in accordance with the Constitution.

Preamble

WE, THE PEOPLE OF INDIA, having solemnly resolved to constitute India into a SOVEREIGN SOCIALIST SECULAR DEMOCRATIC REPUBLIC and to secure to all its citizens:

JUSTICE, social, economic and political;

LIBERTY of thought, expression, belief, faith and worship;

EQUALITY of status and opportunity; and to promote among them all;

FRATERNITY assuring the dignity of the individual and the unity and integrity of the Nation:

IN OUR CONSTITUENT ASSEMBLY this twenty-sixth day of November, 1949, do HEREBY ADOPT, ENACT AND GIVE TO OURSELVES THIS CONSTITUTION.

Note: The word 'Socialist', 'Secular' and 'Integrity' were added to the Preamble by the Forty-Second Constituent Amendment Act of 1976 which came into effect on January 3, 1977.

Main Features of the Preamble

Preamble

- Source of the Constitution
- Nature of the Polity or the State
- Date on which the Constitution was Finalised
- Basic Ideals and Objectives of the Indian Republic

Preamble at a Glance

Source of the Constitution	We, THE PEOPLE OF INDIA (The Constitution is enacted by the People of India)
Nature of the Polity or State	SOVEREIGN SOCIALIST SECULAR DEMOCRATIC REPUBLIC
Basic Objects or Ideals of the Indian Republic	JUSTICE, social, economic and political. LIBERTY of thought, expression, belief, faith and worship. EQUALITY of status and opportunity; and to promote among them all. FRATERNITY assuring the dignity of the individual and the unity and integrity of the Nation.
Date on which the Constitution was Enacted and Adopted	26 November, 1949

Fig. 28.1: Main Features of the Preamble

4. Appropriate Goals

In our Constitution, we have set before us the goals of Socialism, Secularism and Democracy. The Constitution aims at providing equal opportunities to all the citizens irrespective of sex, caste, colour or religion. There are special provisions in the Constitution for the upliftment of the weaker sections of the society.

5. Democratic Republic Based on Adult Franchise

The Constitution of India vests the sovereignty in the people of India.

Indian Republic is based on adult franchise. Article 325 of the Constitution also lays accent on the principle of adult franchise. It says that "There shall be one General Electoral Roll for every territorial constituency". No person shall be excluded from the electoral roll on grounds only of religion, race, caste, sex or any of them.

The Constitution fixed 21 years as the age of adult franchise. The 61st Amendment Act (1989) to the Constitution lowered the voting age from 21 to

18 years. *Thus, as per provisions of Article 326 of the Constitution every person, who is a citizen of India, and who is not less than eighteen years of age and is not otherwise disqualified under any law on the ground of non-residence, unsoundness of mind, crime or illegal practice, shall be entitled to be registered as a vote for elections.*

6. Fundamental Rights

The citizens of India have been guaranteed certain Fundamental Rights. If anyone feels deprived of these rights, the High Court and the Supreme Court can be approached for justice. The provision of these Fundamental Rights in the Constitution acts as a check on arbitrary action on the part of those in authority. The courts can give orders even to the Central or State Government if they think that a citizen's Fundamental Rights are being violated. These rights are very important for the citizens and have been discussed in details in a separate chapter.

7. Fundamental Duties

Rights and duties go together. They are the two faces of the same coin. Every right carries with it some duty. It is from this point of view that our Constitution has outlined the fundamental duties of every citizen.

8. Justice-Social, Economic and Political

The Constitution aims at making laws and taking measures that would ensure that there is no exploitation of the weaker sections of the society. Social justice is secured when there are provisions such as old age pensions, compensation for injury that occurs during work and assistance to social groups that have remained neglected over the centuries.

Our Constitution aims at establishing a socialist society. In our country, there are some people who are very rich. There are others who are very poor. The Constitution aims at providing measures through which these economic disparities may be reduced. It is not the intention to make the rich people, poor. The intention is to raise the living standards of people who are poor or economically backward. There are special provisions in the Constitution that allow the Government to make legislation for protecting the interests of the weaker sections of the society.

Economic justice is ensured through provisions like minimum wages and equal opportunities for employment in commercial establishments etc.

Political justice, implies, that there is freedom to have any political views as long as they do not go against the interest of the country as a whole. Similarly, there is the freedom to vote for any recognised political party in the country.

9. A Welfare State

The Constitution speaks about the establishment of a welfare state. A welfare state is the state which performs functions aimed at the welfare of the people.

10. Directive Principles of State Policy

The Directive Principles of State Policy have great significance as their implementation will lead to the establishment of economic as well as social democracy in India. The Union and State Governments have put them to use for making many laws.

These directive principles provide guidance to the government that certain ideals must be kept in view while framing state policies. In general, these principles provide that the state shall strive to take measures that would ensure an equitable distribution of national wealth, provide employment opportunities to all.

11. India — A Secular State: Religious Freedom and Equality

The Indian concept of secularism is expressed in the following often quoted principles:

(i) '*Sarva-dharma-samata*' or 'Sarva-dharma-samabhava' — equal regard for all faiths and creeds.

(ii) '*Ekam brahma Vipra Bahuda Vadanti*' — God is one, wise men call Him by different name.

Although the word secularism was introduced only in 1976 in our Constitution, our secularism is historical.

Ashoka's secular outlook is one of the landmarks not only of Indian civilisation but also of the human civilisation. He made a passionate appeal for developing a spirit of reverence and tolerance for all faiths.

12. Indian State as a Socialist State

The Preamble declares India as a socialist and secular state. This term, refers to such a political system by which all the sections of the society in general and weaker sections in particular should get an adequate opportunity for development. There should be no exploitation of individuals by individuals.

13. Freedom of Expression

Articles 14 to 32 of the Constitution deal with Fundamental Rights. Articles 19 to 22 relate to Rights of Freedom. Article 19 provides for:

(i) Freedom of Speech and Expression.
(ii) Freedom of Assembly.
(iii) Freedom of Association.
(iv) Freedom of Movement.
(v) Freedom of Residence.
(vi) Freedom of Profession.

14. Impartial and Independent Judiciary

Every citizen, irrespective of any distinction has the right to approach the judiciary for the protection of his rights. Judiciary is a very important organ of the government. It interprets the Constitution correctly, safeguards the citizen's rights, deals with criminals to punish them suitably and at the same time defends the innocent people falsely implicated. Besides, it also plays an important role of keeping the Executive and Legislature in check. The Judiciary decides the matters in case of conflict between the Centre and the States.

All these factors make it important for Judiciary to be impartial and independent of external influences. Our Constitution has made provisions for independence of Judiciary.

15. Federal Structure

A federal structure has two sets of government in a country. One is called the Union Government and the other is called the State Government. Their areas of action are marked out by the Constitution. In India, our Constitution gives us a federal form of Government. It has three lists — the Union list, the State List and the Concurrent List. The Union List contains the subjects which come under the Union Government alone and only Union Government can enact laws on these subjects. Strategically important subjects like defence, atomic energy, foreign affairs, banking, post and telegraph etc. come under the Union List. There are 97 subjects in Union List. The State List includes those subjects on which the State Government can enact laws. It has got 66 subjects. Subjects like police, trade and commerce within the state, local government etc. come under the State List. The third List, namely, the Concurrent List has subjects which are common to both the Union Government and State Government. Both Governments can make laws on these subjects. There are 47 subjects in this List. In case of a conflict between the Central law and State law on a subject of this List, the Central law would be effective. Criminal and civil procedure, education, marriage and divorce, trade unions etc. are some subjects falling under this List.

The subjects left out of all the three lists, leave some powers undistributed. These are known as 'Residuary powers'. The Central Government retains the power to legislate on the residuary subjects.

India is a Union of States. For administrative convenience, the country has been divided into 28 States besides 7 Union territories that are governed directly by the Central Government.

The Central Government, however, has the powers to assume responsibility for the Government of the State, if in its opinion it has become necessary in national interest.

16. Parliamentary Form of Government

The Government at the Centre and at the State level is to be run by the elected representatives of the people. At the Centre, the leader of the majority party in the Lok Sabha is generally invited by the President to form the Council of Ministers. The Council thus formed (with the Prime Minister at the head), is responsible to the Parliament. The Members of the Parliament have the right to question the respective Ministers on matters relating to their departments. The Ministers are duty-bound to answer them. The Council of Ministers can be removed by a motion of 'No-confidence' if the majority of the Members of the Parliament (Lok Sabha) are against it. Similarly, at the State level, the Chief Minister along his Council of Ministers is answerable to the Legislature.

17. Single Citizenship

The citizens of our country have the same political rights, irrespective of their place of residence within the country. They are free to move to any part of the country for the sake of employment, business or residence. However, if a citizen of India decides to live in some other country permanently, he can acquire the citizenship of the other country only after renouncing his Indian citizenship.

In a federation state like the U.S.A., the citizens have dual citizenship; one of the union and other of the state. But we have single citizenship, that of India and not of Punjab, Bengal, Orissa, etc. In India, the Centre has more powers than the States.

18. Liberty, Equality and Fraternity

The Constitution provides that no citizen shall be arbitrarily deprived of his freedom. There can be no arrest or detention without proper authority of law. There is also the freedom of expression and speech. Equal opportunities are guaranteed to all citizens for their full development.

The Constitution seeks to promote the feeling of mutual brotherhood among all citizens.

Liberty, Equality and Fraternity are inter-related. It is only when all citizens are free and bound by a feeling of brotherhood that there can be equality.

Similarly, only citizens with equal rights and equal freedoms can have a feeling of brotherhood for each other. Equality before law, and a feeling of brotherhood for each other alone, can guarantee that there will be real freedom.

The Constitution accepts that all men are born equal and free. So it guarantees to them their basic freedoms.

19. Comprehensive and Elaborate Constitution

No other constitution in the world is so elaborate as ours. It elaborates upon the governmental structure at Central, State and Local levels, citizenship, rights and duties, Directive principles of state policy, Centre-State relations, services, trade and commerce, elections, emergency provisions etc. It covers almost all situations that might arise and leaves little to doubt.

20. Combination of Flexibility and Rigidity

Indian Constitution provides for changes also. It takes into account the changing scenario. Accordingly, keeping in view the modern and contemporary requirements, several amendments (changes) have been made. There are certain matters which need no change. Therefore, an element of rigidity has to be enforced. Changes cannot be made on minor issues which can be solved within the existing framework.

Following procedures are followed for making amendments in the constitution of India:

(i) Certain provisions of the Constitution can be amended by the Parliament by simple majority.

(ii) Certain other provisions can be amended if passed by two-thirds majority in Parliament and then ratified by at least fifty percent States.

(iii) The remaining part of the Constitution can be amended by two-third majority of Parliament. Hence, our Constitution is both flexible as well as rigid.

21. Abolition of Untouchability

Under the Constitution, it is an offence to practise untouchability against any citizen. Every citizen, irrespective of caste, race, religion and sex etc. has equal access to public places like community wells, tanks, hotels, etc. This also applies to places of worship.

22. Common State Language

The Constitution lays down that Hindi shall be the official language of the Union. English, however, has been allowed to be used as an alternate official language as long as it is felt desirable to do so.

Regional Languages

1. Assamese	2. Bengali	3. Bordo
4. Dogri	5. Gujarati	6. Hindi
7. Kannada	8. Kashmiri	9. Konkani
10. Maithili	11. Malayalam	12. Manipuri
13. Marathi	14. Nepali	15. Oriya
16. Punjabi	17. Sanskrit	18. Santhali
19. Sindhi	20. Tamil	21. Telugu
22. Urdu		

23. Due Recognition to State Languages

The Constitution recognises 22 state languages. Thus, it satisfies the regional linguistic aspirations.

24. Written and Lengthy Constitution

Our Constitution is in written form. It is one of the lengthiest Constitution of the world. The Constitution had about 90,000 words when originally adopted. It has grown further in length with the incorporation of amendments. There are 22 parts, 395 Articles and 12 Schedules in it. An unwritten Constitution is not Codified by a Constituent Assembly. It is based on legislative acts, judicial decisions, customs and traditions.

Britain has an unwritten Constitution. Constitution of U.S.A. is written but is very short.

25. Independent Election Commission

As envisaged in Article 324 of the Constitution, an independent Election Commission has been set-up. The political parties have demonstrated their faith in the independence of the Election Commission.

26. Independent Nature of the Comptroller and Auditor General of India

As provided for in Article 148 of the Constitution, the Comptroller and Auditor General plays an important role in controlling public finances.

27. Pubic Service Commission

Article 315 of the Constitution lays down the provision for Union Public Service Commission for the Union and a Public Service Commission for each State. Accordingly candidates for the Civil Service of the Centre and States are selected.

28. Emergency Provisions

Article 352 empowers the President to declare 'Emergency' in the country when the security of India is threatened.

28.4 SUMMARY OF THE SALIENT FEATURES OF THE CONSTITUTION OF INDIA

1. It sets appropriate goals.
2. It establishes India as a democratic republic.
3. It provides Fundamental Rights for the people.
4. It includes duties of the citizens.
5. It aims at economic, political and social justice.
6. It envisages India as a welfare state.
7. It incorporates Directive Principles of State Policy for the general guidance of the government to establish a welfare state.
8. It establishes India as a secular state and guarantees religious equality.
9. It declares India as a socialist state.
10. It guarantees freedom of expression.
11. It provides for impartial and independent judiciary.
12. It distributes functions between the Central and State Governments.
13. It embodies parliamentary form of government.
14. It has a provision for single citizenship.
15. It is based on the values of liberty, equality and fraternity.
16 It is very comprehensive and elaborate.
17. It combines flexibility and rigidity.
18. It abolishes untouchability.
19. It lays a common language.
20. It gives due recognition to state language.
21. It is a written constitution.
22. It provides for an independent Election Commission.
23. It provides for an independent Comptroller and Auditor General for regulating public finance.
24. It includes the setting up of Public Service Commission for the Union and States so that Civil Services are selected in an impartial manner.
25. It provides for emergency powers to meet critical situation.
26. It is derived from various sources.

On account of non-clarification of certain terms, it has led to litigation in some matters.

Notwithstanding certain constraints, the Constitution of India has worked well.

The most important achievement is the successful functioning of democracy.

29

Citizenship—Fundamental Rights and Duties

29.1 MEANING OF A CITIZEN

Literal meaning of a Citizen. The word 'Citizen' literally means a resident of a country who enjoys certain privileges of such residence. But in Political Science it has a different meaning. Citizenship is acquired as per rules of a country. Many Americans are living in India but they are not the citizens of India. Likewise many Indians are living in America but they are not the citizens of America. Every State provides protection of property and life to every individual residing there but every individual is not entitled to all the rights of a citizen.

The following views of scholars throw adequate light on the meaning of a citizen:

According to *Aristotle*, "He who has the power to take part in the deliberative and judicial administration of a state is said by us to be a citizen." In the city-state of Greece, labourers, slaves and peasants were deprived of participation in the activities of the government because they lacked wisdom of running the government. Only the people residing in a city were citizens.

Situation changed in the Roman period. The people of Roman empire, whether they lived in the city or in a village were not distinguished as people in ancient Greek city-states.

According to *Encyclopedia of Political Institutions of Blackwell*, "Citizenship means a full and responsible membership of a state".

In the words of *Sew*, "We define citizen as one who owes allegiance to the state, has access to the civil and political rights and is inspired with a spirit of service to the community."

On the above basis, a citizen may be defined in modern times as one who owes allegiance to the State in which he resides. He has full share of civil and political privileges. Allegiance means the respect on the part of the citizen for the basic ideals of the state. He defends the state in the hour of its crisis. As a citizen is entitled to all civil and political rights, he has also duties to discharge towards the state.

Citizen and Voter

There is a distinction between a citizen and a voter. A voter is a person who has the right to cast his vote at the time of election. However, there may be citizens who are not voters.

29.2 CITIZEN AND AN ALIEN

The residents of a state are broadly classified into citizens and aliens. Citizens own them allegiance to the State in which they reside but aliens residing in the state owe allegiance to some other state. For example, a Japanese residing in India owes his allegiance to Japan and not to India. Besides as already stated, the citizens of a state enjoy all civil and political privileges of the state but the aliens are denied these.

Thirdly, an alien may be expelled from the state for misconduct but a citizen cannot be expelled from his own state.

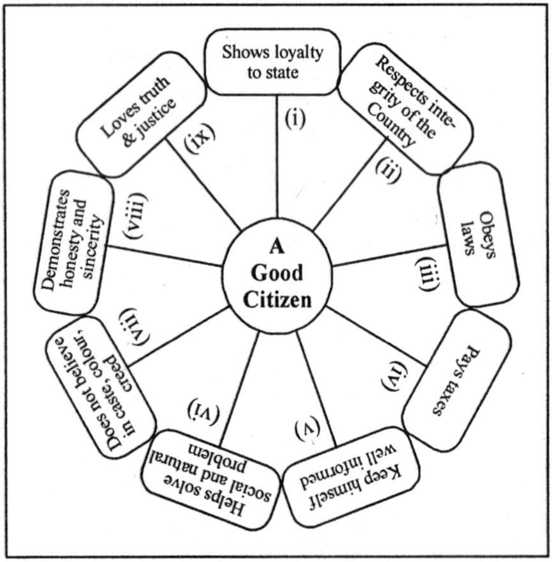

Fig. 29.1: The Qualities of a Good Citizen

Citizenship constitutes the indispensable foundational principle of democratic polity. It involves the individual's full political membership in the State, his permanent allegiance to the State and the official recognition by the State of his integration into the political system. Citizenship brings certain rights, duties, privileges and obligations that do not belong to aliens. All public offices are open to a citizen. He is eligible for recruitment to all public services.

29.3 CONSTITUTIONAL PROVISIONS IN INDIA

Part II entitled "Citizenship" includes Articles 5 to 10 as given below:

5. Citizenship at the Commencement of the Constitution.—At the commencement of this Constitution, every person who has his domicile in the territory of India and—

(a) who was born in the territory of India; or

(b) either of whose parents was born in the territory of India; or

(c) who has been ordinarily resident in the territory of India for not less than five years immediately preceding such commencement, shall be a citizen of India.

6. Rights of Citizenship of Certain Persons Who have Migrated to India from Pakistan.—Notwithstanding anything in article 5, a person who has migrated to the territory of India from the territory now included in Pakistan shall be deemed to be a citizen of India at the commencement of this Constitution if—

(a) he or either of his parents or any of his grand-parents was born in India as defined in the Government of India Act, 1935 (as originally enacted); and

(b) (i) in the case where such person has so migrated before the nineteenth day of July, 1948, he has been ordinarily resident in the territory of India since the date of his migration, or

(ii) in the case where such person has so migrated on or after the nineteenth day of July, 1948, he has been registered as a citizen of India by an officer appointed in that behalf by the Government of the Dominion of India on an application made by him therefore to such officer before the commencement of this Constitution in the form and manner prescribed by that Government:

Provided that no person shall be so registered unless he has been resident in the territory of India for at least six months immediately preceding the date of his application.

7. Rights of Citizenship of Certain Migrants to Pakistan.—Notwithstanding anything in articles 5 and 6, a person who has after the first day of March, 1947, migrated from the territory of India to the territory now included in Pakistan shall not be deemed to be a citizen of India:

Provided that nothing in this article shall apply to a person who, after having so migrated to the territory now included in Pakistan, has returned to the territory of India under a permit for resettlement or permanent return issued by or under the authority of any law and every such person shall for the purposes of clause (b) of article 6 be deemed to have migrated to the territory of India after the nineteenth day of July, 1948.

8. Rights of Citizenship of Certain Persons of Indian Origin Residing Outside India.—Notwithstanding anything in article 5, any person who or either of whose parents or any of whose grand-parents was born in India as defined in the Government of India Act, 1935 (as originally enacted), and who is ordinarily residing in any country outside India as so defined shall be deemed to be a citizen of India if he has been registered as a citizen of India by the diplomatic or consular representative of India in the country where he is for the time being residing on an application made by him therefore to such diplomatic or consular representative, whether before or after the commencement of this Constitution, in the form and manner prescribed by the Government of the Dominion of India or the Government of India.

9. Persons Voluntarily Acquiring Citizenship of a Foreign State not to be Citizens.—No person shall be a citizen of India by virtue of article 5, or be deemed to be a citizen of India by virtue of article 6 or article 8, if he has voluntarily acquired the citizenship of any foreign State.

10. Continuance of the Rights of Citizenship.—Every person who is or is deemed to be a citizen of India under any of the foregoing provisions of this

Part shall, subject to the provisions of any law that may be made by Parliament, continue to be such citizen.

The right to vote and certain fundamental rights are available only to citizens. On the past, citizens have obligations like paying taxes, and defending the nation. All citizens irrespective of the State in which they were born have the same rights and duties all over the country without any discrimination subject only to a few special protections in case of Jammu & Kashmir, tribal areas etc. and the power of Parliament under article 16 to prescribe residence within a State or Union Territory as a necessary qualification for certain classes of employment under that State or Union Territory.

29.4 TWO TYPES OF CITIZENSHIP

Citizenship is either acquired by birth or by 'naturalisation'. Children born in India or born to parents with Indian citizenship get Indian citizenship by birth.

An alien can acquire Indian citizenship by fulfilling certain conditions. One of the conditions is that he must have been living in India for more than five years. He must also know one of the Indian languages. Before Indian citizenship can be acquired, he must give up his citizenship of the other country.

If an Indian citizen acquires the citizenship of some other country, he ceases to be a citizen of India.

Single Citizenship: Some countries allow their citizens to acquire citizenship of another county and also retain their first citizenship. In our country there is no such provision. We even do not have a system of separate citizenship of the State. Every Indian has the same rights in whichever State he chooses to live or work. We are all citizens of India.

Articles 5-8 conferred citizenship on 'every person' who was covered under one of the following categories at the time of the commencement of the Constitution:

1. domiciled in India and born in India—these formed the bulk of the population of the Union of India;
2. domiciled, not born in India but either of whose parents was born in India;
3. domiciled, not born in India but ordinarily resident for more than five years;
4. resident in India but migrated to Pakistan after 1 March 1947 and later returned to India on resettlement permit;
5. resident in Pakistan but who migrated to India before 19 July 1948 or who came after that date but had resided in India for more than six months and got registered in the prescribed manner;
6. resident outside India but who or either of whose parents or grand-parents were born in India.

Thus, Citizenship at the commencement of the Constitution included provisions for Citizenship (i) by domicile (ii) of migrants from and to Pakistan, and (iii) of Indians residing in foreign countries.

29.5 INDIAN CITIZENSHIP ACT 1955

Main Provisions for being Indian Citizens

- Those who were born in India.
- Those whose parents and grand-parents were born in India.
- Those who had been living in India for not less than five years before the Constitution of India came into force on January 26, 1950.
- Those who migrated to India from Pakistan before January 26, 1950 with the intention of permanently staying in India.
- Those who acquired Indian citizenship through naturalisation.

The Parliament is competent to pass laws to regulate the 'citizenship' of India.

29.6 MEANING OF RIGHTS

Definition and Meaning: Among the various definitions of rights, following are the most important ones:

Austin. Rights mean one man's capacity of exacting from another.

Beni Prasad. Rights are nothing more, and nothing less than those social conditions which are necessary or favourable for the development of personality.

Barker. Any particular right which I have is a capacity of enjoying some particular status or employing some particular power of action, which has been secured and guaranteed to me by law.

Bosanquet. A right is a claim recognised by society and enforced by the state.

Green. The power of utility enjoyed by individual or group, which is recognised as essential for all men, by the society or it is considered as delegated by such authority whose protection is considered fully necessary.

Hobhouse. Rights are what we may expect from others and others from us and all genuine rights are conditions of social welfare.

Holland. Rights are one man's capacity of influencing the acts of another by means of the opinion and force of the society.

Laski. Rights are those conditions of social life without which no man can be his best self.

Maccun. Rights are certain advantageous conditions of social being indispensable to the true development of citizens.

Sri Nivas Shastri. In its essence a right is an arrangement, rule or practice sanctioned by the law of the community and conducive to the highest moral good of the citizen.

Wilde. Rights are reasonable claims to freedom in the exercise of certain activities.

Necessity of Rights: Rights are regarded as a bedrock of a democratic system. Rights define the position of an individual in the society. They offer a positive purpose to the state. Through them alone, the state promotes the general welfare of the society as a whole. The presence of rights is a proof that the state exists for the individual and not the individual for the state.

Rights are essential for the all-round development of individual life. The social life is enriched automatically.

Rights also generate a spirit of 'we feeling' towards the state and society. The individuals also feel that they too have some responsibilities or duties towards the society as well as their fellow beings.

The rights are the products of social circumstances. They are conceived in the context of the society. The society recognises claims of the individuals without which they cannot realise their personality. In return of the acceptance of the claims, the individuals have to give something, and that something is termed as 'duty'.

29.7 CHARACTERISTICS OR ESSENTIAL ELEMENTS OF RIGHTS

1. *Acceptability*: Rights are guaranteed by the state. The demand of an individual becomes a right only after it is accepted by the other members of the society and recognised by the state.
2. *Universal Availability*: Rights are available to all and not to a few.
3. *Desirability*: Rights are socially desirable conditions. A good life can be realised only when individuals have some rights or these are favourable conditions.
4. *Changeability*: Rights are neither static nor permanent. They grow according to circumstances. For instance, the right to property in the Constitution of India was guaranteed but in due course this right was omitted from the Constitution.
5. *Rights and Liberty*: It is accepted that rights can be enjoyed in a democratic state where liberty exists.
6. *Complementary Nature of Rights and Duties*: There is a logical correlation between rights and duties. "To protect me against attack from others is to imply", says *Laski*, "that I will myself desist from attacking others."
7. *Justification*: Only that claim can become a right which is essential for one's life and social order.

Summing up the Meaning of Rights

Rights are those conditions of life or claims of an individual which are recognised by the society as essential for the good of the individual as well as the society.

29.8 FUNDAMENTAL RIGHTS

Meaning of Fundamental Rights

Fundamental rights are those legal rights which are framed not by the Legislature but are mentioned in the Constitution. These rights are given to the citizens because without these rights, the complete development of a citizen is not possible.

The rights are fundamental on account of three reasons. First, they are included in the Constitution which is known as the 'Fundamental Law of the Land'. The Supreme Court and the High Court have the power to enforce whenever these rights are violated. Second, the rights are held to be belonging to all citizens, irrespective of caste, creed, race, religion, sex etc. Third, they are indispensable to the all-round development of the personality of an individual.

29.9 NEED AND IMPORTANCE OF FUNDAMENTAL RIGHTS

The importance of these rights is brought out as under:

1. *Necessary for Development of Individuals*: The rights such as right of equality, freedom of religion etc. help in the development of inherent strength of an individual in a democratic country like India.

2. *Essential in a Democratic Set-up*: In a democratic set-up, people choose their own government. For fair reflection of opinion, people need to have certain freedoms which are granted to them through the fundamental rights.

3. *Need for Cultural and Religious Freedom*: India is a vast country having people belonging to different religions and cultures. For national unity, it is required that all people should be free to profess the religion of their choice. There should not be any discrimination on the part of government on grounds of religion, race, sex etc. This is ensured by the fundamental rights available to the citizens.

4. *Difficult to Amend*: By making the procedure to amend these rights difficult, it is ensured that they are protected from the excesses of legislature and the executive. This fact also tells how important these rights are considered, not only for the citizens but for the Indian Democracy also.

Constitution of India and Fundamental Rights

Part III (Articles 12 to 35) of the Constitution of India provides for Fundamental Rights which are illustrated on next page.

Let us now go into some detail to know more about these rights.

1. *Right to Equality*: Right to equality means that all citizens are equal in the eyes of law and they will be equally protected by the laws of the land. The State cannot discriminate against its citizens on grounds of race, caste, sex, religion or place of birth.

Similarly, State cannot discriminate against any citizen with regard to opportunities of employment. But a special provision is made in the form of reservation of jobs for the Scheduled Castes, Scheduled Tribes and other Backward Classes. There are special provisions for women and children as well. The provision for SC/ST/OBCs is made to correct the discrimination of past societies against them and to bring them at par with other citizens. So, those provisions do not go against the spirit of right to equality but tend to remove the existing inequalities.

Right to equality also grants that no citizen will be discriminated against on grounds of religion, race, caste, sex or anyone of them in following respects:

(a) Visiting shops, restaurants or hotels and public places of entertainment.

(b) Using public places maintained by the funds of the state or meant for public use like wells, ponds, bathing ghats and tourist places etc.

Right to equality also mentions the abolition of untouchability. Practice of untouchability offence and anybody practising it may be punished by law. The Constitution has abolished titles except military and academic ones.

Detailed Provisions on Fundamental Rights

Right to Equality	*Right to Freedom*	*Right against Exploitation*	*Right to Freedom of Religion*	*Cultural and Educational Rights of Minorities [Right to Education (Free and Compulsory Education between the age of 6 and 14) (Article 21A)]*	*Right to Property*	*Right to Constitutional Remedies*
1. Equality before law and equal protection before law [Art. 14]. 2. Prohibition of discrimination on ground of religion etc. [Art. 15]. 3. Equality of opportunity in public employment [Art. 16]. 4. Abolition of untouchability [Art. 17]. 5. Abolition of titles [Art. 18].	1. Freedom of speech and expression; assembly; association; movement, residence and settlement; profession [Art. 19]. 2. Protection in respect of conviction for offences [Art. 20]. 3. Protection of life and personal liberty [Art. 21]. 4. Protection against arrest and detention in certain cases [Art. 22].	1. Prohibition of traffic in human beings and forced labour [Art. 23]. 2. Prohibition of employment of children in hazardous employment [Art. 24].	1. Freedom of conscience and free profession [Art 25]. 2. Freedom to manage religious affairs [Art. 26]. 3. Freedom as to payment of taxes for promotion of any particular religion [Art. 27]. 4. Freedom as to attendance at religious instruction in certain educational institutions [Art. 28].	1. Protection of language, script or culture of minorities [Art. 29]. 2. Right of minorities to establish and administer educational institutions [Art. 30].	Article 32 (a) relating to right to property was omitted from Part III by the Constitution 44th Amendment (1978)	Remedies for enforcement of the fundamental right conferred by this part,—writs of habeas corpus, mandamus, prohibition, certiorari and quo warranto [Art. 32].

2. *Right to Freedom*: The right to freedom is actually a cluster of the following six freedoms:

1. The right to speech and expression;
2. The right to assemble peacefully and without arms;
3. The right to form associations or unions;
4. The right to move freely throughout the territory of India;
5. The right to reside and settle in any part of the territory of India; and
6. The right to practise any profession or to carry on any occupation, trade or business.

Right to freedom is the most important of all rights. Other rights become meaningless in the absence of this right. This right is also known as the 'Soul of Fundamental Rights'. All the six kinds of freedoms mentioned above are important. Right to Freedom of Speech and Expression forms the basis of public opinion. Public opinion is the foundation of a democratic nation. This freedom also involves the freedom of press.

Freedom of Peaceful Assembly: This gives expression to right to public debate on matters concerning politics or any other subject. This also helps in formation of public opinion. Freedom to form association, freedom of movement, freedom to reside and settle anywhere in India and right to practise any profession, are the certain rights that give meaning to different aspects of personality of individuals and give them opportunities to develop and prosper.

The right to freedom guarantees some other rights as well. Thus:

(i) No person shall be punished except for the violation of some law;
(ii) No person shall be prosecuted and punished for the same offence more than once; and
(iii) No person accused of any offence shall be compelled to be a witness against himself.

'Compulsion' means what in law is called 'duress'. Duress is injury, beating or unlawful imprisonment to make a person do something which he does not want to do.

No person shall be deprived of his life or personal liberty except according to procedure established by law. Here the expression 'poverty liberty' comprises all those freedoms which are not included in Article 19 based on immortality.

3. *Right against Exploitation*: Forced or bonded labour (beggar) was frequently practised earlier. People were made to work without getting any money in return by wealthy landlords. This happen on from generation to generation. Keeping slaves and buying and selling them was the worst kind of exploitation of human beings. Under the right against exploitation, beggar is now declared a crime.

The Constitution also bars the employment of children below the age of 14 years in hazardous industries or mines. The right against exploitation upholds the dignity of individuals. It ensures the following:

(i) It legally forbids the exploitation of agricultural and other labourers.
(ii) It puts an end to the custom of devdasi.
(iii) It bars the sale and purchase of women and children.
(iv) It forbids the employment of children in factories and mines.

In short, the right against exploitation is provided in the Constitution to uphold the dignity of weaker sections of society.

4. *Right to Freedom of Religion*: India is a secular state. Its Constitution gives the right of freedom to practise any religion through the right of freedom of religion. All religions are considered equal and no religion is given preference over the others. All the citizens enjoy the following religious freedoms equally:

1. Each citizen can have faith in the religion of his choice. He can profess and preach his religion.
2. No religious education will be provided in the state-run educational institutions. No student of such institutions can be forced to take part in a religious activity.
3. All Hindus, belonging to any caste, have the right to enter the temples. Anybody creating hindrance in this is liable to be punished by law.
4. Sikhs are allowed to wear *kirpan.*
5. Each religious institution has the right to form and run charities with the religious objective.

TRUTH IS ONE, PATHS ARE MANY

5. *Cultural and Educational Rights*: This right is meant for the protection of minorities. India is a land of varied cultures and languages. Minorities having a language of their own, have the right to conserve and develop their culture and identity. Majority cannot force its culture on a minority. To achieve this objective, the Constitution has made following arrangements:

(i) Citizens of India, having a language, script or culture of their own, have the right to conserve the same. On this basis, different states have adopted different languages.
(ii) No citizen can be denied admission to a state-run educational institution or one added by it on grounds of religion, race, caste, language or any of it.
(iii) Minorities are given the right to open a school or college according to their will. The state cannot discriminate in giving grants to such institutions. Opening of such institutions helps minorities in preserving and developing their culture.

6. *Right to Constitutional Remedies*: Right to Constitutional Remedies is a very special right. If a citizen's fundamental rights are violated or denied, he can exercise the right of Constitutional remedies to restore his fundamental rights. According to this right, citizens can approach a Court of law to get justice against the wrongs done to them. The court can issue different writs to protect citizens' rights. The Supreme Court or High Court can issue the following kinds of writs:

(i) *Writ of Habeas Corpus*: This writ implies that if a person is arrested unlawfully, he can submit an application in Court against the arrest. If Court is satisfied that his arrest is unlawful, the person is released.
(ii) *Writ of Mandamus*: By issuing this writ, the Supreme Court or High Court can order an employee, corporation, institution or a public body to perform its duties lawfully. The person or body can be made to perform functions or duties not being performed.

(iii) *Writ of Prohibition*: This writ can be issued by the High Court to a subordinate court to instruct it not to act outside its jurisdiction.

(iv) *Writ of Quo Warranto*: According to this writ, the Court can suspend an appointed or elected person from his post until his pending court cases are settled.

(v) *Writ of Certiorari*: By issuing this writ, the High Court can get all the records of an ongoing case in a subordinate court and give its decision on it or ask the court concerned to make a decision in accordance with law and without surpassing its jurisdiction.

29.10 SITUATIONS UNDER WHICH FUNDAMENTAL FREEDOMS ARE CURTAILED

Suspension of Freedom during an Emergency: Under Article 19, the Fundamental Rights guaranteed remain suspended during an Emergency. In other words, the checks laid on the legislative and executive powers are removed.

Situations under Which Safeguards under Article 22 no Longer Exist: This Article enacts two exceptions. First, safeguards are not available to an enemy alien. Second, safeguards do not apply to persons detained or arrested under a law providing for Preventive Detention.

Article 352 authorises the President to issue a Proclamation of Emergency in case of the security of India. Article 358 provides that during the period of Proclamation of Emergency, the State can put restrictions on the enjoyment of freedoms enumerated in Article 19.

Article 368 states that the Parliament can make amendments in the Constitution and deprive the citizens of any freedom. The Forty-fourth Constitution Amendment 1978 deleted the Right to Property.

Article 33 authorises the Parliament to determine by law to what extent any of the fundamental rights shall be restricted or abrogated to ensure proper discharge of duties and the maintenance of discipline among the armed forces.

Thus, it is clear that fundamental rights are not absolute. Each fundamental right is qualified by certain limitations and exceptions.

29.11 MAIN FEATURES OF THE FUNDAMENTAL RIGHTS

1. The rights form an integral part of the Constitution.
2. Fundamental rights are justiciable. In case of violation, one can seek protection.
3. These rights are available not only to citizens, but in certain cases to the foreigners living in India too. For instance right to religion.
4. The rights are not absolute. Each right is given under certain limitations and reasonable restrictions are also provided for.
5. Some rights are positive in nature like right to liberty or religion.
6. Some rights are negative in nature, e.g., abolition of untouchability.
7. Fundamental rights can be amended or even deleted but for this an elaborate process is needed.

8. Rights are liable to suspension. During Emergency, fundamental rights can be suspended.

9. Fundamental rights are comprehensive in nature.

10. Fundamental rights differentiate between citizens and foreigners.

11. Fundamental rights definitely stand on a higher pedestal than the ordinary laws.

12. Fundamental rights put restrictions on the powers of the state also. If the state violates these rights, the citizens can seek redress through the courts.

13. Rights limit the authority of the government.

29.12 DUTIES

Meaning of the Term 'Duty'

Webster's New Collegiate Dictionary gives the following meaning of the term 'duty':

1. conduct due to parents and superiors
2. (a) obligatory tasks, conduct, service, or function that arises from one's position (as in life or in group) (b) assigned service or business specific active military service.
3. (a) a moral or legal obligation (b) the force of moral obligation.
4. A tax especially, tax on imports.

According to *Bhargava's Standard Illustrated Dictionary*, duty means expression of respect, behaviour due to a superior, moral obligation.

Oxford Advanced Learners Dictionary states this meanings of the word 'duty' something that you feel you have to do because it is your moral legal responsibility.

29.13 FUNDAMENTAL DUTIES OF CITIZENS

Article 51A

Fundamental Duties: It shall be the duty of every citizen of India—

(a) to abide by the Constitution and respect its ideals and institutions, the National Flag and the National Anthem;

(b) to cherish and follow the noble ideals which inspired our national struggle for freedom;

(c) to uphold and protect the sovereignty, unity and integrity of India;

(d) to defend the country and render national service when called upon to do so;

(e) to promote harmony and the spirit of common brotherhood amongst all the people of India transcending religious, linguistic and regional or sectional diversities; to renounce practices derogatory to the dignity of women;

(f) to value and preserve the rich heritage of our composite culture;

(g) to protect and improve the natural environment including forests, lakes, rivers, wild life and to have compassion for living creatures;

(h) to develop the scientific temper, humanism and the spirit of inquiry and reform;

(i) to safeguard public property and to abjure violence;

(j) to strive towards excellence in all spheres of individual and collective activity so that the nation constantly rises to higher levels of endeavour and achievement.

(k) who is a parent or guardian to provide opportunities for education to his child or, as the case may be, ward between the age of 6 to 14 (86th Constitutional Amendment 2002).

29.14 IMPORTANCE OF INCORPORATING THE FUNDAMENTAL DUTIES

The importance of incorporation of the fundamental duties has the following merits:

1. *A Lacuna Removed*: The Constitution makers in 1949-50 had not included fundamental duties in the Constitution of India. Several countries like Japan and USSR have provided for fundamental duties in their Constitution. By incorporating the Fundamental Duties, the lacuna in this regard has been removed.

2. *Universality of Duties*: The duties contained in the Constitution are of a universal nature.

3. *Creation of a Sense of Responsibility*: The duties have a psychological impact. They remind the people of India that they must discharge their obligations in their motherland.

4. *Development of Patriotism*: The duties such as to respect the National Flag and the National Anthem develop a sense of patriotism.

Fundamental Duties and Fundamental Rights: Their Status

There is a world of difference between the fundamental duties and fundamental rights.

The fundamental rights impose certain legal restrictions on the State. Fundamental duties impose certain moral restrictions only on the individuals.

The fundamental rights are justiciable but the fundamental duties are not justiciable in the court of law.

Fundamental rights are granted to the individual for the development of his personality. Fundamental duties do not strive for the achievement of the object.

Evaluation of the Place of Fundamental Duties

Merits

1. The duties emphasise the obligations of the citizens towards the motherland.

2. They point out the need to develop patriotic feelings among the citizens of India.

3. These help to follow a code of conduct that would strengthen the nation.

4. They fill up a lacuna in the Constitution: Several countries like Japan provide for the fundamental duties and this aspect was not given its due consideration while framing India's Constitution.

Limitations

1. The fundamental duties are not justiciable. No citizen can be punished for non-observance of duties.
2. They are pious declarations and moral principles such as "thou shall not kill".
3. They are very vague. For example, meaning of phrases like 'composite culture', 'rich heritage', 'scientific temper' etc. is not very clear. These ideals convey different meaning to different people.
4. Most of the citizens are not even aware of these duties.
5. The fundamental duties are not realistic but are simply idealistic.

Summing up: Notwithstanding criticism, it is clear that the Fundamental Duties are a constant reminder to us of the national goals as well as basic norms of civic, political and social life. They may inspire us to inculcate in ourselves a sense of social responsibility.

Our Duty Towards Our Nation

Your country, brother, shall be your love!
Good unto better you shall improve!
Great deeds indeed are needed now!
Word hard, work long in farm and factory!
Let the land be abundant in milk and honey!
Flood the land with goods, all made at home!
Spread your handiwork all over the world!
Are you a patriot? Do not shout it aloud!
Bragging never did anybody any good!
Quietly, do a fine deed instead!
Let the people see it, it is they that decide!

—Dr. APJ Abdul Kalam
President of India,
India 2020—A Vision for the New Millennium

Kinds of Duties

The term duty is used in two senses: moral as well as legal. It is something that we owe to ourselves and to others.

In the words of Benn and Peters, Rules prescribe behaviour, and in so doing are said to impose 'duties' or 'obligations'.

Legal duties like import and export duties are imposed by law.

Moral duties are not enforced by the law of the land, but by a moral sense of the individual or by the force of public opinion of the group or society.

In ancient India, the society was divided into four classes on the basis of their duties or functions.

For an individual, these were four *Ashrams* or stages of life. Each stage had some duties to perform.

Scope and Kind of Duties

(1) *Duties Towards Self*	(2) *Duties Towards Family*	(3) *Duties Towards Society (Neighbour, Village, etc.)*	(4) *Duties Towards the State*	(5) *Duties Towards the World*
1. Towards physical health	1. Due regard to elders and parents	1. Tolerance towards others	1. Abiding by the Constitution	1. Appreciation of interdependence of countries
2. Towards ethical and moral upliftment of oneself	2. Due love to the young	2. Cooperating with other	2. Upholding the unity and integrity of the country	2. Tolerance towards citizens of other countries
3. Towards spiritual pursuit	3. Care towards children	3. Keeping the good of the society in mind	3. Safeguarding public property	3. Working towards international peace
4. Towards self-realisation	4. Supporting family	4. Doing social service	4. Paying taxes	
5. Towards liberation (*Moksha*)			5. Obeying laws of the land	
			6. Cooperating with public servants	
			7. Making proper use of political rights	

29.15 INTERRELATIONSHIP OF RIGHTS AND DUTIES

Gandhiji has very aptly described the need, significance and interrelationship of rights and duties in these words, "I learned from my illiterate but wise mother that all rights to be deserved and preserved come from duty well done. Thus the very right to live accrues to us when we do the duty of citizenship of the world. From this one fundamental statement perhaps it is easy enough to define duties of man and women and correlate every right to some corresponding duty to be performed...."

Prof. H.J. Laski describes the following four types of relationship between rights and duties:

(i) My right implies your duty.
(ii) My right implies my duty to admit a similar right of other.
(iii) I shall exercise my right to promote social good.
(iv) Since the State guarantees and maintains my right, I have the duty to support the State.

Prof. Wilde has explained the importance of the interrelation between rights and duties in these words, "It is only in the world of duties that rights have significance".

Dr. Beni Prasad has very beautifully illustrated the relation is these words, "Rights and duties are interdependent. These are two aspects of the same thing. If one looks at them from one's own standpoint, they are rights. If one looks at them from the standpoint of others, they are duties. Both are social and both are conditions of right living to be secured to all members of society".

(iv) Since the state guarantees and maintains my right, I have the duty to support the State.

Gandhiji once said, "Begin with the charter of duties of man and I promise the rights will follow as spring follows winter.

The relations may be explained on the following lines:

(a) Right of A is the Duty of B.
(b) Right of A imposes a Duty on A also.
(c) If A fails to respect B's right, B is not absolved from his duty to A.

Following are the important arguments which substantiate the interrelation of duties and rights:

1. Group life implies the interweaving of rights and duties.
2. Duty is inherent in right.
3. One's right is one's duty to use it in the right way.
4. Every right enjoyed by an individual involves a duty on his part.
5. Rights are conditioned by social responsibilities (duties).
6. Recognition of guarantee of rights to the individual by the state enjoins certain duties on the individual.
7. Each become meaningless without the other. Both are complementary.

Insistence on rights only is likely to lead to the creation of an anarchist state. There would be chaos and confusion. Likewise insistence on duty without the enjoyment of rights will be a lopsided proposition.

Summing up: It may be stated that:

1. My right is my own duty.
2. My right is other's duty.
3. Both rights and duties are used for individual as well as social welfare.

30

Citizenship Education and Training

30.1 SIGNIFICANCE OF CITIZENSHIP

An examination of social trends and emerging problems indicates that changes are necessary in the process of civic and social education within the schools and outside. The present political and economic conditions in India, the results of invention and technology and our relationships with the rest of the world require a serious study of the needs and possibilities of a suitable type of civic and social education. Never in the history of India has it been so necessary for the schools to readjust their work to accord with the social and economic changes that came with the dawn of the freedom of the country. Moreover in a world in which the products of scientific inventions have so greatly outstripped their social and political controls, a varied and an intelligent programme of citizenship education must be adopted and carried through. In such a scenario Civics can play an active role in citizenship training.

30.2 IDEALS OF EDUCATION FOR CITIZENSHIP

Education for citizenship should enable an individual:

(a) To understand the social, economic and political forces that are shaping the face of the modern world.
(b) To be tolerant and broadminded.
(c) To think clearly and effectively without any kind of prejudice.
(d) To make decisions independently.
(e) To be a patriot in the true sense with a cosmopolitan outlook.
(f) To be a good leader and a follower.
(g) To be devoted to freedom.
(h) To admit his follies, if any.
(i) To understand his rights and responsibilities.
(j) To earn his livelihood in an honest way.
(k) To be firm against heavy odds.
(l) To utilise his leisure profitably.
(m) To act upon principles courageously.
(n) To maintain intergroup understanding.
(o) To have faith in democratic ideals of life.
(p) To believe in the quality of man.
(q) To have a goal to make further progress.

Citizenship Education and Training

The teachers of Civics have to play an important role. They should utilise all the available opportunities to impart this training. The subject of Civics introduces the pupils to the political, economic and social life which they will enter after the school. As a matter of fact the basic goal of Civics is education for citizenship. There are two important approaches for imparting training in citizenship.

1. *The Exemplary Approach*: Generally it is felt that example is better than precept. What may not be achieved by moralising, may be achieved through the examples of the members of the staff. The teachers of Civics should set examples of ideal behaviour in their relations towards others and give an idea to their pupils about citizenship education.

Visits to legislatures may be organised and the students enabled to see how laws are framed by the elected members.

2. *The Experience Service*: Experience is the best teacher. Opportunities for active and responsible participation should be given to the students both in the school and the community. Nobody can deny the fact that civic attitudes are learned and are the result of repetition and reinforcement. Group methods of teaching, class projects and group competition can help a great deal in this respect. A large number of activities should be provided which will train the students in citizenship and develop social interaction varying with the age and ability of the individual to participate and appreciate social experiences. Activities like student councils and parliament, organisation of play activities, the dramatics, the literary dramatic clubs may be undertaken.

Davis Valentine in "The Matter and Method of Modern Teaching" stresses the importance of providing direct experiences for developing understanding, skills and attitudes which are basic to good citizenship and writes that this will build up in the individual a strong and stable sentiment of loyalty to whole community and to varying interests expressed and embodied therein.... It is that experience that is the real centre of the preparation for the larger loyalties of life. The entire process is explained below:

	Experiences and Situations	*Learning Outcomes*
1.	*Student Council.* Sharing some of the functions of school administration with the students in the form of student council which may be responsible for making rules for discipline and work, organising games and sports, planning co-curricular activities, looking after school property, running a cooperative store and a school canteen, preparing school handbook, looking after the school reading room, health and sanitation etc.	Students get practical experiences in the working of representative government, in choosing their representatives, in making and obeying laws made by them and others in formulating their judgement on matters of conduct and learn the necessity of having rules and regulations for our everyday behaviour in various groups and situations.

(Contd.)

	Experiences and Situations	*Learning Outcomes*
2.	*Surveys.* Making surveys of the various needs of the locality.	The students develop the sense of belongingness to the community and the part to be played by them.
3.	*Social Service.* Social service to the school and locality by doing jobs like cleaning the school and surroundings, beautifying school, undertaking social service in community fairs and festivals, rendering first aid to the injured, helping weak children in their studies, making small repairs, digging roads and wells, etc.	The students develop a sense of responsibility and become acquainted with the social and civic problems and the need to tackle them.
4.	*Visits to Legislatures.* Visits to Legislatures, i.e. Parliament, Assembly, Corporation, Municipality or to Panchayat.	This helps children to acquire first hand information of the working of a democratic set-up.
5.	*Morning Assembly.* Holding regular morning assembly and congregational prayers.	This provides a good start for the daily routine of the school. Students develop qualities like God fearing and realise their responsibility to their fellows. They learn audience-habits also. They are inspired to do noble deeds.
6.	*Debates.* Organising debates and discussions.	This enables the students to formulate their own judgement, and to develop habits of thinking independently, scientifically and creatively. Students learn to become good speakers and debators.
7.	*Clubs.* Having clubs for the organisation of musical and dramatic activities	Students develop aesthetic sense.
8.	*Educational Tours.* Organising camps, excursions and educationnal tours.	Students develop a spirit of belongingness to a much large area, their mental horizon is widened. They learn to work together, pool their ideas and to adjust with each other by knowing the qualities or short-comings of each other.
9.	*Student's Days.* Organising student's days in schools and assigning them the teaching work along with other school activities; students themselves acting as principals and teachers; the school personnel being busy with the task of guiding them in the staff room.	This is a very good method of impressing upon the students to learn virtues of self discipline. The students working as teachers on that particular day learn how to control classes and develop qua-lities of leadership.

(*Contd.*)

	Experiences and Situations	*Learning Outcomes*
10.	*Celebration of National Days.* Celebrating national days, community festivals and fairs.	Children become acquainted with the lives of great men and develop a sense of obligation to the heroes and motherland and a sense of patriotism.

By living and working in the school community, the young people learn that rights involve responsibilities, freedom implies restraint and that the membership of the school community carries with it a sense of responsibility for the welfare and reputation of the school as a whole.

Summary

What does 'Citizenship' Denote? Each alphabet of the word citizen denotes as under:

C-denotes: Clear thinking, common good, community feeling, compassion, consideration, constitutional knowledge, constructive thinking, cooperation, courtesy.

I-denotes: Impartially.

T-denotes: Tact, tolerance, truthfulness.

I-denotes: Individual recognition and worth, initiative, intelligent action.

Z-denotes: Zeal.

E-denotes: Equality, etiquette.

N-denotes: National pride.

S-denotes: Self-control, self-discipline, social service, sound opinion.

H-denotes: Hard work, honesty, Humanness, humility.

I-denotes: International outlook.

P-denotes: Patience, patriotism, public spirit, punctuality.

31

Human Rights and Citizenship

31.1 MEANING OF HUMAN RIGHTS

Human rights as commonly understand, are the rights that every human being is entitled to enjoy irrespective of religion, race, caste, sex and nationality, etc. These are moral claims which have been given to shape of legal rights. Because of being a human being, these rights are inherent.

31.2 NEED FOR HUMAN RIGHTS

The need for human right is denoted by the key words which describe the essence of the human rights:

1. Human survival.
2. Human well-being.
3. Human dignity.
4. Respect for humanity.
5. Equality of human beings
6. Liberty of human beings.

It may be observed that for the all-round development of the personality of the individual, above essential requirements must be met. There should be peaceful conditions and security of life. Peaceful conditions have wider dimensions. It is not only absence of war. It also implies equality of opportunity, liberty and freedom from want.

31.3 IMMEDIATE CIRCUMSTANCES LEADING TO THE UNIVERSAL DECLARATION OF HUMAN RIGHTS (DECEMBER 10, 1948)

The Second World War proved to be the most destructive war in history. The desire of the nations to make the world free from future wars and ushering in an era of international peace led to the establishment of the United Nations Organisation (UNO) in 1945. The Charter contained a number of articles related to human rights.

The General Assembly of the UN passed the Universal Declaration of Human Rights on December 10, 1948.

The declaration includes Preamble and 32 Articles.

31.4 BROAD CLASSIFICATION OF HUMAN RIGHTS

(1)	(2)	(3)	(4)	(5)	(6)	(7)	(8)
Civil Rights	Cultural Rights	Economic Rights	Educational Rights	Legal Rights	Political Rights	Social Rights	International Rights

Civil Rights

Article 1 : Dignity of all human beings
Article 2 : Equality without any distinction
Article 3 : Right to life, liberty and security
Article 4 : Prohibition of slavery
Article 5 : No inhuman treatment
Article 9 : No arbitrary arrest
Article 12 : Right to privacy
Article 13 : Freedom of movement
Article 15 : Right to nationality
Article 16 : Right to marriage
Article 17 : Right to own property

Cultural Rights

Article 24 : Right to rest and leisure
Article 27 : Right to participate in the cultural life of the community

Economic Rights

Article 23 : Right to work
Article 25 : Right to standard of living

Educational Rights

Article 26 : Right to education

Legal Rights

Article 6, 7, 8, 10, 11: Right before law

Political Rights

Article 18 : Freedom of thought etc.
Article 19 : Freedom of expression
Article 20 : Freedom of peaceful assembly
Article 21 : Right to take part in the government
Article 30 : Enjoyment of all rights

Social Rights

Article 22 : Right to social security
Article 29 : Duties to the community

International Rights

Article 14 : Right to seek asylum in other countries
Article 28 : Right to social and international order

All religions preach equality, love and affection towards others.

The successful working of democracy depends on the equality of opportunity to citizens.

31.5 BRIEF HISTORY

The idea of the basic rights of human being had been postulated by many poets, writers, philosophers, thinkers and politicians during the last few centuries. But the concept of human rights as it stands today finds its legal foundation in the slogan of the French Revolution, "Liberty, Equality and Fraternity", as well as in the Charter of the United Nations in various Articles. In 1946, the UN established the Commission on Human Rights under the chairperson of Eleanor Roosevelt, human rights activist and widow of former U.S. President Fanklin Roosevelt. In pursuance of its recommendations and Articles of the Charter, the General Assembly of the United Nations adopted at its 183rd meeting on December 10, 1948, a Universal Declaration of Human Rights. December 10 is celebrated as Human Rights Day.

The General Assembly proclaimed the Declaration of Human Rights "As a common standard of achievement for all people and all nations, to the end that every individual and every organ of society, keeping this Declaration constantly in mind, shall strive by teaching and education to promote respect for these rights and freedoms and by progressive measures, national and international, to secure their universal and effective recognition and observance, both among the peoples of member-States themselves and among the peoples of territories under their jurisdiction."

31.6 A HOLISTIC VIEW OF HUMAN RIGHTS

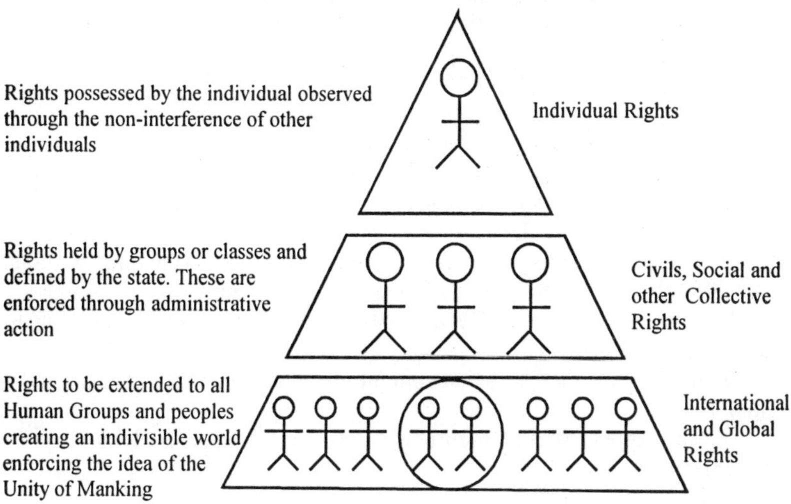

Fig 31.1: A Holistic View of Human Rights

31.7 U.N. AND PROMOTION AND PROTECTION OF HUMAN RIGHTS

(1) UN as a global conscious keeper of human rights

(2) UN as a law-maker agency

(3) UN as a monitoring body of human rights

(4) UN as a nerve center

(5) UN as a researcher

(6) UN as a forum of appeal

(7) UN as a fact-finder

UN adopts the following methods for safeguarding human rights:

1. Conventions
2. Moral pressure
3. Sanctions
4. Laws
5. Education

UN Organisation for Promoting and Safeguarding Human Rights

1. The United Nations Commission for Human Rights (UNCHR) (Since replaced by Human Rights Council – 2006)
2. Human Rights Committee.
3. The High Commissioner for Human Rights.
4. The Office of the High Commissioner for Human Rights (OHCHR).
5. Centre for Human Rights.

Human Rights Council (2006)

The Human Rights Commission set by the UN on June 21, 1946 was replaced by the Human Rights Council at its Sixtieth Session vide Resolution of March 15, 2006. The first meeting of the Council was held on June 19, 2006. It consists of 47 member States and is based in Geneva (Switzerland).

Chief Features of the Work of the Council

1. Promotion of human rights without distinction of any kind.
2. Promotion of human rights education.
3. Serving as a forum for dialogue on thematic issues on all human rights.
4. System of independent investigations of the violation of human rights by Member States of the UN.
5. Broad participation of the Civil Society in upholding the human rights.
6. Commitment of the Member States on human rights.
7. Elected members of the Council to be first in line for scrutiny relating to matters on human rights.
8. Suspension of members that commit gross and systematic violations of human rights.
9. Commitment of the members with the Council and its various mechanisms.

31.8 HUMAN RIGHTS IN INDIA

Recognition and respect for human rights can be traced to the Vedic Age. It is inherent in the ancient prayer which runs like this: 'May all human beings live happily! May all human beings be free from any trouble! May all human beings see goodness'.

Broadly speaking, following three measures have been taken to ensure the availability of human rights to all:

1. Constitutional Provisions.
2. Penal Laws.
3. Establishment of the Human Rights Commission.

Our Constitution incorporates the major ideas of the Declaration of Human

Rights through Directive Principles of State Policy and the provisions of Fundamental Rights which can be enforced through law courts.

Article 14 of the Constitution provides: "The state shall not deny to any person equality before law". This provision reflects the spirit of Article 2 of the UN Declaration of Human Rights. Article 19 of our Constitution gives every Indian the right to move freely, settle and reside in any part of India. This is commensurate with the declaration which provides for freedom of movement and residence.

Other provisions in our Constitution which are parallel to the Declaration of Human Rights include Right of Freedom of Worship and Propagation of Religion (Article 25), Right of Conservation of One's Language and Culture (Article 29); Right of Equal Pay for Equal Work for both Men and Women (Article 39) and Right to have Free and Compulsory Education up to the age of 14 (Article 21A).

31.9 FUNDAMENTAL RIGHTS SIMILAR TO THE UN HUMAN RIGHTS IN THE CONSTITUTION OF INDIA

1. Right to Equality before the Law (Article 14)
2. Freedom from Discrimination (Article 15)
3. Right to Equal Opportunity in Public Employment (Article 16)
4. Right to Freedom of Speech and Expression (Article 19)
5. Right to Assemble Peacefully without Arms (Article 19)
6. Right to form Associations or Unions (Article 19)
7. Right to Move Freely (Article 19)
8. Right to Settle and Reside Anywhere in the Country (Article 19)
9. Right to Practise any Profession, Occupation, Trade Business (Article 19)
10. Right not to be convicted of Offences Not Crimes at Time Committed (Article 20)
11. Right to Life and Personal Liberty (Article 21)
12. Right not to be Detained Without Being Informed of Reasons (Article 22)
13. Right to Consult with, and be Defended by a Lawyer After Arrest (Article 22)
14. Right Against Trafficking in Human Beings and Forced Labour (Article 23)

31.10 NATIONAL HUMAN RIGHTS COMMISSION IN INDIA

The Constitution of National Human Rights Commission is a landmark in the crusade to safeguard human rights.

The Commission started functioning on November 1, 1993.

Composition of the National Human Rights Commission (NHRC)

The eight members would be as under:

1. Chairperson, a former Chief Justice of India.
2. A present or former Judge of the Supreme Court.
3. A present or former Chief Justice of a High Court.

4. and 5. Two members from amongst persons knowledgeable in the area of human rights.
6. Chairperson of the National Commission for Women.
7. Chairperson of the National Commission for SCs and STs.
8. Chairperson of the National Commission for Minorities.

Powers and Functions of the NHRC

NHRC can inquire on its own or on a petition presented to it by a victim or any person on his behalf into complaints of:

(i) Violation or abetment of violation of human rights.

(ii) Negligence in the prevent of such violation by a public servant.

To perform its functions, the NHRC has been given following authorities:

- To intervene in any proceeding involving any allegation of violation of human rights pending before a court with the approval of such court.
- To visit, under intimation to a State government, any jail or any other institution under the control of the State government concerned, where persons are detained or lodged for purposes of treatment, reformation or protection, to study the living conditions of the inmates and make recommendations thereon.
- To review the safeguards provided by or under the Constitution or any law for the time being in force for the protection of human rights and recommend measures for their effective implementation.
- To review the factors, including acts of terrorism that inhibit the enjoyment of human rights and recommend appropriate remedial measures.
- To study treaties and other international instruments on human rights and make recommendations for their effective implementation.
- To undertake and promote research in the field of human rights; spread human rights literacy among various sections of society and promote awareness of the safeguards available for the protection of these rights through publications, the media, seminars and other available means.
- To encourage the efforts of non-governmental organisations and institutions working in the field of human rights. It may also undertake such other functions as it may consider necessary for the promotion of human rights.

Other Commissions

In addition to NHRC, National Commissions for Women, SCs and STs, OBCs, Minorities and Children etc. have been established to protect and promote rights of these specific categories and also to suggest measures for their welfare.

Concluding Observations: India has been making strenuous efforts to fulfil its obligations as provided for in its Constitution which contains a number of rights and Directive Principles of State Policy and also to the UN Declaration of Human rights.

In the ultimate analysis, it must be accepted that for the achievement of best results, it is very essential that we must be fully duty-conscious.

31.11 EDUCATION FOR HUMAN RIGHTS

Education has been specified as one of the fundamental human rights in Article 26 of the Universal Declaration of Human Rights.

Article 26: (i) Everyone has the right to education. Education shall be free, at least in the elementary and fundamental stages. Technical and professional education shall be equally accessible to all on the basis of merit.

(ii) Education shall be directed to the full development of the human personality and to the strengthening of respect for human rights and fundamental freedoms.

It shall promote understanding, tolerance and friendship among all nations, racial or religious groups, and shall further the activities of the United Nations for the maintenance of peace.

(iii) Parents have a right to choose the kind of education that shall be given to their children.

Thus, being a human right, education has essentially 'to contribute to the development of good human rights culture'. This is why all human rights documents have stressed the need for education in human rights at all important stages, namely policy, formulation, curriculum development and actual teaching-learning activities.

31.12 EDUCATIONAL OBJECTIVES OF THE TEACHING OF HUMAN RIGHTS

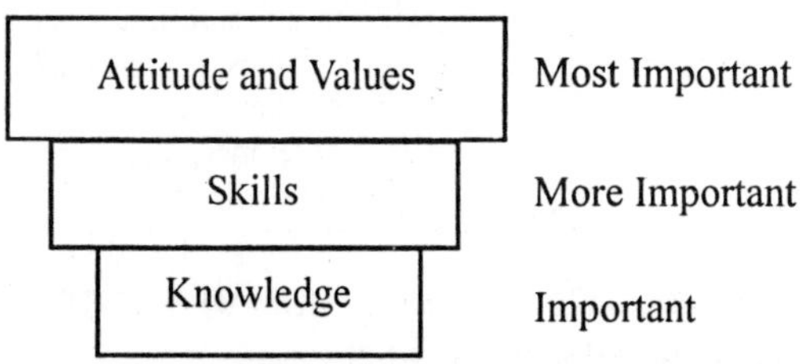

Fig.: 31.2: Hierarchy of Objectives of Human Rights Education

31.13 AIMS AND OBJECTIVES OF HUMAN RIGHTS AND EDUCATION

Education for Human Rights should at imparting knowledge, inculcating right attitudes and values and developing the skills of the students.

A.	*Knowledge*	Concepts	(i)	Historical development
			(ii)	Infringements/violations of Human Rights in one's own and other countries
			(iii)	Concept and scope of Human Rights
			(iv)	Problems of under-developed/ developed countries on Human Rights, their obligations and responsibilities

(*Contd.*)

		Understanding of development process	(i)	Understanding of the environment and human rights over a period of time
			(ii)	International understanding and the cultural heritage of humanity
			(iii)	The United Nations System
			(iv)	Universality of human rights
B.	*Skills*	Intellectual skills		Problem solving, critical thinking and communicative competence
		Action skills		To be able to participate and communicate. It includes the capacity to change the political situation
C.	*Attitudes and Values*	Attitudes		Attitude formation is more important than knowledge acquisition. It includes:
			(i)	Self-respect
			(ii)	Respect of others
			(iii)	Commitment to peace and justice
		Values		Procedural values are considered to be more important than social attitudes. These include:
			(i)	Fairness and respect for truth
			(ii)	Tolerance, freedom and open mindedness

31.14 METHODS OF TEACHING HUMAN RIGHTS

Important methods of teaching human rights are:

(i) *Promotion of Cooperative Practices:* The process of teaching and learning should promote cooperative practices between teachers and students and among students in the classroom.

(ii) *Active Methods*: Teaching and learning methods which are active and process-based should be used to involve students in the investigation of issues and concerns and formulation of solution.

(iii) *Learning Needs and Interests of Students*: Content organisation and teaching methods to be matched to different learning needs and interests of students of different ages and abilities.

(iv) *Oral exposition*: The students to be helped to acquire and develop a language for discussion of human rights issues and to master the concepts associated with human rights.

(v) *Questioning*: Questions should be used as an invitation to students to express their views on an issue to pose questions, and to exchange views with each other, to encourage students to consider sympathetically views which they themselves do not hold, to express their opinions openly and clearly and to pose questions which invite further exploration of an issue.

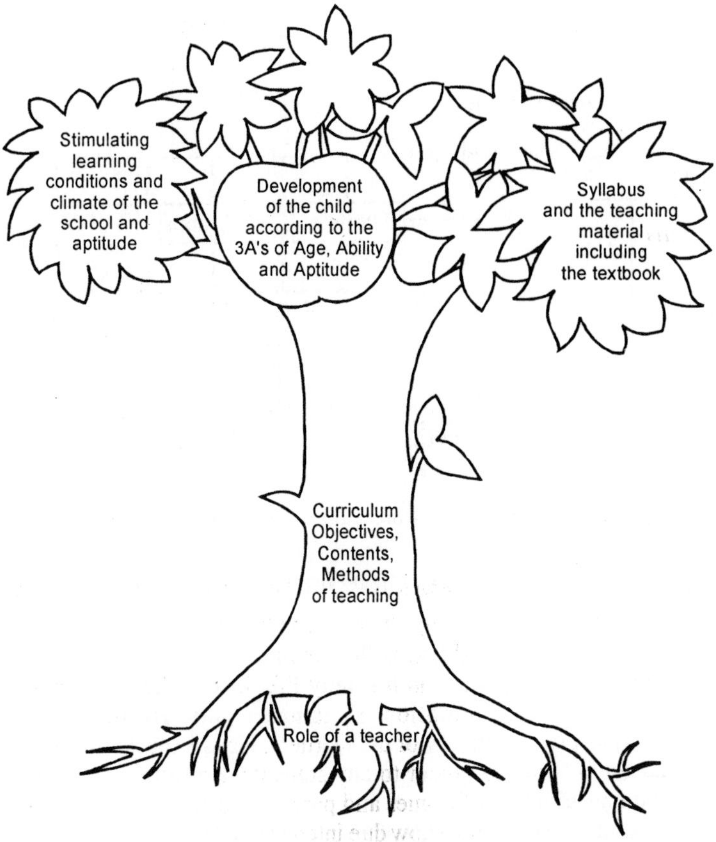

Fig. 31.3: Tree Showing Dimensions or Branches of Human Rights Education

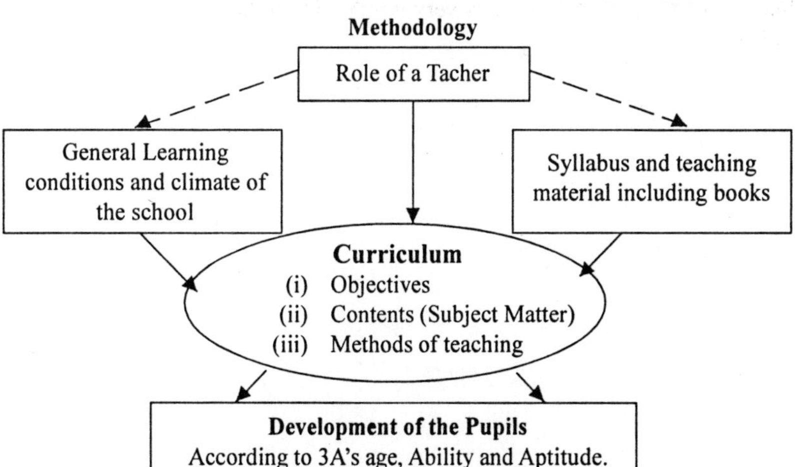

Fig. 31.4: Contents and Methodology of Teaching Human Rights

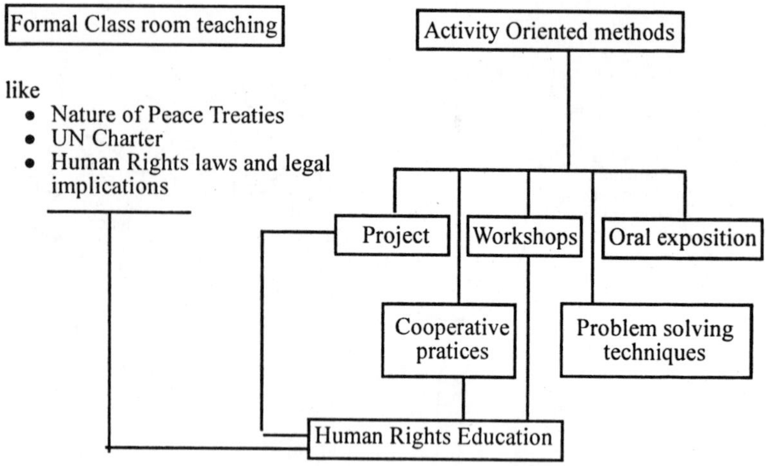

Fig. 31.5: An Overall View — A Theoretical Framework of Human Rights Teaching

31.15 ROLE OF THE TEACHER IN PROMOTING HUMAN RIGHTS

Every teacher can play an important role in the promotion of the values of human rights. The first condition is that he himself not only believes in the human rights but also practise in his daily life. In fact the entire work of a teacher relates to the promotion of human rights. He must give due consideration to the personality of the learners. He is expected to treat them justly. He should show no favour to any students. He should cultivate good human relations with his colleagues and parents and all others with whom he comes into contact. He should show due interest in all the school programmes, especially related to the promotion of human rights. He must keep in mind that duties rightly performed is very conducive to the promotion of human rights.

32

Organisation of Youth Parliament in Schools: Citizenship Training

32.1 OBJECTIVES OF YOUTH PARLIAMENT

The Department of Parliamentary Affairs of the Government of India has been implementing a scheme entitled 'Youth Parliament Competition Scheme for Recognised Educational Institutions in the Union Territory of Delhi'. The objective of the scheme is to strengthen the roots of democracy, inculcate healthy habits of discipline, tolerance of views of others and to enable the student community to know something about the working of the Parliament.

32.2 GUIDELINES FOR THE ORGANISATION OF YOUTH PARLIAMENT

1. Seating Arrangements inside the Chamber of Youth Parliament: The working of Youth Parliament should broadly follow the pattern of the working of the Lok Sabha. It would facilitate the task of the teacher-in-charge of this activity, if he/she and the students, selected to participate in the youth parliament competition could first acquaint themselves with the practical working of the Parliament of the country by witnessing the actual proceedings and make themselves conversant with the arrangements made for the members in the chamber of the Lok Sabha.

The layout of the chamber of their Youth Parliament should resemble as far as possible the layout of the chamber of Lok Sabha. The dias and chair of the residing officer should be on the straight base of the semi-circle. The seating arrangement for members should be in the shape of a horse-shoe as it is in the Lok Sabha. The chamber of Lok Sabha is a semi-circular hall with the speaker sitting in a canopied chair, placed conspicuously at the centre of the diameter connecting the two ends of the semi-circle. There is a dividing space in front of the speaker's rostrum. On the left of the rostrum are the seats for the opposition and on the right are the seats for the government benches. Slightly raised above the chamber of the Youth Parliament for visitors are seats the 'press', the 'diplomats' and the 'distinguished visitors', etc.

2. Agenda: Generally the following items may be included in the agenda for a sitting of Youth Parliament:

1. Oath of affirmation.
2. Obituary reference.
3. Questions.
4. Adjournment motion.
5. Questions involving a breach of privilege.
6. Papers to be laid on the table.
7. Call attention notice.
8. Legislative business.
9. Motions

3. Start of the Session: Like the practice obtaining in Lok Sabha, the session of Youth Parliament starts with the arrival of the Speaker, which is announced by the marshal of the house. The marshal before announcing the arrival of the speaker, ascertains that there is a quorum in the house which should be at least 10 per cent of total membership of the house. Thereafter the Speaker resumes that there is a quorum at all times unless his attention is invited to lack of quorum. In either case bell is rung and the business of the house proceeds only when there is a quorum in the house.

As soon as the speaker arrives in the chamber, marshal announces his arrival with the words "Honourable Members, the Honourable Speaker" or "माननीय सभासदो, माननीय अध्यक्ष जी" in Hindi. Thereafter the entire house stands up. The Speaker before taking his seat first bows to his left, then to his right and then in front of him. He then takes his seat. The members also respectfully bow to the chair before taking their seats.

4. Oath of affirmation by members: The Speaker takes up the business of the house in the order in which it is printed in the list of business. The first item in the agenda is "oath or affirmation by the new members". Before taking the seat in the house every member is required to or subscribe an oath or affirmation in the following forms:

"I... having been elected (or nominated) a member of the House do swear in the name of God/solemnly affirm that I will bear true faith and allegiance to the Constitution of India as by law established, that I will uphold the sovereignty and integrity of India and that I will faithfully discharge the duty upon which I am about to enter".

The members may take oath or affirmation in Hindi or English or in any of the language specified in the 8th Schedule of the Constitution. Before taking the oath the member should bring with him the certificate of election granted to him by the Chief Election Commissioner. Members elected at by-election at the time of making and subscribing oath or affirmation are introduced to the house by the Minister of Parliamentary Affairs.

5. Questions: The first part of sitting each day in the Youth Parliament should be devoted to oral questions, commonly known as 'Starred Questions'. In the Indian Parliament it is the most popular hour for the Members of Parliament and also for the public. From the point of view of a Minister it is the most searching test of his grasp on the items of business allocated to him, his ability to lead as well as his ready wit when answering supplementaries. The question has been defined as an instrument whereby a member can elicit, describe and get information in any aspect of public administration. During the youth parliament competitions the judges give credit for the quality of questions asked and the quality of replies given by the ministers.

6. Short Notice Questions: Where any question relates to a matter of urgent public importance it may be asked for oral answer by a member with notice shorter than the minimum time of 5 days (as far as the minister is concerned) in the Lok Sabha. If the Speaker accepts the urgency, he can admit it at shorter notice after ascertaining the willingness of the Minister to answer it. When it is admitted and placed on the agenda it is called immediately after the question hour.

7. Adjournment Motion: An adjournment motion seeks to raise discussion on some sudden or emergent matter of public importance that has arisen in the country or abroad, demanding the immediate attention of the government and the house. If the motion is in order, and if at least 1/10th of the members present of the Youth Parliament stand up in favour of leave being granted, the motion is admitted. If less than this number rise in their seats, the Speaker informs the member concerned that he does not have the leave of the house to move the adjournment motion.

8. Calling Attention Motions: A member may with the prior permission or the Speaker call the attention of a Minister to a matter of urgent public importance and request him to make a statement thereon.

9. Respect to the Chair: The participants should show utmost respect to the Chair. They should strictly abide by the decisions of the Chair and should have faith in his impartiality and judgement.

Every member while coming to the House for its sitting should bow to the Chair and similarly while leaving the chamber should bow to the Chair.

Members should not sit with their backs to the Chair. When a member wants to speak he should rise in his place to attract the attention of the Chair. No member should speak unless he or she has "caught" the eye of the Speaker and has been permitted by the Chair by name or by a sign to speak.

Every member should resume his seat as the Speaker rises to speak or class out "order, order" and also when any other member is in possession of the floor.

No member should rise or leave the house when the Speaker is addressing the house. The Speaker is always to be heard in silence.

Two or more members should not keep standing at the same time. Members should not distribute within the precincts of the house or inside the legislature questionnaire or pamphlets not connected with the business of the house.

10. No Discussion on Foreign Matters: There should be no discussion on sensitive policy matters affecting the relations of our country with foreign friendly governments or which will prove embarrassing for the country and its present day government.

Unparliamentary Expressions

Arrogant	Brute
Buffoon	Cheat
Blackguard	Coward
Bloody	Criminal
Bluff	Damn

33

Examination and Evaluation in Civics

33.1 SIGNIFICANCE, FUNCTIONS, LIMITATIONS AND SUGGESTIONS REGARDING EXAMINATIONS

Examinations, in one or the other form, have been in existence from times immemorial. In the idealised picture of society portrayed in H.G. Well's 'Utopia', examinations find an important place. The chairman of the Sadler Commission 1917 observed, "To close down examinations would be to give the signal for educational saturnalia. "The Secondary Education Commission 1952-53 was of the view", Nevertheless examinations and especially external examinations have a proper place in any scheme of education. External examinations have stimulating effect both on the pupils and on the teachers by providing well-defined goals and objective standard of education. To the pupil the examinations give a goal towards which he would strive and a stimulus urging him to attain that goal in a given time thereby demanding steady and constant effort. This makes the purpose clear and the method of approach definite. He is judged by external and objective tests on which he and others interested in him can depend. And, finally, it gives him a hallmark recognised by all."

Examinations intend to perform the following functions:

1. To evaluate the achievement of the students.
2. To help in diagnosis.
3. To help in prognoses.
4. To act as motivators.
5. To measure the efficiency of the teacher.
6. To measure the efficiency of the schools.
7. To raise standards of education.
8. To measure fitness of students for promotion and admission to higher courses.
9. To help in selection by competition.
10. To help in guidance.
11. To acquaint the parents with the progress of their wards.
12. To measure some personality traits.

Epithets Given to Traditional System of Examinations

(i) A bane of educational system. (ii) A begetter of rivalry and strife. (iii) A blood sucker. (iv) A dead hand of education. (v) An enemy of creative work. (vi) A glorification of memory. (vii) A growing tyranny. (viii) A necessary evil. (ix) A presumptuous attempt to gauge the depth of human ignorance. (x) An enemy of true education. (xi) An incubus. (xii) An obstacle to learning.

Etymological Meaning of the work: The word examination is derived from the Latin word 'examen' which means the tongue of balance. Perhaps this denotes that in the beginning examinations were conducted orally.

An examination may be defined as a systematic test of knowledge or skill or of special and general capacity whether carried out under the authority of some public body or conducted by the teachers themselves.

In the ancient Vedic system of education, the three processes, i.e., teaching, learning and examination were integrated. The teacher was also the evaluator and the assessment of the students was continuous.

Limitations and Shortcomings of the Examinations

Successive Commissions and Committees have pointed out the following limitations and shortcomings of the examinations:

1. Students and teachers tend to lose sight of the real goals of teaching and learning and tend to substitute the attainment in a subject of high marks at the public examinations as the goal.
2. Element of chance decides the fate of a large number of students.
3. Use of unfair means affects the moral standard of different sections of population.
4. Glorification of memory is predominant.
5. Students begin to depend on cheap notes and do not develop serious habits of study and work.
6. Examinations put heavy mental strain on students.
7. Examinations stimulate an unhealthy competitive spirit.
8. An element of subjectivity in marking leads to wide variability in marking. It led Vernon to point out, "The same script might receive a different mark if read after instead of before dinner." Results are greatly affected by the fancies, moods and whims of the examiners.
9. Examinations are very much limited in their scope and do not test several important aspects of pupil's personality development.

Reforms in the System of Examinations

It has already been stressed that the examinations are very important in the educational set-up. Perhaps they cannot be ended but can only be mended. To mitigate the limitations of the examinations, following measures are suggested. Some action on these lines has already been taken by several examining agencies and institutions.

1. Introduction of objective tests side-by-side, essay tests and short-answer tests.
2. Setting thought-provoking and application questions.
3. Consideration to class work and work done throughout the year.
4. Appointment of examiners who possess the necessary experience of teaching those classes for which examinations are conducted.
5. Prescribing norms of marking and circulating marking schemes to the examiners.

6. Balanced questions in the question paper.
7. Training examiners and paper setters.
8. No overall options in the questions paper.
9. Training students to take examinations on the pattern of proposed examinations system.
10. Provision of weightage in monthly and terminal tests.
11. Maintenance of cumulative records.
12. Reduction in the number of public examinations.
13. Symbolic rather than numerical marking.
14. Multiple sets of question papers.
15. Strict check on the use of unfair means by the students and also by all those who are engaged in various operations like marking, tabulating and declaring results.
16. No overall pass or fail.
17. Compartmental examinations.
18. No compulsory public examination and instead a certificate based on the record of every pupil to be issued by the school.

A good deal of criticism as made earlier relates to external examinations, basically essay-type. These examinations with all their defects have been of great value. They have provided minimum standards for education and have also served as one of the chief means of accrediting educational institutions. The errors present in these examinations are such that they raise serious questions about the utility of examinations. Attempts to change the examination system must take full cognizance of the relationships, such as, exist between the system and the curriculum, the student motivation and learning, teachers motivation and teaching methods etc.

33.2 OBJECTIVE TYPE OR NEW TYPE TESTS AND COMPARISON WITH ESSAY-TYPE EXAMINATIONS

The new type tests are the result of the testing movement which was initiated in an attempt to seek more objective measurements of teaching-learning results. In these tests questions are framed in such a manner that they evoke mental operation separately and to which only one right answer is possible. A large number of items, questions and statements are provided and the students are asked to answer them by making the correct response in some prescribed way, i.e. by ticking the right answer by writing 'yes' or 'no', by writing 'true' or 'false', by drawing a circle round the correct answer, and by completing a sentence etc.

These new type tests are of various forms. The most popular forms are: (i) True False, (ii) Multiple Choice, (iii) Matching test, (iv) Completion test, (v) Single answer, (vi) Best answer test, (vii) Classification test.

A question paper may contain different types of tests.

33.3 DEFINITIONS AND MEANING OF EVALUATION

Shane and McSwam conceive evaluation, "as a process or inquiry based upon criteria cooperatively prepared and concerned with the study, interpretation, and guidance of socially desirable changes in the development behaviour of children..... It is a process within the child as a result of which he responds to the psychological interpretations he makes of his school-community environment."

According to *Good*, "Evaluation is a process of ascertaining or judging the value or amount of something by careful appraisal. 'Values' imply the outcome of the learning activity whereas amount signifies the acquisition of knowledge and skill. It means that evaluation concerns itself with scholastic achievement as well as with behaviour changes."

Chester T. McNernly observes, "The purpose of any programme of evaluation is to discover the needs of the individuals being evaluated and then to design learning experiences that will solve these needs...... Evaluation is an important and delicate process not only from the standpoint of determining the needs and growth of programmes and individuals but also from the standpoint of what it does to the individuals being evaluated... An evaluation cannot adequately be made by using a single check list, an isolated anecdotal record, or a battery of examinations, a complete evaluation will require the use of many techniques."

Thomas M. Briggs and *Joseph Justman* write that evaluation is 'a process by which the values of an enterprise are ascertained'.

Wiles defines evaluation as, "Evaluation is a process of making judgements that are to be used as a basis for planning. It consists of establishing goals, collecting evidence concerning growth or lack of growth toward goals, making judgements about the evidence, and revising procedures and goals in the light of the judgements. It is a procedure for improving the product, the process, and even the goals themselves."

C.E. Beeby describes evaluation as, "The systematic collection and interpretation of evidence leading as a part of process to a judgement of value with a view to action."

In simple language evaluation may be described as a process by means of which changes in behaviour of children are studied and guided towards pre-determined objectives.

33.4 AIMS, NEEDS AND SIGNIFICANCE OF EVALUATION

The primary aim of evaluation is to bring about improvement in the teaching-learning process so that the learner develops his potentials to the optimum level. Following are the broader aims of evaluation:

1. *To Evaluate the Achievement of the Students*: The abilities and the achievements of the students must be evaluated. Evaluations are conducted to discover whether or not the learner has been able to acquire the required knowledge, skill and attitude.

2. *To Measure Personality*: Evaluation is used to test the power of clear thinking, quickness of mind, calmness and perseverance of the students.

3. *To Find Out the Efficiency of Teachers and of the School*: Evaluations provide a suitable occasion for the authorities to judge the efficiency of the teachers. The efficiency of the institution is also judged. They provide a proper occasion to the teachers to know whether or not their methods of teaching-learning are appropriate.

4. *To Help in Diagnosis*: Evaluation helps to discover the specific weak points of an individual or class and thus gives an opportunity to the teachers as well as to the taught to remove these defects.

5. *To Act as Incentives*: Stimulation to work hard is provided to the students through the system of evaluation. Some objectives are placed before the students and for the realisation of those objectives, the students develop in them the habits of constant hard work.

6. *To Help in Prognosis*: Evaluation has a prognostic value also. With this device, the aptitudes of the students are determined.

7. *To Give Uniformity of Standard*: The external evaluation facilitates the problem of uniformity of standards attained by the students of the different institutions.

8. *To Help in Grouping*: Evaluation facilitates the work of grouping individuals for the purposes of teaching by bringing those together who have more or less the same attainment.

9. *To Measure Fitness for Admission to Higher Courses*: Evaluation is designed to determine the capacity and fitness of the candidates to pursue higher courses of general or professional study or training. Evaluations which serve this purpose are called Entrance or Qualifying Examinations.

10. *To Help in Selection by Competition*: Evaluation is also conducted to select the best candidates for appointment to public services or for awarding prizes and scholarships.

Summing up: Whatever be the definition of evaluation, it must serve the following objectives:

1. Assist learners in their learning.
2. Diagnose learning difficulties of learners.
3. Determine readiness for new learning experiences.
4. Assist learners in their problems of adjustment.
5. Prepare reports of learner's achievement.
6. Assist teachers in adopting proper strategies of teaching-learning.
7. Fulfil classroom objectives of instruction.

33.5 MAIN FUNCTIONS OF EVALUATION

1. To make provision for guiding the growth of individual pupils.
2. To diagnose the weaknesses and strengths of pupils.
3. To locate areas where remedial measures are needed.
4. To provide a basis for a modification of the curriculum and courses.
5. To provide a basis for the introduction of experiences to meet the needs of individuals and group of pupils.
6. To motivate pupils towards better attainment and growth.
7. To test the efficiency of teachers in providing learning experiences and the effectiveness of instruction and classroom activities.
8. To improve instruction.
9. To bring out the inherent capabilities of a pupil, such as, attitudes, habits, appreciation and understanding, manipulative skills in addition to conventional acquisition of knowledge.

Components of Evaluation

1. Specifying learning outcomes.
2. Collection of evidence about pupil's growth through reliable data gathering devices.

3. Analysis and interpretation of performance or pupil's growth.

4. Diagnostic appraisal, i.e., indicating the level of performance rather than the judgement on the performance.

5. Redefining and readjusting the instructional objectives on the basis of feedback.

33.6 CHIEF CHARACTERISTICS OF EVALUATION

A publication of the NCERT entitled *Reforming Examinations: Some Emerging Concepts* (1978), lists the following regarding evaluation:

1. Evaluation is a function of the learner and instruction and, therefore, good evaluation is one which is done by the teacher, of the taught as an individual.

2. Evaluation provides quality control at every stage of the teaching-learning process and, therefore, evaluation would be treated as an integral part of the teaching-learning process.

3. Since evaluation provides feedback about the rate of pupil's learning and the effectiveness of instruction, evaluation would be treated as an integral part of the teaching-learning process.

4. As the purpose of teaching is learning by students, focus of teachers' evaluation should be on improvement of pupils' achievement and not on judging their achievement. Therefore, diagnostic testing and remedial teaching should go side-by-side.

5. Pupil's achievement is the outcome of the integrated process of learning within a given set of conditions. Evaluation of pupils' learning should, therefore, be also integrated with regard to both the process and product of learning.

6. Keeping in view explosion of knowledge, the new curriculum stresses the learnability aspect more than the knowledge aspect. Emphasis in evaluation should, therefore, shift from testing to rote memory to that of problem solving abilities and attitude development.

7. For appraisal of the total development of the learner, it is essential that evaluation should not be limited to scholastic achievement alone, but it should encompass all aspects of pupils' development. As such evaluation techniques will have to be extended beyond written and practical examinations to include oral testing, observation, checklists, rating scales and interviews.

8. Since independent learning by students is considered an important method of learning in the new curriculum, self-assessment by pupils of their own learning should be practised in the evaluation system of an institution, so that cooperative assessment of the teacher and the learner is encouraged.

9. Since it is impossible to achieve 100 per cent or even near to 100 per cent reliability of the various tools used for evaluating pupils. It is desirable that students should be classified broadly into 5 to 7 grades rather than using 101 point scale as at present.

10. As every pupil learns at his own rate, he should be judged in terms of his own capabilities and goals and not in terms of the standards of his class, institution or the board of secondary education. As such passing of a student in all the subjects at a time cannot be considered essential.

11. The grades of every pupil indicate only his level of performance which may be satisfactory or unsatisfactory in terms of his own standard. Thus, a

grade howsoever low it may be, cannot be taken as failure but as an indicator of his present level of achievement.

12. Given more time and proper remedial teaching a student can improve his achievement. Therefore, a student should get the opportunity of improving his grade in one or more subjects, if he so desires.

13. The more accurately and meaningfully the evidence about pupils' growth in different aspects of his development is reported to students, teachers, parents, employers and institutes of higher learning, the more appropriate and reliable would be the decision taken for classification, certification and selection of students for different purposes. Therefore, regular recording of pupil performance in various areas of development is a perquisite to every evaluation programme.

33.7 COMPREHENSIVE AND CONTINUOUS EVALUATION

Evaluation is always with reference to the objectives of education and is not done in a vacuum. It has to be comprehensive in a system which aims at the many-sided development of the personality of a child. Evaluation, therefore, must relate to academic and non-academic achievements of the students.

Unlike traditional examinations which are periodical, evaluation is a continuous process. In fact, evaluation to be effective, must be done on daily basis as the chief function of evaluation is not to declare a student 'pass' or 'fail' but to bring about improvement by finding out the deficiencies.

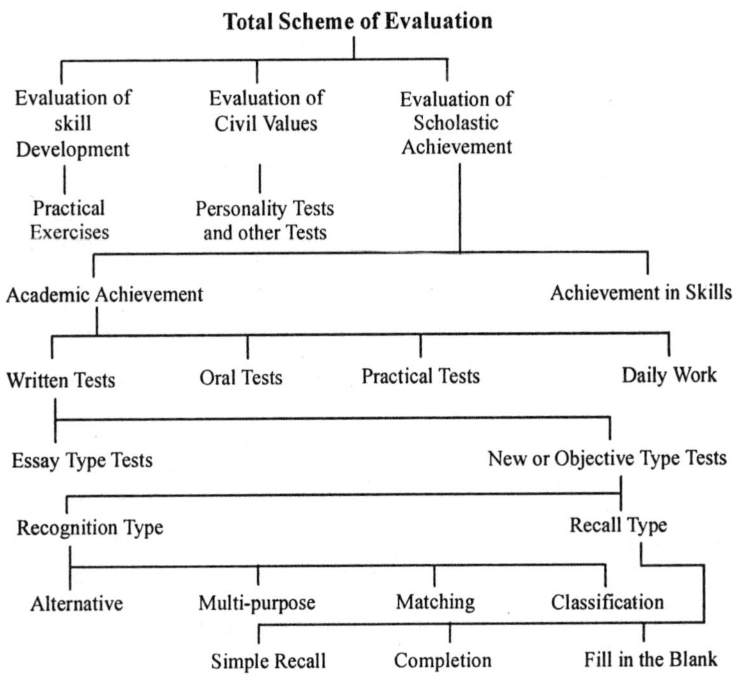

Fig. 33.1: Chart Showing the Total Scheme of Evaluation

Essay-Type Tests

(Already discussed)

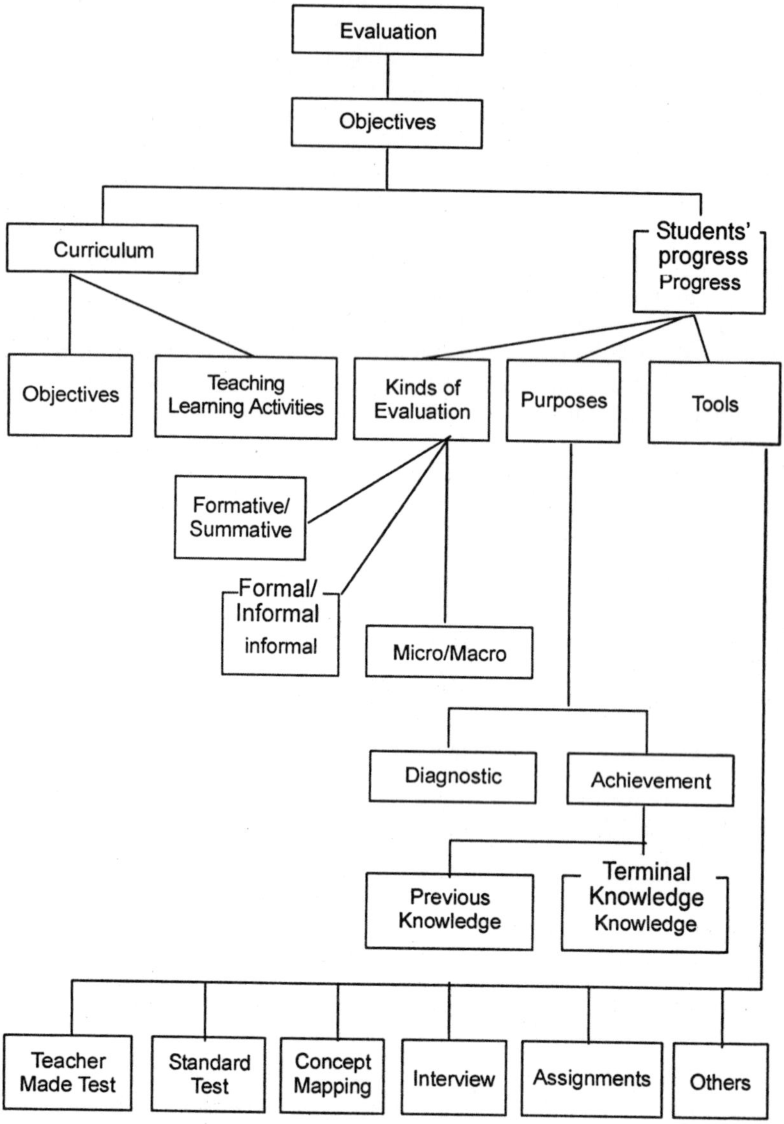

Fig. 33.2: Dimensions of Evaluation

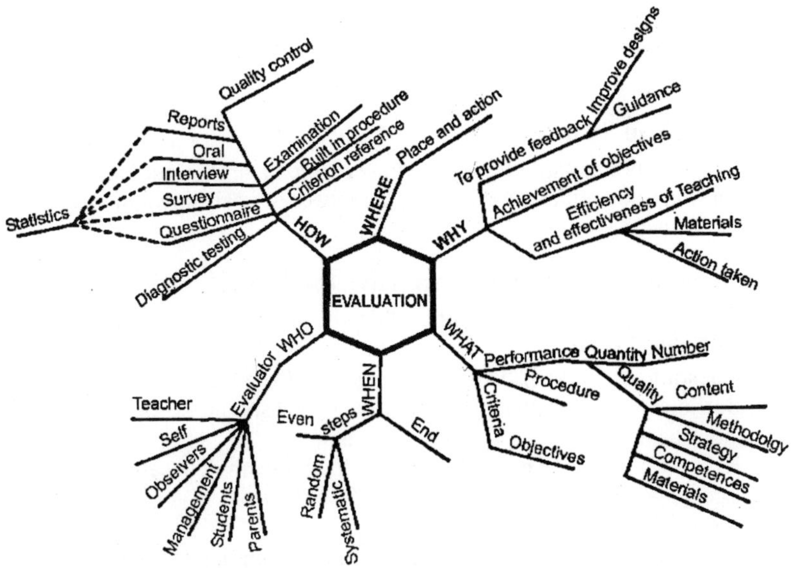

Fig. 33.3: Why, what, who, how, where and when of evaluation?

33.8 SHORT-ANSWER TYPE TEST OR QUESTIONS

Meaning

In a simple language it may be stated that a short-answer type test is between an essay-type test and an objective test. Here we mention a few definitions given by experts to have a comprehensive view.

K.D. Hoppkins, J.C. Stanley and *B.R. Hopkins* in their book, *Educational and Psychological Measurement and Evaluation* (1990) write, "The short-answer test is an objective test in which each item is in the form of a direct question, a stimulus word or phrase, a specific direction, a specific problem or an incomplete statement or question. The response must be supplied by the examinee rather than merely identified from a list of suggested answers supplied by the teacher."

William Wierma and *Stephen G. Jurs* in their book, *Educational Measurement and Testing* (1990) provide this definition, "Short-answer items are considered objective items in that the correct response can be secured objectively. That is preferably there is a single correct answer so that equally important scores would agree on the correctness of a response."

Merits of Short-Answer Tests

1. It is easy to construct them as they measure only simple learning outcomes.
2. They are very useful for the recall of simple memorised facts and figures.
3. They are useful to test the lowest level of cognitive taxonomy, i.e., knowledge of terminology, classification, etc.
4. A large area of subject matter can be covered by the inclusion of a large number of short-answer questions.

5. Marking is relatively objective as compared with essay-type of questions.
6. There is very little scope for the influence of handwriting and spelling etc. on marking.

Limitations and Shortcomings

1. They are not suitable for measuring complex learning outcomes.
2. They are not suitable for judging the power of analysing and reasoning of the students.

Suggestions for Improving Short-Answer Tests

1. The intended answer should be thought first and then an appropriate question formed.
2. Questions should not be picked up exactly from the text-book.
3. Sufficient number of short-answer questions should be asked to cover the content.
4. A direct question is more desirable than an incomplete sentence.
5. Language of the question should be simple.
6. A scoring key should be prepared.
7. The number of words the answer should contain must be specified.

33.9 DEFINITION AND MEANING OF OBJECTIVE TESTS/QUESTIONS

R.L. Ebel and *D.A. Frisbie* (1986) define an objective test as "one that can be provided with a simple predetermined test of correct answers so that objective opinion or judgement in the scoring procedure is eliminated."

Lou M. Carey (1988) defines an objective test as "objective test items require students to work or select a correct or best answer. These items are called objective because they can be scored more objectively than any other type of item used to measure students' performance.... selected response items include alternative response, matching, keyed and multiple choice items".

Gilbert Sex (1989) regards a test objective if "it has a clear and unanimous scoring criteria. Because multiple choice and true-false tests can usually be scored objectively, they are sometimes referred to as objective test."

W. Wiersma and *S.G. Jurs* (1990), "Objective items are items that can be objectively scored, items on which persons select a response from a list of options."

33.10 MERITS OF OBJECTIVE TYPE TESTS

Percival Symonds discusses merits of objective type tests as under:

1. "The newt type examinations are more objective in their scoring, since the responses of pupils are controlled, and since there can be no doubt as to the correctness or incorrectness of their responses."

They are free from the personal factor of the teacher. The mood of the examiner in no way affects scoring. Each question which is asked has only one possible answer. 'Contrast the economic achievements of the Guptas with the Lodis is a legitimate thought-provoking assignment in the essay-type of examination, but there is a great scope for a variability in marking.

2. They may be very comprehensive and can be made to cover a great deal

more material than the old type of examination. Since the pupil does very little writing, he can devote his time to thought and can thereby answer a great many questions than when he has to write his answers out at length."

Chance element is very predominant in the essay-type of examination. Only a limited number of questions are set out of the wide field that has been covered. It is not uncommon to find students preparing fifteen or twenty questions in a subject and securing very high marks and students preparing forty questions but failing miserably. How does it happen and how could it be avoided? The answer is very simple. This happens simply because the number of questions set in the paper is so small that quite a major portion of the course covered remains untested. On the other hand, a large number of questions which are set in a new type of test eliminate of chance and cover a wide field of course.

3. "They are very easy to score as compared with the older type of examination. Notwithstanding the fact that the tests are more comprehensive, they may be scored in less time and with less labour. This itself is a sufficient reason to make them attractive to all teachers".

A key of the various questions may be prepared and then anybody can mark the question papers.

4. "Pupils like them. There is no question as to the accuracy of marks they receive. There is no chance for the teacher to show favouritism or personal bias. The pupils relieved of much writing, find these tests less tiring".

The pupils like the new type of tests because they think that marking will be fair and judicious. Even the students may be asked to mark the papers themselves if key is supplied to them. The general complaints of leniency of marking in one case and hard marking in the other are eliminated.

5. "They are more educative for the pupils. Let your pupils score their own tests directly after they take them by exchanging papers with their neighbours. It is then that their interest is at white heat. After the papers have been scored, the questions may be discussed. The pupils readily see where they need further study".

Besides the five advantages given by Symonds, we might add some more.

6. The new type of tests discourage cramming and encourage thinking, observation and scrutiny.

7. They are more reliable. Same results will be secured whoever may be the examiner. An essay-type of question paper cannot give the same results if it is given to different examiners.

8. Objective tests can be standardised by applying beforehand to a large number of students of the same age group before the actual examination. On the basis of the results of these standardised tests, the authorities of a particular institution can compare the standard of their institution with other institutions of the same area.

33.11 LIMITATIONS

Symonds gives two main limitations of new-type examinations.

1. "The pupil does not have an opportunity to show his ability to organise his thought. He has nothing to do except check over, the truth and falsity of statements or fill in the missing words or incomplete sentences. Pupils miss

the valuable experience of making comparisons, giving explanations or giving definitions. They are not asked to summarise the material or to make applications of principles and of course, these are valuable abilities which we do not want to neglect."

2. "These new types of examinations are not diagnostic in that they do not tell where the pupil's reasoning process goes wrong or where he stops reasoning altogether and starts guessing."

Besides the following limitations may also be noted:

3. It is commonly said that new type of tests fail to check cramming. Once the test is standardised the teaches will coach their pupils on the test, thus making it very little helpful. There is every possibility that 'keys' or 'guides' to these tests find their way in the market. General knowledge guides have already made their entry in the market.

4. It is often argued that use of new types of tests is very expensive.

5. Like the essay-type of tests, these also fail to test the character-building aspects.

33.12 PRINCIPLES OF CONSTRUCTION OF NEW TYPE OF TESTS

1. Prepare a list of all the topics falling within the scope of the examination.
2. Keep in view the most significant items in each topic.
3. Every item should have only one correct answer.
4. Easy questions should come first and then moderate and in the end the most difficult ones.
5. Include different types of objective test, i.e., Recognition, Recall etc.
6. Frame definite and brief questions.
7. Give reasonable time to the students to answer the paper. Ruch suggests the following time

   Recall Type—4 to 8 items per minute.

   True-False Type—10 to 15 items per minute.
8. Give clear instructions.

33.13 CHARACTERISTICS AND COMPARISON OF THE OLD AND NEW TYPE TESTS

1. The number of questions in the essay or old type of tests is very small, generally five or six questions in the paper.

There are a large number of questions in the new type tests.

2. Answers required in the old type of tests are large.

The answers are so short in the objective tests as can be written in a word or two or at the most in a sentence.

3. Essay-type questions are usually broad, general and indefinite. The examinees are at a loss to know how much they will have to write as answers.

Objective questions are specific, narrow and definite.

4. In essay-type tests personal factors like bias, temperament whims, etc. of the examiner influence marking.

Scoring becomes objective in the new type of tests.

5. In the answer of the essay test there is scope for partial credit. Answers may be partially wrong and right.

In the new tests, there is no provision for partial credit. Answers must either be right or wrong and hence full or no credit.

6. In the essay test examinees have to devote a long time.

Questions can be answered in a short time in the new tests.

7. In the essay tests, questions are selected at random and the entire course is covered. Some chapters or questions are completely ignored.

The entire course can be covered by comprehensive questions in new tests.

8. Essay tests put premium on expression. Students hardly find any time to think over the question.

9. Pupils having linguistic skill are at an advantage in the essay tests.

New tests are advantageous to the intellectually smart students.

10. It takes a short time to frame questions in the essay tests.

It takes a long time to frame questions in the new tests.

11. Students find it easier to prepare essay questions. They can safely omit many portions of the subject-matter in the essay tests.

Students have to devote a longer time to prepare for objective type questions as they have to go through the entire course for clear conceptions.

12. Essay tests are very suitable for testing composition, skills, and knowledge of the subject.

New tests are not suitable for testing composition and skill as well as appreciation of the subject.

13. In the essay tests there is relatively less scope for 'guessing' questions. Students prepare themselves from 'Made Easy' books.

In the new type there is more scope for guessing answers.

14. Essay tests take a longer time in examining scripts.

Short answers take less time to examine scripts.

15. Printing cost is small in the case of essay tests.

Since there are many questions, printing is costly in the new tests.

16. Answer scripts cost much as answers are very lengthy in the case of essay tests.

Answers being very short and usually can be written on the question paper itself, this makes the answer scripts less costly.

17. There is less scope for adopting unfair means by the students in the examination hall in the case of essay-type questions.

There is enough scope for adopting unfair means in the new tests.

33.14 GRADING AND RECORDING TEST RESULTS

The Secondary Education Commission 1952-53 made these observations regarding grading, "The present system of evaluating by percentiles, i.e., by numerical marks, out of hundred, may have certain advantages but the disadvantages seem to outweigh the advantages. Firstly, it introduces too many subdivisions which are not only useless but cumbersome; and secondly, it is indeed difficult to distinguish between two pupils one of whom obtains, say, 45 marks and another 46 or 47. This system no doubt gives the semblance of accurate judgement which for most of the pupils it is hardly worthwhile to exercise and is beset with many errors. In this connection we would again invite attention to the Hartog Reports on 'An Examination of Examinations' which fully reveals the limitations and errors of the system. A simpler and better system is the use of the five-point scale to which 'A' stands for Excellent, 'B' for Good, 'C' for Fair and Average, 'D' for Poor and 'E' for Very Poor. In this system pupils are grouped in broad divisions which are more easily distinguishable than the differences indicated by percentile marks. We recommend that this system be adopted for school records."

"For written examinations, whether external or internal, the same scale may be used with this modification that here D and E will be combined to indicate 'failure'. Here A will indicate 'Distinction', B 'Credit' and C 'Pass' and D and E 'Failure' or 'Cases Referred Back'. The value of these categories in terms of percentile marks may be determined by the examining authority. Individual examiners in different subjects may even use the percentile system and then convert the percentile scores in terms of categories."

"The system recommended here will work in almost all cases except where distinctions are to be made for the award of scholarships and prizes. In these cases (whose number will always be limited) the system may be modified to introduce a fine scale which may show the difference between two cases which May be almost similar. It must, however, be admitted that a difference of a few marks on the percentile scale is more often a matter of chance than of exact determination.

33.15 PRINCIPLES OF PREPARING ESSAY-TYPE AND OBJECTIVE TYPE TEST PAPER

E.W. Menzel observes that whether old type or new type, following principles should be observed in preparing a test:

1. It will be general and comprehensive enough to test thoroughly the pupil's mastery of the desired skill or grasp of a subject-matter. It will make it impossible for a pupil to get a good mark just, because he got a few 'lucky questions' and will not fail a good pupil, just because of a few 'unlucky questions'. Very few examinations in India are adequate in this respect.
2. It will reliably grade the pupils into at least six to ten (or more) different classifications according to their ability.
3. It will be as objective as practicable. Some questions of a discussional nature can be given to advantage but there should also be some work which pins pupil and examiner down to answers which can be quite objectively scored. Even in the essay-type of examination, the objectivity can be greatly increased with study and care.
4. Other things being equal, the test which examines most intensively or extensively in the least time and with the least fatigue on the part of the pupil is the best.
5. The test should encourage creative and self-reliant work and discourage mere mechanical rote-memory work.
6. The test should encourage the pupil to put forth his best effort.
7. The test should convincingly reveal to the pupil his deficiencies and encourage him to remove them.
8. The test should examine exactly what it pretends to examine and not handicap pupils for deficiencies in unrelated subjects. The more a test tries to

examine in subjects extraneous to the avowed subject, the less efficiently it examines its own.

9. The standards of a test should be based on actual performance and not upon mere opinion of what a standard should be or on an arbitrary percentage work.

10. The more a test makes it possible to compare the performance of a certain group of pupils to that of other pupils the more revealing it is.

11. Keep in mind that no test is infallible. The daily work of the pupil and an observation of his habits of work are equally important in appraising the work and ability of a pupil.

12. Keep in mind that poor results on the part of a group of pupils indicate a faulty test or one that is not graded to the ability of the pupils or deals with matters the children have not been taught.

33.16 CONCLUDING OBSERVATIONS

The Indispensable Nature of Essay Tests

Essay-type tests govern a wide field of learning—thinking and reasoning, study skills and work habits. Essay tests measure the functional aspects or the application of knowledge. We can evaluate through them the logical reasoning power of the students. The essay tests help us to test the power of expression, verbal facility, use of vocabulary and style of writing. They also help us to evaluate the capacity of the students to organise knowledge to evaluate thoughts and to create new thoughts. The objective tests fail to evaluate these powers.

The Indispensable Nature of New Tests

The new type tests cover the subjects as fully as possible and they offer better and more adequate facilities of sampling knowledge than the traditional type. They also help the teacher to find out where teaching has been defective or learning inadequate. Scoring becomes very objective. Personal preference of the examiners do not matter and subjective factor is completely eliminated and this increase reliability of the tests. In these respects tests have an upper hand over the essay-type tests.

Combination of Essay and Objective Tests

From the above it is quite evident that both type of tests are complimentary to each other. The shortcomings of the essay-type of tests are overcome by the new type of tests and vice versa. Hence a judicious combination of the two is advisable. Essay-type examinations or new type tests do not serve our purpose either singly or independently. A happy combination of these two, therefore, is the first essential to be achieved in the reform of the traditional examination system. We may have the following merits of the combination of the two types:

1. The objective test will make evaluation more reliable by eliminating the subjective element inherent in essay-type tests.

2. Objective tests will cover a wide area of the subject-matter and fill up the gaps left by the essay-type tests.

3. The two types of tests measure two different faculties, the essay-type tests measure the functional aspect and the objective tests measure the theoretical aspect.

4. The scores obtained in the two tests can be correlated and thus the degree of reliability found. This will also check subjectivity.

Limitations of the Two

These tests are tests of knowledge. The various behaviour patterns remain untested. These fail to test the totality of the child's development of personality and character.

These tests should be supplemented by other tests like personality tests, intelligence tests etc. The views of the teachers who guide the students and watch them should be given their due place.

Designs of Civics Question Paper (Including Unit II 'Making of a Modern Nation')

Class IX

1. Weightage to Objectives

S.No.	*Objectives*	*% of Marks*
1.	Knowledge	30
2.	Understanding	50
3.	Application	10
4.	Skill	10
	Total	**100**

Weightage to Form of Questions and Content

S. No.	*Form of Questions*	*Marks for Each Questions*	*No. of Questions*	*Total Marks*
1.	LA	6	4	24
2.	SA	3	12	36
3.	VSA/ Objective Type	2	20	40
	Total		36	100

Weightage to Content	*Marks*
Framing of the Constitution	8
Salient features of the Constitution	8
Government, executive and legislative	24
Judiciary in India	16
Fundamental Rights, Directive Principles and Fundamental Duties	24
Indian Democracy and its Functioning	20
	25 Marks

LA	=	Long Answer Question
SA	=	Short Answer Question
VSA (Objective Types)	=	Very Short Answer Question

Difficulty Level

Estimated Difficulty Level	*Percentage*
Difficult	30%
Average	50%
Easy	20%

33.17 ILLUSTRATION OF DIFFERENT TYPES OF QUESTIONS

A. Essay-Type Questions

1. In what respects are the 'Fundamental Rights' fundament?
2. Bring out the significance of Fundamental Rights.
3. Why should there be duties for the citizens? Can we do away with this provision? Support your answer.
4. "The right to freedom is a cluster of six freedoms." Explain.
5. Explain any three freedoms provided for in the Constitution.
6. Why was the provision for duties made in the Constitution of India?
7. According to Abraham Lincoln democracy is "Government of the people, for the people and by the people." Explain this statement.

B. Short-Answer Questions

1. Mention any five Fundamental Duties.
2. Under what circumstances can right to constitutional remedies be suspended?
3. Explain right to freedom of religion.
4. Explain the functions of a Nayaya Panchayat.
5. State the difference between a Municipal Council and Notified Area Committee.
6. Describe the election procedure of the State Legislative Council.

C. Illustration of Objective Type Questions.

1. Fill in the blanks in the following sentences with appropriate words given in the brackets.
   (a) A State Assembly can be dissolved before the expiry of its term by................. (Chief Minister, Speaker, President).
   (b) The Legislative Assembly is presided over by the................. (Chairman, Speaker, Chief Minister).
   (c) The maximum strength of a State Assembly has been fixed at .... (400, 500, 600).
   (d) Distinguished persons can be nominated to the Legislative Council of the State by the .... (Governor, Speaker, Chief Minister).
2. Write 'Yes' or 'No' against each statement given below:
   (a) Members of the Legislative Council must be over 21 years of age. ☐

(b) Some constituencies are reserved for candidates belonging to Scheduled Caste or Scheduled Tribe. ☐
(c) The Legislative Assembly enjoys more powers than the Legislative Council. ☐
(d) All Bills can originate from the Legislative Council. ☐
(e) The role of the Legislative Council is only advisory. ☐
(f) All States in India have both, the Legislative Assembly and the Legislative Council. ☐

3. Some statements are given under column 'A'. Write the corresponding Fundamental Right under column 'B'.

	A	B
(i)	All citizens have freedom of religious belief.	....
(ii)	Every citizen has the right to form a union.	....
(iii)	No one can be prevented from using a public well.	....
(iv)	People can be made to work only against wages	....
(v)	Every child has the right to seek admission to school managed or aided by the government.	....

4. Some Directive Principles are given in column A. In column B, the broad objectives have been mentioned. Match the two

A	B
Economic Principles	Organisation of village panchayats
Gandhian principles	Living wage
Principles of International understanding	Protecting and safeguarding monuments
Principles of strengthening democracy	World peace and security
Principles of preserving national and cultural heritage	Establishing a uniform civil code

5. Fill in the blanks.
(1) The UN came into existence on .... in the year ....
(2) .... was one of the original member of the UN.
(3) The present Secretary-General of the UN is ....
(4) There are .... official language of the UN.
(5) There are .... members of the UN.
(6) The UN headquarters are ....

6. What does each stand for?
(i) ILO (ii) FAO (3) UNESCO (iv) WHO

7. Best answers test. Put mark against the best answer.
Alexander did not proceed further because:
(a) He did not know the route.
(b) His forces refused to go further.
(c) He was defeated by some king.

34

Bloom's Approach to Evaluation: Writing Instructional Objective Type Test Items

34.1 MEANING OF BLOOM'S TAXONOMY OF EDUCATIONAL OBJECTIVES

Bloom, an American Educationist, revolutionised the educational system through his approach known as 'evaluation approach'. He made an effort to make teaching and testing objective-centred. In the sixties Bloom visited India and held many seminars and workshops in making the new approach popular.

Bloom believed that education is a tri-popular process involving educational objectives, learning experiences and change in behaviour. He made educational objectives as the basis for teaching activities and evaluation techniques. Bloom observed, "Educational objectives are not only the goals towards which the curriculum is shaped and towards which instruction is guided, but they are also goals that provide the detailed specification for the construction and use of evaluative techniques"

Importance of Stating Instructional Objectives

Importance of stating instructional objectives as learning outcomes is that:

1. They provide direction for the instructor.
2. They convey clearly instructional intent to others.
3. They provide a guide for selecting the subject-matter.
4. They provide a guide for selecting appropriate teaching method.
5. They provide a guide for selecting suitable materials to be used during instruction.
6. They provide guides for constructing reliable tests and other instruments for evaluating student achievement.

Objectives provide the starting point on which are based all the learning experiences which in their turn are the material of evaluation. Objectives are the statements which describe the kind of modification that we want to bring about in the learner. Objectives are the policy statements of direction. They provide the foundation of the entire educational structure.

Different objectives. There are many objectives of education like knowledge, understanding, application, etc. While teaching, no objective should be neglected. If learning experiences are based on clear-cut objectives, evaluation is the process of determining the extent to which an objective is being attained and the effectiveness of the learning experiences is provided in the classroom.

34.2 MAJOR CATEGORIES IN THE COGNITIVE DOMAIN OF THE TAXONOMY OF EDUCATIONAL OBJECTIVE (BLOOM 1956):

1. *Knowledge*: It is defined as the remembering of previously learned material. It represents the lowest level of learning outcomes in the cognitive domain.

2. *Comprehension*: It is defined as the ability to grasp the meaning of material. The learning outcomes go one step beyond the simple understanding of material and represent the lowest level of understanding.

3. *Application*: It is the ability to use learned material in new and concrete situations. Learning outcomes in this area require a higher level of understanding than those under comprehension.

4. *Analysis*: It refers to the ability to breakdown material into its component parts so that its organisational structure may be understood. Learning outcomes here represent a higher intellectual level than comprehension and application because they require an understanding of both the content and the structural form of the material.

5. *Synthesis*: Synthesis refers to the ability to put parts together to form a new whole. Learning outcomes in the area stress creative behaviours, with major emphasis on the formulation of new patterns or structure.

6. *Evaluation*: Evaluation is concerned with the ability to judge the value or material (statement, novel, poem, research report) for a given purpose. The judgments are to be based on definite criteria.

Learning outcomes in this area are highest in this cognitive hierarchy because they contain elements of all the other categories, plus conscious value judgements based on clearly defined criteria.

Examples of general instructional objectives and behavioural terms for the cognitive domain of the taxonomy are:

Illustrative General Instructional Objectives	*Illustrative Behavioural Terms for Stating Specific Learning Outcomes*
■ Knows common terms. ■ Knows specific terms. ■ Knows methods and procedures. ■ Knows basic concepts. ■ Knows principles.	Defines, describes, identifies, labels, lists, matches, names, outlines, reproduces, selects, states.
■ Understands facts and principles. ■ Interprets verbal material. ■ Interprets charts and graphs. ■ Translates verbal material to mathematical formulas. ■ Estimates future consequences implied in data. ■ Justifies methods and procedures.	Converts, defends, distinguishes, estimates, explains, extends, generalises, gives examples, infers, paraphrases, predicts, rewrites, summarises.

(*Contd.*)

(*Contd.*)

Illustrative General Instructional Objectives	*Illustrative Behavioural Terms for Stating Specific Learning Outcomes*
■ Applies concepts and principles to new situation. ■ Applies laws and theories to practical situations. ■ Solves mathematical problems. ■ Constructs charts and graphs. ■ Demonstrates correct usage of a method or procedure.	Changes, computes, demonstrates, discovers, manipulates, modifies, operates, predicts, prepares, produces, relates, shows, solves, uses.
■ Recognises unstated assumptions. ■ Recognises logical fallacies in reasoning. ■ Distinguishes between facts and inferences. ■ Evaluates the relevancy of data. ■ Analysis the organisational structure of work (art, music, writing).	Breaks down, diagrams, differentiates, identifies, illustrates, infers, outlines, points out, relates, selects, separates, sub-divides.
■ Writes a well-organised theme. ■ Gives a well-organised speech. ■ Writes a creative short-story (or poem or music). ■ Proposes a plan for an experiment. ■ Integrates learning from different areas with a plan for solving a problem. ■ Formulates a new scheme for classifying objects or events, or ideas.	Categories combines, compiles, composes, creates, devices, designs, explains, generates, modifies, organises, plans, rearranges-reconstructs, relates reorganises, revises, rewrites, summarises, tells, writes.
■ Judges the logical consistency of written material. ■ Judges the adequacy with which conclusions are supported by data. ■ Judges the value of work (art, music, writing) by use of internal criteria. ■ Judges the value of a work (art, music, writing) by use of external standards of excellence.	Appraises, compares, concludes, contrasts, criticises, describes, discriminates, explains, justifies, interprets, relates, summarises, supports.

	Objectives on Traditional Lines	*Behavioural Educational Objectives*
1.	Traditional objectives are very general, broad and vague.	Behavioural objectives are clear, definite and specific.

(*Contd.*)

(Contd.)

	Objectives on Traditional Lines	*Behavioural Educational Objectives*
2.	Social and cultural philosophy is the main source of these objectives.	Psychology is the main source.
3.	They are, by and large common to all school subjects.	Every school subject has its specific objectives.
4.	They can be realised over a very long period.	They can be achieved within the period of classroom teaching.
5.	Examples of such objectives are: development of character and personality, etc.	Examples of such objectives are: acquisition of knowledge, development of skills, etc.
6.	Some outside agency determines these objectives.	Classroom teacher himself determines such objectives.
7.	They do not motivate the teachers because of their indefiniteness.	They motivate the teachers because they are definite.
8.	They do not motivate the learners because of their indefiniteness.	They serve as a motivating force as they are definite.
9.	They cannot be evaluated easily. It is very difficult for the teacher to evaluate the performance and changes brought about in the learners.	It is very easy to evaluate changes in the learners.
10.	They do not specify conditions under which changes in the learners would occur.	They specify conditions under which changes in the learners would occur.

34.3 INSTRUCTIONAL OBJECTIVES OF CIVICS

1. Acquisition of knowledge (Cognitive Domain)
2. Developing understanding (Cognitive Domain)
3. Developing skills (Psycho-motor Domain)
4. Developing interests (Affective Domain)
5. Developing attitudes of an enlightened and intelligent citizen (Affective Domain).

34.4 INSTRUCTIONAL OBJECTIVES OF ACQUISITION OF KNOWLEDGE

At the base of all achievements both in scholastic and non-scholastic fields, knowledge is the basic first element. As a matter of fact, recall, recognition and reproduction of mentally stored facts, terms, concepts, principles, trends, etc. of a particular subject are essential ingredients of all the desirable objectives of instruction. Such knowledge could be stored through deliberate memorisation or empirical experiences. Irrespective of the mode of acquisition, knowledge remains the foundation of the edifice of all educational achievement.

More precisely, the objective and its sub-divisions in terms of pupil's achievement could be stated as follows:

Statement of the objective. To acquire the knowledge (information) of facts, terms concepts, contentions and trends, principles and generalisations, assumptions, hypotheses, problems, processes, etc. in Civics.

Specification of the Objective

To demonstrate the achievement of the above objective, the pupil:

(i) Recalls facts, terms, concepts, principles, trends, etc.

(ii) Recognises facts, terms concepts, principles, trends, etc.

(iii) Acquires information through various forms of representation of data, i.e., maps, charts, diagrams, graphs, etc.

34.5 DEVELOPING UNDERSTANDING

Mastery of concept still remains the prime objective of teaching Civics. Major concepts, principles, terms and generalisations form the foundation for all higher learning. Thus selection of appropriate content to build up the desired concepts and to learn the meaning of terms and principles with exactness is necessary for understanding.

More precisely, the objective and its sub-divisions in terms of pupil's achievement could be stated as follows:

Statement of the Objective

To develop an understanding of facts, terms, concepts, conventions, and trends, principles and generalisations, assumptions, hypotheses, problems, processes, etc. in Civics.

Specification of the Objective

To demonstrate the achievement of the above objective, the pupil:

(i) Discriminates facts, terms, concepts, etc.

(ii) Classifies them.

(iii) Compares and contrasts them.

(iv) Identifies relationships between them.

(v) Understands the points of emphasis and the trends of arguments.

(vi) Cites illustrations.

(vii) Detects errors, fallacies and rectifies them.

(viii) Explains (analyses or gives meaning or clarifies or elucidates).

(ix) Gives reasons or advances arguments.

(x) Interprets data presented in different forms.

(xi) Applies his understanding to unfamiliar situations.

34.6 DEVELOPING SKILLS

It is true that some of the skills stated in the following lines cannot be tested through the written examination but a comprehensive programme of school education should provide for their development as they are necessary for the all-round growth of the pupil's personality. In the achievement of the objective, the pupil should be able to draw or locate information on maps, charts, diagrams and tables. He should be able to present his arguments through effective speech before a group, to understand the procedures of elections and voting and to organise social work or other group work.

Statement of the Objective

To acquire skills both psycho-motor and social related to the subject of Civics.

Specifications of the Objective (Related to Psycho-motor Skills)

To demonstrate the achievement of the above objective, the pupil:

(i) Participates as an effective member of the group.

(ii) Accepts the role of the group leader.

(iii) Displays initiative, spirit of cooperation and sense of discipline in the discharge of the responsibilities if he is a group leader.

(iv) Exhibits organisational capacity in

- planning
- directing
- coordinating
- reporting

(v) Presents his arguments effectively and pursuingly.

34.7 DEVELOPING INTERESTS

Development of interest in the subject can be used both as an end in itself as well as a means for the achievement of further goals. In case of the former, efforts may be made to provide for immediate interests of pupils as also for deep and abiding interests in the subject. When it is used as means, such interests may be used as a vehicle for understanding the working of various institutions and civic principles. Further, we should provide for activities which lead to the application of such principles and the development of interest of the pupils in the school and local life in programmes concerning civic and social problems.

More precisely, the objective and its sub-divisions in terms of pupil's achievement could be stated as follows:

Statement of the Objective

To develop interest in the subject and problems related to the civic and political life on theoretical plane.

Specifications of the Objective

To demonstrate the achievement of the above objective, the pupil:

(i) Voluntarily studies literature related to civics and tries to know about its inherent issues and problems.

(ii) Utilises leisure in trying to know about civic and numerous environmental problems and issues and exerts in finding solutions to them.

(iii) Closely observes civic and political processes and changes at local, national and international levels.

(iv) Discusses and is able to communicate various aspects of every day civic problems and their implications.

(v) Recognises how different civic policies may effect people efforts to meet their daily needs.

(vi) Enthusiastically participates in excursions, visits and field-trips to places of civic and political activities (e.g., Panchayats, Municipalities, State Assemblies, Parliament, etc).

(vii) Enjoys participating in debates, symposia and discussions on civic and political problems.

(viii) Enjoys writing articles and preparing pamphlets, brochures, etc. on topics related to civics.

(ix) Enjoys preparing display-materials related to civic and political life.

(x) Enjoys collecting information about political systems and facts about other localities, regions and countries.

(xi) Appreciates that UNO is playing a significant vole in strengthening world peace and cooperation.

(xii) Appreciates some of the important economic issues vitally related with the political life of the country.

34.8 DEVELOPING ATTITUDES OF AN ENLIGHTENED AND INTELLIGENT CITIZEN

This is one of the most outstanding objectives of teaching of Civics. Living in a democracy, each pupil is expected to develop faith in democratic values, procedures and ideas, and respect for laws. He should possess a sense of healthy patriotism and open-mindedness. A teacher can contribute a lot to the achievement of this goal through explaining and emphasising the need of such social and moral values with the help of a good many examples from the daily life of pupils.

More precisely, the objective and its sub-divisions in terms of pupil achievement could be stated as follows:

Statement of the Objective

To develop desirable attitudes of an enlightened and intelligent citizen related to civic and political life on a practical plane.

Specification of the Objective

To demonstrate the achievement of the above objective the pupil:

(i) Shows respect and concern for the well-being of others:

(a) offers help to others in need.

(b) respects the views, opinions and problems of others.

35

Illustrative Lesson Plans

INTRODUCTION

Some suggestive lesson plans in Civics are given here. As already stated there are several formats/patterns of lesson planning. Pupil-teachers are advised to follow the form as advised by their supervisors.

LESSON PLAN NO. 1

Class VI
Topic: Fundamental Rights

General Objectives

1. To provide the students with intelligent understanding of the various social responsibilities and civic processes;
2. To help the students understand our Constitution and the values enshrined in it;
3. To acquaint the students with the machinery of the government at different levels;
4. To make the students conscious of the actual problems that are facing our country today and instil in them a sense of responsibility towards the community;
5. To make the students identify with the people and their institutions; and
6. To inculcate in the students the values of democracy, secularism, socialism and national integration.

Specific Objective

To enable the students understand their fundamental rights.

Teaching Aids

1. Copy of the Constitution.
2. Chart showing fundamental rights.

Introduction

1. Why does the Government open educational institutions?
2. Why does your school prescribe some rules?

Statement of the Aim

Today we shall study our rights so as to develop qualities of a good citizen.

Section I—Fundamental Rights

Matter	*Presentation*
Every State attempts to provide best facilities to its citizens for the maximum development of their personality. This development is possible only when the citizens have some rights. For example, if a person does not have the right to choose his education or career, he cannot rise to the position for which he may be capable. All governments work for the welfare of their citizens. Promotion of welfare demands that the citizens should have some basic rights that the State shall protect. Think of a society where people can be sent to jail without any opportunity for their defence before a court of justice. In such a society no one feels secure and happy. Right to freedom is thus, a basic right that must be allowed to the citizens. Our Constitution makers knew very well that the ideals set out in the Preamble can be achieved only if the Constitution guaranteed certain basic conditions for peace and prosperity. These basic conditions have been codified as Fundamental Rights. These rights are also called 'Constitutional Rights' because they have been guaranteed by the Constitution. The Parliament or the State legislatures cannot make laws to deprive the citizens of these rights. The High Court and the Supreme Court can give orders to the Governments if it is felt that a citizen has been deprived of his or her Fundamental Rights. The provision of Fundamental Rights in the Constitution acts as a check on the powers of the government. They protect Democracy against any temptation on the part of the government or legislatures to curtail the freedom of the citizen.	1. What facilities are provided to you in the school? 2. Why does the Government aim at providing best facilities to its citizens? 3. What type of facilities should be provided by the Government for its citizens? 4. What are the facilities provided by the village Panchayat, Municipal Committee or Corporation? (Rights will be explained with the help of the chart).
Fundamental Rights: Our Constitution guarantees for all citizens the following Fundamental Rights:	

(*Contd.*)

Matter	*Presentation*
1. Right to Equality. 2. Right of Freedom. 3. Right against Exploitation. 4. Right to Freedom of Religion. 5. Cultural and Educational Rights. 6. Right to Constitutional Remedies. (The Right to Property, which existed when the Constitution was first enforced, has now been deleted by amendment).	

Recapitulation

1. Which right do you consider most important?
2. State any right that you would like to be included in the fundamental rights.

OUR FUNDAMENTAL RIGHTS

Right to Equality

Right to Freedom of Religion

Right to Freedon

Educational and Cultural Rights

Right Against Exploitation

Right to Constitutional Remedy

Home Assignments

1. Why do we need rights?
2. What is the significance of rights?
3. Explain the meaning of right to equality?

LESSON PLAN NO. 2

Class VI—Topics: Fundamental Duties

Introduction

1. Why should you obey your parents and elders?
2. What can you do for the family?

General Objectives. As given in the previous lesson plan.

Specific Objectives

1. *Knowledge Objective*. To develop the knowledge of the students regarding fundamental duties.

2. *Skill Objective*. To develop the necessary skills to perform duties honestly and efficiently.

3. *Attitude Objective*. To develop necessary feelings of appreciation of other's views.

Teaching Aids

1. Copy of the Constitution
2. Chart showing fundamental duties.

DUTIES OF A GOOD CITIZEN

Respects the National Flag

Yotes

Keeps Himself Well Informed

Obeys Laws

Matter	*Presentation*
The fundamental duties are specified in Part IV A of our Constitution. Duties are no less important than rights. As a matter of fact it is possible to enjoy rights only when others are performing their duties. The right to freedom of religion can be enjoyed only if the citizens perform their duty of promoting harmony and spirit of common brotherhood amongst all the people of India, irrespective of their religion. The fundamental duties of citizens in India have been listed under Article 51 A of our Constitution. They can be explained as follows— (i) As a good citizen, we should show respect to our National Flag and the National Anthem. (ii) We should take pride in the ideals that inspired the freedom fighters. (iii) We should respect the sentiment of our fellow citizens of different religions. (iv) All the citizens must join together to defend the country against any foreign attack. (v) We should give equal respect to women. (vi) We should not deface historical buildings and monuments. (vii) We should protect the natural resources of our country. (viii) We should properly use the public properties like parks, railways, etc. (ix) We should settle our differences by peaceful means.	1. What are your duties towards your school? 2. What are your duties towards your town? 3. What are your duties towards your country? (Fundamental duties will be explained with the help of a chart)

Recapitulation

1. Which duty do you think to be the most important one?
2. Why do you consider it to be the most important?

Home Assignments

1. Students will be asked to list duties in their note books.
2. Students will be asked to list four duties towards their class fellows and other students.
3. Students will be asked to list three duties towards their neighbours.
4. Students will be asked to prepare a chart on the duties as given in the Constitution of India.

LESSON PLAN NO. 3

Class VI—Topic: Local Self-Government (Panchayat and Municipal Committee)

Aims of the Lesson

General: To provide knowledge about the working of democratic institutions.

Specific: 1. To acquaint the children with the working of local administration, i.e. Village Panchyat and Municipal Committees.

2. To prepare them to participate in the running of organisations and institutions democratically.

Illustrative Aids

1. A picture of village panchayat at work.
2. A chart showing the sketch of waterworks in a town.

Previous Knowledge. It is assumed that the children know something about the civic amenities provided in the village.

Introduction: To introduce the lesson the following questions will be asked from the students:

1. Who runs the primary school at your place?
2. Who looks after sanitation?

As a result of this conversation the pupils will be motivated to know more about the Panchayats and Municipalities of today and those of ancient times. They will be enabled to correlate the past with the present and know more about local self-government.

Statement of the Aim: At this stage the teacher will declare that they would learn about local self-government (Panchayats and Municipal Committees) today and the Panchayat System and civic administration of olden times.

Presentation: The following subject-matter will be developed systematically in the class in cooperation with the students. Illustrative aids will be used at proper times.

Matter	*Method*
	The Village Panchayat
Village affairs are administered by village elders. They are called Panches. There are five or more Panches in every village Panchayat. They are elected by the people of the village.	Who settles village disputes? After getting the response, the teacher will show the picture of a Village Panchayat at work. He will explain the working of the Panchayat and then put question:
President of the Panchayat is called Sarpanch?	*What is the President of the Panchayat called?*
	Election of the Panchayat
Every adult person of the village whether a man or woman has a vote. A woman can become a Panch or Sarpanch. One of the Panches must be a Harijan. Sometimes there is no voting contest and the villagers select their leaders unanimously. The Sarpanch is also elected by the villagers directly.	1. *How do you elect your secretary of literary society?* 2. *How are the other office-bearers of society elected?* 3. *How are the Panches elected?* The teacher will tell the students that the Sarpanch is also elected by all the voters directly.
	Functions of a Panchayat
A Panchayat is the primary institution of village administration. Disputes of the village are settled by the Village Panches. Only the matters of serious nature go to the Courts. The Panchayat provides various amenities to the village, such as, sanitation, construction of *pucca* streets, wells or hand pumps for drinking water, tanks and so on. Sometimes the Panchayat provides for a primary school also.	*What is the function of your literary society? What is the function of your School Council?* *What should be the functions of a Village Panchayat?* The teacher will deduce most of the information from the students and will then fill the gaps, if any.
	Powers of a Panchayat
A Panchayat has definite powers. It can fine the offenders. It can levy taxes. The State Government helps in the enforcement of the decisions of the Panchayat.	*What are the powers of your School Council?* *What are the powers of a Panchayat?* *How can the Panchayat enforce its decisions?*
	Finances of a Panchayat
The Panches get no salary or allowance. They are honorary workers. But the Panchayat has to spend much on sanitation, education, upkeep of the streets and/or providing various amenities to the village. To meet the expenses, the Panchayat can levy a tax on the villagers. The State Government also helps the Panchayats financially.	*What is the salary of the President of your Council?* *What is the salary of a Panch?* *What taxes do your parents pay?* *Where does a Panchayat get the finances from?*

(*Contd.*)

Matter	Method
Panchayat System in the Past	
Panchayat system existed in ancient India and also in medieval India. Tradition had given many powers to the Panchayats in those days. Our social structure survived due to the Panchayat system. There was peace and tranquility in the villages. But the English did away with Panchayat system.	Children do not know much about the Panchayat system of ancient and medieval India. The teacher will relate the facts.
Advantages of Panchayats	
1. People get training of self-government	*What are the advantages of Students Council?*
2. Many village strifes come to an end.	*What are the advantages of the Panchayats?*
3. Justice becomes cheap, handy and there is no delay in it.	

A Municipal Committee

Matter	Method
Formation	
A Municipal Committee is also elected like a Panchayat. The head of the Committee is called the President or Chairman	How is a Municipal Committee formed?
Functions of a Municipal Committee	
The Municipal Committee arranges for:	
1. The water works.	1. Who arranges for the water works in a town? The teacher will exhibit the chart showing the sketch of water works.
2. The street lighting.	2. Who arranges for the street lighting?
3. Upkeep of the streets.	3. How do we arrange the sanitation, upkeep of the streets, roads in the town and other amenities of the town life?
4. Construction and repairs of roads in the town.	
5. Education.	
6. Medical aid.	
7. Vaccination and precaution against epidemics etc.	
Finances	
The Municipality can levy various kinds of taxes (list of taxes to be given	What is the salary of a Municipal Commissioner?

(Contd.)

by the teacher). Where does a Municipality get the finances from? Civic Administration in Olden Times. There were Municipal Committees in all the towns in ancient times.	How were our towns administered in olden times?

Recapitulation:

Following questions will be asked:

1. What are the functions of a Village Panchayat?
2. How did the Panchayat system work in the days of Chandragupta Maurya?
3. State the difference between the Municipal Administration of the olden times and modern times.

LESSON PLAN NO. 4

Class VII—Topic: Cooperative Society

General Aims

1. To acquaint the students with the advantages of working together.
2. To develop spirit of tolerance and fellow teaching.

Specific Aim. To give the students knowledge of the importance, formation and management of a cooperative society.

Previous Knowledge. Students have some knowledge about the working of other types of business organisation.

Presentation

Matter	*Method*
A cooperative society is an activity in which economic interests are involved. It follows the principle of "one for all and all for one".	What do you understand by "one for all and all for one"?
Salient Features	
The main characteristics of a cooperative society are:	Why is a cooperative society called a voluntary organisation?
1. It must have minimum ten members. The maximum number of members is unlimited.	What is the minimum number of members required in the case of a partnership concern?
2. Its basic objective is to promote the economic interest of its members. It is established for rendering services to its members.	
3. Its capital is raised by issuing shares.	
4. Shares are low prices. So it enables even poor persons to be its members.	Why do we want the poor persons to become its members?

(*Contd.*)

Matter	*Method*
5. Its management is democratic and so the elected members of shareholders look after it. It also follows the principle of 'one man one vote'. So no discrimination is made on the basis of colour, caste, etc.	What is the significance of 'one man, one vote' principle?
6. Its profit is distributed on the basis of every member's dealings with cooperative society and not on the basis of investments. So we can say that cooperative society is an organisation of 'persons' and not 'capital'.	*How is profit distributed in the Company form of business organisation.* Compare the cooperative society with company form of organisation with regards to its capital.
7. A cooperative society has to be registered under the Cooperative Societies Act. Like the case of a Company Law recognises it as a separate person and so it is distinct from its members.	*Is registration compulsory in case of partnership.*
Importance of Cooperation	
The objectives and ideals of cooperative society have particular importance.	
The main points of its importance are:	
1. The basic objective is to improve the economic conditions of the members. This means that the main objective of forming cooperative society is to remove the poverty among the masses and also to develop the cooperative spirit in economic activities.	
2. Cooperative society helps to develop moral qualities like self-dependence, honesty, mutual help, the feeling of brotherhood, equality, social responsibility.	*How is partnership firm and company managed?* *How such qualities will help the cooperative societies?*
3. Service is another important aim of the cooperative society. This service function is not limited to its members but to any one who needs it.	*What is the service function?*
Which are the services given by the government to its people?	
4. It attempts to make its members good citizens.	*How does cooperative society make its members good citizens?*
5. It is moral responsibility to give better services and improve the standard of its products.	

(Contd.)

Matter	*Method*
Formation and Management of Cooperative Society	
Minimum ten members are required to form a cooperative members society. An application for registration must be filled with the registrar on a prescribed form. Here particulars are given regarding the name of the Society, its address, activities, capital, etc.	What is the minimum number of members required in the company form of business organisation?
When the registrar is convinced that all the requirements are met, he issues registration certificate. Management is entrusted in the hands of direction of managing committee, shareholders and employees and the board of directors. The board of directors consists of elected representatives of its members.	How is a company formed?

Recapitulation

1. What is a cooperative society? How is it different from other business organisations?
2. Which are the essential features of the cooperative societies?
3. Why is cooperative society called a voluntary organisation?
4. How are these societies formed and managed?

Blackboard Summary

This will be based on:

(1) Salient features of the cooperative society.
(2) Importance of cooperative society.
(3) Formation of cooperative society and minimum requirements of members.
(4) Management of cooperative society.

Assignments

(1) Cooperative society is an organisation of 'Persons' and not 'Capital'. Explain.
(2) It follows a principal of "One man, one vote". Explain.
(3) "Cooperative society is a voluntary association." Explain.

LESSON PLAN NO. 5

Elections in India: Activity Lesson

Roll No. of the Pupil-teacher ....
Class VIII

Aims of the Lesson

General

(1) To inculcate among students an appreciation for the democratic form of government, secret ballot and right choice of representatives.

(2) To develop the right attitudes of cooperation, obedience to law, toleration and fellow feeling.

Specific

To teach through the Project Method how elections are conducted in India.

Illustrative Material with the Teacher

(1) Ordinary Classroom Apparatus
(2) Empty Ballot Box
(3) Ballot Paper
(4) Voters Lists
(5) Polling Booth

Correlation

The lesson will be correlated with the immediate social environment of children.

Pupil's Previous Knowledge

The pupils know that in India general elections are held after every five years in case of local bodies and every five years in case of State Assemblies and Union Parliament.

Introduction and Announcement of the Aim

The lesson will be introduced by announcing to the students that in compliance with an order from the Headmaster, they are required to elect one representative from their class for the Students Council in that very period. All preparations have already been made for the election.

Presentation

I Step. The teacher will ask the class to propose the names of the students whom they wish to elect for the Students Council. No name will be accepted for election unless it is seconded by one of the voters. Names of candidates duly proposed and seconded will be written on the blackboard.

II Step. One student of other class will be chosen to act as Presiding Officer and two as Polling Officers respectively. They will occupy their respective seats in the polling station. The polling will begin after the duties have been explained to the polling personnel. The students will come to the polling station one by one. The first polling officer after consulting the voters list will put an ink mark on the little finger of each voter and then ask him to go to second polling officer. This polling officer after seeing that mark will issue him the ballot paper. With this ballot paper the voter will go to the place where the ballot box has been placed under the direct control and supervision of the Presiding Officer. The voter will affix the seal on the ballot paper and put it in this box. In this way all the students will cast their votes.

III Step. After the voting is over, the ballot box will be opened by the Presiding Officer in the presence of the candidates concerned. The candidate securing the maximum number of votes will be declared duly elected. His name will be written on the blackboard.

Generalisation

The teacher will then tell the students that this is exactly the way of elections in India, for local bodies, State Assemblies and the Union Parliament. Election Symbols will be shown to them.

LESSON PLAN NO. 6

Our Foreign Policy

Class: X

General Objectives

As in other lessons

Specific Objectives

INDIA'S DEFENCE AND FOREIGN POLICY

Knowledge: Through the content the child will be given the following knowledge:

1. India has vast boundary and has its peculiar problems.
2. Modernisation of armed forces, e.g., army, navy and air force, and maintenance of unity is necessary for the defence of the country.
3. The foreign policy of our country has to sub-serve its interests, both economic and political.
4. India adheres to the policy of non-alignment and 'Panch Sheel' in national interests.
5. India has a role in the United Nations for maintaining peace in the world.

Understandings: To enable the child to develop the following understandings:

1. Preservation of freedom, territorial integrity and sovereignty is first concern of every State.
2. Only strong nation can defend its freedom and territorial integrity.
3. The strength of a nation lies in the unity and solidarity of her different units and high morale of its people.
4. Mental and physical preparation on the part of nation is very necessary for effective defence of the country.
5. Preparation for defence against aggression is closely related to the country's industrial and scientific development.
6. Indian foreign policy is based on principles of non-alignment and co-existence.
7. India's foreign policy is the projection of her national interest, including her defence and economic development.
8. India does not believe in aggression but will certainly defend its territorial integrity against any aggression.

9. India's interest of defence and security requires that her border areas should be clear of all doubtful elements and be invulnerable to neighbouring propaganda, infiltration and sabotage.

10. Foreign Service of India and her Intelligence Service have to improve their efficiency in national interests.

Skills: To help the child to acquire the following skills:

1. To acquire the skill of reading maps and to locate and distinguish natural boundaries of India with neighbouring countries.
2. To inculcate among the students the skill to participate effectively in the National Fitness Corps and other programmes of the schools.
3. Ability to participate, in discussion and debates with a view to give expressions to one's own ideas.
4. Ability to distinguish between propaganda and truth.

Attitudes and Interests: To help the child to develop the following attitudes and interests:

1. To inculcate among students the spirit of preparedness for the defence of the country.
2. To inculcate among students an interest to join organisations like NCC, Scouts and Guides.
3. To develop respect for the principles of non-alignment and the Panch Sheel.
4. To develop better relationship with the foreigners in the country.
5. To appreciate the efforts of international agencies for the solution of racial problems and colonialism.
6. To create an interest in the students to read the biographies of Nehru, Kennedy, Attlee and others who have been the architects in making foreign policies of their countries.

Teaching Aids

1. Chart showing Panch Sheel
2. Political map of the world.

Teaching Hints

Activities: The following are a few suggestive activities and a teacher may adopt one or more according to his ideas, resources and school situation:

1. To exhibit a film show on "India and her neighbours".
2. To use a map of India showing the boundaries of India with Pakistan and China.
3. To exhibit a film show on the modernising of defence, equipment, ordnance factories.
4. To use a map of India on which places having defence factories are located.
5. To use world map to show various countries with which India has friendly relations.
6. To prepare a chart in which five principles of Panch Sheel may be inscribed.
7. To prepare a chart in which the major agencies of the United Nations may be shown.

8. To prepare a map showing countries where UNO has worked in eradicating colonialism and racial discrimination.

9. A chart may be prepared in which aims and objectives of UNO may be shown.

10. Group discussion may be organised to discuss the relations of India with other countries.

11. Some foreigners, who happen to be on tour, may be invited to deliver a talk or persons from different foreign missions (embassies) or some experts on foreign policy may also be invited to give a talk.

12. An army or naval or air force officer may be invited to give a talk on the organisation of defence and our border situations.

13. Mock-sessions of various agencies of UNO may be organised in the school.

14. Students may be asked to read daily newspapers or periodicals concerning the topics.

15. Encouraging the students to read the foreign policies of various countries. They may be asked to draw out familiarity and differences among various nations.

16. Flags of various nations may be shown in the class.

17. A debate may be organised on our foreign policy.

18. To develop a date line showing some important events vis-a-vis India and different countries.

19. To prepare a list of different projects or production units in India which have been started with the collaboration of other countries.

20. To collect pictures, quotations of eminent statesmen and prepare scrap book, album, and give a brief narration of each.

21. To have the activities like:
  (a) reading of news in morning assembly.
  (b) writing of important daily events on blackboard.
  (c) to fix up photos, news items on bulletin board.
  (d) to prepare wall magazines on the major world events.

22. The study of Article 370 of the Constitution relating to Kashmir.

Evaluation

Multiple Choice Type

1. China invaded in the year:
   (a) 1950
   (b) 1954
   (c) 1962
   (d) 1964
2. Russian armed intervention of Hungary took place in the year:
   (a) 1952
   (b) 1954
   (c) 1956
   (d) 1958
3. The country in which Bandung is situated:
   (a) Japan

(b) Indonesia
(c) Burma
(d) Sri Lanka

4. Indo-Pak war was stopped at the instance of:
(a) Security Council
(b) Russian Pressure
(c) American Pressure
(d) Colombo Powers
5. The very important factor that has shaped India's relations with the Soviet Union was:
(a) American fear
(b) love for communism
(c) fear of Chinese invasion
(d) that it is her powerful neighbour
6. India followed the polity of non-alignment due to:
(a) her strategic situation
(b) Pt. Nehru's liking
(c) her military weakness
(d) her historical tradition
7. India criticised US bombing in Vietnam because:
(a) she believes in non-interfering in other nation's matter.
(b) because Russia and China also criticise
(c) because she has a liking for communist expansion
(d) because Dr. Ho was friendly to India
8. India sent her army units on US Peace Mission to:
(a) Korea
(b) Germany
(c) South Africa
(d) Pakistan
9. Indian is against the manufacture of Atom Bomb because:
(a) she believes in peaceful coexistence
(b) she cannot afford
(c) she has signed the Test Ban Treaty
(d) Russia and America are ready to give us bombs
10. India's first Atomic Plant was started at:
(a) Trombay
(b) Chittaranjan
(c) Cochin
(d) Madras
11. Identify in order of priority the dangers to national security—infiltration; sabotage; anti-national propaganda; strikes; hartals and gheraos; corruption in public services.

Short Answer Type

1. What do you understand by the term foreign policy? Why does a country need a foreign policy? Explain in ten lines.
2. What does the term Non-alignment indicate?

3. What is Government of India's policy towards manufacturing of Atom Bomb?
4. Write a short note on Kashmir issue.
5. Describe India's role in solving the Korean problem or the Indo-China problem.
6. Write a short note on India's defence preparation since 1962.
7. Which countries are sometimes considered as India's immediate enemies?
8. What is Tashkent agreement?
9. Write short notes on the following terms:
   Balance of Power, Peaceful Co-existence, Panch Sheel, Non-alignment, Truman Doctrine.
10. What are the proposals for Indo-China Border issue?
11. Name the countries in which India has rendered assistance in maintaining peace.

Essay-Type

1. What are the requirements of national defence?
2. What changes would you suggest in India's foreign policy from the point of view of national defence?
3. Describe India's role in world affairs.
4. Describe India's defence achievements.
5. Write a short description of India's relations with her neighbouring countries.
6. How is India cooperating with the US?

(*Source*: '*Improving Instruction in Social Studies*', NCERT, New Delhi, 1969)

LESSON PLAN NO. 7

Religions of the World

Objectives

Knowledge

1. To acquaint the students with the conditions which led to the birth of important religions of the world.
2. To acquaint them with the life sketches of the founders of all religions and also the prominent saints connected with the development of all important religions.
3. To give them the knowledge of the main tenets of these religions.
4. To bring out the essential unity of all religions by a comparative study of their basic principles.
5. To acquaint them with the cause of rise, spread and decline of some of the religions.
6. To acquaint the students with the significant contribution that religion has made to different spheres of life.
7. To develop the feeling of respect and toleration for all religions.
8. To develop international brotherhood through the study of all religions of the world.

9. To develop sympathy, love, kindness, respect, tolerance, fearlessness, etc. for mankind.

Understandings

1. Religions in the primitive times have been characterised by superstitions and rituals.
2. The character of all the religions in the beginning was simple but complexities and inflexibilities creeped in with the lapse of time.
3. The aim of all religions is the salvation of mankind.
4. As there is a basic unity among all religions, man can be knit into a brotherhood.
5. Religion satisfies the conscience of man and leads him to a moral path.
6. The observance of religious practices depends upon the sentiments of an individual.
7. Indulgence in worldly pleasures tending to immorality has been denounced by all religions.
8. In spite of basic unity among all religions and their principles of religious tolerance, there have been religious conflicts on account of different forms of rituals and lack of understanding of other religions.
9. All the great religions of the world had their birth in Asia.
10. Religion has influenced mankind in many walks of life.
11. Throughout the ages religions have been subjected to changes from within giving rise to numerous sects within a religion.
12. Religion has helped to lead moral and ethical lives.

Skills and Abilities

1. To create an ability to understand the basic principles of all religions.
2. To enable the students to study the present form of worship among different religions.
3. To develop ability to discuss the basic values common in all religions.
4. Ability to explain the different forms of worship.
5. To draw out a map showing the distribution areas of all religions and to point out the important place of pilgrimage.
6. To make them able to draw a time-line on the origin and the developments of great religions of the world.
7. To prepare a chart explaining the similarities and dissimilarities among different religions.
8. To develop the ability to get along with people of different faiths.

Interests and Attitudes

1. To create an interest in the comparative study of all religions.
2. To foster a spirit of toleration and respect towards other religions.
3. To create an interest in visiting the religious places.
4. To know about the inspiring incidents of the lives of great saints.
5. To create an interest in the study of important sayings of saints and savants.
6. To develop an interest in reading the biographies of saints.

Teaching Hints to the Teachers

1. To arrange discussion in the class on:
   (a) basic principles of all religions.
   (b) basic unity among all religions of the world.
2. To arrange talks on the fundamental unity of all religions by inviting scholars and eminent teachers.
3. To arrange visits to local sites of religious importance including temples, mosques, gurdwaras etc.
4. To locate the following places in the outline map of the world:
   (a) Birth places of important saints of all religions.
   (b) Places of religious importance.
5. To collect and prepare an album of the pictures of saints and seers.
6. To arrange celebrations of anniversaries of great prophets and saints in the school.
7. To present tableaus depicting different features and activities from the lives of saints and prophets.
8. To organise programmes in which all students may participate in religious songs, Bhajans, Prayers, etc.
9. Pictures of saints of all religions should be displayed in the school.
10. Film shows depicting the lives of saints may be arranged in the school.
11. Students may be encouraged through competitions to memorise couplets and sayings of great saints.
12. Celebrations of all religious festivals in the school.
13. All the important books of all religions should find place in the school library.

Evaluation

1. 'Jainism and Buddhism were popular social revolts against Hinduism.' Explain the main teachings of these two faiths with reference to the above opinion.
2. Throw the light on the teachings of Christ. Compare these with the main principles of Islam and Judaism.
3. Write an essay on the contribution of the religion to the intellectual, social and cultural life of mankind.
4. Write briefly on the ethical principles of Judaism.
5. Discuss the principles of Islamic teachings.
6. Write short notes on:
   (i) Animism. (ii) Shankaracharya's Advaitvada. (iii) Hinayana and Mahayana. (iv) Torah. (v) Protestantism. (vi) Bhakti Movement. (vii) Sankhya Darshan. (viii) Concept of Non-violence.
7. 'The ethics of Confucius have deeply affected the course of Chinese life throughout the ages'. Do you agree?
8. Arrange the following names of religions correctly against their founders.

Religion	*Name of the founder*
Christianity	Mohammad
Islam	Buddha
Buddhism	Mahavir
Jainism	Christ
Confucius	

9. Arrange the following dates of birth correctly against the names of the religious leader:

Mahavira	4 B.C.
Buddha	570 A.D.
Christ	550 B.C.
Mohammad	470 A.D.

10. Fill up the blanks selecting the most appropriate word from the lists of words given: India, Mecca, China, Sixth Century B.C., Medina, Jews.
   (a) Judaism is a religion of the...........
   (b) Jainism is confined to...........
   (c) The birth of Mohammad took place in...........
   (d) Mohammad fled from Mecca to...........
   (e) ....was an age of religious reformation in different parts of the world.
   (f) Confucius was a resident of ....

11. Tick mark the correct alternatives in the following:
   (a) Ahimsa is practised in its extreme form in Hinduism/Christianity/Islam/Jainism.
   (b) Eight-fold path is the middle path of Judaism/Confucianism/Buddhism/Islam.
   (c) Moses was an exponent of the philosophy of Judaism/Jainism/Christianity/Islam.
   (d) In the pre-historic ages, the religion of the Egyptians/Sumerians/Aryans was not guided by fear from the forces of nature.
   (e) Christianity was declared as a state religion by Nero/Constantine/Julius Caesar.
   (f) The sermon on the Mount was delivered by Buddha/Mahavir/Christ/Mohammad.

(*Source*: *'Improving Instruction is Social Studies'*, NCERT)

LESSON PLAN NO. 8

Our Growing Industries

Class: VII

Background and objectives: Children have studied about the different States and Union Territories of India. They know that all the States have many small and big factories and that new industries are also being established. Things of daily use like cotton, cloth, hosiery goods, lanterns, electric fans, etc. are produced in these factories. Industrial goods make our life more comfortable and the workers have to undergo much less drudgery. The purpose of this topic is to acquaint the children with a few important industries in our country.

Expected outcomes: Children will gain the following understandings through the study of this chapter.

1. Our country is progressing through the establishment of new industries.

2. New industries provide new jobs to a large number of the people.

3. The standard of living of the people of our country is being raised as a result of industrial advancement.

4. In the Five-Year Plans provisions have been made for the development of our industries.

Teaching Hints: 1. Show on the map of India the industrial centres referred to in this chapter.

2. You may also explain the reasons why a certain industry is located at a particular place. Illustrate it through the example of the Iron and Steel Industry. Let them understand the relationship between the availability of raw material and the location of Iron and Steel Industry.

3. The children know about several other industrial products also. Through class discussion you may acquaint them with other industries of the country as well.

4. Collect some samples of industrial goods as well as handicraft goods and let the children note the difference between the two. You may also explain the difference through discussion.

5. If possible take the children for a visit to a factory. It will help them to see the big and small machines used in the factory. They will also see how the workers work cooperatively. The visit will also help you to explain how machines can produce much faster and on a large scale.

6. Children know that many people work in the factories. This could form the basis for discussing the effect of increasing industries on employment of people. They will thus understand that growing industries provide new jobs to the increasing population and help to accelerate progress in the field of agriculture.

7. You may ask the children to make a list of the products of different industries. The various uses of the industrial products may be discussed to help the children understand how the industry helps in raising the standard of living.

8. With the help of the latest year-book on India some intelligent children may make a list of all these industries which have been started under the plan period.

9. Make a list of those places which are known for handicrafts.

10. With the help of the information given at the end of the text-book make a list of the places which are known for producing oil; fertilisers and textiles.

LESSON PLAN NO. 9

Preamble of the Constitution
Syllabus Unit—Unit 2

Class X

Teacher's Note: This lesson aims at developing the cognitive ability as well as emotional maturity of the adolescents. Some basic principles and ideals with which our national movement had started will be explained so as to develop faith in our national destiny. Teacher will combine lecture and dialogue method for intellectual development, with dramatisation and technology for emotional development.

Specific Objectives of the Lesson

(i) To inform the students of the goals and ideals before our national movements.

(ii) To analyse how these goals and ideals are enshrined in our Constitution.

(iii) To make the students aware of how the Preamble is being implemented and the difficulties in implementing the same.

(iv) To develop a healthy emotion in the students, that cooperative and active and alert citizens are essential for achieving the goals and ideals of the Constitution.

Introduction of the Lesson

On the display board the teacher will fix a chart with a few lines of the 'Tryst of destiny speech' of Nehru written on it. Then the record of the speech will be played twice, and students will be asked to read the lines written on the chart. Teacher will then explain the background and the meaning of the speech.

Aids and equipments for the lesson. 1. Record of Pt. Nehru's Speech. 'Tryst with Destiny'.

2. A picture showing Republic Day Celebration with the Preamble written under it.

3. Picture of the Constituent Assembly.

Presentation of the Lesson

The teacher will draw the attention of students to another picture with the Preamble written on it. Students will read the lines along with the teacher. Then the teacher will explain the meaning and significance of Preamble. Thereafter he will put these developing questions:

1. Who made this solemn resolution?

2. When was this resolution made?

3. Why is this resolution made?

(The last question is of reflective type).

Teacher will then explain the meaning of the terms 'Sovereign', 'Democratic', 'Republic', 'Justice', 'Liberty', 'Equality', 'Fraternity', 'Socialism and Secularism'. He may explain this way:

Sovereign: The people of India are sovereign and independent. The Constituent Assembly was given sovereign powers by the people. It was not dependent on the direction or order of any queen, or emperor or governor general of the country.

Democratic: India is a democratic country because every adult citizen has the right to vote and send his representatives in the legislature. Thus through his representative he participates in deciding the policy of the nation.

Republic: India has a system of government in which the elected representatives of the people are supreme, with a non-hereditary head and the powers of the state are divided between the union and the states.

Justice: Justice is secured to people of India as the government promises not to deprive or favour certain people or group in consideration of caste, colour, race, religion or sex. The fundamental rights, directive principles and various acts of the Parliament aim at securing social and economic justice to the people.

Liberty and equality: The constitutional provisions and policies of the government endeavour to secure individual's freedom of speech, expression, thought and faith and equality in dignity and rights.

Fraternity: The Preamble seeks to promote fraternity or brotherly feeling of common bonds and goals uniting comrades.

Socialism: It means (i) nationalisation of some selected industries, (ii) providing equal opportunity to every individual for progress, (iii) freedom from exploitation,

Secularism: It means freedom of religion and conscience. It means free play for all religions subject only to their not interfering with each other.

While explaining these concepts, teacher should cite practical examples from our day-to-day life to show how the Preamble of the Constitution is given practical shape, say; (i) free and fair election; (ii) election of the new president; (iii) protection by the police as well as the court to individual's freedom of speech, movement, life and property; (iv) abolition of untouchability; (v) improvement of the living standard of workers and farmers; (vi) abolition of slavery and bonded labour; (vii) celebration and holidays during religious festivals of different religions and communities.

Recapitulation: When one concept has been explained, teacher will put question from the list given below:

1. Give one proof to show that our people are sovereign.
2. Who decides the policy of our State?
3. How can you show that our country is a republic?
4. Why is England called democratic but not republic?
5. Mention some provisions of the Constitution that endeavour to secure our liberty and equality.
6. Give one example from your day-to-day life to show that you have liberty.
7. Why does India have no state religion as Pakistan has?
8. Mention one policy of the government to prove that India is a socialist country.
9. What do you mean by 'justice'?
10. In which sphere justice is secured in our State?

Assignments

In your school you are organising a 'human rights' society to implement the UN ideals of protecting human rights. Write the Preamble of that society incorporating the ideals and goals of the society.

2. Collect from newspapers or magazines ten pictures indicating the violation of the ideals enshrined in our Preamble.

LESSON PLAN NO. 10

Our Transport and Communication
(Hints for Lesson Planning)

Class VII

Background and Objectives

Children know the different means of transport used for carrying people and goods. The purpose of the unit is to tell the children how the developed means of transport and communication help towards the progress and defence of the country and how they promote national unity.

Expected Outcomes

Through the study of the lesson of this children are expected to acquire the following:

Understandings

There is a network of rails, roads and air routes in the country. These routes link different parts of the country.

Modern means of transport have brought the different parts of the country closer.

Modern means of transport are helping the development of industry and trade.

Modern means of communication help to bring closer people of different parts of the world.

Modern means of communication bring to us the latest news of the country and the world.

Improved means of transport and communication promote national unity.

Skills

To study the map of India.

To follow the traffic rules.

To consult railway time-table.

To use telephone.

To write the telegraphic message.

To read the newspaper.

Attitudes

Feeling of unity among the people of different parts of the country.

Feeling of interdependence of different parts of the country.

Introduction. This unit may be introduced through conversation and discussion. The following type of questions will help in initiating and developing effective discussion.

How do you go from your village or town to the other big cities of your State?

How are the things made in distant parts of the country brought to your village/town?

How do the factories of your town get the raw materials?
How do you get the news from different parts of the country?

Projects and Activities

The following activities may be helpful in promoting the desired understanding.

1. Let the children collect pictures of different means of transport and communication.

2. Let the children make a plan for an imaginary trip to some distant place in the country. Encourage them to plan the tour programme with the help of rail, road and air-route maps of India.

(Adopted from *Social Studies, Manual for Teaching, Book Two*, NCERT, New Delhi, 1972).